CW01263446

A FORTUNATE MAN

A FORTUNATE MAN
ISMAIL MEER

With a Foreword by Nelson Mandela

ZEBRA

Published by Zebra Press
an imprint of Struik Publishers
(a division of New Holland Publishing (South Africa) (Pty) Ltd)
PO Box 1144, Cape Town, 8000
New Holland Publishing is a member of the Johnnic Publishing Group

First published 2002

1 3 5 7 9 10 8 6 4 2

Publication © Zebra Press 2002
Text © estate late Ismail Meer 2002

Cover photograph © George Hallett

All rights reserved. No part of this publication may be reproduced,
stored in a retrieval system or transmitted, in any form or by any means,
electronic, mechanical, photocopying, recording or otherwise,
without the prior written permission of the copyright owners.

PUBLISHING MANAGER: Marlene Fryer
MANAGING EDITOR: Robert Plummer
EDITOR: Ronel Richter-Herbert
COVER AND TEXT DESIGNER: Natascha Adendorff
TYPESETTER: Monique van den Berg
INDEXER: Frances Perryer

Set in 10 pt on 13,5 pt Plantin

Reproduction by Hirt & Carter (Cape) (Pty) Ltd
Printed and bound by Robprint

ISBN 1 86872 664 9

www.zebrapress.co.za

Log on to our photographic website www.imagesofafrica.co.za for an African experience

CONTENTS

FOREWORD vii
INTRODUCTORY NOTE xiii
ABBREVIATIONS xv

1	Waschbank	1
2	Durban	21
3	Political Activism	31
4	Events During World War II	53
5	Johannesburg	69
6	Passive Resistance	87
7	The End of Indian Passive Resistance and the Beginning of Apartheid	109
8	Violence and Unity	113
9	Settling Down to Family and Work	127
10	The Defiance Campaign	141
11	The Verulam Practice and Some Cases	157
12	Freedom Charter	167
13	The Treason Trial and the Family	177
14	Sharpeville, the State of Emergency and the Birth of Umkhonto we Sizwe	215
15	Students Take Over	225
16	Travelling Abroad	239
17	Moving into Non-Racial South African Democracy	259

EPILOGUE 267

APPENDIX 1
    An address at Mr IC Meer's
    eightieth birthday celebrations
    by Chief Justice Ismail Mahomed   269

APPENDIX 2
    IC Meer in the KwaZulu-Natal
    Legislature by Dr Michael Sutcliffe   271

NOTES   274

GLOSSARY   277

INDEX   279

FOREWORD

Ismail Meer was my friend. We were young men together, young law students. There were times when I stayed with him in his flat in Kholvad House. These were important times for both of us, for not only did we come to know each other, we also came to appreciate our different cultures and learnt the valuable lesson of unity in diversity.

It would be true to say I never really knew Indians until I met Ismail. Living in the racial climate as we all did, I had prejudices, though never against Ismail, who became a very dear friend. Through him, I came to love the Indian people as people, as fellow South Africans. I met Dr Dadoo, Molvi and Yusuf Cachalia, Goolam and Amina Pahad, the young Ahmed Kathrada and JN Singh, and they all became very good friends and fellow freedom fighters. Ismail refers to the first meeting I addressed in Durban, at 'Red Square', and correctly recalls my surprise at the very large Indian attendance.

Ismail gave me a new perspective on South African Indians. I knew Johannesburg Indians as rich shopkeepers and thought all Indians to be the same. From him I learnt about Natal's Indians, who constituted by and large a working-class population. I learnt about their slave-like origin in this country as indentured labourers. It was through him that my image of Indians as exploitative capitalists eroded, and I came to see them as part of the large black working class, discriminated against and oppressed by the white government, though in different ways.

I learnt a lot from Ismail – he was a universalist who loved humanity without distinction; he was uncompromising in his belief in human equality.

Ismail writes about my exclusivism at the time we first came to know each other: 'I sympathised with Nelson's Africanism and did not see it as racism, but as a legitimate claim for African ascendancy in an African country. I could not, however, sympathise with his refusal to co-operate with us in strategic demonstrations for the elimination of pass laws, for freedom of speech, and for the right to franchise, simply because the campaigns did not originate with the ANC.'

He was a devoted member of the African National Congress, even at a time when it did not admit him as an Indian and reserved membership for Africans alone. He was passionate about non-European unity, and writes: 'I was more than prepared to realise non-European unity, to which I aspired, through the ANC. The ANC, however, was not prepared, at that time, to open its doors to non-Africans.'

But he persisted, patiently and doggedly, to lead me into the broad unitarian approach to which he was committed. Ismail's search for a non-racial home and his attraction to socialism led him to the Communist Party, where he enjoyed the camaraderie of whites, Africans and Coloureds.

Ismail was a member of the Communist Party when I met him, but I never found him to be a doctrinaire Marxist. He had an open mind and I found that attractive. He spoke as easily about Marxism as he did about Gandhi's Ahimsa or Nehru's socialism or Bose's militancy. All these ideas converged when he analysed the freedom struggle in India, and we discussed the parallels to be drawn in our own struggle in South Africa. It was through him that I learnt about Gandhi's contribution to our freedom struggle and about the Natal Indian Congress, which he had founded even before the formation of the ANC.

Ismail was politically ahead of me, and I acknowledged that when he, JN Singh, Zainab Asvat and Abdul Haq Patel interrupted their studies to give their full attention to the passive resistance struggle. Ismail and JN were law students like myself; Zainab and Abdul Haq were medical students. I admired them and was inspired by them.

Ismail writes of the struggle he and his political colleagues waged against the conservative Indian political leaders – the Old Guard, as he calls them – and I think of our own parallel struggle in the ANC as youth leaders against the conservatives.

Had not the youth in the two organisations taken over the reins of leadership in their respective Congresses, it is highly unlikely that the ANC and South African Indian Congress would have united in action when they did, and thereby spurred our people on their path to liberation.

Ismail had a wonderful mind; his thinking was clear and crisp and his analysis of political problems made a significant impact on our joint committee meetings. His oratory at public rallies was spellbinding.

When relaxed, he was a great companion, light-hearted and amusing, with a treasure trove of anecdotes that could keep you entertained for hours. These were the qualities I took into consideration when I invited him to be my travelling companion and speech writer on my trips abroad after my release from prison.

In his autobiography he emphasises his early religious upbringing and the influence of Islam on his political thinking.

At the age of six, the young Ismail was formally introduced to his religion at the local Madressa, the father handing him over for instruction with the words, 'Make something out of this boy. The bones are mine, the meat is yours.'

The lesson he was taught that first day guided him throughout his life: 'This is the Quran. It says all humanity is one, and that no one is superior to another.'

He attributes his grasp of socialism to Islam as explained to him by his father: 'When I asked him what is Islam, he said it was sharing,' and he gave Ismail a demonstration in which he was taught to share his two apples with a friend, Mandlenkhosi, who had none. 'So now you are equal, you both have an apple each. That is Islam. To share and be equal.'

'That lesson,' Ismail writes, 'lived with me throughout my life,' and it attracted him to socialism, which became his social and political goal.

I do not recall his ever pressing his religious beliefs on our political discussions, either moralistically or as some sort of special insight. It remained an unparaded private inspiration while he pursued his thoughts in a secular mode common to his comrades.

I knew Ismail as a man of great integrity, both in his personal life and his political thinking. One cannot help feeling that if there had been more people with Ismail's attitude, our transition to a normal society would have been much easier. His tolerance and generosity are evident throughout his life, but became more pronounced as he grew older and wiser.

Gandhi was another influence. Through his father and his uncles, Gandhi was no distant figure but a real person who came into their lives. 'Gandhi's popularity knew no bounds in our family when he became one of the leaders of the Khilafat movement,' which 'united Hindus and Muslims as never before and never since. We felt close to Gandhi and his goodness and courage.'

Later, at the beginning of his long silencing, barred from publishing and speaking, he searched for ways to occupy his new-found time, and, amongst other things, delved deeply into the world's religions, discovering in them their common truths. 'I followed the Quranic Surah, which stated all religions to be equal, and different paths leading to salvation.'

Inclusive when strategies suggested the opposite, broad in vision when many around him saw the detail and not the whole, he persisted in challenging small-minded attitudes whenever he encountered them. This did not always make friends, though it gained respect even from those who differed in opinion. Politically he never deviated from his beliefs. Expediency was not a word he knew.

Even when he differed, you knew that he was presenting a view that was based on careful thought. He had the ability to accord respect to those whose viewpoint he differed with in debate, and he had a sharp eye for tactically splitting his opposition to gain support for his viewpoint.

In 1950 I was wary of joint action between the ANC and the other Congresses and the Communist Party. In the wake of the banning of the Communist Party and the bans slapped on individual leaders, the idea of a campaign called the Defend Free Speech Convention grew. In the ANC we had reservations about the campaign because we feared that it was led by communists and the Indian Congress. We felt that any joint action should clearly be led by the ANC. Our suspicions were heightened when the campaign was announced in the media and, despite our concerns in the ANC, the then president of the Transvaal ANC, CS Ramohanoe, publicly called on ANC members to support the campaign.

This, to us, was going too far. We decided to have a joint meeting in order to get the campaign called off. Walter Sisulu, Oliver Tambo and I went along, determined to get our way. We itemised our criticisms of the way the campaign was planned and announced, and we did not conceal our anger that, behind our backs, the organisers had gone and obtained the public support of our president. Ismail and JN Singh responded by readily acknowledging our concerns, and appealing to us not to walk out of the campaign in the interests of the struggle. Walter broke ranks – he responded by recognising the harm that would result if the campaign was now called off. That was all Ismail needed. He pursued the point with great tact, ensuring that he gained and consolidated the ear of Walter. At the same time he made sure that he fully accepted our concerns. Oliver and I persisted. We wanted the campaign called off. But Ismail had split our ranks. And he gave us no opening to fight back.

Oliver and I were left with the consolation of showing our disgust with Walter by refusing to walk with him as we headed for Park Station to take the train home. We left Walter to walk alone on the opposite pavement, while between the two of us we vented our spleen at the shrewd and tactful way Ismail had outmanoeuvred us.

Like so many of us, he made use of his times in prison to rethink his life, welcoming the chance 'for contemplation, taking stock of my life and replanning'. During his first imprisonment, discussions centred on the various branches of the liberation movements in order to evolve strategies for the future. 'We could not deny that Indians and Africans, even within the Congresses, were not without prejudices,' he writes. 'There had to be attitudinal changes. We activists deemed ourselves freed from prejudice but we knew this was not shared by our peoples.'

His joy was obvious when, in 1950, the ANC called for a National Day of Protest to commemorate the eighteen people killed during the Freedom Day strike. He talks of the 'sense of triumph' he felt when we invited other organisations, the African People's Organisation, the Transvaal Indian Congress, the Natal Indian Congress and the Communist Party, to join us. In Durban we worked together to canvass support for the planned strike. It was on that occasion, as he recalls,

FOREWORD

that I met his future wife, Fatima, in Pinetown, where she lived with her parents. Fathu struck me as a highly capable, brave and independent person, who did not hesitate to express her views, however unpopular, on a wide variety of issues.

My initial impression has since been confirmed by her sterling commitment and service to our country. As long as we have persons of her calibre, South Africa will continue to shine.

Ismail was proud of her and very obviously in love. Later, when I fell in love with Zamie,[1] I introduced her to him on the telephone, as he recalls. We both married strong-minded women. Ismail writes that though he and Fathu, as he called her – and I was the only other person to join him in this – agreed on most things, they disagreed on the position of the Non-European Unity Movement, which questioned our motives and dismissed our campaign as counter-revolutionary. 'We dismissed the NEUM rhetoric as puerile,' Ismail writes. 'Fathu respected the NEUM and I found this painful.'

Zamie too, as I saw it, had her flirtation with the NEUM, but she became a staunch member of the ANC, as Fathu did of the NIC. It is to Ismail's credit that he did not interfere with Fathu's independent thinking and political independence, for their relationship was based on mutual respect and love. 'While I continued to resent her penchant for the NEUM, which could have threatened our marriage had our love not been as strong as it was, I knew that she was far too strong-minded and could never be brainwashed, and, most importantly, she would not commit herself to their Ten Point Programme as a precondition of membership. She was not one to commit herself to an exclusive "doctrine", and she placed the Ten Point Programme in that category; she wanted to keep a free mind.'

Their marriage was based on two free minds, and the letters between them during periods of long separation are touching in their tenderness and revealing in the insights they provide into the daily, ordinary lives of two people seldom out of the gaze of public scrutiny. At different times, both needed this normality to counteract the very abnormal situations they found themselves in – prison, the Treason Trial, banning, intimidation and attempts on their lives.

Ismail was a true friend. I spent some days with him and Fathu during the time that I was in the underground, and experienced the love and concern of their children, who, upon noticing the dilapidated state of the face-cloth I was using, clubbed together their pennies to buy me a new one. During my internment, Ismail and Fathu were among those friends to whom I turned with confidence and ease to help my family, and they never turned me down.

When we comrades were free to work together, we stimulated each other with our exuberant energy and were charged with a confidence that emboldened us to overcome any adversity. The banning of our organisations and our personal bannings changed our lives in ways we had not imagined. Some of us went underground and planned armed resistance, were arrested and imprisoned; others went into exile and continued the battle both diplomatically and militarily; others remained in South Africa in the outside world and adjusted as best they could.

Ismail, banned and listed, and prevented from writing and speaking, continued nonetheless to write and speak. His column in the *Leader*, appearing week after week continuously for forty-five years, was our historical voice. He never gave up on his belief in the unity and equality of humanity, and he continued to involve himself in actions that implemented this, using religious ideology when he could not use the political. His autobiography, completed by Fathu, is the portrait of a man who was indispensable to our struggle for and realisation of our democracy.

NELSON ROLIHLAHLA MANDELA
SEPTEMBER 2001

INTRODUCTORY NOTE

In the last weeks of his life, Ismail began dictating notes to his daughters, Shamim and Shehnaz. Neither he nor I knew how little time we had.

Ismail had not got far with his dictation when quite unexpectedly, and to my great shock and inconsolable grief, he left us. I resolved to complete his autobiography. 'Would it be a biography or an autobiography?' Shamim asked. I said, 'Your father had started his autobiography and I will complete it.'

Anant Singh had arranged to interview him about a year ago. Six hour-long videotapes were completed with Hassim Seedat as the interviewer. In addition there were the articles he had written in the *Leader* over a period of forty-five years, which were a biographical record of the history of South African Indians. Over and above that there are his numerous personal letters to his family, and finally there were the almost fifty years I shared with him. They were filled with his writing, his public speeches, his informal anecdotes in private and public, his teasing, disciplining, loving and scolding. I came to know his strengths and weaknesses, his vulnerabilities and advantages, his vanities and modesties. He could be distant and forbidding, and he could be warm, appealing and utterly charming. I loved him intensely and will continue to do so until the end of my life and beyond; though living with him was not easy. He was domineering, a typical patriarch, whose patriarchy particularly centred on me. I had to find my space and independence within that patriarchy, often stealing it and feeling guilty about it, at times breaking away from it, though never wholly. But he was also most supportive of all I did, and I survived my confrontations with apartheid and the security police because I was always assured of his protection. I was secure with him. It was an evolutionary process; there was nothing revolutionary about it. I wanted to be happy with him and happiness came on his terms. The fact is that I could not conceive of happiness without him.

So, taking all this into consideration – the rich autobiographical records left by Ismail and my being an eyewitness to events that enabled me to fill in the gaps – we have the autobiography of Ismail Chota Meer.

His life, however, is his own, and so he tells it. I have helped him to do so, leaving in everything that he has recorded and introducing nothing he has omitted. No biography or autobiography is a complete record. It is an abstract from the entirety, and so is this autobiography.

FATIMA MEER
AUGUST 2001

ABBREVIATIONS

AAC	All Africa Convention
ANC	African National Congress
APO	African People's Organisation
BI	British-India
CBSIA	Colonial Born and Settler Indian Association
CMT	Cut-make-and-trim
COD	Congress of Democrats
CODESA	Convention for a Democratic South Africa
COP	Congress of the People
CPC	Coloured People's Congress
CPSA	Communist Party of South Africa
FOPS	Federation of Progressive Students
ICU	Industrial and Commercial Workers Union
MCC	Middlesex Cricket Club
Nats	National Party
NEUF	Non-European United Front
NEUM	Non-European Unity Movement
NIA	Natal Indian Association
NIC	Natal Indian Congress
NIO	Natal Indian Organisation
NRC	Native Representative Council
NUSAS	National Union of South African Students
PAC	Pan African Congress
PRC	Passive Resistance Council
PSC	Primary School Certificate
SABC	South African Broadcasting Corporation
SACTU	South African Congress of Trade Unions
SAIC	South African Indian Congress
SASO	South African Students' Organisation
SRC	Students Representative Council
TIC	Transvaal Indian Congress
UDF	United Democratic Front
UDW	University of Durban-Westville
UNISA	University of South Africa
Wits	University of the Witwatersrand

ONE

WASCHBANK

1918–1931

*'Hum ko malum hê Waschbank ki hakieket,
lekin dil ke khush rakne ko liayê Isma-iel khyal acha he.'*

*'I know the state of affairs in Waschbank, but to indulge
my heart, Ismail, I entertain happy thoughts'* – *with
apologies to Ghalib*[1]

THE BEGINNING

The village of Waschbank, near the town of Dundee in the province of KwaZulu-Natal, lies at the foot of the Indumeni Mountain, which forms part of the mighty Drakensberg mountain range. Indumeni means 'where the thunder rolls', and it is here that I was born on 5 September 1918. I was named after my uncle, Ismail Meer, who had died just prior to my birth. This was in keeping with the custom of commemorating the dead by naming the most recent addition to the living after him.

Waschbank gave me many pleasures, but I left it at the age of thirteen with bitter memories of the pain it had caused me. I was born a prince, but left it a pauper.

My father Chota Meer was the youngest of Ahmed Meer's four sons, born of his second wife, Sarah. All four sons came to South Africa from India, but only my father settled here. There was an elder brother born of my grandfather's first wife, Sulaiman Meer. He never came to South Africa, but his son Cassim became a prominent businessman and community leader in Dundee. He was very close to his uncles.

My father's eldest brother, Mohamed Ahmed Meer, was the founder of the Meer clan in this country. He arrived in 1882 at the age of seventeen, a strikingly handsome youth without any capital but with a strong determination to succeed.

He established businesses in Durban, Johannesburg, Dundee and Waschbank. While this may seem exceptional, it was fairly typical of the nineteenth-century Indian immigrant who tried his luck in commerce.

Practically all the land in Waschbank was the property of one white farmer, and he had it declared a township in the 1880s. Mohamed Meer bought a plot for £2000, a phenomenal price in those days, which set tongues wagging and eyes ogling. No one had paid that kind of money for a plot of land before, not even in Durban. Mohamed Meer knew that the price was inflated because he was an Indian; but this was only one of the many disadvantages he had to suffer in that part of the British Empire where all the opportunities were stacked in favour of Europeans. On the mines, non-Europeans could not trade within a five-mile radius of a European store; in addition, mineworkers were paid a substantial portion of their wages in 'concession store' money, which obliged them to buy from the white concession store. In the Waschbank area, this amounted to a sizeable custom: from the surrounding regions of Burnside, Elandslaagte and Wesselsnek.

But Mohamed Meer had formidable tenacity, tremendous self-confidence and keen foresight. He was already running a flourishing business in Dundee's main street, McKenzie Street. He saw Waschbank as the potential hub of the collieries sprouting in the surrounding area. He reckoned that the £2000 investment in the land would more than pay for itself in a few years despite the concession stores he had to contend with.

He built a wood-and-iron shop and began trading. When he saw business picking up he called my father, his youngest brother, in Surat, and made him a partner on a 60:40 basis; he taking the lesser share since he was the 'sleeping' partner, and my father, whom he placed in charge, the active.

When Mohamed Meer returned to India in 1906, he left with £20 000 in gold sovereigns. It was a fortune and it helped to establish him in his home city in the style of a nawab [noble man]. He purchased the estate of a Raja – Rajawadi – pulled down the decaying 'palace' and replaced it with his own mansion. When the brothers dissolved their partnership, my father continued to pay his brother a goodwill of £1800 a year for several years.

THE COMMUNITY OF WASCHBANK

My father opened his general dealer's business, under the name CA Meer, in 1893 – the year Mohandas Karamchand Gandhi came to South Africa. You could find everything in our shop, from the proverbial needle to an elephant.

Just as his brother had helped him establish his store, my father helped others to establish theirs. Among those whom he helped were his maternal nephews, the Malls and Amins, who came from the village of Garah, near Surat, and

Ramsevak Singh, an indentured Indian who had worked on the mines and earned the reputation of Sirdar[2] of Waschbank because of his great learning. Ramsevak overcame all the obstacles placed in his path and became a landowner. He settled one of his sons, Baijnath, as the village blacksmith, and the other, Ranjith, as a general dealer. Success in adversity was the hallmark of those pioneers, both indentured and passenger.[3]

When I was a child, there were serveral Indian shops in the village besides those of the Malls, Amins and Singhs; one was that of Amod Saheb, a very popular and kind man, and another that of the greengrocer, Desai Chacha, who was also the village humorist. These shopkeepers pursued their businesses co-operatively and in friendship, not competitively, nor with any trace of conflict.

The customers of these stores came from the mines close to Waschbank and from the farms. They shopped on Saturdays; the African mineworkers walking or travelling in donkey carts, the Indians atop the coal in the coal trucks. They were all served a meal after the conclusion of their shopping, and those who had far to travel and could not leave because of darkness were accommodated for the night in the frugal restrooms adjacent to the shops. They liked dealing with the Indian shopkeepers because of the bargaining. It worked both ways: the shopkeeper felt he got his price, and the customer felt he got a bargain.

The European farmers were given long-term credit facilities. They paid annually when they reaped their crops and turned them into cash. They never paid any interest, for interest was haraam [forbidden] in Islam, and my father would not dream of charging it. The Europeans appreciated this and my father formed close friendships with some of them.

I remember three Europeans who regularly came to our shop: Oom Nel, Mr Hansen and Lotjie de Jaager. They would talk, drink coffee and do their business. When the Anglo-Boer War broke out in 1899 and Indian shopkeepers began leaving the district, Oom Nel said to my father, 'Chota, you are not leaving. You are coming to stay with me on my farm. You are not like the other Coolies.' My father did not take up the offer but he never forgot Oom Nel's kindness and often referred to it.

When my eldest sister, Äpa, married our cousin AI Meer, Hansen gave her some diamond jewellery. They were the only diamonds we ever possessed, our preference being for gold.

Chota Meer, Ramsevak Singh, Lotjie de Jaager and the umfundisi[4] George Mashaba were all staunch opponents of British imperialism, each for his own reason – my father and Ramsevak because of India's colonisation, Mashaba because of British injustice to the Africans, and De Jaager because of the concentration camps during the Anglo-Boer War. When they met at the shop, they could be heard castigating their common enemy.

In the evenings, CA Meer's shop became a 'university'. All nineteen Indian male members of the Waschbank community assembled there. The orphans of the late Ismail Meer, Moosa and Ahmed, or MI and AI, as they later came to be known, and who were my father's wards, were the stars of the 'university'; they read important items from the newspaper and explained the contents, and they recited poems.

Ramsevak Singh, a commanding figure with his great curled moustache and mountainous white turban, usually came a bit late, and when he arrived everyone stood up and sat down only after he sat down.

I asked my father why everyone stood up when Ramsevak Singh arrived and why this did not happen when the others arrived. My father said we had to respect not only the person but also his learning, and Ramsevak was the most learned of us all because of his knowledge of the Vedas. Ramsevak often preceded whatever he said with 'Hamara Ved kehtha he ....' ['as the Vedas say ...']. Whether what he said came from the Vedas or from Ramsevak's mind was questionable, but it did not matter since no one knew any better. Years later, I met Comrade Buirski in Johannesburg who invoked Lenin when he wanted to stress a point, though Lenin had said no such thing: It gave him authority.

The year of my birth in 1918, besides bringing the First World War to an end, also brought a wave of influenza that struck my father. My cousin MI resigned his work as a shop assistant in Ladysmith and came to nurse him. I watched MI with deep veneration as he applied hot poultices to my father's chest to relieve the congestion that had built up there.

MOULANAS – WHAT IT IS TO BE A GOOD MUSLIM

My father was very concerned about our education. He employed tutors and brought in Moulanas[5] from abroad – Moulana Afriki, Moulana Bashir Siddiqi, Moulana Ahmad Mia Osman and Moulana Sema – to ensure that our family and the community were well guided in Islamic theology and morality. Moulana Osman later settled in Ladysmith and wrote copiously on Islam; Moulana Cassim Sema went on to become the principal of the Darul Uloom[6] in Newcastle and translated the Quran into Zulu.

There was great excitement in our village when we welcomed Moulana Abed Mia from Lourenço Marques. The shop was cleared and prepared for the jalsa [reception]. The guests arrived, and among them were of course Ramsevak Singh with his five sons, my father's cousins, Salehba Mall from Douglas, Amjaloo Mota from Toleni and Sardiwala Chacha from Hlatikulu, and neighbours, Desai Chacha from across the road, Ismail Master the baker, Dubree the hide and skin merchant, Amod Saheb the butcher and Jawoodeen, and so many others from as far afield as Dannhauser, Dundee, Ladysmith and Newcastle.

The local young talent, Kalloo and his music makers, began the proceedings. Kalloo played the sarangee [violin] and sang the only song he knew, 'Aji bahaare baaghe duniya chundd roz' ['This world which is a garden'], proclaiming the transient nature of the 'worldly garden' of humankind. We lustily sang in support of Turkey and the Khilafat[7] and that night we destroyed the Greeks with our words, 'Qatal kar Greek shaytaanko' ['Destroy the Satanic Greek']. We were united with our Gandhiji and Mohammed Ali and Shaukat Ali as we sang their praises, 'Bôliê amma Mohamed Ali kie, jaan dê daw bêta khilafat mê' ['Mohamed Ali's mother said, "My son, lay down your life for the khilafat"'].

During his one-year stay in Waschbank, Moulana Abed Mia gave many lectures and wrote copiously in Urdu. We were sad to lose him to the Amods of Ladysmith, from where he continued to dispense knowledge and Unani[8] medicines.

But for all the Moulanas, it was my father who imbued me with the universal ethics of Islam, and it was he who taught me to be both a Muslim and a socialist. When I asked him what is Islam, he said it was sharing and gave me a demonstration. He asked me, 'How many apples have you got?' He knew how many I had because he had just given me two. But I answered dutifully, 'two'. And how many apples does your friend Mandlenkhosi have? I said none. Now give him one apple. Now how many apples do you have? 'One,' I replied. And Mandlenkhosi? 'One,' I said. 'So now you are equal. You both have an apple each. That is Islam. To share and be equal.' That lesson lived with me throughout my life.

Our hardest worker was Jim Ndlovu and it was said that he was receiving the highest wage in our area. My father insisted that Jim Ndlovu should have the first helping when food was served and he gave him the same quality of clothes he wore himself. When a consignment of military coats arrived, Jim was given the first pick. This was Islam to my father.

I recall going to Dundee with him on one occasion. In the evening our host, his shop assistants, my father and I sat down to supper. We all had generous helpings of Canadian wonders, a standard fare on the Meer menu. There was also a small pot of chicken curry on the table and our host kept urging my father, 'This was especially prepared for you.' My father ignored the invitation and did not touch the chicken, saying he preferred the beans. I preferred the chicken curry and was eager to get into it. But I dared not. When the shop assistants left, my father turned on our host and said, 'Don't you ever insult me like this again. I will not eat special food while everyone else is served red beans. You must understand what Islam teaches us.'

When I was about six years old my father took me to the local Madressa[9] and told the Molvi Sahib,[10] Moulana Afriki, 'Make something out of this boy. The bones are mine, the meat is yours.' The Moulana opened a huge red book and told us, 'This is the Quran. It says that all humanity is one, and that no one is superior to another.' When I had grown into a man and was arrested for treason, I was greatly disappointed at the Moulana's timidity when I went to him for a testimonial. He lived at Madina Manzil in Durban. He was very nervous on seeing me and asked if anyone had seen me entering his home. I understood the cause of his distress. I told him, 'Moulana, when I was a child, you introduced me to the red book and to the truths contained in it. I have been arrested for practising those truths. I shall tell the courts to arrest you, for you indeed are the cause of my alleged treason.'

The Moulana was most apologetic. He relaxed. I was welcomed, tea was served, talks followed; he displayed his usual courage, criticised the government of the day and gave me the required testimonial.

MADRESSA AND MALINGA'S SCHOOL

Tender as were our ages, mine and my sister's and the other children who joined us, we were taught Arabic, Urdu and Persian by Moulana Afriki. Later, at high school when we learnt the poetry of Omar Khayyam, a fellow student told the teacher that I knew the poem in its original language. Without batting an eyelid, I recited the only Persian poem I knew. Our English teacher was most impressed. 'See how Fitzgerald has maintained the original rhythm,' he said.

The brightest pupils in our Madressa were Hoosen Mall and Ayesha Meer, both of whom brought credit to their Ustaad.[11] Hoosen took an active part in assisting Moulana Cassim Sema to translate the Quran from Arabic into Zulu, and Ayesha went on to run a very successful Madressa.

Ayesha and I had a special bond. She was two years my senior but we were very close. She was by far the smarter; I was regarded as something of a simpleton, easily manipulated. Our mother would settle us down with our special treat, a saucer of condensed milk to be shared between us. Ayesha would give me a matchstick and direct me to eat with that – 'It won't dirty your fingers and it is much tastier that way,' she convinced me. It never occurred to me to question why *she* used her finger. I struggled with the matchstick, the condensed milk refusing to wrap around it and dripping off while Ayesha lapped up the condensed milk with her finger, leaving me, to my dismay, with an empty saucer!

I began my secular education at Malinga's school where I was instructed in Zulu. I clearly remember beginning with words identifying the different parts of the body. We would chorus after Mr Malinga with gusto as he pointed to his head, 'ikanda', and his arms, 'izandla'. I learnt to speak Zulu before I spoke English. My Zulu, learnt in primary school, stood me in good stead with my Zulu-speaking clients when I began my legal practice in Verulam and travelled out to the court in Indwedwe.

A few years ago I had a letter from a fellow pupil from Malinga's school. He reminded me that I had beaten him in our last stick fight, and challenged me to another in our hoary age so that he could reclaim the title!

ADAM CHACHA AND MRS VAN VUUREN

I have told you about the good Europeans in Waschbank; now let me tell you about one who, like many others, strutted about with superior airs.

Adam Chacha, the greengrocer, was outwardly obsequious when the arrogant Mrs Van Vuuren entered his fruit shop. He advised her on her purchases. Behind her back, he winked mischievously. 'She thinks herself very clever, but I will make her buy my rotten bananas,' he said in Gujarati to others in the shop, and turning to Mrs Van Vuuren with a most engaging smile, said, 'You make banana pudding? These best bananas,' pointing to the overripe ones.

'Is that so, Adam? Give me half a dozen.'

When Mrs Van Vuuren left, they all burst out laughing. When my father heard this, he was very angry and scolded Adam Chacha for cheating Mrs Van Vuuren, however arrogant she might be.

It was a hot summer's morning. The sun was ascending to strike the noonday heat. I was at the station, standing where the engine coupled the first coach. Coopasamy, from Burnside, was standing on the platform close to the coach. Adam Chacha, the village greengrocer-cum-carriage taximan, was waiting to transport the bulky Mrs Van Vuuren and her luggage. Mrs Van Vuuren alighted and collided with Coopasamy, almost throwing him to the ground, but instead of apologising to him, she burst out, 'You Coolie, can't you see where you are going?' Coopasamy was going nowhere. It was Mrs Van Vuuren who was going, knocking into Coopasamy. There was an argument and Coopasamy was justifiably upset. Adam Chacha was outraged but kept his cool. After all, she was his profitable customer. But that evening at our 'university shop', he fulminated against the gora log [white people] who thought they could behave as they liked. 'That gojie kuthrie [dirty bitch]!' he spat.

'You will serve her with smiles tomorrow!' one of the company challenged. 'You will never call her "gojie kuthrie" to her face. I challenge you.'

'Done,' he said.

Adam Chacha was never one to back away from a challenge: 'I will call her "gojie kuthrie" to her face on Saturday when she comes to collect her weekly supply of fruit and vegetables.'

Two witnesses were appointed to observe and report on the challenge. Saturday came, and Mrs Van Vuuren ambled into Adam Chacha's shop, her dog following. Adam Chacha served her with a smile, as always. The witnesses, and a number of others who had collected for the fun, waited. The smile never leaving his face, Adam Chacha said, 'Missus Van Vuuren, Missus Van Vuuren, you bitch, very dirty.'

The witnesses were on pins and needles. There was a momentary silence as they looked apprehensively at Mrs Van Vuuren's arrogant face. Mrs Van Vuuren said, 'Yes, Adam, my bitch is very dirty; I will give her a bath when I get home,' and she paid for her fruit and vegetables and left with her purchases and her dog. The observers were confused, but Adam Chacha, who claimed that he had never lost a bet in his life, shouted with glee, 'See, I called her a gojie kuthrie, a dirty bitch to her face!'

The observers were impressed. Adam Chacha had called her a dirty bitch and she hadn't batted an eyelid. But one of the witnesses who had a slightly better understanding of English said Adam Chacha had called her bitch dirty. He had not called Mrs Van Vuuren a dirty bitch. The others who could not distinguish between 'you' and 'your' remained confused. Did Adam Chacha say, 'Missus Van Vuuren, you are a dirty bitch,' or did he say, 'Missus Van Vuuren, your bitch is very dirty'?

And for days there were arguments for and against Adam Chacha's claim that he had called Mrs Van Vuuren 'gojie kuthrie' to her face, and no matter which side you took, Adam Chacha's reputation as the village humorist went up in everyone's estimation.

LANGUAGE AND TRANSPORT

Our Waschbank Indians did not speak the Queen's English. In fact, it could be said they did not speak English at all. They strung together nouns and verbs and managed as best they could when forced to communicate with customers in English.

We traded with the wholesalers in Durban, large European firms like Randle Brothers, Butchers, JW Jaggers and so on. Few northern Natal traders could write in English; they corresponded in Gujarati: 'Beloved Rundle Bhai' [brother] or 'Beloved Jagger Bhai', etc. The European wholesalers engaged Gujarati-speaking interpreters who replied in Gujarati. Some of the interpreters graduated to become their brokers and agents. Prominent among these was Amod Bhayat of Pietermaritzburg, who had worked closely with Gandhi as a passive resister and also had an office in Durban at 137 Grey Street, next to the *Indian Views*; AI Kajee (Pty) Ltd, Kazi's Agencies, Hajee Rooknoodeen (our Adam Chacha's brother) and MH Ismail (the only person I knew who had come from Bengal to South Africa) were some of the others.

We blacks pronounced English words differently from the English-speaking whites. The Zulus, for instance, never said Dundee; they said 'Daandi'. To us, Johannesburg, Pietermaritzburg, Dannhauser, Verulam and Sydenham were respectively Jonoosbaagh, Morrisbaagh, Dunnhoss, Willum and Sillum. And tomatoes united the blacks even with the Afrikaners because, for all of us, it was tamatees, not tomatoes. When Sir Kurma Reddy pronounced 'world' as 'wurrelled', we knew that he was a pukka Indian – that he was not from London, or even Durban for that matter, but from Madras.

Both at Ramsevak's store and at Chota Meer's, some customers found difficulty in communicating with the shopkeepers in their Tamil and Telugu … but this was Africa and the people drawn here from the north and south of India conversed easily in Zulu, which had become their lingua franca in their adopted country. In the 1920s, as now, the majority of Indian South Africans were born in Natal.

Years later, when Dr Monty Naicker visited Surat and met my sister Amina, who was married and living there with her husband AM Meer, they conversed in Zulu, the only language common to both.

There was only one hotel in Waschbank, and that was for 'Europeans Only'. The Indian agents had to find accommodation with the shopkeepers who reserved rooms for that purpose, as we did. MH Ismail was a frequent visitor and we formed a lifelong friendship with him. Later, when we moved to Durban, both my brother AC and his son Haroon joined his business for a while.

Our shop was the centre where the commercial travellers exhibited their samples. These were usually brought by the representatives in huge wicker containers. The samples were displayed in our large sample room, and shopkeepers from the adjacent areas – Hlatikulu, Toleni, Douglas, Matiwanskop, Elandslaagte and other villages – came to view them and place orders. It was always a very busy time for us during the few days that the samples were displayed. We extended our hospitality to the visiting retailers, serving them food and putting them up for the night when necessary, and Adam Chacha's 'carriage taxi' was equally busy.

Adam Chacha took MH Ismail from Waschbank to Pomeroy, where the generous Hindu businessmen, the Budhoos, accommodated him and cooked special halaal food for him.

In Durban, the rickshaw was the more common mode of transport; Indian traders also used it to deliver goods. If, however, you announced to your host that you had arrived by Essop Omar's gadee [car], everyone knew that you had come on your two God-given legs, for Essop Omar always walked to all his manzils [destinations].

Very few Indians possessed cars in the late twenties and early thirties, and if you saw an Indian woman driving a car, it could only be Mrs Bhailal Patel, and the car would be a Baby Austin. If you saw an Indian family riding in a Rolls Royce, it could only be Ismail Moosa's, who was married to my cousin EM's[12] wife's sister. That also qualified us to get a ride in it when in Durban. In the days when Indians were criticised for not conforming to Western standards, Ismail Moosa set a high standard. In the absence of hotels for non-whites, his house in Clarence Road welcomed Indian dignitaries. Professor Gopal Krishna Gokhale stayed there in 1912, as did Gandhi, and members of the Paddison and Habibullah commissions in the early thirties.

MOHANDAS KARAMCHAND GANDHI

One of the most treasured documents in my father's safe was a letter from Gandhi thanking him for his assistance during the Great March of 1913. My uncle MA Meer was the organiser of Gandhi's Natal Indian Congress (NIC) in northern Natal. He admired Gandhi greatly, as did my father. MA Meer was, however, critical of Gandhi's obsession with all things British, and is reported to have told him: 'Gandhi Bhai, you are doing wonderful work, but when you praise the British, we don't like it.'

Gandhi also relied on MA Meer to report to him cases of maltreatment of Indian mineworkers on the collieries, as is seen in the following letter to Herman Kallenbach, his lifelong friend and confidant:

October 30, 1913

MY DEAR LOWER HOUSE,

I sent you a full message from Ingogo which I hope you received. Mr Mahomed Meer is at Waschbank. He has the 'phone. It was he who gave the information about the Ramsay Collieries assault.

Please inquire further. You know that I telegraphed to the Protector at Durban and the Interior.

You may now inquire further through Meer and if there [be] any workers, send one to make local investigation.

MK GANDHI

Gandhi's popularity knew no bounds in our family when he became one of the leaders of the Khilafat movement. He addressed vast masses at the Juma Masjid in Delhi, exhorting the people to demand that the ill-gotten gains of World War II were not divided between the English and the French. The Khilafat movement united Hindus and Muslims in India as never before or since.

When the Indian National Congress adopted the Purna Swaraj [complete independence] resolution moved by Gandhi, and when Gandhi marshalled his forces for non-cooperation and civil disobedience in India, we celebrated.

MI Meer read out a letter to us from our uncle Mohamed Meer, who was at the time residing in Surat. He wrote that Gandhiji, the Mahatma, had addressed a huge meeting at Surat, and had cancelled a scheduled visit to a temple to visit 'my Mohamed Seth from Natal' at Rajawadi in Rampura. We felt close to Gandhi and his goodness and courage.

We followed the Great Salt March in Dandi with keen interest. Our Karodia Chacha, however, confused Dandi with Dundee and lost a precious £5 as a result. He had just performed his Fijr Namaaz.[13] Immaculately dressed as always, he was seated outside his shop in Victoria Street with the *Natal Witness* in hand when he espied Mr Englishman Lawyer coming along. Karodia Chacha called out to him.

'Look! Look! Lawyer Sahib, Gandhi come back to Dundee. Very good, very good!' he cried out, pointing to an item in his paper.

Mr Englishman Lawyer, somewhat perplexed, took out his reading glasses and seriously perused Karodia Chacha's copy of the *Witness*. He then burst out laughing. 'No, no, Karodia, Gandhi arrives in Dandi in India, not Dundee in Natal,' putting an end to Karodia Chacha's joy, but Karodia Chacha was happy to hear that Gandhi was to challenge the British. His happiness, however, was short-lived when a little later Mr Englishman Lawyer's messenger brought him an account, which read: 'To perusing the *Natal Witness* and to explaining the contents thereof including the exact location of the place Dandi ... five guineas.' This story was told over and over, but no one from Waschbank checked its veracity with Karodia Chacha himself.

SAROJINI NAIDOO

In 1924, the Indian community was agog with excitement. Sarojini Naidoo, the nightingale of India, had arrived in South Africa at the invitation of the South African Indian Congress (SAIC). She was the most important Indian leader after Professor Gokhale to visit the country. My father spoke of her eloquence and her intelligence and I heard it repeated again and again how, when at a public meeting in India she had called for India's freedom, an Englishman had jeered, 'You are asking for the moon.' Her spontaneous retort had been, 'I am not asking for the moon. We will pluck the moon from the heavens and wear it on the diadem of India!'

'What presence of mind!' my father exclaimed, his eyes sparkling like the jewels on that diadem. 'What language! What brilliance! What wit!' he drooled.

He told another story, how, when asked why she did not confine herself to women, she had retorted, 'What will the poor men do then?'

We heard that Sarojini Naidoo was to visit Glencoe and that my father's nephew Cassim Meer was the key organiser of her reception. We also heard that his daughter Afoo was to recite the welcoming poem. My father said we had to go to Glencoe and support Cassim in his efforts and, above all, meet Mrs

Naidoo. So we set off in our elegant carriage. In my mind, that jalsa [celebration] was the best I had ever attended. I was as spellbound by Sarojini Naidoo as my father was.

The next day Sarojini Naidoo was due to leave for Durban. Her train would pass Waschbank; it would not stop there, but everyone was eager to see and greet her. During our evening session at the shop, they reminded my father how, when Professor Gokhale's train had passed through Waschbank in 1912, he had arranged with the stationmaster to slow it down so the locals could greet him, how Sirdar Ramsevak had led the welcome, how he had stood on the platform, tall and majestic as the Indumeni in his imposing turban and curled moustache, and how he had led the cheering in his fine, clear, strong voice, how they had all joined in, how Gokhale had waved graciously from his window. They now urged my father to make similar arrangements again. I thrilled at the prospect of being a participant in welcoming Sarojini Naidoo in Waschbank.

My father was more than ready to comply. He was as eager as the rest to give Mrs Naidoo a rousing cheer. So he negotiated with the stationmaster.

'I won't press you on the payment of that account.'

'What do you want, Chota?' the stationmaster asked, knowing full well that nothing was given for nothing.

'When the Durban-bound train approaches Waschbank on Sunday, slow it down so that it passes very slowly through our township. There is a very important lady travelling on it and we wish to cheer her.'

The stationmaster acquiesced.

Desai Chacha prevailed upon the company gathered at our shop to give him the honour of leading the cheer party. I could see that my father was hesitant, but Desai Chacha pressed so hard and so graciously that it became difficult to refuse him.

We saw the train approach and slow down. We had assembled four hours ahead of time. Our hearts swelled in expectation. We had practised our hurrahs to perfection. The train drew nearer, it slowed down and proceeded at a snail's pace. We saw Mrs Naidoo seated at the window; we waited for our signal. Our cheer-leader, Desai Chacha, had to say 'Hip! Hip!' before we could say 'Hurrah!' But Desai Chacha was so overcome by the history of the moment that the 'Hip! Hip!' got stuck in his throat. Disciplined as we were by my father, we dared not break rank and say 'Hurrah!' We looked anxiously at Desai Chacha and waited. We saw Mrs Naidoo smile at us, expecting some greeting. Nothing came. Our hurrahs remained suspended in our throats, awaiting Desai Chacha's signal. The train picked up speed and we were looking at the back of the last coach as it disappeared, leaving the dreary, empty rail track. Then we heard a limp squeak, 'Hip! Hip!' There was no point in following with our 'Hurrahs'. If only we had left our leadership to our Sirdar; Ramsevak's voice would never have remained trapped in his throat.

My father was furious. Desai Chacha never lived down his ignominy. It pursued him to the end of his life. I wondered how my father, whose instincts were usually so correct, had gone so wrong in allowing himself to be misled by Desai Chacha.

CLEMENT KADALIE AND THE INDUSTRIAL
AND COMMERCIAL WORKERS UNION

The Reverend George Mashoba introduced my father to the Industrial and Commercial Workers Union (ICU). My father sympathised with the Africans and saw their colonial history paralleling his own in India. Though he was a shopkeeper, not a worker, an Indian, not African, he supported the ICU and created space in his shop for the organisation to establish an office. Samuel Masabalala, organiser-in-chief of the ICU, took charge of that office. Waschbank became the rural centre of the union in Natal, and AWG Champion and Selby Msimang became familiar figures in the area, organising on the mines and holding meetings on Sundays on the ground opposite our shop. Champion was a police constable in Dundee and he gave up his job to throw himself fully into the ICU. He brought Clement Kadalie to Waschbank. It was a great event and there was great excitement. I went to the meeting with my father and older brothers. We were all very impressed by Kadalie. Even as a child, I felt the effect of his charismatic oratory.

Kadalie came to our shop after the meeting. We were opening goods that had just arrived – among them were four Decca gramophones. They were £7 each. Kadalie purchased one on credit and I recorded his name and address, for it was my job at that time to send out monthly statements to our debtors.

Many, many years later I travelled to Europe and on the plane was Kadalie's granddaughter, a university lecturer who wanted to know whether I had known her grandfather. I replied, 'Most certainly, I could not forget him because for months I sent him regular statements for £7 for a Decca gramophone, for which he never paid.'

MI MEER ATTEMPTS TO JOIN THE TURKISH ARMY
IN DEFENCE OF THE KHILAFAT

There were strong feelings against the British in our family; the speaking of English was decried, and there was an old cousin of my father's who spent hours reading the paper and meticulously scratching out 'Great' each time it appeared before Britain. This was during the time when the Muslim world was outraged by the British attack on the Caliphate. Muslim hearts were roused to high passion and they were ready to be martyred in the Islamic cause. In Waschbank, my cousin MI Meer, considerably older than me, volunteered to join the Turkish army.

MI Meer rejected the evil of imperialism with all his heart, and his thoughts on the matter had appeared in print in the *Dundee and District Courier* under a nom de plume. Everyone in the village knew that this was the writing of MI Meer, who also contributed articles to the *Muslim Gujarat* of Surat, earning praise from its well-known editor, Munadee.

It was a moonlit night, but a unique one in that the earth had cast its shadow on the bright clear face of the moon, sailing through flimsy clouds to the heavy darker ones over the snow-covered peak of the Indumeni, as if to hide her blemished face from the world. We were gathered on the verandah of our shop on the night of the eclipse, watching it, when Chota Meer informed his nephew, MI, that he had discovered the latter's move to take up the sword in defence of the Khilafat. The uncle had accidentally come across the correspondence of the nephew. 'It is not our vocation to be soldiers,' he told MI, but he was gentle with his nephew, advising him to think carefully before taking the next step. The decision must be his and his alone, he emphasised. Though my father was a keen supporter of the Ali brothers, he was not about to sacrifice his nephew to their movement.

I remember how the next day MI and I walked silently for a long time in the valley that we loved. We knew every tree and every hillock in the valley and the shaded slopes of the forested Hlatikulu. That day he decided to abandon his plan of entering the battlefield of Turkey, deciding instead to go to Kimberley where his maternal uncle was a wealthy merchant and a highly respected resident on account of his social-mindedness. MI left us to join his brother AI and my eldest sister whom AI had married, and who had preceded him to Kimberley. We missed the two orphans of my uncle Ismail Meer.

In 1926 Waschbank celebrated with pride the news that MI had accepted the editorship of the *Indian Views*, an English/Gujarati weekly founded in 1914 by Mohamed Angalia and owned by the Jeewa brothers at the time.

The young man who had talked to us about the French Revolution, of Rousseau and Voltaire, who loved Charles Dickens and Victor Hugo, was no more to share his knowledge with Waschbank alone, but with the whole of southern Africa and beyond.

PREJUDICE AND POLITICS – THE LOSKOP KILLER

Fear swept the country shops throughout Natal when the shopkeeper Sulieman Ismail Kharwa was murdered by the 'Loskop Killer', who remained mysterious and at large, claiming the lives of four more Indian shopkeepers within a few months.

There was a stillness in our house and conversation in the 'university shop' was unusually subdued. There was the fear: who next? Indians had no doubts about the origin of the killings. The Loskop Killer was set on them by the Europeans who wanted to get rid of them, especially the Indian traders. It was a time when the Round Table Conferences were in progress between India and South Africa, the main purpose of which was to repatriate Indians.

We in Waschbank had by and large remained isolated from the events erupting in the larger cities. European voices were raised against Indians. A Bill was being introduced in the European parliament to segregate us and to deprive us of our businesses. We listened and read and waited. The leaders looked to India to intervene. In the 'university shop' there was much heated discussion. There was general agreement that the 'gora log' were odious. My father said, 'Not all,' and he was thinking of Steven and Bower, two deserters from the British army, who had become members of our extended family and who served us loyally. Steven was our groom and kept our horses in splendid condition; Bower eventually married the daughter of Clement Khuzwayo and became integrated with the local population.

There was consternation about the statements made by some of the delegates at the 1927 Round Table Conference. George Mashaba, Chota Meer and Ramsevak Singh were dumbstruck to hear that the Indian Agent General in South Africa, VS Srinivasa Sastri, had said: 'The Union Jack wherever it flies has brought peace and goodwill.' The Sirdar's immediate reaction was to ask whether Sastri came from the same country where the Jalianwala Bagh[14] massacre had taken place, and whether India was not in fact asking for Purna Swaraj [complete independence], and why would she, if Britain was so wonderful? De Jaager, leaning on the counter, said, 'Your Mr Sastri is to the Indians what Smuts is to the Afrikaners, the spokesman of the British, not of his people.'

We missed MI. He would have explained the situation clearly to us. In his absence, Ramsevak and my father discussed the issues while we listened. They told us that at least the Indians were uniting; they had strong organisations – the Natal Indian Congress, the Transvaal Indian British Association, the Cape British Indian Council – and these had come together to form the South African Indian Congress. India had sent the finest brains and they were all working together, and something would come of it despite the Loskop Killer. We drew hope.

DR ABDURAHMAN AND THE NON-EUROPEAN UNITY CONFERENCE

In December 1930, Mr AWG Champion visited us in Waschbank for the last time. He had come to consult George Mashaba en route to the Third Non-European Conference in Bloemfontein, convened by Dr Abdurahman. I went to the station to meet AWG Champion with my older brothers, HC and AC. Mr Champion, as usual, ruffled my hair (which I never liked), and then lost all interest in me. His mind was preoccupied with the conflicts in the ICU, between him and Kadalie and between Kadalie and Ballinger. I recalled an earlier visit when Mr Champion had brought Mr Ballinger and the two men had been put up in our 'guest quarters'. They were so friendly. Now Mr Champion, who was leading the ICU Yase Natal, was vehemently denouncing Ballinger and blaming him for problems in the ICU, saying that as long as Ballinger attended their conferences there would always be trouble. Mr Champion stayed the night and left the following day for the conference.

Years later when I joined the Communist Party, I understood the Champion–Kadalie–Ballinger conflict. The Communist Party saw the conflict in South Africa in class terms, complicated by race. Africans saw it in terms of race and pointed to all the race laws that restricted and persecuted them but did not affect white Party members. A white communist qualified for election as a Native representative to the white parliament, but a 'Native' communist could not represent Natives. African leaders within the ICU wanted to attain higher economic status and resented accusations by white communists that they, Kadalie and company, were using the ICU to enrich themselves.

My father was interested in the conference and read out the report that appeared in the *Indian Opinion* to Ramsevak Singh and Reverend Mashoba. They listened. I also listened. They discussed the report. The conference had begun with the singing of *Nkosi Sikelel' iAfrika*. Mashoba said it was a hymn composed by the gifted Enoch Sontonga in 1897. My father read that it was a great conference, and all the African leaders who mattered had attended it – Reverend Z Mahabane, Professor Jabavu, Clement Kadalie and, of course, AWG Champion, who had attacked Ballinger and blamed him for the problems of the ICU. Dr Abdurahman, who had opened the conference, had denounced the laws against Africans aimed at keeping them as slaves on white farms, and warned the whites of impending disaster if they continued their oppression.

Dr Abdurahman was ahead of his time. When other leaders were thinking in terms of ethnic organisations, he was making an impassioned plea for the unity of the disenfranchised in one powerful organisation to defeat racism.

Dr Abdurahman had criticised, in particular, the government's use of banishment to deal with non-European opposition. AWG Champion had been banished from Durban to Kingsley in northern Natal from 1930 to 1933. Mashoba commented that that had just about finished the ICU Yase Natal. There was criticism too of the white government's 'civilised labour' policy.

I would meet Champion again in Durban, at my cousin MI's *Indian Views* office where MI would generously help him with his printing, and then much, much later, when I was a qualified lawyer and he engaged me to handle his business affairs in Inanda. We would work together, he as president of the Natal African National Congress, and I as an executive member of the NIC, to bring order among Indians and Africans during the 1949 unrest in Durban.

For all my awakening interest in politics, I played happily in my father's shop and in the grounds around our house, conscious of the harassment suffered by our community elders, but not seeing it as my business. The grown-ups would handle the problems and keep us safe.

DEPRESSION AND INSOLVENCY

When I was old enough to travel by train on my own from Waschbank to Glencoe, my father enrolled me in the Indian school at Dundee, where Ephraim Thomas was the principal. I only reached class two when tragedy struck our family and I had to leave school. The depression had been crowding in on us and we were caught in its web. That and Hertzog's civilised labour policy impacted directly on Indian traders and workers alike, and the drift from rural to urban areas started. In Waschbank we saw the pitiful consequences of replacing Indian workers with white workers on the railways and on the coal mines. Many Indian shops closed down and the families moved into the cities. In later years, many young sons would pursue a college education and become doctors and lawyers, and I would be fortunate to be one of them. But in the 1930s, the universities and colleges in South Africa were closed to non-Europeans, as we were called, and the first shopkeeper's son to move into a profession, Dr Cassim Seedat, graduated in England.

The depression of the 1930s struck the world and insolvency became endemic. Roosevelt alone seemed to have a solution for his people as he inaugurated his New Deal in the United States of America. There was no deal to rescue us; our Waschbank empire collapsed and we faced dire poverty.

My father had nurtured his business and the business had stood us in good stead for thirty-eight years. He could not hold on any longer. His two sons, AC and HC, who could have taken over from him, could not help. They went their own ways, each taking his wife and only child with him. They had lost faith in the business ever reviving. The times had changed and they could no longer live in our father's time or pursue his life. They set out to make lives of their own.

My father sold all his possessions and paid his creditors in full. The *Natal Witness* reported on the 'insolvent' who was 'solvent'. My father could have compromised and retained his business, but his conscience would not allow him to do so. We were reduced to penury. The Malls bought our shop, lock, stock and barrel.

Our last possession was my father's much-loved rooster. I took this rooster around from house to house to sell it but nobody would buy it. I was thirteen years old and forced to earn our keep. I took a job with the Malls in the shop that had once been ours, and we were accommodated in a room in the shop assistants' quarters, and received food from their kitchen.

I was moved to the Farms Store in Douglas. The customers liked me and there were those who insisted on being served by me alone and would wait until I was free to do so. This flattered and pleased me. However, I wanted to be close to my parents who needed me, so when Ismail Master offered me a job in his bakery, I left the Malls. I worked at the bakery for a year and expected to be paid a lump sum at the end of it. There was a bucket in which my boss kept all the small change, usually pennies. On Eid Day, he put both his hands in the bucket and withdrew as much of the change as his hands could hold and offered this to me in a gesture of generosity. It added up to eight shillings and three pence and that was my whole year's wage! My bonus was that I learnt to make macaroons and bake bread.

My brother AC, who had moved in with his in-laws, the Amras, made his appearance in Waschbank on a December day and announced that he was taking us to Durban to live with him. He had set up a cut-make-and-trim (CMT) home 'factory', and I could help him.

ALWIDA [FAREWELL] WASCHBANK, 1931

The sun has set on my Waschbank and I am about to begin a new phase in my life in Durban. My father had spent almost forty years in that village and though I had spent only thirteen, it was the whole of my life.

As I prepare for my departure, pictures from the past flit through my mind. It is Saturday afternoon – the coal train from Burnside steams towards our village; as it ascends the high ridge, I see seated atop the heaped coal in the open trucks, dignified red-turbaned Indian men and graceful sari-clad Indian women, their jewellery sparkling as they are touched by the sun.

The picture changes and I see them at our shop: Indian mineworkers – men, women and their children – seated in rows along the long trestle table. The lunch is on the house and as usual consists of bread, tinned sardines and tasty home-made pickles, followed by a steaming cup of hot tea. Shopping begins after refreshments.

In the shop window photographs are stuck from newspapers showing the Abdurahman-led delegation of the South African Indian Congress in India. Much interest is shown in the photographs, and some caustic comments are made on the Round Table Conference.

Night descends on Waschbank … In the absence of MI Meer and AI Meer the evening gathering has lost much of its lustre.

A gramophone in the distance plays my favourite Urdu record, which ends with 'Mera naam Peearoo qawal he' ['My name is Peearoo qawal'] – as if anyone else could be mistaken for this maestro.

I remove the brown wrapper from this week's light-blue coloured cover of *Indian Views* and lie on my bed reading this journal … and I am back with MI Meer sharing the exploits of Victor Hugo's Jean Valjean, as he walks in the streets of Paris and cries his heart out … in Gujarati, translated by MI and Farooqi Mehtar.

It is Wednesday. Waschbank is closed in the afternoon and I am proceeding to Dundee to do our weekly banking in the company of Shewlal Maharaj, better known as Frank Maharaj, who comes from a Hindi-speaking family in Greytown, but is perhaps the best Gujarati-speaker of Waschbank, as is his brother Kundanlal, who lives in Glencoe and is an old subscriber to *Indian Views*. When we reach Kundanlal's house we find him the centre of attention in a group of Zulu, Tamil and Hindi listeners. He is loudly translating the Gujarati of *Indian Views* into Zulu, which every listener, Indian and African, can follow and fully understand.

Here, in this part of Africa, the thoughts and feelings of CF Andrews, Victor Hugo, JBM Hertzog and others are being communicated in Zulu from Gujarati.

Ramsevak keeps on emphasising how immoral the caste system is, both in India and in South Africa, and insists that the Rig Veda, the oldest book of man, and the Vedas as a whole, nowhere sanction man's inhumanity to man, as practised in the caste system. He continues in his own way on the inhumanity of race prejudice. He sees the political happenings, poised to ruin the Indian people, as a conspiracy between the British Raj and the racist Afrikaners.

Chota Meer speaks of the British atrocities in India and in the whole of the Muslim world; Mashoba continues his harangue about how they were left the Bible and robbed of their land; and Lotjie de Jaager harps on about the British concentration camps in which Afrikaner women suffered and died.

When our final departure is at hand, Lotjie de Jaager, the Nationalist farmer whose farm stretches from Waschbank to Glencoe, comes with a serious offer to Chota Meer to move onto his farm, where he has a house for him and where he can retire. This touching offer is declined with thanks.

Chota Meer has spent the best years of his life in the village; its surrounding fauna and flora have become part of his psyche; the Indumeni Mountain is contoured on his face and in his mind and the Busi River flows in his heart.

Ramsevak Singh, the Sirdar of Waschbank, is no more, having joined the ranks of the immortals. The lifelong friendship of Chota Meer and Ramsevak Singh is now reflected in my brother AC's bond with Ramsevak's son Ranjith, both of whom have proceeded to Durban and will, for a period, occupy neighbouring flats in Market Building in Etna Lane.

I make the journey to Durban at night with my parents. Our coach, in rhythm with the rail on which it is travelling, keeps reminding me: 'Hum ko malum hê Waschbank ki hakieketh, lekin dil ke khush rakhne ko liayê khyal acha hê' ['I had known poverty in Waschbank and I had known hardships, yet

Waschbank continues to have a magical ring for me']. I carry rich memories of the beloved village.

The train steams away. I am leaving my birthplace to be swallowed up by a strange great city.

The train whistles and moves on in a moonlit night, making the distance between it and the imposing sentinel Indumeni larger and larger, and the Indumeni smaller and smaller, until it disappears out of sight, as does the Busi River, the place of so many childhood picnics. I will never know Waschbank again.

TWO

DURBAN

1930s

THE MEERS IN DURBAN

Parting from Waschbank was painful: parting from Surat must have been equally painful for the sons of Ahmed Meer – the common ancestor of all the Meers in South Africa – the first of whom emigrated to the colony of Natal in the nineteenth century. One son lies buried in Waschbank, another in the Indian Ocean with the ship that sank with all its passengers off the coast of Mauritius; my father is buried in Durban and his eldest brother and mentor in Surat.

In 1931 there were fifteen grandchildren of Ahmed Meer, the Surat patriarch, in South Africa bearing his surname. MI Meer was Ahmed Meer's first grandchild to settle in Durban at a time when the rest of the kutum [clan] was scattered in northern Natal, Kimberley, India and Burma.

I arrived in Durban with my parents in 1931. AI and his family came soon thereafter from Kimberley. Many years later Mohamed Meer's sons, EM and Alif (married to my sister Amina), returned from Burma to Surat and from Surat arrived in Durban, where they settled with their families. The call of the kutum was powerful and they gathered around MI Meer. Twelve of Ahmed Meer's fifteen grandchildren found their way to Durban, leaving two behind in Dundee – Amina, the daughter of Mohamed, married to GH Peer, and my sister Fatima, married to SM Motala.

Mohamed Meer's two sons-in-law, GH Peer of Dundee and MI Meer of Durban, collectively provided the South African Medical and Dental Council with so many members that the compilers of the Guinness Book of Records could find their contribution noteworthy.

In Durban, the ten of us – my parents and I; my sister Ayesha who had joined us because of trouble with her in-laws; my brother HC and his wife and daughter, Zohra; AC, his wife and son, Haroon – fitted into the two rooms rented by AC in Pine Street as best we could. Our flat overlooked Nicol Square, which would become famous as the 'Red Square' of so many historic meetings and events addressed by Monty Naicker, Albert Luthuli and Yusuf Dadoo. It was the Square to which HA Naidoo, George Ponnen and PM Harry would rally the workers of Durban and which would become the Hyde Park of the city.

From our home, the office of MI Meer and the *Indian Views* at 137 Grey Street was only a three-minute walk. We went there often, as did so many others who gravitated there to get first-hand information of happenings in South Africa, India and the world.

SCHOOL AND WORK

I was eager to continue my education. I was fortunate to find that my old school principal, Ephraim Thomas, was now the principal of Carlisle Street Government School in Durban. I went to see him. He was very friendly and most encouraging. He said I was a bright pupil and if I co-operated and worked hard, he would put me through the six years of primary school that lay ahead of me in four years. I had left school in Dundee in class two. I took up the challenge with a passion. I worked hard, harder than anything Mr Thomas could have imagined. I worked two shifts – the first shift at school and the second at my brother's 'factory' at home. We made shirts at one shilling and sixpence a dozen. The shopkeepers in the Grey Street casbah supplied the fabric, cotton and buttons. It was my duty to collect these and deliver the completed shirts. The shopkeepers weighed the material carefully and recorded the weight. When I delivered the completed shirts, a second weighing was done to ensure that no material loss had occurred, that we had not short-changed them by even a thread or a button. I hated their implied aspersions on our honesty.

My job in the factory was to make the buttonholes. Every night I worked on the high-powered buttonhole machine. There were eight buttonholes to a shirt. The work was laborious and left me little time for my homework, yet I passed my PSC (Primary School Certificate) in 1935 with a first class in English, Arithmetic and General Knowledge. I was seventeen years old.

My primary-school days were the most difficult of my life. My secondary-school days would open up new horizons and would be the most seminal, but there were hurdles to be crossed before that could happen.

We moved house from Pine Street to Little Grey Street, now known as Baker Street. The name change occurred because Grey Street was clearly an Indian street, residentially and commercially, and the whites living on Little Grey Street did not want to be confused with Indians. This despite the fact that Sir George Grey, after whom the street was named, was a highly respected governor of the Cape Colony.

I suffered my first great loss in Baker Street; I lost my father, and it was as if the ground had been swept away from under my feet. Although the grief was shared by the family, I felt terribly alone and insecure. The others busied themselves with the rituals and found solace in these. I just missed my father. I thought of his misery during his last four years when he had lost his independence and had become a dependant. I, too, was a dependant: my brother's. I could be his dependant only so long as he allowed me to be. I suddenly found that my brother could no longer support me. His CMT business had proved a disaster, and he threw in the towel. He closed shop. He and his family moved in with his in-laws. My brother HC and his family moved in with MI. My sister Ayesha, my mother and I appeared to be homeless. My PSC, the gateway to secondary school, suddenly became useless. I found myself confronted with far more serious problems than my education. I had no means of survival, nor did my mother and sister. I began looking for work.

I was offered a job as a shop assistant in Waschbank at £3 a month. I saw no alternative but to take it. I began my round of goodbyes to my elders, among them my cousin MI, who was then the editor and proprietor of the *Indian Views*. His head was bent over his writing, and he didn't lift it all the while I was saying my goodbyes and explaining why I was leaving. When I had finished, his writing stopped, and his pen remained momentarily poised in mid-air – it was one of those old-fashioned pens with a detachable nib. He had wound cotton around the part where his fingers gripped it to form a protective pad against blistering. He looked at me for a few seconds, then said, 'Ismail, don't go to Waschbank. There is nothing for you there. I'll pay you £3 a month. You come to the press tomorrow and start writing out the subscription reminders.' I was amazed. I had not expected this. Suddenly my PSC became valuable. If I earned money, I could go to high school.

We Meers are not a demonstrative people. I sort of mumbled something in lieu of a thank you. MI would have been embarrassed if I had been more explicit. He had done what he believed he had to do, and it did not merit any gratitude. I believe he would have offered me accommodation as well, but I knew he was in no position to do so. He was living in Convent Lane at the time and running a very full house, which, apart from his family, included my eldest brother Hussain (HC) and his wife, Gorie Äpa, and their daughter, Zohra; and Chota Motala and MC Meer, both from Dundee, schooling at Sastri College. For full measure there was also Karodia Chacha, the shopkeeper of Dundee/Dandi fame, now down and out and dependent on anyone who would shelter him. There was obviously no room for me in MI's house; he did not say so, but I knew. The very fact that he did not say 'move in' was confirmation enough.

I went to my sister Äpa. I told her I had a job, but nowhere to stay. She said I shouldn't worry. She would speak to 'your' Mota, meaning my brother-in-law – her husband and MI's younger brother, AI. He had just bought a wood-and-iron house at 62 Ritson Road, the first Meer to purchase a property in Durban. It had five bedrooms, two of them very small, a living room and a breakfast room. AI had no hesitation in taking me in. He also took in my mother and my sister. Suddenly my life changed per favour of the two orphans of Waschbank, MI and AI. But for them, I may have disappeared into the world of shop assistants; instead I entered the world of journalism, and high school, and was on my way to becoming a lawyer.

SASTRI COLLEGE

Secure in my material needs, I enrolled as a student at Sastri College, the only high school for Indian boys in southern Africa at the time. It had been built with great pride by the Indian community and was named after the first Indian Agent General in South Africa, VS Srinivasa Sastri, who had inspired it. Sastri was stationed in Pretoria, but when he came to Durban he took up residence at the elegant home of EM Paruk on the Berea, since not a single hotel would accommodate him as a 'Non-European': the hotels were reserved for 'Europeans Only'. Later on, an exception was made for the Indian Agent, but this had never been extended to Sastri.

EM Paruk was a philanthropist, a founding member of the NIC, and its longest-serving president. There was an open invitation to all who desired to lunch at his shop, and many guests gathered there daily for the midday meal. AWG Champion, when down and out, was cared for by Paruk Seth,[1] who provided his family with free accommodation. Champion never forgot that kindness and often referred to it.

Each evening Indian merchants gathered at 330 Currie Road, when the Agent was in residence, and sat at the feet of the silver-tongued orator of the British Empire. Most of them did not understand English and depended upon those among them who did to translate his erudite counsel. During one session the revered Agent pointed out that there was not a single high school for Indian boys in all of southern Africa, which included Nyasaland (Malawi), Kenya, Uganda and the two Rhodesias (as Zambia and Zimbabwe were then known). 'South African Indians will never truly progress until they have university graduates,' he warned, 'and to prepare for this, you have to have a high school.'

'What does he say?' one of the merchants enquired.

'He says we must build a high school,' his colleague interpreted.

'Tell him,' the enquiring merchant said, 'we have built forty-eight schools. We will build one more. That is no great task.'

So Sastri College came into existence in 1930 as the forty-ninth school to be built by the Indian community. It is today a living monument to the India–South

Africa relationship. There were no teachers in South Africa to teach at this prestigious Indian high school, so India sent out a team of educators to staff it.

Indian boys came from all over southern Africa to Sastri College.

The community had initially planned to build a hostel for boys adjacent to the college, but the City Council had not granted sufficient land to incorporate this, so the students were left to make their own boarding arrangements. AI's house in Ritson Road was only a stone's throw from Sastri College. AI, who had left the *Indian Views* by then and set up business on his own, was struggling to keep the home fires burning. So he and Äpa took in boarders, of whom there was no shortage.

The boarders at AI's occupied two of the three large bedrooms in the house. I had one of the small rooms all to myself. Life at Ritson Road and at Sastri College was busy, bubbly and invigorating. The company was congenial and the food good – my sister served it piping hot directly from the stove to the table. We ate in silence while AI remained at the head of the table, but when he left we broke into animated discussion and joked and pulled each other's legs. I came to know a lot of students from northern Natal and the Transvaal.

I loved my days at Sastri College. My buttonhole-making chores came to an end. My evenings were my own and I filled them with social and political interests. MI gave me all the time I needed to take part in the many extra-curricular activities that attracted me. He provided me with my material needs and gave me intellectual guidance. He encouraged me to write, and my pieces were published in his *Indian Views*. My office hours were from 2.30 to 5 pm every weekday, my weekends free. I paid my school fees and bought my textbooks and clothing from the money I earned at the *Views*.

Apart from sports – I was never a sportsman – I participated fully in all other extra-curricular activities. I was a keen member of the dramatic society and was cast in prominent roles by our 'director', CR Warriner. I was also a prominent member of the debating society and represented the college at all debates. The college magazine, which was always edited by the English teacher, was entrusted to me, and I was appointed its editor in recognition of the fact that I was already a practising journalist.

INDIAN VIEWS

The *Indian Views* was founded by Mohamed Angalia, who had succeeded Gandhi as secretary of the Natal Indian Congress. They had differences over the issue of the annual subscription of members. Gandhi had wanted the subscription fee lowered so that Indian workers could afford to subscribe. On losing the motion, Gandhi left the NIC and formed the Natal Indian Association (NIA). This was in 1903.

Mohamed Angalia founded the *Indian Views* in opposition to Gandhi's *Indian Opinion*. He saw the *Opinion* as the mouthpiece of Gujarati Hindus and established the *Views* as the mouthpiece of Gujarati Muslims. Both papers as such represented the passenger Indians and not the indentured, whose languages were Tamil and Hindustani. Mohamed Angalia's son, Cassim, took over the paper from his father, but, unable to run it, sold it to the Jeewas, who employed MI as its editor and then, in 1932, sold the paper to him. MI developed the weekly and increased its circulation substantially in South Africa, and extended it to other southern African countries and to Mauritius. He travelled by car to the Rhodesias, Nyasaland, Mozambique, Kenya and Zanzibar. He never learnt to drive and the faithful Omar Khan, who drove him to all these parts, was both friend and son to him. MI returned from his subscription-collecting trips with rich stories about the hazards encountered and the people met.

The *Indian Views*' office was a vantage point from which one observed and learnt all about the goings-on in the Indian community. It was also a very stimulating place because of its many and varied visitors – almost all interesting, and ranging from the Indian Agent General, Sir Kunwar Maharaj Singh, to merchants, trade unionists and the reigning Indian politicians.

I was busy making out receipts one day when a tall European walked in. I recognised the gentle Reverend CF Andrews, who had worked with Gandhi. I noted the deep respect with which MI greeted him, and then he introduced me to him. Andrews handed in an article he had written on the outbreak of smallpox in Durban, a week after his arrival from India. MI and Andrews discussed the epidemic and the unhygienic conditions in which most Indians lived in Durban. MI published the article prominently on the main page of the *Views* under the heading 'A Message to *Indian Views* by Reverend CF Andrews'. The Gujarati translation, as requested by the author, appeared alongside the English.

Another distinguished person of Gandhi fame who frequented the *Views* was Albert West,[2] who often contributed articles to the journal, and at times wrote its editorials.

In 1935 the *Views* was in trouble. MI published a report alleging a criminal case against Cassim Angalia, and Angalia slammed MI with a libel suit for £3000. MI lost the case but the damage awarded was for a far smaller amount than demanded.

The *Indian Views*' office and Mullah's Cafe were places of call for Transvaal Indians after booking passage to India on the British–India (BI) ships at Shaik Himad's. *The Views*' office, they claimed, provided them with much food for thought, and Mullah's Cafe with samoosas, biryani and Mullah Chacha's famous Bombay Crush.

The visit to the *Views* was also made on their return from India or Mecca. Such visits often paid handsome dividends when their names were featured in the social column.

Many of the BI passengers in 1936 took, besides other items, cases of pineapple jam to India to distribute in the villages as murabba, the Gujarati version of jam. Most Indians travelled third class on the deck and cooked their own food or contracted with the caterer on board: £6 for the twenty-one days for 'Muslim weesee' [contract], and under £5 for 'Hindu weesee', which was vegetarian.

The arrival of the BI boat in Durban was the pleasant signal for letters and newspapers from India. We looked forward to the rickshaw loads of 'exchange copies' of all the leading newspapers and journals, which came from India and were disgorged out of the huge mail bags: there was the *Bombay Chronicle* of BG Horniman, the *Kesari* of Poona, the *Statesman* of Calcutta and the *Hindu* of Madras. They told us about Nehru and the state of the Indian freedom struggle. The exchange copies were read voraciously by MI and his assistant editor, Farooqi, and later by Alif when he and my sister Amina and their daughters arrived from India, and settled in a rented flat in Azad Court. I have the sense that for all our technology today, we were better informed on national and international matters in those days.

I met Chamberlain Nakasa at the *Indian Views*. He was the English language compositor. We became good friends. One day we went to the Avalon Cinema, part-owned by AI Kajee, who was then secretary of the Natal Indian Congress and probably the most important Indian political figure. We were given seats apart from each other. We went to the ticket counter and asked to be seated together. We were told there was special seating for 'Natives' – 'manager's orders'. I caught sight of AI Kajee. I went up to him and complained. He took off in righteous indignation and swore at the ticket attendant, ordering him to give us seats together. Later the ticket attendant told us that it was at Mr Kajee's instruction that they segregated Africans in the theatre.

All his life Chamberlain remained a restless soul, interested in publishing and writing, and he received much encouragement from MI. But it was not Chamberlain, but his nephew Nat, who became South Africa's well-known African writer. I remember Nat in his early teens, coming to the *Views* on Saturdays and helping Chamberlain with typesetting. He died tragically in New York.

In 1937, Chamberlain Nakasa spent his savings on launching a monthly journal called *New Outlook*, with an editorial board consisting of himself, B Asher, Dr Goonam, Farooqi Mehtar and myself. The journal was welcomed by both the *Views* and the *Opinion* with favourable reviews. I was very proud when my article was published with my photograph, and under it the caption 'the author'. Apart from the *Views* and *New Outlook*, my journalistic activities extended to the *Indian Opinion* and letters to the editor of the daily papers.

PHOENIX SETTLEMENT

My first trip to the Phoenix Settlement took place in January 1936; it was an unforgettable experience. I went to this historic place with MI to meet his friend Molvi IA Cachalia, who was visiting the settlement with SB Medh. SB Medh was recuperating after fracturing his arm and leg in a motor collision on the Pretoria–Johannesburg road.

He had been an inmate of the Phoenix Settlement during the time of Gandhi. Molvi IA Cachalia was the son of the famous AM Cachalia, to whom the Mahatma had paid his highest respect in his book, *Satyagraha in South Africa*,[3] dedicating a whole chapter to him.

Molvi Cachalia was later to play a vital role in the Transvaal Indian Congress (TIC) and would be honoured by the government of India with a Padma Shree.[4] I was very impressed by the Molvi's very liberal approach to all religions. He and MI were of one mind in their understanding of Islam. They were both strongly influenced by Moulana Abul Kalam Azad. MI was critical of the conservative Molvis and took them on fearlessly. He had just written a book on Islam and non-Muslims in which he stressed the universality of all religions. Molvi Cachalia agreed with his analysis and complimented him.

Omar Khan drove the car through the sandy track in between the tall cane. On a rainy day, the 'track' became quite unmanageable, and on that memorable day the car became bogged down. Khan had considerable trouble digging it out and moving it.

I walked the historic grounds at the Phoenix Settlement and saw the house in which Gandhi had lived, the simple wood-and-iron Sarvodaya[5] of world fame. I visited the press where the *Indian Opinion* was printed, and found the same flatbed machine at work as at the *Views*' press, with sheets of newsprint being fed manually. Though rivals, the *Views* and *Opinion* helped each other when either of their machines broke down. I met Sushila Behn, Manilal Gandhi's wife, during that visit, and saw the important role she was playing at the press. Both the *Opinion* and the *Views* had dedicated staff. It was indeed a very sad day when years later the *Opinion* ceased to publish and the same fate befell the *Indian Views*. Both were family-run weeklies, and both had depended largely on Gujarati-speaking subscribers, who were on the wane by the 1940s.

As we drove back to Durban, my mind dwelt on the great lesson of sacrifice that MK Gandhi had left us.

VICTORIA STREET MARKET

I was often sent to the squatters' market in Victoria Street by my sister-in-law, Gorie Bai. During market hours the whole of Victoria Street was cordoned off against motor traffic, of which there wasn't much in those days, and the market gardeners put out their vegetables, which they brought by foot or donkey-drawn carts, on the pavements and road.

I was particularly intrigued by an article in the *Natal Advertiser* (that was the name by which the *Daily News* was known at the time) about Karamchand, a 108-year-old Indian market gardener, who lived at 25 Wandsbeck Road, Sydenham. I went to investigate.

Karamchand didn't look as ancient as I had expected. He was quite strong and in control of all his faculties. He attributed his longevity to frugal living and not acquiring too many worldly goods. He told me that at one time he had been offered the ground on which the Durban Town Hall stood. He could have bought it at £5 an acre, freehold, but did not think it worth his while. The soil was too sandy, not good for cultivation, so instead he bought land in Sydenham, which then fell outside the Old Borough of Durban. The soil was good, he said, and for years he supported his family with the sale of the vegetables he grew on it.

He had come to Natal as an indentured worker on board the *Ailsa* in 1874, when he was forty-seven years old. I wrote a story about him, but MI said it had been killed by the *Advertiser*. However, he translated the article and it appeared in the Gujarati section of our paper.

DURBAN'S FLEET STREET

A year or so after AI had bought his house in Ritson Road, MI bought his house on the same road. AI's address was 62, MI's 84. Later still, my cousin, EM Meer, arriving from India, purchased a property at 26 Ritson Road.

By the time the Meer kutum had moved into the 'Meer Fariya' [neighbourhood], Ritson Road had taken on something of the character of a 'Fleet Street' in Durban. It was from Ritson Road that I, in 1939, and my successor, Ranji S Nowbath, in 1940, edited the Sastri College magazine. From 84 Ritson Road came the editorials and columns written by MI Meer, and from 64 Ritson Road, Dhanee Bramdaw edited his *Leader*, which hit the streets of Durban with its catchy placard, 'Bridegroom Ducks Wedding', in 1941.

AI Meer, as far as I know, became the first Indian South African to be appointed as a correspondent for a foreign newspaper, the *Blitz of Bombay*, and he sent his dispatches from 62 Ritson Road, 'Press Collect' to Bombay. He also wrote copiously for local newspapers.

Ranji Nowbath graduated to writing columns in the *Leader* from 64 Ritson Road, and from around the corner, at Azad Court in Mansfield Road, came the creative writings of Alif Meer in Gujarati, both in prose and poetry, both serious and humorous.

I myself often operated from Ritson Road. During the 1946 passive resistance campaign I dispatched the editorials of the Transvaal-based *Passive Resister*, which I was editing, and at the same time covered news for the *Cape Standard* and *Guardian*.

Indeed, Ritson Road had been converted into our 'Fleet Street' at a time when there were only a handful of black journalists in the whole of South Africa. There were no black journalists on any white daily or weekly; the sole exception was Dhanee Bramdaw on the *Natal Witness*.

Of all the journalists I have referred to, the one with the least formal education was MI Meer, having completed only Standard Five, and yet he was admired by all his colleagues as a brilliant writer in English, Gujarati and Urdu. His prose and poetry continue to receive acclamation to this day.

In March 1936, years after the demise of the *African Chronicle*, its former editor, PS Aiyar, walked into the *Views*' office with a copy of his new publication, the *South African Indian Review*. MI was very excited; he introduced me to Aiyar and said this was a red-letter event. MI Meer had the highest regard for PS Aiyar. The two men held similar political views. MI welcomed Aiyar's new publication under the heading 'Mr Aiyar's Come Back'.

THREE

POLITICAL ACTIVISM

1937–1944

FIRST POLITICAL MEETING

I was introduced to South African Indian politics within the year of my arrival in Durban. My brother AC and my cousins MI and AI were going to a meeting in the town hall, and they took me along. I felt grown up and important for I had been allowed to accompany my 'elders'. MI and AC talked about the trouble among the Indian politicians. I heard them mention the names Kajee, Pather, Christopher, Rustomjee, Godfrey and Manilal Gandhi, and learnt that they were our current Indian political leaders. I also learnt that there was a lot of infighting among them. I gathered that my elders were critical of them. They said they fought over nothing.

We found seats towards the front. My eyes were riveted on the great long pipes at the back of the stage – organ pipes, as I came to know later, but on my first view of them, I thought them sinister. What if a person fell into one of them? What would happen, would he disappear? My attention was distracted from these foolish thoughts by a wave of clapping and I saw the cause of it, a stockily built man who took his position before the microphone. AC whispered, 'That is AI Kajee. He is very important and very clever.' I was impressed by Kajee's energy, his bombast and anger at the way Indians were being treated. His speech was received with great applause. I joined the clapping vigorously, but then angry voices overpowered the clapping. The voices became people and they rushed onto the stage, and fighting broke out close to where we were sitting. It was getting very dangerous; not only were words being used, but also fists, and fruit and vegetables were being thrown onto the stage. The hall was full; there appeared to be thousands of people and they began milling into each other. I was sure we would be crushed and wondered why we were not leaving before we were caught in a stampede.

Then a lady come to the stage and took the microphone. She looked very important. Her voice carried over the yelling and howling, and the yelling and howling subsided; all eyes were riveted on the lady. Her voice was firm and commanding: 'You should be ashamed of yourselves. India is ashamed of you. This is not the way to solve your problems!' She said a great deal more that I cannot recall. I was highly impressed by the sight of her and the impact she had on a hall full of men. It was my first experience of the power of woman. In our family the men talked, the women listened. Nowhere in my experience had I seen a woman who talked and men who listened. MI, seeing me entranced, told me she was Kunwar Rani Maharaj Singh, the wife of the Agent General of India.

IMPERIAL CONFERENCES:
INDIA–SOUTH AFRICA ROUND TABLE CONFERENCES

Back home, I asked my elders what the furore had been about at the City Hall, and MI explained to me that Indian political leaders had become divided over the Cape Town Agreement between the governments of India and South Africa. MI told me, 'The white people want to get rid of Indians and the Cape Town Agreement allows them to do so. It has set up the Colonisation Commission, which is looking for another country to which Indians can be expatriated.' I was shocked. I said I thought they wanted to expatriate us to India. MI confirmed that that was so, but Swami Bhawani Dayal had reported that Indian expatriates were suffering in India. 'India is overcrowded. So now the leaders were divided between those who supported the Colonisation Commission and those who opposed it. Kajee and his NIC support the Commission.' I looked at AC. 'You admire Kajee? Do you support the Commission?'

'No,' he said, 'Kajee is clever. You saw that yourself. He is a good politician. But on this issue he is on the wrong side.'

MI explained that there were two sides to the Agreement. 'The other side is that the South African government has undertaken to "uplift" Indians who remain in the country. Kajee is concentrating on the Upliftment Clause, and overlooking expatriation. The Colonial Born and Settler Indian Association (CBSIA) is vehemently and correctly opposed to the Colonisation Commission. There is, however, no integrity in that lot either.'

And then MI laughed and said, 'Aiyar, of course, says the only upliftment there is comes from our Indian women who uplift their heavy baskets onto their heads and raise money to educate their sons. Sirkari Naidoo[1] is one such person.'

I thought of the time when I'd peeped into the bar. The stairway of our flat led directly into the shopping area. At the corner was the bar. I was given strict instructions not to go near it. Bad things happened there, I was told. I was curious to know the bad things, so I slowed down when I neared the bar and, after ensuring that the Muslim shopkeepers were not watching, I sort of looked in. I was surprised to see Indian women, the vegetable and fruit vendors who came up our stairway to sell their wares, drinking at the bar, their heavy baskets, which they carried atop their heads, momentarily resting on the ground. I saw them emerge from the bar, wiping their mouths, erect and full of pride after a hard day's work. I thought of them 'uplifting' educated sons on their heads instead of their baskets. I remained full of respect for those women all my life.

INDIAN POLITICAL PARTIES IN NATAL

I began reading about local Indian politics. MI guided my reading and directed me to articles in past issues of the *Opinion* and the *Views*. From these, I gained a fair understanding of the dynamics of the Indian political process.

Gandhi had founded the Natal Indian Congress in 1894. It was not only the oldest anti-colonial political organisation in the colony of Natal, but also in the country and in Africa. It was dormant for six years after Gandhi's departure and was revived in 1921, in the main by Sorabjee Rustomjee and Swami Bhawani Dayal. I also learnt that South African Indian politics, unlike African and Coloured politics, was influenced from abroad; that South African Indians maintained strong links with India, and the Indian government took a protective interest in our affairs. India was an equal member of the Imperial Conferences set up by Britain after World War I to muster unity among her dominions.

India had contributed significantly to the Allied victory, both in terms of capital and manpower, and her delegates at the Imperial Conference pointed out that unity was impossible in the Empire so long as some of the dominions, namely Canada, Australia, New Zealand and South Africa, discriminated against Indians. The treatment of Indians in South Africa was a major issue at these conferences from 1917 onwards. The *Views* and the *Opinion* reported on the exchanges between General Smuts of South Africa and Sir Tej Bahadur Sapru of India on this issue.

AI Kajee entered the political arena as a backroom boy during the first Round Table Conference and later became an office bearer of the South African Indian Congress.

The conflict between the opposing sides worsened in 1924 when the Union government introduced the Class Areas Bill, the mother of the Group Areas Act of 1950, which finally deprived Indians of their capital accumulation in real estate. In 1924, Indians reacted by uniting their provincially based political organisations under the SAIC, and elected Sarojini Naidoo president and Dr AH Gool vice-president. Sarojini Naidoo was also elected president of the Indian National Congress. This was the only time that the two Congresses shared a common president.

India did not see the Class Areas Bill as a domestic issue, but as an imperial issue, and as a hostile act of one dominion member against another. India demanded equal rights for South African Indians.

The British prime minister, Lloyd George, held that there could be no discrimination in the Empire on the basis of race or civilisation, but the South African delegates rejected this. Their argument was that they could not extend equality to Indians without extending it to Africans as well, and that was unthinkable. British principles were easier enunciated than implemented, and when it came to the crunch, white British opinion sympathised with South Africa's whites and supported them in their racism.

In the face of this impasse in the international arena, Sarojini Naidoo recommended a Round Table Conference between India and South Africa, and this resulted in two conferences in 1927 and 1930, during which the irritant, the Class Areas Bill, was suspended. There was agreement on a Round Table Conference in 1950, but it never took place. When South Africa did not agree to suspend the Group Areas Act, India felt a conference was not appropriate and the matter went back to the United Nations.

The first conference culminated in the Cape Town Agreement and the second in the Colonisation Commission, which sought the repatriation-cum-expatriation of Indians, thereby hopefully reducing the Indian population to a bare minimum, which the South African government promised to 'uplift'; that is, educate and Westernise.

AI Kajee and PR Pather had wrested the leadership of the NIC by then, and they accepted the Cape Town Agreement and co-operated with the Colonisation Commission. The serious conflict that erupted over this issue resulted in Albert Christopher and Sorabjee Rustomjee setting up the Colonial Born and Settler Indian Association in 1932. As I saw it, both groups were conservative, inward-looking and self-centred.

The first two Round Table Conferences were held before we left Waschbank and before the churning of my political consciousness.

The post–Colonisation Commission years were hectic, and the feuding conservative political organisations had a Mafia-like quality about them. Their meetings were boisterous and invariably broke up because of personal wrangling.

I was attending to my work in the *Views'* office one afternoon when an excited Farooqi Mehtar rushed in all hot and bothered. 'They're fighting like dogs!' he exclaimed. 'There's Angalia standing on the hood of his car, castigating Kajee and hundreds of people watching the tamasha [spectacle].' MI's only comment was, 'What's new?'

MOVING TOWARDS SOCIALISM

When I moved into political activism, the people around me saw my obvious choice as being between one of the two dominant Indian political groupings in the community – the Kajee-led Natal Indian Congress or the Christopher-led Colonial Born and Settler Indian Association. I had no respect for the leadership of either; I was repelled by their opportunism and fickleness, their concern with personal power and apparent disregard for the Indian people they supposedly represented. Moreover, I was brought up in a fairly multicultural environment in Waschbank. This steered me away from a uni-racial organisation. I found myself veering towards multiracial, leftist groups.

While I had been raised in comfort, I had also experienced penury. I therefore identified easily with the poor and working class. Small and isolated as Waschbank was, its very smallness and isolation had brought neighbours of different races close together. I had no problem mixing with non-Muslims, unlike the average Durban Vohra[2] Gujarati-speaking Muslim, whom I found to be very conservative, very closed in and snobbish. The wealthy among them were bonded in the Orient Club, where they relaxed, played games and organised pleasant social gatherings. We Meers were the poor ones, struggling to maintain a sort of middle-class existence, which we sustained only through our interdependence as an extended family-cum-clan. The only one worth anything among us was MI on account of his writings, intellectualism and quiet leadership. The Orient Club hierarchy could not ignore him. He was invited to the club with his guests and he took his cousins with him in his car. His was the only car in the 'clan', and we all shared it. They could not ignore us, either, on account of our education and knowledge. Both MI and AI were sought after to interpret national and international affairs, particularly when these impinged on the businesses of the Orient Club members. Our cousins, AM and EM, educated in India, with their understanding of Urdu literature and being poets in their own right, could not be ignored. My cousin AM couldn't get over one Seth's ignorance about the famous seventeenth-century poet, Ghalib. After listening to AM's rendering of some of his poems, the Seth commented, 'I suppose you are in continuous correspondence with him!'

With my Waschbank grounding, and the non-ritualistic, rational Islamic approach that my father had nurtured in me, I reached out easily to non-Muslims and formed friendships across religious and racial lines. It was therefore not at all surprising that I became part of a multiracial group of young people who yearned for a society where men and women would live in equality. The colour bar we experienced angered us. This group, together with my early indoctrination in Islam, laid the basis of my orientation towards socialism, which remained consistent throughout my life.

LIBERAL STUDY GROUP, 1937

In 1937, I was nineteen years old and at high school. We formed the Liberal Study Group, a non-racial think-tank. The founder members of this group were HA Naidoo, Dawood Seedat, Cassim Amra, AKM Docrat, Wilson Cele, George Ponnen, PM Harry and myself. We were joined by Jacqueline Lax, Beaver Timol, Pauline Podbrey, Leslie de Villiers and Debi Singh, who later became the secretary of the NIC.

We were inspired by Fay King Goldie, who chaired the group. We met every Thursday and we learnt to articulate and share our thoughts, to tease out and crystallise our ideas, analyse and write reports, conduct meetings, keep minutes and speak with confidence and authority. We held debates and tested our skills in public speaking. We studied socialism and Marxism and we popularised the Communist Party, which did not have the capacity to attract the kind of people we were attracting, namely young non-Europeans.

The Communist Party of South Africa (CPSA) of the 1930s in Natal had at its heart a core of ageing white communists, and that, combined with their intellectualism, put off young non-Europeans. Party meetings were moreover not open meetings, as they were organised into cells. We in the Liberal Study Group were, by contrast, young non-Europeans who combined intellectualism with activism. We went out into our communities and related to our people.

We established our office in Pembroke Chambers, between West and Saville Streets. The rooms were stuffed with our thoughts and smoke as we consumed cigarette after cigarette, and penned thought after thought on paper. We published our own weekly, *The Call*, as well as the newsletters of a number of trade unions, and pamphlets of the India League headed by Dawood Seedat. All we needed for our publications were a duplicating machine, stencils and a typewriter. We managed to acquire these.

HA Naidoo was the political editor and I was the overall supervisor of the 'publications division', having had experience in writing. I knocked out articles on our old typewriter. I never learnt to type properly; I remained a two-finger typist, but I found it functional. All of us tried our hand at writing and typing, but it fell to me to pass the final drafts before publication. Many of those working in the movement did not have a very good command of the English language and their writing required correcting. On the whole, they did very well. On one occasion I missed a serious error. An editorial appeared proclaiming 'we must forge the chains of our oppression'. I pulled up the author. 'Forge' means 'make' the chains of oppression. Surely he didn't mean that!

My comrade insisted that forge meant to break. He further insisted that forge was a stronger word than break and therefore better. I patiently informed him that a blacksmith forges, welds together. He does not break. He makes. But it was not until I brought out the dictionary and showed him the word 'forge' and the meaning attributed to it that he reluctantly accepted his mistake.

'No problem,' I told him. 'That's how we learn.'

'But,' he said, 'we have already printed two thousand copies.'

'Two thousand copies!' I exclaimed. 'We will have to pay heavily for your learning. We will have to cross out "forge" and replace it with "break" by hand, on all two thousand copies.'

We didn't go home at the usual time that afternoon. Instead, 'with all hands to the pump' we worked late into the night until every copy of the trade union newsletter had been corrected.

When we worked late and had money, we would treat ourselves to a snack at Cafe de Move On, a cafe on wheels that was stationary until midnight on Victoria Street, or at the Crystal Cafe in Alice Street or Peter's Lounge in Grey Street. Then we would make our way to our separate destinations, in Acorn Road, Wills Road, Mansfield Road and Ritson Road.

Peter Abrahams, a talented young poet and writer, joined us and we virtually adopted him, paying his rent and sharing our food with him. We published his first collection of poems, *Tell Freedom*. It was dedicated to Cassim Amra. I wrote the foreword and NV Mehta of Universal Printing Press printed it at the behest of DA Seedat, and the cost was 'payable when able', which was never.

We knew what fascism was all about. Italy had attacked Abyssinia (Ethiopia), and the civil war was raging in Spain, with Britain and France following the path of cowardly non-intervention. We were distressed by those events and inspired by Jawaharlal Nehru, who, when accepting the office of president of the Indian National Congress in 1936, had said: 'I am convinced that the only key to the solution of the world's problems, and of India's problems, lies in socialism and when I use this word I do so not in a vague humanitarian way but in a scientific, economic sense.' He influenced me to read up on socialism. We read about Nehru's visit to Burma (Myanmar) and Malaya (Malaysia), and the following year to England, where his daughter Indira was studying at Oxford. In Europe he made his stand clear to the Western world, and it was a stand with which I easily identified.

In my first year at university Dr Mabel Palmer introduced me to the writings of Beatrice and Sydney Webb: *Soviet Communism – A New Civilisation?* and their subsequent work when the question mark was dropped and Soviet communism confirmed as a new civilisation. I was greatly influenced by the Webbs. I also read Hewett Johnson's *Socialist Sixth of the World*. At about this time, the *Views* was publishing articles by Hawa H Ahmed under the pseudonym Muslim Girl. She was putting across socialist thought to an essentially Muslim readership. She aroused a great deal of interest and many challenged her female identity.

Only a man could write like that, they asserted. The Muslim Girl's identity was revealed when she married Dr Goolam Gool and the *Views* published a photograph of both bride and groom. My readings in leftist literature advanced and expanded as I joined the Left Book Club and later the Communist Party.

One of the issues that bothered us in the 1930s was what we South Africans should be called. African was not popular; the ANC was founded as the Native, not African, Congress. I recall AWG Champion taking umbrage at one of our meetings when I introduced him as an African. He corrected me emphatically, proudly declaring, 'I am not an African, I am a native of this country,' as if he was being deprived of his claim to the country as its indigenous inhabitant. The African People's Organisation, the APO, alone laid claim to African; as did its leader, Dr Abdurahman, who, though Indian in origin and perceived as Coloured, referred to himself as African.

We tried to find a name inclusive of all groups and appointed a commission headed by Cassim Amra to go into the matter. After some three months of deliberation, they came up with the designation Afri-Eurocola. The term was laughed out of court.

THE NON-EUROPEAN UNITED FRONT, 1938

I was still at high school in 1938 when I was invited to join the Non-European United Front (NEUF). My first reaction was not to join the NEUF, since it excluded Europeans. But when I saw that this non-European body had as its treasurer a European, Sarah Rubin, its 'racism' fell away and I joined, and became committed to it.

The NEUF was formed in 1938 in Cape Town by Zaibunisa (or Cissy) Gool, as she was popularly known, at a national conference, attended by 125 delegates from eighty-three organisations. She was elected president of the NEUF with Moses Kotane as secretary, BG Baloyi vice-president and WH Andrews treasurer. HA Naidoo and Dr Yusuf Dadoo, who headed the Natal and Transvaal branches respectively, were elected to the executive.

I met Cissy Gool when she came to Durban to help us with our membership drive in Natal. Dawood Seedat and Cassim Amra had taken leave for three months to organise in northern Natal. I was assigned to help Cissy Gool on the North Coast. I was overawed by her. She was the daughter of the famous Dr Abdurahman, who had worked with Gandhi, organised the Non-European Conference in 1930 and been part of the SAIC delegation to India. She was married to Dr AH Gool, a former president of the SAIC. Like her father, she too had been elected to the Cape Town City Council. The people took to her because of her oratorical skills, and, I am certain, her beauty. Cissy Gool was a huge success on the North Coast.

I never met Dr Abdurahman but heard him speak at the Muslim Institute in Queen Street. The hall was packed to capacity on that occasion; there was not even standing room. I was struck by Dr Abdurahman's sincerity and impressed by his call to the oppressed classes to consolidate themselves into a united front if they were to compel the Europeans to accede to at least some of their demands. 'The group system,' he said, 'has led to destruction. By uniting the African, Coloured and Indian, we can gain much.' I think my decision to join the NEUF was in part influenced by him.

The cub reporter of the *Daily News*, Aida Parker, was covering our Natal membership campaign. She was following us in a police van, which we found objectionable. We stopped our car and I went to speak to her. I told her that we objected to her mode of travel and unless she changed it she would not have our co-operation. She abandoned the police van.

Cissy Gool stayed with AI Kajee during that visit. We didn't like this as we were opposed to Kajee's conservative policies. But then none of us could accommodate her in the style to which she was accustomed. Kajee could. There were no hotels for non-whites at the time. Her parents (her mother was of Scottish descent) stayed with EM Paruk when they visited Durban, as did all important visitors in those days. Others stayed with relatives or friends, and when one did not have these, Muslims could claim hospitality at the two Musaffar Khanas [traveller's lodges] built by two family trusts, the Haffejee family in Alice Street, and the Randeree on the corner of Grey and Victoria Streets.

In 1939, the NEUF had made sufficient impact to draw the attention of the Indian National Congress, which moved a resolution supporting the participation of Indian South Africans in the Non-European United Front. The resolution, however, was opposed by Gandhi for reasons I could not support. His opposition received a great deal of publicity. It fitted neatly into JH Hofmeyer's[3] warning to Indians a few years earlier not to become involved with Africans and Coloureds, but to remain distinct and separate. I discussed Gandhi's opposition with both HA Naidoo and Dr Dadoo and urged that we should respond to it. Both declined, not wanting to be at odds with the Mahatma. But where angels fear to tread, fools rush in, except that I didn't see myself as a fool. Both men, seeing my insistence on the matter, relented somewhat and agreed to my writing a letter to the press, under my initials, not my full name, since I was too well connected with the NEUF, and by implication my letter would be associated with that organisation. My letter was published in the *Daily News*. Gandhi eventually changed his views on Indians throwing in their lot with non-Europeans in general and supported non-European unity.

TRADE UNIONS

The outbreak of war and the rapid growth of secondary industries in Natal saw a tremendous upsurge in trade union activities. HA Naidoo and George Ponnen, coming as they did from a background of factory employment and the working class, were ideally placed to mobilise and foster this movement.

The Falkirk Strike in 1937 demonstrated to us that unity between Indian and African workers was an absolute necessity. The Europeans were united in their racism, and therein lay their strength; the non-Europeans remained divided and therein lay their weakness. Non-European strength lay in unity, which was still to be realised. My mind turned to Dr Abdurahman and his appeal for unity, and I pondered on the meaning of our long struggle. I was more convinced than ever that we would get nowhere as a people if we allowed the Kajee–Pather and Rustomjee–Godfrey groups to continue misleading the Indian people.

The Falkirk Iron and Steel Workers' Union struck for better working conditions. The employers responded by firing fifteen Indian and African workers, resulting in 350 workers striking on 26 May 1937. The strike lasted thirteen weeks. This was the first time Indian, African and Coloured workers had united against their bosses. Conservative as it was at the time, the SAIC supported the workers by holding a mass meeting at the Victoria Picture Palace and providing emergency relief in cash and kind.

My 'friend' Champion played a most reactionary and racist role. He ordered the African workers to return to work, and not to join the Indians, who were 'shopkeepers' and 'exploiters'. The workers countered, saying that none of them had shops, but Champion did, so he was the exploiter.

In 1942, twenty-nine African workers were brought to court for striking at Morton's Jam Factory in Rossburgh. They were represented by Advocate Harry Bloom, instructed by Albert Christopher. HA Naidoo managed to settle the dispute with an increase in the wages of workers.

In the 9 December 1942 Dunlop Strike, the bosses used African workers against Indian; they fired thirteen Indian activists and reduced their Indian employees by half (eventually stopping all employment of Indians in their company). They brought in Africans from the rural areas to replace the Indians. HA Naidoo, Pauline Podbrey, RD Naidoo, George Ponnen and Ramsunder joined the picket line. The NIC under AI Kajee held a supportive meeting at the City Hall and provided emergency relief. One hundred and forty-seven Indians were charged for holding an illegal strike and 350 Africans were charged under the Masters and Servants Act. The fact that Indians and Africans had stood together and the strikers were supported as a body, inspired a measure of Afro-Indian unity.

Most of us in the Liberal Study Group became trade unionists. We studied trade unionism and visited factories and focused our energies on organising workers. Dawood Seedat, NG Moodley, George Ponnen, HA Naidoo, Cassim Amra, SV Reddy, Pauline Podbrey and I all became secretaries of trade unions.

In my first year at university I was surprised to see a large number of ageing gentlemen there. I found that they were teachers in government-aided schools; their salaries were pegged at £5 per month. They were studying to advance their qualifications in the hope of getting appointments in government schools, where conditions of employment were better. I pointed out to them that the majority of Indian schools were government aided and hence only a few of them, regardless of their qualifications, would be absorbed into government schools. I advised that they should work to improve their conditions of employment in the aided schools. I wrote to the Department of Education to clarify the position of aided school employees. I got the reply that the department had nothing to do with them. This immediately relieved the teachers of the regulation that prohibited civil servants from forming trade unions.

In 1940, at a well-attended meeting of teachers, we founded the Natal Teachers Association. I was elected secretary. Since the salary of Indian teachers was pegged at £5 a month, they decided to pay me £6 a month to drive home the point that anything less was not a living wage. My income trebled overnight and I felt rich. I was the first Indian trade union secretary with a matric, NG Moodley the second.

Things became 'fairer' when the Woman's Liberal Study Group was formed in March 1942. Debi Singh and I were very flattered when we were asked to address its first meeting at the Gandhi Library. If there was an air of condescension in our approach, this was quickly dispelled by Dr Goonam. She stood out among her fellow members in her vivid colours, puffing away stylishly at a cigarette at the end of a long silver holder. She was sharp, and it was clear that no man, or, for that matter, woman, could dominate her. But she was at the same time fun loving and a generous hostess. She liked arranging parties at her house and invited us around. We found these parties relaxing and enjoyable. Radhi Singh, a fellow BA student, was in the chair of the Women's Group when Mrs Jithoo spoke on the need for non-European women to unite. Miss Minnie Ramawthar, a student at the Girls High School, addressed the group on the need for women to play a greater role in the community. We were all invited to a special function organised in honour of Misses Irene Godfrey and Gertrude Lazarus, who were leaving to study at universities.

Needless to say we enjoyed these excursions into femininity; and we were not beyond romancing those we fancied and who responded.

LEFT BOOK CLUB

Fay King Goldie was married to Andrew Goldie, who ran the Gollancz Left Book Club. Inspired by this, we formed our own Left Book Club and took turns reviewing books. At one of our meetings I was reviewing a book by Palme Dutt; I was flattered to see AI Kajee in the audience. Though essentially a businessman, Kajee took an interest in intellectual pursuits and kept a fine collection of left-wing books in his home in Ryde Avenue. He invited us to borrow these books.

At the time, Kajee's political career was on the rise. Under his leadership, the NIC appeared to be developing as a people's organisation, involving itself with the problems of workers, helping Indian trade unions and taking up issues of education and housing, apart from protecting Indian property interests. It was difficult to know to what extent his activism was inspired by pure political rivalry. One suspected that AI Kajee was trying to upstage Albert Christopher, who had taken the lead in organising Indian workers, marching with Gandhi and the striking Indian coal miners at the turn of the century. He had established the South African Federation of Non-European Trade Unions in 1928.

Yet when Indian unemployment reached crisis proportions it was Kajee who, through the NIC, organised a massive protest of unemployed Indians, filling the City Hall and marching the workers to the residence of the Indian Agent General to lodge their protest. It was as if he was tweaking his nose at Christopher and saying, 'You may be the trade union fundi, but I have the workers.' BLE Sigamoney was another early trade unionist. While we of the Liberal Study Group did not initiate trade unionism among Indians, it certainly matured with us and took on a militant dimension, and we provided it with a Marxist theoretical base.

THE COMMUNIST PARTY AND COMRADES

I became a member of the Communist Party during my second year at the University of Natal, non-European section, without knowing that I had done so. George Ponnen introduced me to HA Naidoo, and he in turn invited me one evening to a lecture by a University of Natal professor in his house on the Berea. What I learnt from that one lecture was mind-boggling.

The lecturer pointed out the massive exploitation on which the economy of the world was run. He spoke of the wastage inherent in the capitalist economy. He spoke of the vast quantities of coffee that were dumped into the sea in Brazil in order to preserve coffee's high price. I was shocked by the lunacy of it. He went on to relate an example nearer to home, the fishing monopoly in South Africa at the hands of Irving & Johnson. The price of fish, he informed us, was kept high by dumping fish back in the sea if there was an over-catch. He extolled the lack of monopoly under socialism, where production was planned to meet the people's needs and not for the profit of capitalists. There was lively discussion in which I also took part.

The evening proved both fascinating and enjoyable. I listened in disbelief that people could go to such diabolical extremes to accumulate wealth; that they would actually throw food away rather than feed the poor; that they would create a false scarcity in order to keep prices up and accumulate profits. It went against everything I had learnt as a Muslim.

After the discussion, the person who appeared to be the chairman of the group looked enquiringly at my friend and asked whether I was to remain for the rest of the discussion. HA responded, 'He is one of us and can remain.' On our walk back home, HA explained to me that I had participated in a communist cell and I was now a member of that cell and of the Party.

MI, always respectful of my freedom to think and associate and never interfering, for the first time sounded a warning note when he heard I had joined the Party. We used to gather at his house on Sundays. Within the Meer family, there was a great divergence of views and these were aired, at times, quite passionately. He now said to me, 'There is a great deal of good in the communist ideology, but you are a Muslim and it leaves God out of its reckoning. Can you live with that?' This put me in a dilemma. The family was deep within my psyche and I could not in any way be alienated from it. Islam was at the centre of the family and I could not be parted from that either. I was caught on the horns of a dilemma. What I had heard at the lecture resonated deeply. I was angry with the economic system that dominated the world. I wanted to do something about it. HA convinced me that I could do so through the Party. I was attracted to the Party. It was non-sectarian, inclusive of all humanity without restrictions on race and religion: the Party offered me the political home I sought. I liked what I heard; I liked the people I had met. I had been stimulated by the lecture and had enjoyed the multiracial company. I debated the issues in my mind and finally reached a decision. I told HA I was pleased to be in the Party but that I would remain a Muslim. The two would coexist in my person. HA assured me that that wouldn't be a problem.

Harry Rubin was a Marxist and a Stalinist, and when he died his instructions were that he should be cremated. This was before the advent of Jewish Reformism, and at a time when, as far as I knew, no Jewish person had been cremated in Durban; all Jews were buried. The Jews refused to attend Rubin's funeral and it was left to the left wing in Durban to cremate him. The only Jew present at his funeral was Roly Arenstein.

GEORGE PONNEN AND HA NAIDOO

George Ponnen was one of the most active trade unionists in the early forties. He worked in Magazine Barracks among the municipal workers. Ponnen invited me to a meeting he was addressing. I took two buses to get there. I looked at the leaflet and it was in Tamil, which I could neither read nor understand. Magazine Barracks was a new experience for me. The Corporation[4] housed its workers in appalling conditions. The meeting was held on an open piece of land. The residents had put out benches and these were quite full. I took my seat next to one of the Corporation workers. Ponnen had told me he would be talking on Marxism. I had quite absurdly imagined he would speak in English, but the lecture, like the leaflet, was also in Tamil! Had he addressed them in English, no one would have understood. As it happened, I was the only one who did not understand. Ponnen saw my disappointment and said he would make it up to me. He accompanied me on the bus home, and repeated the lecture in English during our journey. It was simplified Marxism, on a level that simple working people could understand. I was impressed.

I have fond memories of HA Naidoo; his brilliance, his range of contacts, his high sense of discipline, his oratorical skills, his integrity and his passion to eliminate poverty. They were quite a pair – George and HA. Both were South Indians, both were trade unionists working among the poor Indian workers, and both were involved with white women. George was married to Vera Alberts, HA was courting Pauline Podbrey; both women were members of the Communist Party and the Liberal Study Group.

Vera was a chain-smoker, swore like a trooper and was very domineering, but she had a heart of gold and was generous to a fault. She was warm, kind and passionate about things she believed in and the people she loved.

George was her direct opposite. Where Vera was loud and garrulous, George was quiet and rarely spoke. There was a mystique about him on account of his quietness, so that when he did speak, every word seemed valuable. Where George was restrained and non-judgmental, Vera was voluble, assessing and classifying people into good or bad. If one passed Vera's test, one passed the test of acceptability in general; she had that kind of authority. Together the Ponnens displayed such strength of character that one thought of them as the bedrock of the Party. They lived in a block of flats in Wills Road, their neighbours being lower-middle-class Indians. They were very popular. Vera's friends ranged from the voluble Dr Goonam to the sedate Mrs Moosa, whose husband owned a prosperous departmental store in Berea Road. Was he not a capitalist in conflict with our workers? But when it came to personal relations, Vera relaxed Party doctrine.

The Ponnens kept open house for all the members of the left-wing fraternity, and I enjoyed visiting them. I was introduced to Christmas dinner at the Ponnens. I was particularly charmed by the Christmas pudding, brought in flaming, the tickeys crunching in my mouth when I got lucky. Everyone celebrated my luck.

The Ponnen daughters, Indira and Marsha, were beautiful and quite clearly Indian. One felt that Vera's passion for Indian rights was closely linked to her passion for her daughters.

Pauline was very different from Vera. She was strikingly beautiful, refined of speech, sophisticated. I remember her best in her vivid red coat and matching lipstick. Both women were dedicated to the Party. Pauline's closest friend was Leslie de Villiers, very pretty and gentle. The two of them took a keen interest in Indian women, believed them in need of 'liberation' and volunteered their services to liberate them in a very practical way, beginning with literacy. They spent a great deal of time with AKM Docrat's wife; my sister Ayesha and my niece Zohra were also among their 'pupils'. I don't know what Pauline and Leslie did with them, but whatever it was, it did them good, for they glowed after each 'visit'.

I accompanied HA Naidoo to Mt Edgecombe and helped him form the Sugar Workers Union. Indian and African women weeders were paid 7 pence a day. We discovered that the Industrial Conciliation Act prohibited 'pass-bearing natives' from unionisation. African women did not carry passes at the time, so they could join our union, and we went out of our way to enrol them.

HA was doing an excellent job when he was promoted to the executive of the central committee of the Communist Party. This required him to move to Cape Town. He and Pauline were in one sense happy about the move, for Cape Town was more liberal in its attitude to mixed marriages. They were finding it difficult to settle down in Durban as a married couple. They could do so with relative ease in Cape Town.

I continued to go to Mt Edgecombe. The people there missed HA, for he was an excellent trade unionist and had won their confidence. On one of my dues-collecting visits (the system of stop orders collected and paid by the employer came later) one of the women members enquired, 'Bhaiya [brother], where is HA?' I told her that HA had gone to Cape Town and would not be coming any more. 'Aiyau!' she said. 'How can you take a mango tree from Natal and plant it in Cape Town? It won't grow.' Her words were prophetic. HA, who had shone in Natal and led the trade union movement, faded in the Cape. Some put it down to his marriage, others to his estrangement from his cultural roots. Whatever it was, HA's light dimmed in the Cape.

A FORTUNATE MAN

OLD GUARDS AND YOUNG TURKS IN NATAL

In 1939, the two dominant Indian political organisations, the Natal Indian Congress and the Colonial Born and Settler Indian Association, were united at a mass meeting attended by 2000 people as the Natal Indian Association (NIA),[5] which then became the official Indian political body recognised by officialdom in India and South Africa. But unity was short-lived; the NIC re-emerged as an independent competing body and the Indian political scene was dominated by two groups of conservatives. This would continue for three more years until the CBSIA would disband, amalgamate with Kajee's Congress and come to be known as 'The Natal Indian Congress founded by MK Gandhi in 1894'. But in early 1940, the two-party spectacle continued.

The problem the community faced was that of institutionalised segregation. Though it was segregated up to the mid-1940s, this was more by custom than by law. A segregatory Bill, the Asiatic Land and Trading Bill, was in the offing and the leaders of the NIC and NIA humiliated and demeaned the Indian people by not rejecting the Bill outright. Instead, they followed a course of appeasing the government and co-operating with its commissions, and presenting elaborate defensive reports that they were not a threat to Europeans, they were not 'penetrating' into white areas and threatening white commerce, 'so please *baas*, don't pass a law against us'. Their humiliating pleadings reached intolerable proportions when they undertook to subject Indians to voluntary segregation. Despite this, the government passed the Pegging Act, which temporarily pegged all property transactions between Indians and other race groups, while it prepared legislation that would isolate Indians permanently in their Indian ghettos. Understandably, Indians were agitated, and both the NIC and NIA organised competing mass meetings at which thousands gathered to back personalities rather than policies, since there were no differences in policies. The NIC and NIA were equally conservative and equally keen to collaborate with the government. Fighting often broke out at these meetings. Into this equation, we of the NEUF brought a third force, distinct and different from that of the NIC and NIA. We were the radicals challenging their collaboration with the racist government, which included supporting the war. We came to be referred to as the 'Young Turks' against their 'Old Guard'. We were committed to establishing a socialist society in South Africa that would eliminate all inequality, both of class and race, and place our country and her destiny firmly in the hands of her people.

THE NATIONAL BLOC, 1940

Towards the end of the thirties, JW Godfrey, a colourful lawyer of the time, shifted allegiance from the NIA to the NIC and became an enthusiastic Kajee supporter. He berated the youth of the NEUF and said that we were not fit to wipe Kajee's shoes. We stood our ground; we were introducing new political thinking that would revolutionise not only local Indian politics, but also impact on non-European politics in general. Kajee realised this; there was a part of him that was attracted to us, but he was too entrenched in his conservatism to cross over. In 1937 we were still a few years away from the confrontation that would explode between us and the Old Guard. Kajee didn't quite realise our potential. In the meanwhile, he dealt with us by having us beaten up by his henchman Cassim Angalia. But we were not beyond defending ourselves in like manner. We had the intimidating PM Harry, chairman of the Falkirk Workers Union, large-bodied and tough like Hanuman himself, reinforced by his trade union stalwarts. They formed a powerful guard against our adversaries.

We infiltrated the Christopher–Rustomjee-led NIA, and in 1940 established the National Bloc within the NIA and challenged its leadership.

THE THREE DOCTORS: NAICKER, DADOO
AND GOONAM ARRIVE FROM EDINBURGH

In the mid-1930s, three Edinburgh graduates, Doctors Naicker, Dadoo and Goonam, returned from their studies and became active in South African Indian politics. While Doctors Dadoo and Goonam entered left-wing non-European politics almost immediately, it took Monty Naicker somewhat longer. He dallied on the fringes, spending his first year with the Hindu Youth Movement, but he also joined the Natal Indian Association where he became radicalised by the NEUF members. He not only joined them but he became the leader of the National Bloc.

On 11 February 1940 Dr Naicker made what I believe to be his maiden speech in a packed City Hall. He took his stand clearly and forcefully against non-Europeans supporting the war, and vigorously attacked the NIA leadership for collaborating with the white authorities to enforce voluntary segregation on Indians. At a second meeting, on Sunday, 9 June 1940, at the Royal Picture Palace (the old Rawat Bio Hall), he seconded HA Naidoo's resolution condemning the Christopher–Rustomjee fraternisation with the Provincial Council to prevent Indians from buying properties in 'white areas'. Quietly but firmly, and with his typical humility, Monty Naicker asserted the right of Indian South Africans to live and trade where they wanted, and rejected the concept of 'penetration' into European areas. 'It was the racist Europeans,' he contended, to rousing applause, 'who were encroaching on Indian rights and Indian freedom.' Only the *Indian Views* published both his speeches. I sat up and took note of this rising star with whom I would later work closely. As his PRO I helped him with his press statements and speeches throughout his political career.

DR DADOO AND THE CONSERVATIVES IN THE TRANSVAAL, 1939

A parallel confrontation was taking place in the Transvaal between the conservatives in the Transvaal Indian Congress, led by SM Nana, and radicals of the NEUF, led by Dr Dadoo. Like Kajee and Rustomjee in Natal, Nana, in the Transvaal, was negotiating voluntary segregation to prevent the passing of the Anti-Asiatic Land Act. Dadoo formed the National Group[6] within the TIC in 1936. The two blocs in Natal and the Transvaal, led respectively by Doctors Naicker and Dadoo, by contrast, were taking an aggressive attitude and preparing for passive resistance. Dadoo was ably supported by EA Asvat, an old Satyagrahi who had worked with Gandhi.

The late thirties saw Dadoo and Nana locked in battle over their opposing policies. As in Durban, public interest was high and attendance at political meetings and rallies ran into thousands. A significant factor in the Transvaal was the large turnout of women, initiated, strangely enough, by the Nana group to increase their support. Dadoo proposed passive resistance against the government in 1939, and Nana stringently opposed it. Dadoo had popular support but postponed his campaign on the advice of Gandhi, who hoped to negotiate respite for Indians from the South African government. This did not happen. The Transvaal Nationalist Group, in the meanwhile, settled for a sort of mini passive resistance in 1941, and vendors set up fruit stalls close to the City Hall in defiance of the law that excluded them from trading in white areas. The story goes that, unfamiliar with commerce, one of the gentleman vendors, Sulieman Desai, cleared his supply of oranges within the hour by selling them at 15 pence a dozen instead of 50 pence!

When the conflict between Nana and Dadoo appeared to be reaching danger point, my cousin MI Meer agreed to mediate between the leaders of the two groups, both of whom he admired and knew well. If anyone could have reconciled them, he could. The mediation meeting was held on 15 May 1939 at the home of EI Patel. Lengthy and friendly discussions followed. MI proposed that two resolutions should be put to the mass meeting scheduled for 28 May 1939: the first ensuring that those in favour of passive resistance (Dadoo group) 'shall be at liberty to carry on their struggle and those opposing them would neither oppose them nor deny them sympathy, support and help to which they are entitled by their heroic resolve to suffer and sacrifice in the cause of Indians in South Africa'. The second resolution was that 'Congress will come to no settlement with the government on any question appertaining to Indians in the Transvaal except with the consent of the passive resistance struggle'.

The mediation failed, for all MI's skills. Less than twenty days later, on 4 June 1939, SM Nana's supporters allegedly attacked Dadoo's supporters outside Osrin's cinema in Ferreirastown with chains, knuckledusters and knives.

Dayabhai Govindjee, twenty-five years old, was disembowelled. Dadoo put his intestines back into position and he was rushed to hospital, where he died. Eight Dadoo supporters were injured. Five of the attackers were arrested and found to be relatives of Nana and AI Kajee respectively. However, the charges against them were dropped in suspicious circumstances.

For all the violence and skulduggery, the future was in the hands of the radicals, and the immediate future in the passive resistance struggle, as events unfolded.

The conflict between the prevailing conservative leadership and ourselves continued. In Pietermaritzburg, other NEUF activists were arrested for holding an illegal meeting. We responded by holding an 'illegal' mass meeting to protest the arrests.

GENERAL SMUTS INTRODUCES THE ASIATIC LAND AND TRADING BILL

The 1940s opened with Indians facing the first parliamentary enactment against their land and trading rights. General Smuts prepared to pass the long-threatened Asiatic Land Tenure Act, which would confine Indians to their racial ghettos. The Old Guard dreaded the proposed legislation. They were concerned, above all, about their business interests and were therefore prepared to do a trade-off: accept residential segregation voluntarily if the Bill was withdrawn and their commercial interests left intact. We radicals, the Young Turks, raised our voices at every racial assault and criticised the 'sell-outs'. Our support increased among the people.

The Old Guard was an elitist club of merchants representing themselves and their interests. Then again, they were isolationists who devoted their attention to Indians alone, and ignored the fact that Coloureds and Africans were also assailed with exploitative segregation laws.

SORABJEE RUSTOMJEE'S BRIEF DALLIANCE WITH THE YOUNG TURKS

In the Transvaal, the TIC leader, SM Nana, negotiated with the central government to withdraw the pernicious Pegging Act, and with the provincial government to stay ordinances imposing statutory segregation.

In the midst of this, Sorabjee Rustomjee, a key NIA collaborationist, intimated his desire to join the radicals. He organised a mass meeting in Durban for Dadoo.

Sorab was wooing the radical Dr Dadoo, whose popularity was on the rise. Sorab planned to fill the City Hall and Dadoo was his draw card. He was scoring a point against Kajee. He saw himself bringing Dadoo to Durban as his protégé. We of the National Bloc understood Sorab's motives very well, but we overlooked them for he was also serving our interest. The City Hall would be full, the meeting would not cost us a penny and the platform would be our platform since Dadoo was our man.

On Friday, 24 April 1943, the mail train from Johannesburg to Durban left Park Station with almost a full coach of persons who were to attend the 'Paruk–Lockhat wedding' and the mass meeting against the Anti-Asiatic Land Bill at the Durban City Hall.

The NIA and NIC, with large memberships drawn from the well-to-do members of the Gujarati-speaking Vohra Muslims, arranged their social occasions to coincide with the political, to conveniently ensure full attendance at both.

Sorabjee left no one in any doubt that he was the organiser-in-chief of the train journey. He came to our compartment and gave us details of the Durban programme. He had many surprises up his sleeve and was enjoying keeping us in anticipation of the rabbits he would pull out of his hat.

It was now supper time on the Johannesburg–Durban mail train. And again Sorab was up and about with another surprise. Unbeknown to the passengers, he had arranged with the catering department of the railways to take on board huge pathilaas [pots] containing biryani, jardaa, samoosas, kebaabs, kalias, hand-made rotis, pickles, chutneys and papads. And a smiling Sorab saw to it that all his passengers were treated in grand style.

After supper he proudly displayed the illuminated copy of the Atlantic Charter.[7] It had taken my team of six students three whole days of combing Johannesburg before finding that copy at the Information Office of the US Consulate. We had assumed he would frame the Charter and display it in his home in Johannesburg. He had come to my flat at 13 Kholvad House to fetch the copy. He now displayed it to us in our compartment with great pride.

And later came a surprise unplanned by Sorab. At Estcourt the train was grounded. It was now Saturday, 25 April 1943, the day of the wedding, and the stationmaster at Estcourt said that there was a derailment. He therefore could not give any guarantee as to when the train would reach Durban.

Sorab was back in action. A telephone call from him brought not only a leading merchant to the Estcourt station, but with him came a fleet of taxis to take Sorab's passengers to Durban, where they arrived well in time for the nikah ceremony.[8]

The City Hall was jam-packed. Dadoo was at his charismatic best and his speech received thunderous applause. We were justifiably proud of him. Sorab was almost as good that evening. His voice boomed through the hall. In his hand was the scroll of the Atlantic Charter. In clear, indisputable words, he said, 'The Atlantic Charter is not worth the paper on which it is written!' and, very deliberately, took the beautifully printed copy of the Charter and, to my horror, tore it up and scattered the pieces on the stage! If that was his intention, I thought, why did he not tear up a blank piece of paper? Who would be the wiser? But for Sorab, only the genuine article would do.

The Anti-Asiatic Land Bill had hung like the sword of Damocles over Indians for several years. AI Kajee, in control of the NIC, took his own peculiar action in the matter and provoked a storm of protest. He went into a huddle with General Smuts and the two came up with the Pretoria Agreement in March 1944, which was rejected by both whites and Indians.

Kajee gave Smuts the 'assurance' that he and the NIC would persuade Indians to accept voluntary segregation if Smuts withdrew the Anti-Asiatic Land Bill. This gave Smuts a way out of the embarrassing situation he faced in the international forums, where he was respected as a liberal.

The exposure of this Agreement brought the skies down upon Kajee's head. He became the target of Indian working-class anger. Not that his opponent, Rustomjee, was any different in his tactics. He had actually served on the Lawrence Committee of the Durban City Council to monitor that Indians did not purchase properties in white areas.

We of the NEUF/Nationalist Bloc joined the fray with vigour. We opposed and exposed the collaborators so stridently that the NIA expelled Dr Naicker and his followers, thereby intensifying the conflict between the radicals and conservatives.

ANTI-SEGREGATION COUNCIL CONFERENCE, 1944

The expulsion only strengthened our position. We went on to form the Anti-Segregation Council in 1941, and held its first conference in Durban in May 1944. Dr Naicker and George Singh gave the keynote addresses. I helped to draft the comprehensive resolution, which set out our minimum demands: the repeal of the Pegging Act, which had for years frozen all property transactions between Indians and non-Indians; the abrogation of the Pretoria Agreement; and the removal of the provincial barriers and colour restrictions in all spheres, such as universities, industry and trade unions.

The Council instructed its executive to rouse world opinion against South Africa's racist government. We also moved to appoint a full-time organiser to orchestrate a national membership campaign. The Anti-Segregation Council had twenty-nine organisations with which it was affiliated, mostly trade unions, and these provided an effective organisational network. We focused on building a national Indian organisation representative of all economic groups, both trade unions and merchants' associations. We formed branches throughout Natal. We were determined to be a force to be reckoned with. We were also determined to oppose the new Anti-Asiatic Land Act as strongly as possible.

FOUR

EVENTS DURING WORLD WAR II

1939–1944

UNIVERSITY OF NATAL NON-EUROPEAN SECTION, 1940

In 1939, I wrote my matric examination. I was twenty-one years old, probably three years older than the average matriculant. There were only a hundred Indians who wrote the matric examination in the entire country that year. I had spent four years at Sastri College as a secondary-school student, and it was during those four years at high school that I had matured politically.

I was the first member of the Meer family to matriculate. My elders were almost as ambitious for me as I was for myself. We discussed my future: MI, AI, my brother AC and my brother-in-law YC. Medicine was rated the highest profession, law came second, and there the choice of professions ended for Indians. Architecture and engineering were entirely out of their scope, not only because the courses were not open to non-Europeans, but also because they could not possibly hope to make careers in these fields. One didn't think of teaching as a career because it paid so little. Medicine was out of the question for me; it would mean raising board and lodging fees apart from the tuition fees, since there was no medical school in Durban. In fact, non-white doctors in those days all qualified overseas. We decided that I should enrol for law at the University of Natal. I would continue to work for MI at the *Views*. Between my salary at the *Views* and the Teacher's Association I had enough money to pay for my expenses. I could continue to live with AI at no cost to myself.

I enrolled at the University of Natal in 1940. I was sorry to leave Sastri College; it seemed to me that I had spent the best part of my life there. But then I didn't quite leave, as the non-European section of the university, established in 1936, was based at Sastri. We were not allowed on the main campus with European students. We couldn't be full-time students. Our lectures began in the afternoons when the lecturers, having taught the full-time white students, descended from the Berea hills to teach us non-whites. Our lecturers were Dr Mabel Palmer, the organiser of the classes, Mrs McDonald and Professor Sneddon. They were highly committed.

Dr Palmer could lecture on any subject we requested, or so it seemed. She lectured us in political science, philosophy and economics. She was a Fabian socialist. She had personal contact with George Bernard Shaw and there was a snapshot on her mantelpiece of her with Shaw on a hiking trip. Yet she tolerated the racial attitudes of white society. She warned us not to talk to white girls. 'The time of Rag[1] is full of jocularity,' she said, and instructed me that there was to be no dancing between white and non-white students. I had been elected president of the non-white SRC in 1940, so the responsibility fell on me. 'You must not ask a white girl to dance with you, and if a white girl asks to dance with you, you must decline.' I knew very well why, yet I asked in pretend-innocence, 'Why?'

'Because European parents will be outraged and we are dependent on their funding to run the university.'

Our socials were supervised by lecturers who made certain that barriers between Europeans and non-Europeans were not infringed. We had an overseas visitor at one of our socials, blond, blue-eyed and every bit European. He asked me whether he could ask one of the Indian girls for a dance. 'Go ahead,' I said, and I watched Dr Palmer's reaction from the corner of my eye. She was nervous when the blond European took the dusky Indian girl onto the dance floor, but did not move a muscle, knowing that any bad publicity abroad would be worse than coping with white prejudices at home.

Although we were segregated, we maintained some contact with white students at Howard College, particularly through the National Union of South African Students (NUSAS). In 1942, our university students, for the first time in Natal's history, took part in the NUSAS conference held in Johannesburg. I was elected by both the non-European and European students at Sastri and Howard Colleges as their best speaker. I was excited; my cousins, MI and AI, and my brother AC, were very proud. The competition was stiff. I thought the other speakers were so much better. I was placed second; Cape Town was honoured with the first position.

I wrote an article in *Dome* magazine in which I argued that it was necessary to free India to enable her to rally maximum support against fascism. I criticised British imperialist policy. The principal of the University of Natal did not like my article and that issue of *Dome* was banned. That was the first banning of my writings and it did not come from the government, but from the principal of a liberal university.

Rag came and we participated, raising funds and building a float, which drew considerable attention because of the political statement it made: a battalion of

EVENTS DURING WORLD WAR II

non-European soldiers scrubbing the floor, our placard reading, 'Arm them, do not harm them!' Non-Europeans were being enlisted but were not allowed to be armed. The prospect of a non-white shooting a white, even if a Nazi, was too terrible for whites to contemplate.

KHALASIES AND BLACK MARKETEERS

We lived through the Second World War with its shortages and black marketeering, and black nights. We would sit huddled in the dark on the bed and tell stories. There would be the occasional knock, an inspector at the door: 'There is a chink showing in your blackout. Very dangerous.' We agreed, and immediately took steps to seal it.

The Suez Canal was closed during the war, and ships, forced to round the Cape, would stop at Durban. There were interesting visitors. Troops from India on their way to the war zone were highly admired and sumptuously entertained at the Orient Club. The Rampura Regiment paraded down the streets in the Indian business area bearing arms, and we all turned out to applaud them.

The khalasies (Lascars), survivors from torpedoed ships, who swam or rowed to shore, or who came off their ships anchored at the port, were neglected and exploited.

They were given all sorts of strange accommodation, even being put up at the Depot Hospital where conditions were quite grim. Our student union formed a research group and exposed their fate in Durban. We applied such pressure that the Minister of the Interior, Harry Lawrence, made a trip to Durban and requested us to take him on a conducted tour of the places where they were housed. The minister was shocked; he took immediate action and relief followed.

Among the Lascars were some very good musicians. At times when we walked on the docks, the stillness of the night was broken by the beat of the tabla [drum]. Harry Devodutt arranged qawali [traditional music] sessions to entertain the Durban Indian community and help the khalasies earn some much needed money.

On one occasion a ship anchored in Durban harbour, and manning it were a group of Jewish Lascars. The authorities alerted the local Jewish community. They came enthusiastically to give comfort to their fellow Jews, but when they discovered they were dark and Indian they withdrew, and their welfare was left to our committee.

The war years brought scarcity and in turn the scarcity led to hoarding and black marketeering.

AM Motala – nicknamed 'Fishaan' on account of his small size – upon hearing of the plight of the poor from MI, imported a large quantity of rice and sold it at cost price to the poor. We took up the issue of black marketeering. We addressed mass meetings on its evils and carried out raids on the hoarders, opening up boxes and bags of food and forcing the owners to sell the produce at control prices. JN and I continued food raids when we went to Johannesburg, assisted by the CPSA and TIC, and Bram Fischer and Joe Slovo were among the more enthusiastic participants.

CHIEF ALBERT LUTHULI

Dawood Seedat initiated the India League during the war years. Palme Dutt had formed the League in London and later stood for parliament. George Bernard Shaw had written to him saying that he would vote for him knowing full well he would lose, simply because intelligent people like him did not stand a chance. Shaw visited South Africa. I attended the meeting he addressed at the Gandhi library. He offered miscegenation as the solution to the South African race problem!

We began to observe India Independence Day in support of the Indian freedom struggle. We planned a public meeting at the Avalon Cinema in Durban on 26 January 1942. Paul Sykes and the Reverend WH Satchel, both of whom had connections with India, and Dawood Seedat and I met at a planning meeting at AI Kajee's office. We set the time between the matinée and evening shows so as not to interfere with box office revenue. I said I had read that a man called Albert Luthuli had visited India, and we should ask him to be one of the speakers. I had up to then not met Chief Albert Luthuli. Paul Sykes undertook to contact him and invite him to our next planning meeting. Two days later I met Luthuli at AI Kajee's office in Albert Street, Durban. That was my first meeting with Chief Albert John Luthuli. I was greatly impressed by his quiet dignity. He listened intently to Sykes and Satchel's reasons for supporting the Indian struggle. He did not ask any questions; he didn't have to, as both Sykes and Satchel were pretty garrulous. After they had finished there was a pause, neither too long nor too short. I had the feeling that Luthuli had been considering the matter all the while, and he was forming his response in his mind. He had been introduced to me and had taken my hand firmly in his, but it was the two men he turned to because they had done all the talking while I, like him, had only listened. Then, with slow deliberation, he said he would be happy to speak at the meeting. He respected the struggle of the people of India. He admired Gandhi and Nehru.

I thought to myself, 'There is more to this man than appears on the surface,' and I was proved right in the years that followed, when we worked together.

The India Independence Day meeting was highly successful, I believe, because of Luthuli's spellbinding speech. He had a beautiful voice, his oratory was awe-inspiring. His impact on the audience was electric. I was asked to make a contribution as a student leader. I talked about India's freedom and how the lack of it was hampering India's full contribution against the fascists and Nazis. Luthuli talked about India's great civilisation and how it was a blot on humanity that such a great country should remain chained by colonialism. I was drawn to Luthuli and I sought him out whenever I could. I found in him a most attractive blend of serenity and moral authority. We began working closely together when he became president of the Natal ANC, which also had its office in Lakhani Chambers, on the same floor as the NIC.

I grew close to Luthuli. He would come to my home when some new Bill or new issue perplexed him, or he was not quite sure about some new strategy or policy. He had confidence in my evaluation and judgment; on such occasions he would sleep over at our home, occupying the ottoman in the front room. I would know him in life and I would be with him in his mysterious death, rushing to Groutville and breaking down in an unexpected flood of tears over his coffin.

I had assumed that the India Independence Day celebration was the first multiracial meeting the Chief had addressed, but when I asked him he laughed heartily and then told me of the first mixed gathering he had addressed. It was, of all places, in Dundee, when he was a young teacher. 'There was a tailor in Dundee, Nathoo Morar.' I said I knew Nathoo Morar; he was a tailor by trade but always gave his occupation as Commissioner of Oaths.

'The same,' Luthuli confirmed, his eyes twinkling a smile. 'He was a very good businessman. His main clients were African teachers. He would travel long distances to measure them and then make a second journey to deliver the suits and collect his last instalment. The suit cost £3, but the teachers paid 10 shillings a month. He struck on an excellent idea one year. He persuaded us to hold our conference in Dundee and undertook to help with the arrangements. We agreed. He put a lot of effort into that conference. He arranged a public reception, presided over by the mayor, and there was a mixed gathering of Africans, Indians and whites, apart from us African teachers.'

'And Morar profited handsomely,' I added.

Luthuli said Morar had brought in helpers and there were six very busy people with measuring tapes at that conference.

'He measured over a hundred teachers. You can work out how profitable that was. Besides, it saved him many trips.'

I found a report of that conference in the *Indian Views* of 26 July 1935. Nathoo V Morar had arranged the reception at the Dundee Theatre Supper Room on 4 July. The Supper Room was packed to capacity and the president, Mr Luthuli, thanked Mr Morar 'for the excellent reception', and expressed the hope for a continued good relationship between Indians and Africans. Another speaker was BW Vilakazi, who expressed pleasure at seeing all races together at the function. But that India Independence Day meeting was certainly the first mixed gathering Chief Luthuli addressed in Durban.

When I began work at the *Indian Views* I found that AWG Champion was a regular visitor at 137 Grey Street, Durban, the headquarters of MI Meer and the *Views*. I also learnt that because of the old Waschbank connections, MI was doing all the printing for Champion's ICU Yase Natal free of charge. Chamberlain, our chief compositor, set the monotype. Champion was living in Grey Street at the time, much to the annoyance of the Corporation, and his Social Club (essentially political and barely social) in Old Dutch Road was flourishing. He continued holding ICU meetings in the grounds opposite the Carlisle Street School.

When Champion was president of the Natal ANC I went to see him and told him that I wanted to become a member of the ANC. He said that I could join the ICU but not the ANC. Had the ANC opened its membership to Indians in the 1940s, I believe many would have joined it.

I was fond of AWG Champion – he was a friend of the family. The fact that he had been my father's friend weighed heavily on me, but Luthuli was so much more admirable. I could see that Champion was an impediment in the development of the ANC. He operated like a dictator. I began canvassing for Luthuli as the next Natal president, and found that there were others who shared my thoughts. I attended the 1950 provincial conference of the ANC. Champion was in the chair, pompous and arrogant as always. He did not think for a moment that he could be displaced. But displaced he was. Cocksure that Luthuli could never defeat him, he exercised his prerogative as chairperson and ruled that there would be no secret ballot. He instructed all those for Luthuli to come on the left-hand side, and the first person to walk to that side was Mangosuthu Buthelezi. Luthuli had a clear majority when the walking was over. I was reporting for the *Guardian* and I interviewed Champion afterwards. He was gracious about his defeat and told me he would never oppose Luthuli as long as he was president of the Natal ANC, and he kept his word.

THE ANTI-WAR CAMPAIGN: THE ARRESTS OF DADOO
AND SEEDAT IN SOUTH AFRICA AND NEHRU IN INDIA

A key area of conflict between us and the Old Guard was the issue of the war. We vehemently opposed the war; they supported it and canvassed funds and recruits. Our stand on this issue was the same as that of the Congress in India and of Gandhi and Nehru – to distance ourselves from it as long as we remained fettered.

Nehru's stand was, 'No participation without responsible government.' He was imprisoned because of his anti-war pronouncements. Dadoo similarly described the war as 'an imperialist war and therefore an unjust war'. Non-whites in South Africa were recruited as menials and not as arms-bearing soldiers. Dr Dadoo published the anti-war position succinctly in an NEUF pamphlet, 'An Appeal to all Non-European People of South Africa':

> You are being asked to support the war for freedom, justice and democracy. Do you enjoy the fruits of freedom, justice and democracy? What you enjoy is pass and poll tax laws, segregation, white labour policy, low wages, high rents, poverty, unemployment and vicious colour bar laws.
>
> European recruits receive 3s 6d per day (beer allowance). You are expected to give your life for 1s a day.

Dadoo, at the time heading the Transvaal NEUF, was charged for his anti-war statements under the emergency regulations. He stated in court:

> This war is not a war to free the people, but to maintain and extend imperialist domination. This war could only be transformed into a just war for the preservation of democracy and the defeat of fascism when full and unfettered democratic rights are extended to the Non-European people of this country and when the oppressed people of India and the colonial and semi-colonial countries are granted their freedom and independence.

Dadoo was sentenced to four months' imprisonment with hard labour, with two months suspended. He continued his protests against the war after his release from prison, and was charged again under the War Measures Act for 'inciting Natives' in Benoni not to join and help the government win the war. This time he was sentenced to two months' imprisonment with hard labour. The suspended sentence came into force and he served a total term of four months' imprisonment.

On 30 April 1941, Dr Dadoo stepped out of the Benoni jail, twenty pounds lighter in weight, but apart from that quite the same man who had entered prison. Thousands of Africans gathered at the prison gates and gave him a resounding welcome. The membership of the NEUF increased and exceeded that of the ANC.

In 1941 a contingent of NEUF representatives, led by Dawood Seedat, attempted to take over a Natal Indian Association meeting at the City Hall, but Rustomjee successfully defended his platform, bellowed his resolution and obtained majority support. Dawood Seedat and his followers, undeterred, surged onto the platform and fighting broke out, which was only brought to order when the police intervened. Dawood Seedat and his supporters were ordered out of the hall. Undeterred, they marched to Bond Street where Dawood addressed the crowd using the English language very colourfully; the 'colour' landed him in trouble. He called Smuts 'a clever, cunning crook'. The government was not amused by his alliteration. He was arrested. We engaged Harry Bloom to defend him. Harry Bloom explained that there was a time in England when it was an offence to criticise the head of state. He referred to a case where a man was charged with taking Queen Victoria to a brothel. He had done so by paying the prostitute with coins that bore her image! But such a law was now archaic, he explained, and got Dawood off, but that did not keep Dawood out of prison.

At another meeting, protesting the arrests of Nehru in India and Dadoo in Benoni, he said, 'The British Empire is not an Empire, it is a vampire.' He was charged under the War Measures Act and his case was adjourned to a later date.

I was working at the *Indian Views* at the time and one day found a hefty Afrikaner looking for me. He brought me a letter from Dawood written in Gujarati. It said, 'Bhai, I am hungry. Please send some puri patha [an Indian savoury] with the warder.' I borrowed money from Farooqi Mehtar and satisfied Dawood's craving for Indian cuisine.

INDIRA NEHRU (GANDHI) IN DURBAN

In the midst of our escalating activism and our irrevocable breach with the Old Guard, Indira Nehru stepped off her ship, briefly berthed in Durban, en route to India. She gave us her wholehearted support and boycotted our enemies. Her arrival, unexpected and sudden, was an exciting interlude in our young, protest-filled lives.

Early on the morning of 31 March 1941, a very excited Dawood Seedat urged me to come to his home at once. He likewise alerted Cassim Amra in Acorn Road. Both of us lived within walking distance of Avondale Road, where Dawood lived with his mother, his wife Fatima and their burgeoning children. Curious to know the cause of his excitement we rushed to his house situated at the edge of the morning market. Its hustle and bustle invaded the house, except when Dawood's mother shut the door on the noise. We stepped into the front room, which rose directly from the pavement and served as the only entrance to the house and as a sitting-cum-bedroom. Inside it were two large beds.

We were met by a beaming Dawood and he led us into this room. The beds were occupied by a number of attractive young men and women who were Indian, all right, but certainly not South African. For one thing, they did not sit like South Africans, who would have sat on the edges of the beds, their legs dangling down. These young people sat in cross-legged comfort on top of the beds, quite at home with Dawood's large mother and talkative aunt, Bibi, who was serving them cups of steaming hot tea, helped by Dawood's wife, Fatima. Included in the strange group was Indira Nehru, Jawaharlal Nehru's only daughter. Close to her was Feroze Gandhi, who would become her husband and give her the name by which she would become famous. They had been advised in London by the India League to contact the India League in Durban, and had found their way to the only address they knew, the home of Dawood Seedat, head of the Durban India League.

They were students, on their way to India from Europe. We suddenly found ourselves in charge of this illustrious group that every important Indian organisation wanted to host. The community was soon alerted to their presence. Dawood Seedat's humble home became inundated with high-profile callers: Mr Kajee, Mr Rustomjee, Mr Manilal Gandhi, and so on.

INDIRA REJECTS PRO-WAR OLD GUARD

The Old Guard, supported by the affluent members of the community, people who 'mattered', saw themselves as the obvious hosts of Nehru's daughter, but she snubbed them. Rustomjee had rushed to the boat, garlands in hand, but Indira and her fellow students had refused to have anything to do with him because he was supporting the war effort and collaborating with the racist government. Her father, Jawaharlal Nehru, was in prison in Dehra Dun for opposing the war, on account of India's continued status as a colony.

The *Indian Opinion* gave a full account of Indira's rejection of the Old Guard. It was rumoured that Sorab, in his usual majestic way, had threatened that he would report her to Gandhiji and Pandit Nehru, to which Indira is supposed to have replied, 'Then you too will have to go to the prison at Dehra Dun.'

Rustomjee was not only enlisting men in the Indian community for the war, but, to make matters worse, he was justifying his collaboration by claiming he was following Gandhi. He pointed to Gandhi's participation in the ambulance corps in 1906 during the so-called Zulu Rebellion.

I found much confusion among many people on MK Gandhi's role in this rebellion, and I can do no better than to quote his own words from *Satyagraha in South Africa* to explain his position. 'I joined the army with a small corps of twenty or twenty-five men,' he writes. 'We found that the wounded Zulus would have been left uncared for, unless we had attended to them. No European would help to dress their wounds ... The Zulus could not talk to us but from their gestures and the expression of their eyes they seemed to feel as if God had sent us to their succour.'

This had happened thirty-five years before Indira arrived in South Africa.

Indira's group, in a discussion later on the day of their arrival, declared that they would prefer to be the guests of the Non-European United Front in preference to the India League. This brought forth an approving smile from Natal's leader, HA Naidoo. We found kindred souls in each other; we shared political ideas; we were against imperialism and colonialism and were vehemently opposed to supporting the war while our country and people remained bonded. We were all young together and filled with the sort of idealism that had become jaded in the Old Guard.

Like Indira's father, our Transvaal leader, Dr Dadoo, was also in prison for opposing the war, and Dawood Seedat was out on bail and due to appear in court on a second charge of opposing the war.

INDIRA INFLUENCES MANILAL GANDHI TO SUPPORT THE NEUF

Herman Kallenbach, Gandhi's close friend, made arrangements to accommodate Indira and her group at the Marine Hotel, but they declined on the grounds that they would not accept as a special favour something denied to non-whites.

Manilal and Sushila Behn Gandhi hosted a social at the Surat Hindu Association Hall. Gandhi's son arrived in a dress suit to meet Nehru's daughter, clad in a simple khadi sari. The tables were laid elegantly with knives and forks, but the guests used their fingers. Manilal was clearly put out by their implied criticism of his Western ways.

With great politeness, Indira also declined an invitation to stay at the Phoenix Settlement. Indira said that she would not stay there as long as its occupants remained vague on the war issue and opposed the Non-European United Front. She was also averse to accepting Manilal's invitation to visit Phoenix, but following a lengthy discussion with our 'group' – as I recall, Beaver Timol, George Ponnen, AKM Docrat, Dawood Seedat, HA Naidoo, PM Harry and myself – Indira not only agreed to meet Manilal and Sushila Behn, but she also undertook, with her colleague, Chandra Gupta, to influence Manilal to change his attitude – both to the war and to the NEUF – and they succeeded.

Instead of his total opposition to the NEUF, Manilal Gandhi, in his editorial of 11 April 1941, stated for the first time that the colour bar affected Africans, Coloureds and Indians, and that 'such colour bar can effectively be opposed only by a united front of all Non-Europeans'. The comment from the Liberal Study Group was that Nehru's daughter had succeeded with Gandhi's son where others had failed.

Manilal and Sushila Behn invited Indira and her group to Phoenix for lunch, and this time Manilal turned the table on us. He seated us on grass mats on the floor and served us rice and dhal on banana leaves. I had never seen such thin dhal; it ran off the banana leaves and we were hard-pressed to block it from running down our legs. Indira, and more notably her companion, Parvathi

Kumaramanglam, thought Manilal a strange man, but they laughed and made a joke of the whole incident.

We hosted Indira Nehru and her group for the four days they stayed in Durban. Few of us had any money, but we pooled together our meagre resources and rose to the occasion. We took them to the cheapest restaurant in town, Kapitan's Vegetable House, where for three pence one could get a slice of bread, a saucer of curry and a cup of tea. Our guests did not mind the frugal fare. There was a spontaneous rapport between us; they were keen to know about us and our lives in South Africa. Our lively interest in each other more than made up for any shortcomings in creature comforts.

INDIRA VISITS HOWICK FALLS
AND MAGAZINE BARRACKS

We arranged a trip to Howick and hired two taxis. To our pleasant surprise, the taxi drivers declined to charge us and said it was an honour to drive Nehru's daughter. The Falls enchanted Indira; we lazed about in the park-like environment and engaged in happy small talk.

The photographs taken at the Falls with a small box camera are the only photographs that exist of that historic visit of India's future prime minister. The simple khadi-wearing group was shunning all publicity and they would have opposed any formal posing at a photographic studio.

The next day we exposed the group to something very different – from the scenic to the squalid. We took them to Magazine Barracks, where the Durban municipality housed its Indian workers in abysmal, overcrowded conditions. The Barracks had been condemned as far back as 1914, and would be condemned again in 1944 by the Durban Health Commission as unfit for human habitation and a serious danger to public health.

Indira Nehru walked in the dusty, sandy lanes between the rows of rooms, some in dilapidated wood and iron, others in hollow block under iron, with the barest of ablution facilities, communal taps and communal shelters for toilets; no water-borne sewerage, electricity or proper cooking facilities; and entire extended families living in grossly overcrowded single rooms.

Indira Nehru was a quiet, very private person, but the conditions at the Barracks so appalled her that she came out of her shell and empathised with the people. I saw ensconced in that frail form the potential leader. Her unassuming demeanour belied her strength.

We had wanted to organise a public reception for Nehru's daughter, but our enthusiasm had been dampened by her adamant refusal to speak at the function. She said she had never spoken in public, and our attempts to convince her that there had to be a first time left her unconvinced. Now she turned to me and volunteered to speak, setting us in a flurry of activity to arrange a venue and distribute leaflets and press releases to ensure a bumper turnout.

HA Naidoo considered the MK Gandhi Library and Parsee Rustomjee Hall as the appropriate places to give Indira a public reception, but he had not realised that Rustomjee, who controlled the venue, would go to the extent of refusing permission. Rustomjee did not want any anti-war speeches and he behaved as a self-appointed censor.

The *Indian Opinion* observed, 'Strange to say that while the Marine Hotel was quite willing to accommodate Miss Indira Nehru, the Hall which bears the name of Mahatma Gandhi ... was refused for a welcome reception to Miss Nehru. The management was unable to allow the use of the Hall without knowing the agenda of the meeting and what kind of speeches would be made.'

HA Naidoo was, however, not without influence and respect, even among the affluent members of our community, and he approached AI Kajee for the Avalon Cinema as the alternative venue.

Though Kajee had been rebuffed, he understood very well the political significance of the meeting we were organising. He placed his Avalon Cinema at our disposal at the end of the matinée show at 5.30 pm. It was a good time and an excellent venue. The 1200-seater hall was packed to capacity.

HA presided over that historic reception and Manilal Gandhi, speaking in Hindi, presented a bouquet of flowers to Indira. DA Seedat and I, representing the NEUF, spoke out stridently against the war. When HA Naidoo saw AI Kajee in the audience, he showed his usual tact and invited him to the platform of the NEUF, and Indira heard AI Kajee praise Jawaharlal Nehru's fight for India's freedom.

Indira Nehru condemned the war as imperialistic, and listed the numerous national leaders in India who were in prison, while Gandhiji, still outside, continued the resistance campaign.

After criticising the British imperialists, Indira Nehru continued: 'One of your leaders, Dr Dadoo, is now in prison for the greatest of all crimes – the crime of telling the truth.' Amidst tremendous applause from the packed Avalon Cinema, she pointed out that in India, the 'workers and peasants have to bear the brunt of imperialism's assault'.

The visit to the municipal barracks and the sugar estates led to Indira saying to the audience, 'What little we have seen of the intolerable and humiliating conditions of the Non-European people has convinced us of the necessity of united action of all peoples against our common enemy ...'

The people rose as one at the end of Indira's speech and applauded her enthusiastically as she concluded: 'Our enemy is clever. We must not, we shall not allow him to divide us. Indians and Africans must act together. Common

EVENTS DURING WORLD WAR II

oppression must be met with the united and organised power of all the exploited peoples. We are not alone in our struggle. We have, as our allies, the whole international working class fighting against tremendous odds. Our enemy is weakening. Let us unite and strike the last blow.'

Thus Jawaharlal's *Priyadarshani of the Glimpses of World History* spoke on that memorable evening, and the *Indian Opinion* has preserved for posterity all that happened during those four historic days in its issues of 4 April 1941 and 16 April 1941.

After the meeting we wound our way to our homes in the darkness of the blackout, thankful for the great experience the Non-European United Front had provided for us at that public meeting.

Because no one was allowed to talk about ships and shipping in the war years, I don't remember the name of the ship on which Indira and her party travelled. In fact, the harbour and Durban Bay were prohibited areas during the war. Nothing was allowed to be taken in or out of a ship or the harbour area without clearance from the censors. All the incoming newspapers to the *Views* and *Indian Opinion* in Gujarati, Urdu, Hindi and Marathi, and other papers also, had to be censored, and Indian language censors were especially appointed for that purpose.

MY FIRST ARREST

There was a sequel to Indira Nehru's visit. On 4 April 1941, Indira's ship, which was anchored in the bay, lifted anchor and prepared to sail. In our cluster of organisations, I was in charge of publicity. I realised that in all the excitement of hosting our guests, we had overlooked to ask Indira Nehru for a message. A small group of us went by ferry to bid Indira and her group farewell. We either had forgotten about the war restrictions or ignored them. When we came close by the ship, I could see Indira Nehru, perpendicularly above me, high up as I bent my head back as far as it would go. I called out to her, and she leaned over as far as she could to narrow the distance between us. 'Indira!' I shouted. 'We need a message from you!' Indira and Chandra Gupta got into a huddle with the other students, and I could see her writing her message on a piece of paper, which was lowered to the ferry by a fisherman's hook and line. I unhooked the message and read it aloud: 'All good wishes and success to the Non-European United Front in their struggle against oppression.' When the boat reached the jetty we were confronted by members of the Security Branch who had been keeping us under telescopic observation. I was arrested and detained in a police cell. Indira Nehru's note was confiscated.

This was my first political arrest. After keeping me in detention for almost two hours and questioning me, I was released without being charged. From the jetty via the Point Police Station, the farewell party returned to the city with the *Daily News* as their first stop. The story was given to the cub reporter, the young and very conservative Aida Parker, well-known to the Liberal Study Group (she later joined the *Citizen* and then ran her own newsletter). The story was given prominence. Indira's last message to us appeared under her photograph taken at Howick Falls, in a special edition of the *Indian Opinion*. The special edition of the *Opinion* of 16 April 1941 is a valuable document recording our history in the making.

MK Gandhi had made his debut in public speaking in Pretoria; Indira Gandhi, as she became known, made it in Durban. Her visit to Durban left a lasting impression on the young Indira Nehru. Years later, in the seventies, when she was prime minister of India and my wife Fatima visited her, she referred to her time in Durban. I had sent her some photographs taken at Howick Falls, and she acknowledged these graciously. The photographs were prominently displayed in her home, which became a museum after her assassination. Sonia Gandhi, Indira's daughter-in-law, told Fatima that she had found the snapshots among her belongings after her assassination, and remembered how fondly Indira had spoken of her Durban visit. She had told Sonia how she had made her maiden speech there and how very nervous she had been. Many years later my grandchildren visited the museum, and I playfully complained to the youngest, Ayesha, 'You didn't take me to India,' and she said, 'But Pappa, you were there. We saw you in the photographs.' She was referring to the box camera snapshots Fatima had taken to Indira Gandhi on her first visit to India in 1972.

Shortly after the Indira Nehru group departed, Dawood Seedat appeared in court for the second time. I gave evidence in his defence, but it did not help; he was sentenced to three months' imprisonment for his anti-war stance.

THE COMMUNIST PARTY REJECTS ANTI-WAR POSITION

When the war broke out in 1939 the Communist Party saw it as an imperialist war, waged between imperialist powers. In South Africa, the Party opposed the war, as did the NEUF.

When Germany attacked Russia in June 1941 and Churchill pledged his support to the Soviet Union, the imperialist war became the People's War overnight in the eyes of the CPSA, and the stand of the CPSA swung from opposing the war to canvassing non-European support for it. The NEUF was more or less ordered to follow suit. The Central Committee of the CPSA imposed its unilateral decision on all political formations it influenced.

Dawood Seedat in Natal and YM Dadoo in the Transvaal had both been imprisoned under the War Measures Act for their anti-war statements. Now it seemed that the heroic stand they had taken had been in vain. It didn't make sense, particularly to the non-Europeans. Nothing had changed in their lives – why then the change in CPSA policy?

I found the directive difficult to accept, let alone sell to the non-European people, but one did not argue against the decision of the Central Committee of the CPSA; I was not comfortable with that either. I realised I could not be the disciplined cadre the Party expected me to be.

More followed: we were instructed to disperse the NEUF and build national, ethnic organisations. It seemed to me we were going backwards instead of forward. I was unhappy with the situation, unhappy to find myself unable to support the thinking of the Party's hierarchy.

In 1941 the Non-European United Front headed by Dadoo was the most popular organisation in the Transvaal, attracting popular African support. The Party obliged us to abandon it and strengthen the national ethnic political organisations – the APO (Coloured), the Indian Congress and the ANC. Later, following the banning of the Party, a separate white organisation, Congress of Democrats (COD), was formed as part of the liberation movement.

Dr Dadoo accepted the party line and threw himself into propagating support for the war, much to the confusion of the people. He got a rough reception at a mass meeting in Pietermaritzburg, where he was called a traitor. The Indian weeklies banner-headlined this. But coinciding with this confusion was the unexpected arrival of the young Indira Nehru, and our lives were momentarily brightened, particularly in view of the fact that she brought with her the anti-war position of the Indian National Conference.

And as Dr Dadoo walked out of prison on 30 April, Dawood Seedat walked in, taking the same stand on the war issue. He was a founding member of the NEUF and leader of the India League. He was quite fearless. Some described him as careless and foolhardy. I knew him as passionate, honest, generous and very likeable.

On 17 July 1941, a large crowd gathered outside the Durban Central Prison to welcome Dawood Seedat. The prison doors opened at 8 am, and Dawood emerged looking thin, all the more so since they had shaved his head in prison. We surged forward and shouted our hurrahs; the guards, not used to this, didn't know how to react. Dawood dismissed our concerns for his well-being and kept reassuring us, 'It was okay. It wasn't so bad.'

That afternoon we welcomed him formally at a meeting in the MK Gandhi Library called by a number of organisations – the Liberal Study Group, the Nationalist Bloc, the Left Book Club, the NEUF, the May Day Unity Committee and the CPSA. Among the speakers was the new recruit to the NEUF, Manilal Gandhi, recruited by Indira Nehru.

Both Dadoo and Seedat were lucky that they were not interned like John Vorster (later National Party president of South Africa).[2] But both received 'certificates' confining them to the magisterial districts where they resided and prohibiting them from engaging in the activities of the political organisations to which they belonged.

Within a few days of his release, Dawood was regaling the Liberal Study Group with his prison adventures in violation of his order, which banned him from the Group. He was once more in court, charged with having violated his ban and sentenced to forty days or £20. We decided we could no longer afford to have him locked up; there was far too much work to be done. So we paid his fine and got him back into our working fold. No more 'resting' in prison, we told him.

FIVE

JOHANNESBURG

1943–1946

UNIVERSITY OF NATAL CANCELS LAW LECTURES FOR NON-EUROPEANS
The year 1942 brought me to a crossroads in my personal life. I was happy in Durban. I was attending law classes with JN Singh and Ahmed Bhoola at Sastri College, the non-European section of the University of Natal. I was president of the Non-White Students Representative Council, with NG Moodley as vice-president and JN Singh one of the secretaries. All three of us were also active in the Liberal Study Group and the Left Book Club. I was also one of a three-member committee elected to raise funds for students who could not afford to pay their fees. I had joined the newly established International Club, which had added a new dimension to my social and cultural life. The club was a venue where people of all races could meet, share a cup of tea, or settle down to lunch, something they couldn't do in any other place in Durban. I enjoyed the club and the many intellectual and cultural evenings it organised. I had formed new friendships with white and African friends beyond our left-wing fold. Nessa Pillay exhibited his paintings at the club and we shared in the pride of his work. HK Naidoo held his first operatic recital there and the city's celebrated conductor, Edward Dunn, introduced him.

When that year ended and a new year began, I found that my participation in all these organisations was terminated by a racist act of the Natal Law Society. I had passed five law subjects when I was informed by Dr Palmer's secretary that she wanted to see me. I went to her office and found her in a highly distressed, tearful state. She gave me the shocking news that all lectures in law subjects had been cancelled for non-Europeans. It was now my turn to be distressed.

'Why?' I asked.

Dr Palmer explained that the Natal Law Society was against non-whites entering the legal profession. My mind flashed back to 1894 when the very same Law Society had unsuccessfully opposed Gandhi's application to practise law in Natal. Dr Palmer was still explaining: 'The council of the university bowed to the wishes of the Law Society.' I said to Dr Palmer that this was the pettiest and most malicious kind of racism and that it would never succeed. 'I will practise as a lawyer in Natal; and there will be hundreds of non-white lawyers,' I prophesied belligerently.

My thoughts now centred on myself. My first thought was: What about my law degree? If Natal University shut its doors on me, my ambition to be a lawyer would be jeopardised. I wouldn't be able to study anywhere else. But almost as soon my mind turned to the larger problem: this would affect all non-Europeans. It was yet another racial barrier to obstruct our path. There were ten law students enrolled at the university. I thought of the other students. The Law Society's demand and the university's acquiescence threatened all of us. We were all in the same predicament. We would all have to make alternative arrangements. I was able to study law at Natal because I had an income from the *Indian Views* and from the Teacher's Association, and I had free board and lodging at my sister's. If I wanted to continue with my studies in law, I would have to go to the Transvaal or the Cape. Where would I find the money? I realised too that if my personal life was not in order, I would not be able to contribute significantly to the community either.

A new attack on our people briefly distracted my attention from my personal concerns. In May 1942, the Durban City Council, backed by the Central Housing Board, slammed the community with expropriations in Riverside, Merebank, Wentworth, Sparks Estate, Springfield and Sydenham. The expropriations sent Indian leaders into a flurry of activity, unfortunately competitively rather than co-operatively. We, the Young Turks, organised meetings, protested and issued statements, but it all fell on deaf ears. The government continued with the expropriations, and thousands of Indians were made homeless. We realised that we would continue to be victimised so long as the political leadership remained in effete hands.

We discussed the weaknesses of the Indian political situation hard and long – Dr Monty Naicker, Debi and JN Singh, HA Naidoo, Cassim Amra, AKM Docrat, George Ponnen, PM Harry, Dr Goonam and I, among others. Radical changes would have to be made on the non-European political stage. Our goal was the elimination of racism. We were convinced that this could only be done through a united front consisting of all democrats. We worked for this through the Communist Party and, more specifically, through the Non-European United Front. We were very concerned about getting this message through to the Indians. In the 1940s there were as many Indians in Durban as there were Africans, and Indians had the lowest per capita income of all the race groups. In numbers they contributed equally to the labour force. The Dunlop and Falkirk strikes clearly demonstrated, if any doubt remained, that Afro-Indian unity was imperative in the assault on racism. On the labour front, Indian and African workers would be pitted against each other by employers. This strategy of divide and dominate would be extended to the communities at large with devastating results. To forestall that eventuality, we worked out a plan of action that required us to take over the Indian political leadership monopolised by the merchant-class conservatives, who were prepared to sacrifice Indian honour and general Indian interest to preserve their economic interests.

PARTING OF WAYS

At the same time, the Liberal Study Group, the centre of radical planning in Natal, lost some key members: Cassim Amra and HA Naidoo left for Cape Town. I too had to leave, although I was as yet undecided where I would go. But though Natal would lose us temporarily, we would contribute to non-European politics in the Transvaal and the Cape respectively.

My personal problems remained. I was in a quandary when Dr Coopan, who had been my teacher at Sastri College, asked me to join him. He had been given a niggardly grant of £100 per annum by the Human Sciences Research Council to undertake a two-year study into Indian education. He had to raise additional money if he was to do the study. He had decided to pursue his studies on a part-time basis and work as a waiter in Cape Town to raise the balance of the money he required. He suggested I join him; we could work to see ourselves through our studies. I discussed the idea with MI and AC. They didn't appear enthusiastic, but they said I could give it a try.

Dr Coopan and I set out for Cape Town in 1944. For some reason I cannot recall, we first went to Johannesburg, where Dr Coopan visited Molvi Mia's Waterval Islamic Institute. The Molvi became very interested in Dr Coopan, and when he learnt of his dilemma he offered him financial assistance. This relieved him of having to work as a waiter.

I did not fancy waiting on tables in Cape Town on my own. I gave up the idea. My colleagues from Sastri, JN Singh and Ahmed Bhoola, planned to enrol at the University of the Witwatersrand. My thoughts also turned in that direction.

MY RELATIVES IN JOHANNESBURG

I arrived in Johannesburg at the beginning of 1943, and sought out my relatives, GH Meer, the brother of Cassim Meer and my father's nephew. He and his wife had left Dundee and settled in Johannesburg. My last recollection of GH was of the two of us conspiratorially gorging mithai [sweetmeats]. It was someone's wedding, I do not remember whose, but mithai had been hidden away to be used for a special purpose. GH knew the hiding place and was going for it. Spotting me, he pulled me towards him and we both moved stealthily into a small room. Closing the door behind us, GH had filled his topi [fez] with choice portions of the delectables. I then followed him furtively to the safety of his house, where we consumed the laddoos and burfee [sweetmeats].

GH Meer now lived in Fordsburg, on Lillian Road. Both he and his wife, Bhabie [sister-in-law], as we called her, were very happy to see me. They welcomed me and made it clear that their home was mine, and that I was free to stay for as long as I wanted. Although this would have solved my accommodation problem, I had no intention of living with them. My family in Durban had warned me about Bhabie's domineering nature. She kept GH firmly under her thumb, and it was said of him that he was less than a man, though generous and loveable. I had no intention of being with them longer than necessary.

DOCTOR DADOO AND HIS HOUSEHOLD

I went to see Dr Dadoo, whom I knew well. When I first met him in 1938 when he came to Durban, I had taken an instant liking to him, and I think the feeling was mutual. I went to consult him. Dadoo greeted me effusively; even with a measure of excitement.

He convinced me that I should pursue my studies in Johannesburg. He said he needed me to help him with his political work and offered me accommodation. 'There's enough room in my house,' he said. 'If you can fit in with us, you are welcome to stay.'

The 'us' included his major-domo, who styled himself after his employer. His employer's trademark was his pipe, which he smoked very impressively, removing it to make a point and then returning it to its previous position while he listened. Boxer, as the major-domo was called, attempted to do the same, only he never had any points to make.

I accepted Dr Dadoo's invitation as a temporary solution.

Dadoo was a much sought-after doctor, and the veranda of his house, which served as a waiting room, was forever full. But the doctor barely stayed to serve the waiting patients. He would see a few before he would be called away on political business by the NEUF or CP or the TIC.

His living habits were simple and there was an openness about his nature. He was never doctrinaire in his thinking. He was a man of action rather than of theory, and a wonderful public speaker, direct and clear. Closest to him were Goolam Pahad and Molvi Cachalia. Of the three, Molvi was perhaps the most intellectual. I never knew him to lead a prayer in a mosque. Goolam was foremost a businessman, but his commitment to the cause was unstinting. His wife, Amina Bai, was one of the strongest women in the TIC, a wonderfully generous hostess and the first among us to court imprisonment.

JOHANNESBURG

I thought to myself, 'This is a peculiar situation. Here is a doctor who doesn't practise medicine, a boxer who doesn't box and a Molvi who doesn't preach.'

I discovered that Dadoo's immediate circle was made up of Gujarati-speaking Vohras like myself. He introduced me to them and they embraced me as their own. I was literally adopted by a number of families, welcomed into their homes, regularly invited to stay for meals and even presented with items of clothing. There was, in particular, Chotie Bai Bhayat, Amina Bai and Goolam Pahad, and Molvi and Yusuf Cachalia. They became my family. I relaxed and joked with them and discussed issues of the time, especially with the Cachalia brothers. I sounded my ideas against their keen intelligence and their wide-ranging knowledge of current affairs, histories of civilisations and liberation struggles.

THE KHOLVADIANS

I found the Johannesburg Vohras different from those in Durban; they were less conservative, more open to outsiders and simpler in lifestyle, with very little inclination to snobbishness. Unlike the Durban Vohras who had emigrated largely from Kathor and Surat and were politically conservative, the Johannesburg Vohras came in the main from Kholvad and, to a lesser extent, Dhubel and Alipur. Though they had a greater sense of identity in terms of place of origin in India than Durban Vohras, they were more open to outsiders, because, I think, of Dadoo's influence. I got on very well with the Kholvadians, Dadoo being one of them. He was assured of their support, especially of the women's. I think they were largely attracted by his handsome looks and cared practically nothing for his Marxist ideology, though they were passionate about their rights in South Africa. I didn't know a single Vohra Muslim woman who knew anything about Marxism. Dadoo, it seemed, didn't peddle his 'doctrine' among them. He struck a note of aloofness and this added to his mystique. Dadoo, however, was innocently ignorant of the impact he was making on the fairer sex. If you mentioned it to him, he dismissed it with an amused smile.

I got on well with Dadoo, as in fact everybody did. He had a fun-loving side, which relaxed me, and I had a sense of humour that he enjoyed. We complemented each other.

I MOVE IN WITH DADOO

I wrote to MI that I was settled in Dr Dadoo's house, and that took care of my board and lodging. However, I required money for my university fees. I would try to find a job, but until then I had a problem. MI replied promptly and said that between himself and YC, the only other member of the family with means, they would send me a monthly allowance to cover my fees. He enclosed a cheque for the necessary amount. He was, however, not happy with my staying with

Dadoo. He feared it would make me politically obligated to him. He wanted me to be free in my choices. But he agreed that I should stay with him temporarily until they came up with something else. I enrolled at Wits and settled in with Yusuf Dadoo.

Dr Yusuf Dadoo had returned to South Africa after obtaining a medical degree in Edinburgh in 1936. Strongly influenced by Kemal Ataturk, he, like his mentor, pronounced that Muslims should stop wearing the fez. As much as Muslims admired Ataturk, his views on Westernisation did not sit well with South African Muslims. Dadoo was rescued from Ataturk by the writer PS Joshi, who introduced him to Molvi Cachalia. Molvi immediately grasped Dadoo's enormous potential. He saw in him the leader that the Transvaal Indian community needed and invited him to join the TIC. As Molvi had anticipated, by 1946 Dadoo was leading the Congress.

Dadoo lived in a small cottage in End Street. He wasn't fussy about food, though he enjoyed a good meal and ate with relish at the homes of the Pahads, Bhayats and Cachalias. At End Street there was one standard meal. John, the other member of the Dadoo household, put on a large pot of soup that remained on the boil the whole day, with continuous additions of bones and vegetables. Anyone who desired could help himself to a cup of hot soup. Thus one never went hungry in Dadoo's house.

Dadoo was a bachelor at the time – he had a knack for being a bachelor even when he was married, much to the chagrin of his wives, of which there were three in succession.

I recall a time during the 1952 Defiance Campaign when Manilal Gandhi stayed with Dadoo for a few days. Manilal, after a great deal of soul-searching – because the Campaign was deemed to be communist-led – had joined it. Meetings were held at End Street. Dadoo would take off every now and again. Manilal would ask, 'Where are you going?' and Dadoo would answer, 'Just here, just here.'

During one meeting, Manilal exploded. 'There is a lack of trust among us; while we meet together, Dr Dadoo disappears, and when I ask him where he is going to, he says, "Just here, just here." Where is this "just here", and with whom is he meeting and what secret agenda is he pursuing?'

Everybody kept silent. We knew in our minds that Manilal was thinking that Dr Dadoo was consulting with a communist cell. I took Manilal aside. 'Manilal Bhai,' I said, 'let me explain. Dr Dadoo is courting a young lady. He respects you too much to tell you that he is going out to meet her. That is all there is to his disappearances.' That dispelled Manilal's doubts and set his mind at ease.

KHOLVAD HOUSE

I had spent a few months with Dadoo when YC Meer came to see me. He said he had rented a flat, 13 Kholvad House, which he would be using occasionally. He would share it with me on those occasions, but other than that, the flat was all mine. I was thrilled with the offer. He also told me that he and MI would send me a regular allowance to meet my other expenses.

I became a happy householder in 13 Kholvad House. Armed with a recipe book I picked up at a sale, *A Hundred Ways of Making Eggs*, I could face any emergency, unexpected guests or hangers-on. I moved out of End Street, but my involvement with Dadoo did not weaken; in fact, it strengthened.

My flat in Kholvad House became a sort of socio-political centre and a think and talk place, as comrades from the Communist Party, the TIC, the APO and ANC congregated, shared ideas and planned action.

While our discussions were intense, they were never humourless. They were punctuated with a great deal of light-heartedness, joking and laughing. We would think hard and plan intensely, and then we would 'roll up the carpet' and have a party.

JN and I joined the local branch of the Communist Party, and with such comrades as Bram Fischer, Joe Slovo and Ruth First, carried out raids against the black marketeers, an activity we had pioneered in Durban under Dr Naicker. My flat, being in the heart of the downtown commercial area, was invariably used as the meeting point. This and the anti-war activities kept me loyal to the Party, but when the Party changed its stance on the war and, following that, instructed the closure of the NEUF, which we had nurtured with such firm conviction, directing us to build 'national-cum-ethnic' organisations instead, serious doubts emerged and my loyalty waned.

MICHAEL SCOTT

Among those who came to Kholvad House was the strikingly handsome, very tall Reverend Michael Scott. He was a member of the Royal Air Force in India, where he had connections with the Communist Party. I met Michael Scott at the TIC office. He was a soul attracted to people suffering injustice, and even more to people standing up against injustice. We were in the midst of passive resistance at the time, and were both suffering injustice and standing up against injustice, in a manner which complied with his Christian conscience. He came to our very busy TIC office, with the cyclostyle machine whirring and the typewriter tick-ticking away under my two fingers. I was editing the *Passive Resister* at the time. There was JN and Molvi, who was as religious as the reverend, in the Islamic idiom. Ahmed Kathrada,[1] or Kathy as he was known even then, was a high-school kid still in his teens, who came daily after school and put in a man's work. I had met Kathy earlier, when I had accompanied Debi Singh[2] while organising support for the Bengal famine relief. The office steamed with our energy. Bajee [Father], as we came to call Michael Scott, merged his energy with ours. He became one of us. When we called it a day and I prepared to leave, I asked him where he was going. I discovered that the place where he was living was much too far away, so I took him home with me to 13 Kholvad House where Kathy was staying with me at the time. That is how we acquired the honour of Bajee's company.

He stayed and worked with us. Everyone at the Passive Resistance Council and TIC offices loved him. He appeared to have the purest of hearts and a childlike innocence. He was attached to the St Joseph's Home at the time, administered by the St Alban's Mission. The Church was very slow in awakening to the injustices of racism and Michael Scott was far ahead of it in 1946. He was granted leave by his superior, H Leach, who was in sympathy with him and admired and respected him, unlike his fellow clergy who became very critical of Scott's involvement with passive resistance and Indians. They said he was encouraging lawlessness, but Leach defended him. He said: 'We who know Father Scott have only the highest respect for his unselfish devotion, his sincerity and courage.' Leach described the laws passed by the South African government as akin to those of Nazi Germany, and said that passive resistance was not only an Indian issue, but that it affected all non-Europeans.

Bajee's and our food needs were frugal, but there were times when, as frugal as they were, we didn't have money to purchase any food. Bajee had one possession, a movie camera, and we pawned it repeatedly to buy packets of soup.

In 1946, Michael Scott put the ethics cat amongst the Christian Church's docile pigeons, and this ultimately led to the changed role of the Churches. But in 1946, that was more than a decade away.

JN Singh and Nelson Mandela were among the young people who moved in and out of the flat, and Bajee got on very well with young people; in fact, he thrived in our company.

Bajee was the easiest guest I have ever known, and the most absent-minded. A friend lent him a car and he couldn't remember where he had parked it, or what kind of car it was. He walked to my flat with his problem. I mustered help and we went in search of a car we knew nothing about, but somehow hoped to find. We had to find the car and return it to its owner. We eventually did, by a process of gathering clues in detective fashion. On the occasions that I accompanied Bajee in his car, I sat next to him, tense and nervous. He would let go of the steering-wheel and look for sweets in the cubby-hole. He had served as a pilot in the war and I thought that he drove the car as if it was an aeroplane.

When the Nationalists announced a boycott of Indian traders in the Transvaal, he volunteered to visit the country towns and check on how the Indian traders were doing. He went from shop to shop enquiring about the health of the businesses and returned with a carefully compiled report. We had a merry time listening to it, because we found that those shopkeepers we knew were doing well had reported disaster, and those who were suffering had reported good business and affluence. This was typical of our Indian traders. Those doing well were afraid some evil eye [nazar] might strike their good fortune if they appeared to be boasting, and would therefore say, 'Well, we are struggling. What can we do against the boycott? It is crippling us,' and those who were really being crippled were afraid of their creditworthiness being jeopardised, and reported good business.

When we met Bajee, he was already involved with the Herero chief, Hosea Kutako, and Tshekedi Khama of Bechuanaland (Botswana). They were bitterly opposed to the incorporation of their territories into racist South Africa. He discussed his mission in those countries with us, and we also became involved in the South West Africa problem.

Bajee wanted to visit Tshekedi Khama and discuss his representation to the UN on behalf of the Botswana and the Herero people. Yusuf Cachalia commandeered Kathy to drive Bajee. The police at this point were watching Michael Scott. So Yusuf was extra careful. He wouldn't even tell Kathy Bajee's destination. He told Kathy that Bajee himself would instruct him at the appropriate time. Kathy drove Bajee to Botswana and they went to see Tshekedi Khama, where Bajee received his instructions. Then he instructed Kathy to drive him to Salisbury (Harare), in the then Rhodesia, from where he planned to take an aeroplane to New York. But then Bajee suddenly remembered that he was due to address a meeting near Johannesburg. So he instructed Kathy to drive him all the way back to Johannesburg. I was awakened in the early hours of the morning and there, standing in the doorway, were two very weary travellers. I was surprised. 'What happened?' Kathy appeared somewhat fed up and went to bed, leaving Bajee to explain the situation to me.

Bajee's plans now had to change. He had to leave from Johannesburg if he was to make the UN on time. He had returned with a bag full of small change and he counted this up, declaring that it was enough to purchase his ticket. I wasn't paying much attention at that point. I was busy rounding up some friends to give Bajee the send-off he deserved. He was going on a historic mission.

I contacted Essop Nagdee. He was the only person I knew with a car, and I told him our problem. He drove us to the airport along with Bajee's small suitcase. At the airport, Bajee sought my opinion. Did I not think he should carry some cash with him? 'Of course you should,' I said in considerable agitation. 'Hasn't Tshekedi provided you with sufficient cash?'

'No, all the money he gave was enough for my ticket.'

'You must have money on you,' I said. 'You can't go all the way to New York with no money in your pocket. Let me see what I can do.'

I made a collection there and then from the handful of well-wishers we had gathered to bid him goodbye. The total amount came to £27. It was better than nothing. Bajee thought it was a great deal of money, even too much!

We all said our goodbyes. Bajee parted from us and walked towards passport control, when a call came over the public address system. 'Will Reverend Michael Scott please come to the information desk.' We were shocked. We thought the worst, and it was. He was told that he could leave for the States provided that he surrendered his passport. We urgently telephoned Dr Lowen, a senior Johannesburg advocate, to seek his advice. He said Bajee should under no circumstances surrender his passport.

So Bajee and I, crestfallen, returned to Kholvad House. It was now Kathy's turn to look surprised.

Kathy had to make another trip all the way to the South African–Rhodesian border. But this time he extracted a promise from Bajee that he would not ask him to take him back to South Africa.

Kathy returned to Johannesburg to find a telegram awaiting him: 'Unable to get flight to USA.' Kathy and I sent him a telegram in reply: 'Proceed to your destination even if you have to walk.'

The rest is history. Father Scott was successful in his mission. Years later, in the 1980s, when Fathu and I were given passports, I went to London and visited Michael Scott.

I AM A STUDENT AT THE UNIVERSITY OF THE WITWATERSRAND

I enjoyed my student days at Wits. I found the atmosphere exciting and invigorating. I became active in student politics. I formed many friendships, some lasting, others passing. JN Singh and I were invariably together. We were particularly drawn to students who were members of the Communist Party or inclined towards left-wing politics. We formed a radical students' organisation, the Federation of Progressive Students (FOPS) – Harold Wolpe, Ruth First and Joe Slovo were on the committee.

Ruth and I became very close. We respected each other's ideas, enjoyed each other's company, had similar interests and shared common values.

Our registrar, Glynn Thomas, was elected president; Violaine Junod, chairperson; and I organising secretary. I formed a lifelong friendship with Violaine Junod. She became godmother to my eldest daughter, and although she left South Africa in the sixties we always kept in touch through correspondence wherever she settled: in Rhodesia (later Zimbabwe), the USA and Britain. It was a friendship that Fathu and I and the children valued.

FOPS became the most popular student organisation. It went beyond the timid politics of NUSAS. Meetings organised by FOPS filled the Great Hall. We invited prominent politicians from both parliamentary and extra-parliamentary parties, such as the CPSA, TIC, APO and ANC, who gave students first-hand opportunities to understand their programmes and enter into direct debates with their representatives. But for FOPS, white students would have remained ignorant of black aspirations.

While Natal had segregated classes for non-Europeans, the classes at Wits were integrated, but there was discrimination in other respects. Non-whites could not use the swimming pool and were not allowed into the residences. The year that I was on the SRC, the administration considered putting up residences for non-white students. I was informed one day that the principal, Mr Raikes, wanted to see me. When I arrived at his office I saw the SRC representative of the medical students, who happened to be African, also waiting to see him. When I was admitted to his office, he told me that he wanted to discuss the university's plan to build a residence for Indians. I thought it strange that he would want to discuss that with me. 'Sir,' I said, 'I represent law students on the SRC, not Indian students. Your approach strikes me as racist.' Mr Raikes apologised. Residential facilities were subsequently provided for African students but not for Indian students, who had to find accommodation in the community.

I participated fully in Rag. I went out selling tickets for a car raffle to raise funds for the annual Rag charity. I asked Dr Vallabhbhai Patel for £50.

'Why £50,' he asked, 'when the tickets are a pound each?'

'Because I want a donation of £50, and you can afford it.'

Vallabhbhai said, 'I'll give you £1 for Rag and £50 if you will start a bursary fund for a student to enter a discipline that is closed to non-Europeans.'

I accepted the additional £50 and deposited it in a separate bank account. It was quite a challenge I had accepted. Not only was I required to raise the necessary funds, but also to force open disciplines blocked to non-Europeans. I convened a meeting of a group of my fellow students and we founded the University Students Bursary Committee. We went out canvassing for donations. We had generous support from the Indian community.

Our first bursary was allocated to Abba Raidoo for land surveying. There were no non-European land surveyors. Herman Kallenbach, Gandhi's close friend, who had joined him in the great march of coal miners and who had given him Tolstoy Farm as a base for his Satyagraha and a refuge for Satyagrahis, helped us to open up the Institute of Architects for Non-Europeans and remove its colour-bar clause.

My somewhat prominent position at university, and growing prominence in the community, resulted in people seeking my help. I must admit that it flattered me, and I sometimes stepped into situations where I had no place being. A medical student pleaded with me to accompany him to speak to the father of his lady love, who had become pregnant. He was a boarder at their home. This was serious business and he thought that I could help to ease the father's anger. He, of course, thought wrong. The father was not prepared to entertain me.

'Were you present when he defiled my daughter?' he demanded.

And when I meekly answered, 'I was not,' he ordered me out of his home.

'I will deal with this guilty young man myself!' he thundered. 'Without any defence from you.'

The young man was forced to do the correct thing, to marry the daughter.

NELSON MANDELA

One of the most impressive students I met at Wits was Nelson Mandela. He was a fellow law student on campus and, off campus, a member of the African National Congress Youth League. I was more attracted to him in his capacity as an ANC member. We were both non-Europeans, about the same age, and members of disenfranchised communities. As such, our destinies were linked. I knew this, he did not; but as our friendship matured and our talks deepened, he realised this too.

I invited him to stay at the flat whenever he needed to. He lived in Orlando, which was far from town, and it was convenient to sleep over at the flat. We would then talk late into the night. He would tell me about his youth and his life in the Transkei. He told me a great deal about Thembu customs. I was particularly fascinated by his account of the Thembu circumcision ceremony in which he had participated. I told him about my circumcision experience. We were intrigued by the fact that we had both been circumcised and that circumcision was a custom in both our cultures.

I told him about my life in Waschbank, about how I had become literate through the Zulu language, sitting alongside Zulu boys, taught by a Zulu master. He was impressed by my fluency in Zulu. I told him about Champion and Kadalie, and he was fascinated.

Nelson was strongly Africanist at the time, but this in no way affected our friendship, nor did the fact that I was a commoner and he an immaculately dressed Thembu prince. There was a sale at Vrededorp. Ahmed Bhoola, JN and I were excited about the bargains we would pick up. I invited Nelson to join us. He looked down his nose and said, 'I shop at Markhams.' It was a choice man's shop, as I discovered later, but at that time I hadn't heard of it. It was then that I realised precisely how aristocratic this Thembu prince was.

Nelson was beginning to develop a passion for revolutionary writings, and he was probing the relation between Europe, Asia and Africa – to understand how

Age six, with my father and my youngest sister Ayesha, Waschbank

Age six with my sister Ayesha and our cousin AM Meer

My mother and her daughters-in-law, Gorie Bai and Gorie Äpa

Our family shop in Waschbank

Age seven – my bicycle and I

At age fourteen, with
my nephew Haroon, Waschbank

1937, while at high school, walking down
West Street, Durban, with a fellow student

At Howick Falls with Indira Nehru. She is sitting second from right
between me and Dawood Seedat, 1941

With Pauline Podbrey at Curries Fountain
before a mass meeting, 27 September 1942

Botanic Gardens, Durban, 1942

At Sastri College with my fellow students. JN Singh is seated on the right and I am behind him

Students' Representative Council, University of the Witwatersrand.
I am seated on the far left

My Muslim marriage – Nikah ceremony – at which the bride is absent. I am seated between Molvi Bashir, who performed the marriage ceremony, and JN Singh. 11 March 1951

Fathu and I on our wedding day, Pinetown

colonialism dominated and degraded. He was keenly interested in India's struggle for independence, her burgeoning nationalism and the thoughts of Nehru and Gandhi. I gave him Gandhi's *Ahimsa* and *Satyagraha in South Africa*, and some of Nehru's writings. He was already making a serious study of Marxist literature. We discussed the theories and liberation movements in relation to these theories. We were both students learning about change and how best to effect it.

Nelson took a keen interest in our activities when we began organising passive resistance, and was deeply moved when JN, Zainab Asvat, Abdul Haq Patel and I gave up our studies to give our full attention to the campaign. By now he had met Dadoo and often came with me to Goolam Pahad's flat in Orient House, where he met Amina Bai and acquired a taste for her curries.

After his twenty-seven years in prison, when he was fêted as the president of South Africa, he would say, in the middle of a speech to amuse and relax his audience and draw them into laughter, 'And Ismail Meer, I remain eternally grateful to him for he taught me ...' And this would be followed by an eloquent pause that held his audience in suspense, who expected some great Eastern wisdom that I had imparted to him. Then, breaking the silence, he would say, '... to eat curry.' And the audience would erupt with laughter.

The colour bar in public transport had never been easy to understand. In Durban, the three back seats in the trams were reserved for non-Europeans, but the back seats became front seats on the return journey, and we had to move to the 'front' in order to be at the 'back'. If there was no stability between back and front, where was the guarantee that black would remain black and white, white, and never the twain would meet?

In Johannesburg, non-Europeans were not allowed on trams, but if an African maid accompanied her European mistress, to help with her baby, she became kosher, as did an African male servant accompanying a European man. Indians and Coloureds, however, were not allowed to 'carry' African servants, as the process was known.

So one day JN Singh, Ahmed Bhoola, Nelson and I boarded a tram. The conductor accosted me and warned, 'You are not allowed to carry a Native!'

'Who is carrying a Native?' I remonstrated.

'Isn't this your Native?' the conductor asked, pointing at Nelson.

'No,' I said, outraged.

'This is Mr Nelson Mandela, a Thembu prince and a student of law,' JN butted in. 'Don't you see that Mr Mandela is walking on his own? Nobody is carrying him? And he is an African, not a Native!'

Nelson was not beyond using some choice expletives, and he now contributed some, but fortunately the conductor was focusing on JN and me, and he didn't hear him.

Then Ahmed joined in and all four of us were engaged in a verbal attack on the conductor. When the bus stopped at the next stop, the conductor ordered all of us out and handed us over to a policeman who was waiting for us. I was charged with interfering with the transport service. They took Nelson aside and tried to persuade him to turn prosecution witness against me. They had no idea who they were dealing with.

I contacted Bram Fischer, whom I knew from the Communist Party, and he represented us in the trial that followed. We entered the court, feeling uneasy, not quite knowing how things would go, but the welcome the magistrate accorded our defence counsel set me at ease. 'Oh, *Meneer* Fischer,' the magistrate drooled, 'I was with your father yesterday.' He adjourned the court to have a private session with Bram Fischer, whose father was the Judge President of the Orange Free State, and whose grandfather had been the president of the Orange Free State.

The case was as good as won. The prosecutor deposed that our interference had resulted in a loss of fares.

'How did that come about?' my counsel questioned.

'Well, sir,' the conductor testified, 'I lost seven fares.'

'How did you come to that calculation?'

The conductor said that he had seen seven men carrying seven suitcases and he had counted them. The magistrate was in no mood to believe him and found his explanation implausible. 'I have never seen such a thing, seven men carrying seven suitcases, indeed! I am not prepared to accept such stories in my court.'

The case was dismissed.

Years later, while Nelson was incarcerated, I received a letter from him that I have treasured and which I now share with you. He wrote to me on learning of the assassination of Indira Gandhi.

On 31 October 1984, Indira Gandhi was assassinated upon leaving her home for her customary reception of people who assembled in her garden to bring their problems personally to her. The young Miss Nehru had become one of the most impressive, though controversial, prime ministers of India, and it was in the flames of that controversy that she was assassinated.

Nelson, in his cell at Pollsmoor Prison, had learnt of her death and wrote to me to pass his condolences on to the family. It was the only letter I received from him from prison, though he and Fathu corresponded regularly. The letter, to the best of my knowledge, never reached Rajiv, but Fathu was able to give it to Sonia Gandhi when she attended the Indira Gandhi Memorial Conference in 1991 at the invitation of Rajiv. He was assassinated by the time the conference was held.

/82: Nelson Mandela
29 January 1985

Dear Ismail

I've missed you so much these 22 years that there are occasions when I even entertain the wild hope that one good morning I will be told that you are waiting for me in the consultation rooms downstairs.

I watch the world aging, scenes from our younger days in Kholvad House and Umgeni Road come back so vividly as if they occurred only the other day – bending endlessly on our textbooks, travelling to and from Milner Park, indulging in a bit of agitation, now on opposite sides and now together, the fruitless polemic with Boola and Essack,[3] and I kept going throughout these lean years by a litany of dreams and expectations, some of which have been realised, while the fulfillment [*sic*] of others still eludes us to this day.

Nevertheless, few people will deny that the harvest has merely been delayed but far from destroyed. It is out there on rich and well watered fields even though the actual task of gathering it has proved far more daunting than we once thought. For the moment, however, all that I want to tell you is that I miss you and that thinking of you affords me a lot of pleasure, and makes life rich and pleasant even under these grim conditions.

It is about that tragic 31 October 1984 that I want to talk to you. You will, of course, appreciate that my present position does not allow me to express my feelings and thoughts fully and freely as I would have liked. It is sufficient to say that when reports reached us that Indirabehn had passed away, I had already exhausted my 1984 quota of outgoing letters. This is the only reason why it took me so long to respond.

Even though Zami[4] may have already conveyed our condolences (please check), I would like Rajiv to know that he and the family are in our thoughts in their bereavement, that on occasions of this nature it is appropriate to recall the immortal words, which have been said over and over again: when you are alone, you are not alone, there is always a haven of friends nearby. For Rajiv now to feel alone is but natural. But in actual fact he is not alone. We are his friends, we are close to him and we are fully aware of the deep sorrow that has hit the family.

Indira was a brick of pure gold and her death is a painful blow which we find difficult to endure. She lived up to expectations and measured remarkably well to the countless challenges which confronted her during the last 18 years.

There must be few world leaders who are so revered but who are lovingly referred to by their first name by thousands of South Africans as Indira. People from different walks of life seemed to have accepted her as one of them and to them she could have come from Cato Manor, Soweto, or District Six. That explains why her death has been so shattering.

I'd hoped that one day Zami and I would travel all the way to India to visit Indira in person. That hope became a resolution especially after 1979. Although the years keep on rolling away and old age is beginning to threaten, hope never fades and that journey remains one of my pride and dreams.

I wish Rajiv well in his new office and we sincerely hope that his youth and good health, his training and the support of friends from far and wide will enable him to bear the heavy work load with the same strength and assurance as was displayed by his famous mother over the past 18 years. Again, our dearest sympathies to Rajiv, Sonia and Priyanka.

Lastly, I must repeat that I miss you badly and I hope you are keeping well. I look forward to seeing you some day. Until then our love and fondest regards to you, Fatima, the children and everybody. Please do tell me about Nokukhanya[5] and her children.

Very sincerely,
Nelson

Ismail Meer, 148 Burnwood Rd, Sydenham, 4091

Nelson introduced me to Anton Lembede, an intense young man with a brilliant mind. The ANC Youth League was made up of a number of brilliant young men, but there was none as brilliant as Anton Lembede. He was working in Dr Seme's office in Johannesburg when I met him, having carved out a career in law, which he was never to realise fully, for he would die prematurely. On that summer morning, as we talked on our way to the Wits campus, Anton Lembede described his dream for our country. We entered the library and he was so moved that he literally trembled. He saw the law books in the original Dutch and said, 'This is what the bastards have kept away from me.' We went to Amina Pahad for lunch. He later wrote me a letter thanking me. 'The day was full of wonders, but what moved me most was to see all of you eating with your fingers. Unless we respect our own culture we will never be able to respect ourselves and we will never be free.'

Anton Lembede was the original Black Consciousness philosopher of our country.

Off campus, Yusuf Cachalia, Nana Sita, Molvi, Goolam Pahad, I and others set up the Transvaal India League and commemorated India's Independence Day. We celebrated Nehru's release after he had served 1041 days in prison. We felt all that much closer to him because of the four pleasant days we had spent with his daughter a few years earlier. His message to us South African Indians made a deep impact on me: 'One can never accept anywhere in the world the status of inferiority. No Indian worthy of his country can thus demean himself and his motherland.'

I had never been to India, but my father had come from there and I hoped one day to visit it. I was South African but India had great meaning for me, particularly because of her freedom struggle and the leaders of that struggle – Gandhi, Nehru and Sarojini Naidoo.

SIX

PASSIVE RESISTANCE

1945–1946

THE RADICALS TAKE OVER INDIAN POLITICAL LEADERSHIP
The year 1945 marked the beginning of the Dadoo–Naicker era. The two men were elected president of the TIC and NIC, respectively, towards the end of that year. But remaining obstacles had to be overcome. By the mid-1940s, the Anti-Segregation Council in Natal had enlisted about 30 000 paid-up members and had twenty-nine branches, mostly trade unions. There was no questioning its popular support. We were poised to take over the NIC. The Old Guard knew this, and knew too that at the next election, which they were obliged to call according to the constitution, it would be a walk-over victory for the Anti-Segregation Council. Their only recourse to maintain power was not to convene the conference.

According to the NIC's constitution, the annual general meeting had to be called in October. When the NIC failed to do so, the Anti-Segregation Council sought a court order to force its hand. The applicants were Dr Monty Naicker, AKM Docrat and BT Chetty. We won the application and the court set October 1945 as the date of the annual general meeting.

It was a meeting JN and I could not miss, and we motored down from Johannesburg to Durban. The grounds and stadium of the Curries Fountain sports ground overflowed with almost 8000 people who had come to vote in the new NIC. It was as if they were voting in a new government. There was a festive atmosphere.

DR NAICKER IS ELECTED PRESIDENT OF THE NIC
AT THE CURRIES FOUNTAIN SPORTS GROUND
The Old Guard had resigned a week before the elections, conceding defeat. They did not attend the historic meeting and Dr Naicker was elected president unopposed. My cousin AI was elected joint secretary with MD Naidoo. Of the

eighty-member committee, a significant number was drawn from the old Sastri students and members of the Liberal Study Group.

The new NIC was organised along democratic lines; the branches were responsible to their constituencies and there was a full-time office with a full-time staff. The NIC had never had an independent office. Even in the time of Gandhi, the NIC secretary had operated from his legal office. Kajee had made the NIC an appendage of his business. The new NIC, with a full-time secretary and staff, was available to all its members. It inspired them to come and give their time to the organisation.

We rented offices in Lakhani Chambers, and Debi Singh, who gave full-time service in a purely honorary capacity, headed the staff, which included the paid clerks, Ganas and Green. Pembroke and Lakhani Chambers stood back-to-back on Saville Street, off Grey Street. There were more than twenty paid, full-time organisers in those two buildings, most of them trade unionists. The Liberal Study Group, which was in the twilight of its existence, contributed richly to the executive of the NIC.

I made short trips to Durban during this time to maintain first-hand contact between the key leaders – Dadoo and Naicker – and the key political groupings. The Secretariat met daily at five in the afternoon. Decisions were taken democratically, responsibly and in transparency. New branches were being formed all the time and the membership was expanding. Debi was a giving person. He had the mannerisms of an aristocrat. His father had left him several plots of land and he sold these as he needed money, which he spent like a lord until he became a pauper. He liked his alcohol, a little too much at times, but that did not keep him from his work. He had separated from his wife and was sharing his flat with a friend. When relaxed, he would entertain us with the one and only song he knew, 'Nadie kinare bagla bêthê choon choon machlie khai' ['The bagla sits on the river bank and eats fish, choon choon']. Not much of a message, but great fun after a drink and a bite. And talking of singing, there was Toti Khan who taught us to sing an Afrikaans *liedjie* [song], which we sang with great gusto, crazily and meaninglessly: 'Donker kamer sonder kers, daar lê die ding, daar lê die ding' ['A dark room, without a candle, there lies the thing, there lies the thing']. We never knew what the thing was and it didn't matter. It was the rhythm we went for.

Monty kept talking about urumbu, some sort of lizard-like reptile, which he said was such a delicious dish. I don't know if urumbu ever materialised on his table. I didn't much care what it was, the importance of urumbu was not urumbu but Monty's predilection for talking about it. After a few drinks Monty and Dr Thegie Chetty would lighten up and, squatting on the floor with tabla and harmonium, break into concert. They were hilarious evenings that relieved the tension and hard planning in the smoke-filled offices of Lakhani Chambers.

PASSIVE RESISTANCE

DR DADOO IS ELECTED PRESIDENT OF THE TIC

In the Transvaal, the deaths of the two key conservative leaders, EM Valod and SM Nana, left the field wide open for Dadoo. SM Nana was a greatly admired leader, and, despite his conservatism, we radicals mourned him. Dr Dadoo was elected president of the TIC two months after Dr Naicker had assumed leadership of the NIC. Dr Vallabhbhai Patel and I were elected joint secretaries. We were now close to our goal, to forge non-European unity and topple the racists. I didn't know then that it would take almost half a century more to do so.

Originally Dadoo's house, his surgery and the TIC offices were under one roof. The TIC offices later moved to Market Street in Barkley Arcade. The ANC offices were close by in Rosenberg Arcade. We then moved the office to Kort Street and then Diagonal Street, where we had larger premises.

RADICALS TAKE OVER THE SAIC

In February 1946 I joined our large contingent of delegates to attend the SAIC conference. We travelled by train to Cape Town. I enjoyed the long journey in excellent company. We joked, played cards and discussed the stratagem we would adopt at the conference. There were Doctors Dadoo and Naicker, Debi and JN Singh, MD Naidoo, Billy Peters and AI Meer. The conservatives had lost Natal and the Transvaal to us, but they still retained the parent organisation, the SAIC. It was an untenable situation. It meant that while the two major sections agreed on a policy or strategy, it could be vetoed nationally. The conservatives were confident they would retain their hold on the central body. We radicals were equally confident that we would wrest control from them. The conservatives and radicals faced each other and deliberated. The entire Indian political leadership was assembled in conference in Cape Town. It was an impressive assembly; the debate was eloquent and of a high standard. If the conservatives had expected the Young Turks to be wild and irresponsible, they were disappointed. The conservatives pressed for a Round Table conference, which we considered futile. We pressed for passive resistance. 'They will not respond to words,' we argued. 'Let us give them action as Gandhi had given them.'

The conference proved to be the best organised ever.

The conference resolved to launch passive resistance and mobilise all the resources of our people to fight the Ghetto Act, and to send delegations to the USA, UK and India to rouse world opinion against the racism practised in South Africa. There was unanimity on the key resolutions, but a dispute broke out among the conservatives over the selection of persons to make up the delegations. Who would go where, and who would lead? We radicals had our work cut out for us. We planned to set up passive resistance councils in the provinces and launch passive resistance. We kept out of the delegations that left for the USA, UK and India; we campaigned for funds and recruits to empower resistance.

In the Gandhian tradition, a large delegation met the prime minister, General Smuts, to prevail upon him to withdraw the Bill and warn him that we would launch passive resistance if he did not. The message was delivered in the most conciliatory tone. The prime minister did not have the power to withdraw the Bill – parliament had, and we knew it. Our meeting was a gesture from both sides.

THE XUMA–DADOO–NAICKER PACT

After Dr AB Xuma's return from the UN and before our two doctors set out on their Indian tour, I was asked once again to approach Dr Xuma, this time to discuss a joint declaration of co-operation between the Congresses. The result was the Three Doctors' Pact signed on 9 March 1947 by the president general of the ANC, Dr Xuma, and the presidents of the NIC and TIC, Doctors Naicker and Dadoo respectively, to co-operate on specific issues. Time alone would tell if there was any reality to the Pact. In retrospect, the Pact may be deemed as having been premature.

At the time, I considered the Doctors' Pact important, as laying the foundation for joint Afro-Indian political action, and indeed Dr Xuma supported our (the CPSA, SAIC and APO) call for a National Assembly to extend franchise to all South Africans. Likewise, Dr Moroka, who succeeded him as the president general of the ANC, presided over our 'Defend Freedom of Speech Convention' in Johannesburg in 1950, despite the opposition of the ANC executive. Though members of the TIC considered that a coup, I was uncomfortable with it, for I could see it could result in tension. It was as if we had hijacked the president from his executive. I was cautioned by the terrible fissure that had occurred in the Transvaal ANC when its president, CS Ramohanoe, supported our 'Assembly of Votes for All' in the face of his executive's expressed opposition to that conference. Bitter conflict erupted when a vote of no confidence was moved against him.

DR XUMA FOR THE UNITED NATIONS

Sorabjee Rustomjee returned to South Africa from India, which he had visited as part of the SAIC delegation, profoundly influenced by Pandit Nehru, who, in a message to the South African Indian people in September 1946, had advised them to co-operate with the African majority. 'The struggle in South Africa is ... not merely an Indian struggle ... It concerns ultimately the Africans who have suffered much by racial discrimination and oppression.' He emphasised this to Rustomjee, saying, 'Indians in South Africa should co-operate with the African people. If you consider yourselves their superiors then others will consider themselves your superior.' It is to Rustomjee's credit that he took this advice to heart, and on returning to South Africa he sought me out in Johannesburg to discuss how, in some meaningful way, a start could be made towards implementing what Nehru had in mind. I wondered whether I should tell him that we had been working in that direction for years, and that unity was our goal. But he knew that, and he also knew that unity was the key difference between the Old Guard and the new. 'You know,' I said, 'your delegations overseas would gain you far more support if you made it a mixed delegation of Indians and Africans.' Rustomjee was a big man with big ideas and his mind raced in the opposite direction to mine. I was thinking of a delegation that would include an equal number of Africans and Indians. He thought of one 'big' African, whose existing high status would make an immediate impact. His eyes shining, he said, 'You know Dr Xuma? I will provide all the money he requires. Persuade him to go to the UN.' And that is how I came to make repeated visits to Dr Xuma at his home. He was always busy and I had to fit into his time. While he breakfasted, I pursued Rustomjee's mission, which I saw as implementing Nehru's advice in a small way.

Dr Xuma found the idea appealing. He named his cash needs and I was given a suitcase of money to deliver to him. I had, of course, discussed Rustomjee's proposal with Dadoo, JN, the Cachalia brothers and others on the executive, and they were fully supportive of the plan. The Xuma delegation in November 1946 included HA Naidoo and Sorabjee Rustomjee.

The post-war period created volatile situations in the cities, particularly in Durban and Johannesburg. Excruciating conditions in the rural areas resulted in an exodus of Africans into Johannesburg and Durban, where a lack of housing and inadequate transport erupted in massive strikes and large-scale shack settlements. We in the TIC and on the Passive Resistance Council could not ignore the miseries of the African communities, who faced high transport costs and acute shortages of basic necessities.

I was editing and publishing the *Passive Resister* and the *Cape Standard* at the time, as well as co-ordinating resisters and arranging their travel to Durban, where resistance was taking place. The recruits travelled by car and made MI's house in Pinetown their port of call, where they spent the night, breakfasted and then left for Durban. In the evening they occupied the resistance tents in Gale Street in defiance. They spent the night that followed in police cells before being brought to court the following morning.

PASSIVE RESISTANCE

For South African Indians, 1946 was an eventful and historical year. In January, General Smuts announced his government's intention to introduce the dreaded

Asiatic Land Tenure Act to replace the Pegging Act that was about to expire, and which had frozen all property transactions between Indians and whites for years. Exceptions were made through special permits, but these were difficult to come by and required generous bribes.

On 25 March General Smuts moved the second reading of the Asiatic Land Tenure and Indian Representation Bill. On the same day India gave formal notice of the termination of the 1938 trade agreement with South Africa, and thereby became the first country in the world to apply sanctions against South Africa's racism. In time, international sanctions would become a powerful weapon against apartheid. On 24 May 1946, the last Indian High Commissioner, Deshmukh, sailed for India.

The NIC and TIC prepared for mass resistance when the Bill became law. Natal set up the first Passive Resistance Council (PRC) in March to conduct the passive resistance campaign. Dadoo confided to me that he was having trouble setting up the Transvaal PRC. I discussed this with JN. Preparations for resistance were proceeding well in Durban. Johannesburg could not lag behind.

When Dadoo had first asked me to join the TIC, I had hesitated; I did not fancy joining an organisation that limited its membership to Indians. Dadoo, however, drew my attention to the constitution of the TIC, which said every Indian was a member of the TIC. 'Do you wish to opt out?' He pointed out that according to the NUSAS constitution every student was a member of the organisation. I hadn't opted out of NUSAS, he challenged. 'Why then this different attitude to the TIC?' I had no defence. Both JN and I joined the TIC. I was soon on its executive and, for a while, served as its secretary. We had to set up the Passive Resistance Council. Dadoo could find only two persons prepared to serve on the council. He discussed his problem with me. I, in turn, discussed it with JN.

We observed that Johannesburg had a wonderful leader in Dadoo, a most responsive Indian community and the same revolutionary plan of action pursued in Natal, but it lacked the support base and the kind of expertise that the Liberal Study Group had provided Monty.

JN and I were both active in the Communist Party at the time, carrying out food raids, attending meetings and, of course, enjoying socials; we were also very active in student politics. We realised that if we took on another organisation our studies would be seriously affected. We discussed our priorities and, like the Soweto youth who would succeed us some four decades later, we decided to place 'liberation first, education later'. We gave up our studies temporarily and devoted ourselves to the passive resistance campaign full time. We felt we couldn't continue the luxury of being full-time students while matters in the community stood as they did. We decided to suspend our studies and devote our time entirely to the struggle.

The NIC and TIC declared that they would oppose the Bill once it became law, through passive resistance.

While JN and I worked in the TIC, we did not restrict ourselves to Indian politics; we were far too rooted in the NEUF tradition. Our goal was not simply the removal of Indian disabilities, but freedom for all the disenfranchised people. We helped to organise the Anti-Pass Campaign in 1944 and we supported the Alexandra bus boycott against rising bus fares. Some of us joined Dr Dadoo in walking with the protesting communities. We fully supported the 1946 mineworker's strike and suspended our regular activities in the TIC and Passive Resistance Council to help the mineworkers, who went on strike in August 1946. We collected resources for the strikers. Of the 300 000 mineworkers who worked on the gold mines, 50 000 went on strike, and they needed all the support we could give them. We were eager for the strike to succeed. We worked closely with JB Marks and David Bopape, who were both members of the Communist Party. Unfortunately, the strike was crushed in three days. Among those arrested were JN, Dr Dadoo and Mohamed Vania.

We concentrated all our efforts on the passive resistance campaign, working day and night. For three months, JN and I joined Molvi Cachalia, Solly Nathie and other Transvaal activists and scoured the country towns near Johannesburg, holding meetings and canvassing support for the campaign. Within two weeks a fifteen-member Transvaal Passive Resistance Council was established, and the Transvaal was poised to make a proud contribution to passive resistance. During 1946–1947, JN and I moved between Durban and Johannesburg, co-ordinating affairs between the NIC and TIC. Attendances at mass meetings were most encouraging. Other PRCs followed in Cape Town, Port Elizabeth and East London.

Recruiting resisters was not easy. In Durban, at mass meetings, hundreds of hands went up when the call was made, but when it came to registration the number was halved, and when it came to the point of defiance there was a further dwindling in numbers. There were times preceding the actual launch of the campaign when we despaired that we would have sufficient recruits to launch the campaign. Fortunately, both in Natal and the Transvaal the volunteers at leadership level grew, and therein lay our hope. We had wonderful stalwarts and together with them and through them, we roused public enthusiasm. We worked relentlessly all through March and April, co-ordinating our efforts in Durban and Johannesburg. At the open-air mass rallies, resolutions were passed condemning the Bill scheduled to become law in early June, abolishing our right to own and occupy property. The Bill also offered us communal franchise, which we rejected as beneath our dignity. As South African citizens, we claimed the right to full franchise on the common roll.

A FORTUNATE MAN

As the days of the resistance campaign drew closer, I found myself making many trips to Durban. Fathu, in her matric year, had thrown herself fully into the campaign. She was developing into quite an independent thinker. She always demanded her slice of my attention whenever I was at her home in Pinetown. She kept me abreast of her school activities. The matriculants from her school and Sastri College had formed a Students Passive Resistance Council and were raising funds for the campaign. I was pleased that the family had not raised any objections to this mixed-gender working.

'We are putting on a play,' she told me. 'I am Anne Boleyn and Dhun is Henry VIII. My head gets chopped off.'

'Good thing too,' I teased. 'You talk too much. That will silence you.'

'I don't talk so much,' she countered. 'I talk as much as I need to.'

I had to concede that. She protested that I wasn't taking her seriously. She told me about her teacher, Miss Hammond. It was Miss Hammond this, and Miss Hammond that.

'We are staging *Macbeth* at school. I am Lady Macbeth,' she told me.

I told her she was Lady Macbeth because she was Miss Hammond's pet.

'No! No!' she protested. 'Miss Hammond isn't like that.'

'No,' I teased. 'She is just a cry-baby.' Behn[1] was visibly upset.

'How can you say such a thing?'

'Well,' I said, 'we had a debate, Sastri versus Girls High, and we beat the girls. There was Zulie Christopher and Irene Godfrey and Miss Hammond – they all huddled in one classroom and cried.'

This was too much for Behn. She saw it as an attack on her gender, on the senior students she admired and on her school.

'We are not like that. We are having a debate against Sastri College – Jessie, Ivy and I are the speakers from our side. We'll beat the boys, you will see.'

I knew they would and I told her so, and declared a truce.

We were especially encouraged by the large turnout of women at our meetings in Johannesburg. Five thousand people rallied at the Natalspruit Football ground where we organised a march, and there were five hundred women among the marchers.

FIRST RESISTANCE MARCH IN DURBAN, 31 MARCH 1946

On 30 March I travelled to Durban with a car-full of Transvaal supporters to attend the special conference of the NIC, which elected the Natal Passive Resistance Council. The next day, Sunday, 31 March, we held a mass meeting at Red Square. Bhaboo (Behn's mother) had told me that Behn was going to speak at the meeting. Her Gorapappa (AI Meer) had urged her to do so. 'Your Bhai Mota (MI) has written her speech and she knows it well.' I looked forward to hearing her make her debut in public speaking.

The meeting saw one of the biggest crowds ever on Red Square. When the time of the meeting arrived, AI helped Behn onto the lorry and she took her position alongside the other speakers. She looked minute. I saw the pride reflected on the faces of Bhaboo and Budie, Behn's two mothers. Monty made his speech. He was unusually charged that afternoon, and the crowd cheered enthusiastically when he said, 'There are too many black marketeers, bloodsuckers. They all need to be locked up and the foodstuff they hoard distributed to the poor.' He went on to attack Kajee and his gang. He spoke for twenty minutes. Goonam was our next speaker. As usual, she was strong, strident, impelling the energy of that large multitude into one loud freedom roar. Our tiny Behn spoke next. She grew taller on the stage. If her father had written her speech, she made it her own. It came across clear and sincere. The people loved her and had they not already been standing, they would have given her a standing ovation. We were all very proud of her. Monty was exuberant in his praise. He insisted that she lead the march with him and Goonam, and so there she was leading us all, 6000 strong.

On 2 June the obnoxious Bill became the obnoxious law, which Indians referred to as the Ghetto Act. The next day, the NIC met at an emergency session in Durban and decided to launch passive resistance on 13 June. The third South African passive resistance campaign was accordingly launched in Durban. The campaign was preceded, in the Gandhian tradition, by a Hartal [Day of Prayer] when all economic activity among Indians came to a stop.

JOHANNESBURG RESISTERS LEAVE FOR DURBAN, 12 JUNE 1946

On 12 June there was a lot of activity in the offices of the PRC and TIC. JN and I were working overtime in constant consultation with Yusuf Dadoo. Molvi Cachalia was on hand attending to problems as they arose. In Fordsburg, Chotie Bai Bhayat, a powerful matriarch, large with a booming voice, was giving last-minute counsel to the women resisters, among whom was her pretty eighteen-year-old daughter, Zohra. She was having last-minute misgivings as to whether she had done the right thing by encouraging Zohra to be a resister. She was so delicate and pampered, and they were in the throes of arranging a marriage for her, but Zohra had told Dr Dadoo she wanted to be a resister before she got married. Chotie Bai had been proud of her, but now that they prepared to leave for Johannesburg, she had her doubts.

Amina Bai Pahad was leaving her young sons, Ismail, Essop, Aziz, Nasim and Zunaid, in the care of her husband. She was somewhat apprehensive. He needed more attention from her than they did, and now she was off for three weeks or more and actually expecting him to care for the boys. Was he up to it?

The young Zainab Asvat, a medical student at Wits, was bustling around, somewhat like a 'sergeant-major bringing her company to order'. It included, apart from Zohra, Zubeida Patel, Mrs PK Naidoo, Lutchmee Govender, Veeramah Pather and Jamila Bhabha. That evening there was a large turnout at the station to give this first batch of women resisters from the Transvaal, who would be among those launching the campaign, the kind of send-off they deserved. They were heroines, all. I thought of the batch of women who had travelled from Tolstoy Farm in 1913 and defied the provincial barrier, inviting arrest. There was an excited, expectant atmosphere on the platform, and my mind went back to Waschbank when we had awaited the arrival of Sarojini Naidoo. Here we were bidding goodbye to five Sarojini Naidoos. The train readied to depart – there was a lot of embracing and giving of last-minute instructions. The women entered their compartment and leaned out of the windows, waving their excited goodbyes. Soon we were looking at the back of the last coach.

JN and I, though up to our ears in work, could not bear to remain in Johannesburg and miss the launch in Durban. Six of us set out that evening in Essop Bhabha's car. He was a daredevil driver, but we arrived safely in Pinetown just as dawn was breaking. We drove into the poinsettia-flanked driveway, the house came into view, still and quiet, with most of its occupants sound asleep.

MI had bought a large rambling house with a wraparound veranda, set in twenty-five acres of land. But as large as this house was, it was still not large enough, and it brimmed with people as had the houses in Ritson Road and Convent Lane. A house is as large as the heart of its owner, and MI's heart was limitless.

Bhaboo and Budie had just risen from their musallahs [prayer mats]; I could tell from the large namaaz awdnies [head scarves] that were still draped around them.

MI was in his room, writing. I paid him my respects, then joined Budie and Bhaboo to help them with the breakfast and show the 'guests' to their beds.

The next day, Sunday, was very busy. I left early with the Transvaal recruits, to help with arrangements. JN and I went straight to the NIC office and I was involved in work as if I had never left. Debi, MD, Monty, the talented, young Bobby Naidoo, and too many others to remember, were going about their separate duties in a methodical way.

Matters were very much under control, but as I arrived Debi immediately put me in charge of publicity. I assumed my usual position behind the typewriter in the office and knocked out press releases, which I then arranged to be sent off to the respective newspapers.

MEETING GENERAL SMUTS

Before launching passive resistance, and adhering closely to the Gandhian formula, we requested a meeting with General Smuts to test if there was any room for a negotiated settlement. The general agreed to meet our deputation. That was the first and last meeting he had with radical Indians. Dr Naicker led our delegation. MD Naidoo presented our memorandum calling for universal adult franchise and the withdrawal of the Anti-Asiatic Land Act. Smuts read the memorandum. We have no record of Smuts's impression of the NIC, but our delegation (both JN and I were working in the TIC at the time and were not part of the delegation) found Smuts pleasant and attentive. General Smuts responded by taking the delegation on an inspection of the building. Then, standing at the window of his office in the famous Union Buildings and waving his hands across the length and breadth of the observable expanse of his empire, he said: 'This city was not built in a day.' This is as MD told us. It seemed to me that the general had adroitly side-stepped the issues and charmed our boys with his patriarchal presence.

FIRST RESISTANCE BATCH

The mass meeting on 13 June was scheduled for 6 pm. By 4 pm, Red Square, as we had re-christened Nicol Square, was almost full. We were 15 000 strong. The lorry, our platform, was parked in readiness. JN tested Kathree's sound system, the best available at the time. The speakers arrived and were positioned on the lorry. There was resounding applause. The first batch of resisters followed. The crowd was stunned to see so many women, and especially Muslim women, among them. The Johannesburg group was joined by the Durban group. The applause was now deafening. The resisters were garlanded.

The Meer family had turned out in full, especially the women; all my sisters and cousins were there, as were the children.

The resisters left the platforms and formed the first phalanx in preparation of the five-kilometre walk to the selected resistance plot on the corner of Umbilo Road and Gale Street. The people, almost 20 000 of them, formed phalanxes behind the resisters in endless rows. I was among the large contingent of marshals and our work was cut out for us as we helped them into position. We were as disciplined as Satyagrahis were expected to be. The people were good-natured, their spirits elated by the sense of history in which they were participating. They sang robustly and lustily shouted anti-government and anti-Smuts slogans. The people were well behaved and did not require much controlling.

We reached the resistance plot; the marshals guided the marchers away from the plot and they dispersed. A few hundred, however, remained. We saw to it that they were clearly off the resistance plot, as we ourselves were. We didn't want any accidents with 'non-resisters' being arrested. We had fifty marshals on hand and we knew they could manage affairs. The resisters occupied the two tents, one for the men and one for the women, and by that act occupied land reserved for whites, thus breaking the law.

We now waited for the police – a law had been broken, arrests had to follow. Nothing happened. The police looked on but did nothing. We kept an eye on the situation, ready to take any necessary action. More than an hour passed – nothing. After a while Monty and MD became restless; they came to talk to us. MD posed the question, 'What if they don't arrest us? Should we not have an alternative plan?' We discussed this and concluded that the PRC secretariat would have to decide, but for the night the resisters should just sleep it out. The Women's Action Group arrived with the evening dinner. The resisters were in jocular mood. They ate outside their tents. Zainab and the women decided to retire for the night. They were quite exhausted by the train journey and the excitement of the day. They made their beds on the floor of the tent. The men walked around the tent. It was one of those beautiful Durban nights, the sky relatively black, sparkling with stars. We continued our vigil. MD and his male resisters also retired for the night. All was quiet. Debi struck up a tune rather noisily; some of the guards joined him. JN told them good-naturedly that they should quieten down. The resisters were probably having a rough time trying to sleep as it was, without the noise they contributed.

Dawn broke. Life stirred in the tents; Zainab was the first one up and about. As I suspected, they had had an uneasy night. Arrangements had been made for the resisters to bathe, freshen up and have breakfast. Their hosts arrived to collect them.

WHITE HOOLIGANS ATTACK RESISTERS, 17 JUNE 1946

JN and I also left for our respective homes. We arranged to meet at the NIC office in about two hours' time. I had to prepare the press statements and then take them to the newspapers. I snatched a few hours' sleep and was back again at the resistance site. Another night passed. The government continued to ignore our resisters. It was hard on them, the waiting, and the realisation that each day in the tent meant an additional day given in the struggle. The Women's Action Group brought lunch. The women resisters chided them for taking all the trouble. 'And what was the need to bring samoosas and halwa?' one of them protested. 'Eat dear sisters, eat. We don't know what you will be getting in prison, whether you will eat at all. You are doing so much for us. Let us do this little for you.' Supper followed. Still the police did not move. At the NIC office our clerk, Green, carefully placed telegraphic messages of support from the Indian National Congress and the Muslim League in the incoming mail tray for our attention. Saturday night passed. The resisters left their tents briefly and were taken away to bath and breakfast. The crowd at the tents swelled on Sunday and, as the day came to an end, thinned out. Day four passed and the resisters prepared for the fourth night. The police remained on their 'perch'. More police arrived in their vans, smoking, watching. We waited, tense, expecting some action. It was 8.30 pm.

JN was the first to see them, a gang of white youths approaching the tent. 'There is trouble,' he said, and alerted the marshals; they sprang into action and began forming a cordon, arm-in-arm. Suddenly there was an invasion of about a hundred youths, many rushing in from the bush where they had been hiding. Our marshals were not strong enough; they broke through the cordon and overran the tents, tearing them down, knocking into the resisters, pulling their blankets, grabbing their pillows. The crowd that had gathered in support was incensed; we could see they were raring to take on the white hooligans. We instructed the marshals to restrain them. 'We must remain non-violent!' we shouted. The four policemen remained inert, watching, taking no action, neither protecting the resisters nor restraining the attackers. The white hooligans – for there was no other word to describe them – retreated, leaving a mangle of canvas and poles behind. We moved in. Monty was attending to the injured. Dr Goonam had joined him; they attended to the shocked and battered resisters.

Mrs Govender, one of the women resisters, said, 'They flew in like ants.'

An uneasy calm followed, pregnant with expectation that more was to come. The four policemen present were joined by more; the hooligans returned, emboldened by the 'support' of the police who had taken no action against them.

All of us on the spot, onlookers and marshals, surrounded the camps and formed a protective shield, arm-in-arm. More police arrived. The hooligans returned and tried to push through us, but this time we were strong; they could not push through. They now began swearing and used the foulest language as they tried to break our cordon. Two or three of them held MD by the shirt and shook him up. More police arrived. Mrs Veeramah Pather, who had served as a resister under Gandhi, was knocked down by a collapsing tent. She lay weak and concussed on the ground. Both Doctors Goonam and Naicker were at her side.

Amina Bai Pahad and Zainab Asvat were also injured; the two doctors advised them to leave the tents, but they insisted on staying. Veeramah's age was against her, so she returned home.

I telephoned Dadoo and reported on the situation. He flew into Durban the next day, 18 June, and his presence strengthened the resisters, especially the Johannesburg women who bore the brunt of the attacks.

We had an emergency meeting of the executive of the PRC. We decided that we should send in batches in quick succession, led by high-profile leaders, as soon as the first batch was arrested. We were certain the police would act after the violence. We called a mass meeting at the resistance plot. One thousand five hundred people turned up.

The attacks were repeated with increased ferocity on the evenings of the 18th and 19th, and on both occasions the police stood by observing, neither restraining the attackers nor protecting the victims. It seemed that the authorities wanted to expose the resisters to maximum brutality so that they would give up and move out. But that didn't happen. The Indian people were aroused as never before. The resisters inspired them with pride and courage. They gathered on the resistance plot daily in increasing numbers, and the number of volunteers swelled.

THE RESISTERS ARE ARRESTED

On 21 June, eight days after the launch of the campaign, the police acted. Dr Naicker and his batch of thirteen resisters were arrested, including Zainab Asvat and Jamila Bhabha. Dr Dadoo took Monty's place and led the second batch.

The police were now fast on the job, arresting resisters no sooner than they occupied the plot. New contingents of resisters replaced those arrested. The magistrate became very busy as batch after batch of resisters was brought before him for sentencing.

Monty's first batch of resisters was, surprisingly, cautioned and discharged. They returned to resume their defiance on the resistance plot. Dr Naicker and Dr Goonam were each sentenced to six months' imprisonment with hard labour. MD Naidoo, Dr Dadoo, RA Pillay and Zainab Asvat were sentenced to three months. The leaders were charged under the Riotous Assemblies Act; their followers were charged with trespassing and fined £5 without the option of imprisonment. If they did not pay their fines, they were told their properties would be attached. This did not deter the resisters.

Admiration for the resisters intensified. Thousands visited the camp, money poured in, European consciousness was roused and a Council for Human Rights was set up to support the resisters and educate the whites. Mahatma Gandhi called on the South African government to stop the hooligans.

The attacks by the hooligans continued, then worsened. On 21 June, a plain-clothed Indian policeman, Krishensamy Pillay, was beaten unconscious and left in the gutter. He was taken to hospital, where Debi Singh, the Reverend Michael Scott and Dr Dadoo spoke to him. He said he had been beaten up by Europeans between Frere and Davenport Roads, yet the police said they had not taken a statement from him because he never regained consciousness before he died.

Thousands of mourners attended his funeral. The campaign had produced its first martyr. On the 22nd, the Indian movement was slightly changed when Michael Scott and my fellow student from Wits, Benny Sischy, joined the resisters, led by Dr Goonam. The hooligans were again on the attack. Dr Goonam and Michael Scott were arrested, but within an hour Michael Scott was released.

He returned to the resistance site and reported that he saw five resisters, knocked unconscious by white hooligans, lying in the gutter. Among them were two Indian girls. They had not retaliated and referred to the Europeans as misguided.

The worst attack occurred on the night of 23 June, when the batch led by J Joshi was attacked. The hooligans stoned cars, broke windows and left many resisters and their supporters concussed and confused. That evening Dr Dadoo addressed a mass meeting at Red Square; volunteers and money poured in. The people were as enthusiastic as ever.

THE MOVEMENT GROWS

Eight hundred women gathered at the Avalon Cinema where Zainab Asvat and Dr Goonam led the fray. Zainab Asvat's words rang out in courage and tolerance when she told the audience that she didn't blame the whites for the attack; she blamed the colour madness of a section of whites. An African woman spoke up from the mass of Indians. She expressed her admiration for the fight the Indian people were waging and said, 'We (meaning the African women) are with you.'

My niece Zohra was one of the speakers; Miss Khatija Mayat spoke in Urdu.

It was an impressive meeting. The resistance had truly taken off. On 5 July, 152 volunteers were sentenced to terms of imprisonment ranging from six weeks to four months. This brought the total in jail to 158.

On 4 August, Cissy Gool led the first Cape batch.

By September, 594 resisters had been convicted. In November, a delegation comprising HA Naidoo, Sorabjee Rustomjee and Dr Xuma, president general of the ANC, went to New York to advise the Indian delegation tabling the case of racism in South Africa before the world community.

In October, to coincide with the opening of the UN Assembly, 355 volunteers resisted, and a special court was appointed to deal with them.

In Johannesburg the executive of the PRC met, and we mapped out our plans to send more resisters to Durban. They left in batches by car, their first stop in Standerton at Pochees Cycle Works, where Mahomed Pochee welcomed them to breakfast. In Ladysmith, Dr AH Sader's mother hosted them for lunch. They reached Pinetown in time for supper and sleep.

The resisters spent the night and part of the next day with MI and his family, enjoying the walks in the large grounds and the gracious hospitality of my cousins. The credit for this must go to the two Mrs MI Meers: Budie, MI's first wife and my cousin, the daughter of MA Meer; and Bhaboo, as we called his second wife,

Behn's biological mother. All I had to do was telephone Bhaboo and say a certain number of people were coming, and they would have beds and meals ready.

The Transvaal resisters drove into Durban to the Congress office and attended the mass meeting. Accompanied by thousands of supporters, they marched to the plot in Gale Street and occupied the resistance tents. Their arrest followed; they spent the night in police cells and appeared in the magistrate's court the next morning. The magistrates followed a standard procedure: rank-and-file resisters were convicted to three months' imprisonment. The public gallery at the court was always full to capacity, but in deference to the court's rule of no cheering, the supporters were restrained. But the resisters knew by their presence the great support they had from the people.

AI MEER LEADS HIS BATCH

AI Meer, the NIC secretary, led his resistance batch. He was a man with many interests. He was involved with my brother AC in founding the Buzme Adab, which organised Mushairas, or the gathering of 'poets'. These were open to anyone, regardless of whether he or she was a poet or not. The gathering inspired the writing and reciting of poetry. A couplet was given, bearing the metre in which the poem was required to be written. Our family was very involved in the Urdu language and Urdu poetry, and four of my cousins, MI, AI, EM and AM, were recognised poets in the community. EM's son, Unus, also joined this company and for years headed the Buzme Adab, following in the footsteps of AI and Farooqi Mehtar.

AI had also enrolled at the University of Natal in the arts three years previously. The women in the family joked about him and said he was undergoing his second youth when they saw him running around in his undergraduate gown, shaking his box for Rag donations.

On one of my visits to Durban, I found all my women cousins and cousins-in-law gathered at AI's house, making samoosas. They explained that the samoosas were for AI to take to a special dinner at Adam's Mission. The only semblance the non-European students had of college life was when they spent the annual week at Adam's Mission while the Mission's students were on holiday.

It was customary to hold a special dinner at the end of the stay, and AI was contributing 500 samoosas. He hung around taking pleasure in watching the progress of the women, chatting away happily as they filled the samoosas.

I was very happy to see how well he had integrated into college life. He also attended meetings and socials much in the way I had done before. He too was a member of the International Club. He invariably took Behn with him. With these changes in his life, I was not surprised when he was elected secretary of our new Congress at the historic Curries Fountain meeting. I knew his strength.

The Indian resistance movement inspired many national songs. We had meetings each night to keep up our spirits, and there were individuals who rendered musical items. Suryakala Patel's rendition of a song, recounting the massacre at Jalianwala Bagh in India, was a top favourite. The words, in translation, went something like this: 'When charged with the hunger of freedom, you were fed the bullets of Jalianwala Bagh.' AI usually chaired these sessions.

I recall an evening when he took me aside and gave me a lecture on how important it was to audition performers before putting them on stage. Once, three rather portly women had volunteered to recite a poem. AI had introduced them with a great flourish and the three belles had proceeded to recite: 'Ding dong bell, General Smuts, he go to hell.' That was the poem in its entirety, the one sentence repeated several times. AI was very embarrassed.

He and his batch were arrested and brought before the court. AI addressed the court: 'I am charged for trespassing on the resistance plot. Our forefathers, when they came to this country, found it there. Persons of all colours trespass that plot and they are not charged. Yet we have been singled out for prosecution. What is the explanation? Trespass is not a crime. The only object in charging us is that we are defying the Asiatic Land Tenure Act.'

'Why then,' he asked, 'were we not charged under that Act?' He supplied the answer: 'Because a world tired of the Nazi doctrine of race superiority, which it fought to destroy, will no longer tolerate such laws; they have said so by their verdict at the United Nations.'

He and his batch were found guilty and sentenced to three weeks' hard labour. He served his sentence in Bergville.

I RESIST

In January 1947 I took time off from my editorial and organisational work in Johannesburg and became a passive resister. I travelled to Durban to defy the Ghetto Act.

There was the usual meeting of some thousands of people at Red Square. Speakers made it clear that this was a struggle for the liberation of all the oppressed people of the country, denied access to land, and for the extension of democratic voting rights to all South Africans, regardless of race.

We then marched to the resistance plot and took our positions in the tents; our supporters hung around but kept clear of the marked boundary so as not to contribute accidentally to our numbers. We did not have to wait long before we were arrested and taken to the Umbilo police cells, where we spent the night. We appeared before the magistrate at the Durban court the next morning. I addressed the court as leader of my batch. We were sentenced to imprisonment with hard labour for three weeks, since no resister offered to pay the alternative fine. We were then removed to Durban Central Prison.

We settled for the night. I was disturbed early in the morning.

The order was curt: 'Get your belongings!'

'No belongings, sir,' I answered.

'Then come along with me,' the tone still curt.

But before I could go along I was handcuffed and my legs shackled with ball and chain, the likes of which I had only seen in Laurel and Hardy comic books. I had suddenly become a dangerous criminal. I was shoved into a police van and taken to the station, where I was put into a third-class coach to Stanger with two guards. I was driven from Stanger Station to the local jail, where the prisoners were assembled in the yard, breakfasting on yellow mealie meal porridge. I joined them and I too received my bowl of porridge, without sugar or a spoon. I wondered how I would eat the porridge. I saw that some prisoners had spoons and so I asked the warder, 'Please sir, may I have a spoon?'

My request was met with an unexpected burst of anger. 'You bloody Coolie, you eat with your hands all your life, now here in prison you want a spoon!' I thanked him for reminding me of my culture. I later learnt that only the old-timers had spoons, which they made themselves out of wood. This was before the plastic era.

I joined the road gangs. We cleaned the gutters of Stanger and repaired the roads. My stay was short; I was released after three weeks, but served some extra hours because JN Singh, who had come to fetch me, had an altercation with one of the warders, who decided to teach the 'bastard' a lesson.

The first Sunday after both AI and I had been released from prison, on 23 March 1947, the entire Meer clan gathered in Pinetown at MI Meer's sprawling homestead overlooking the roses, asters, dahlias and sweetpeas that MI had so lovingly cultivated.

RELAXING IN PINETOWN

Molvi Cachalia was also present. He had come down from Johannesburg and was due to lead his batch of thirty resisters the next day. But on that Sunday he had come to talk with MI. In another part of the house, AI and I were regaling the women and children with our prison adventures. It felt good to be treated like heroes by our kith and kin.

In the afternoon we watched the children, organised by Behn, playing charades in the study. She had grouped the children into competing teams and they dramatised scenes, mimicking various members of the family. We had to identify the real-life characters represented.

There were a lot of children: MI's eight children – he had nine in all, but his eldest, Ismail, was away in India, as was AI's elder son Unus, both starting out at

PASSIVE RESISTANCE

Aligirh College in preparation for university. Then there were the five Mall children, who were regarded as family – their eldest brother Hassan (later Judge Mall) was away at Fort Hare – and MI's cousin's five children, who had come from Kimberley to live with him because their parents were having trouble. Both MI and AI had lived with their maternal Uncle Amod Mohamed in his good times and it was taken for granted that they should care for his grandchildren when he was no more. Then there was my brother AC's four sons, my brother HC's daughter, and my sister Ayesha's son, who was stuck with the unlikely name of Bubbles because of the saliva that had drooled from his mouth as a baby. I think I have listed them all. They were really a mob.

The family days at Pinetown were always long and exuberant. MI was the only one with a car, and his driver, Omar Khan, spent his time making several trips fetching us in the morning and then returning us to our homes in the evening.

We had re-established some of the Waschbank atmosphere in Pinetown, and transferred it to Ritson Road when MI was forced to vacate his property because of racial laws. Our cousins, the sons of MM Meer, AM and EM, had left India and settled in South Africa. My brother AC was living in a flat in Etna Lane, within walking distance from Ritson Road. They met regularly on Sundays, and I joined in when in Durban. We discussed religion and politics. Our ideas were so different. MI and AI were radical in their approach to religion, intellectual, not ritualistic, and presented their ideas logically. The Mahomed Meer 'boys', EM and AM, were passionate and found it difficult to be cool-headed when their beliefs were challenged. They became very emotional and raised their voices. AC was the listener. He always had an amused, quizzical look on his face. I didn't enter into their arguments except when specifically asked to. They discussed and argued about India's freedom.

The end of the war brought changes in British imperialism, and India was one of the first colonies to win independence. But the movement towards independence was charged with violence as Muslims and Hindus divided and the pressure for an independent state of Pakistan intensified.

The British mediation between Hindus and Muslims was a major issue of political dissension. Where MI supported Mohamed Ali Jinnah,[2] AI, Behn – who was beginning to take strong political positions – and I supported Gandhi and Nehru. Where AI voted for an undivided India, MI wrote passionate editorials in support of Pakistan. He had the fullest support from AM and EM. AC inclined towards our position, but also tended to support MI.

In India, our cousin Moosa Mohamed Meer supported neither Jinnah nor Gandhi, but Subhash Chandra Bose.[3] MI Meer's great tolerance kept the whole family united with a healthy agreement to disagree.

105

The community celebrated the departure of the British and the independence days of India and Pakistan. There were three kinds of gatherings: those celebrating the freedom of India, those celebrating the freedom of Pakistan, and those organised by the NIC and TIC, celebrating the freedom of both countries jointly. All the celebrations were joyous, with street processions, flag hoisting and waving, and bugle blowing and drum beating.

DADOO AND NAICKER LEAVE FOR OVERSEAS

Towards the beginning of 1947, when our campaign was strong and its organising in the firm hands of the executive committees, we decided that it was time for Dadoo and Naicker to visit India, consult with Gandhi and Nehru and canvass the strongest possible support from the subcontinent.

Sarojini Naidoo, the former president of the SAIC, was a key organiser of the Asian Relations Conference scheduled for March 1947 in New Delhi. We thought it would be useful for Dadoo and Naicker to attend the conference.

But in 1947 the Smuts government instituted new punitive measures against people whose policies they did not like by refusing to issue them passports. My entire family, my children included, would later become victims of this persecution. It meant that we could not leave the country – not that we had the money to take holidays abroad, but there were invitations to conferences paid for by the hosts that Fathu was unable to accept.

The *Leader* had begun a regular commentary, 'The Crack of the Sjambok', and the first crack it reported was the refusal of passports to Doctors Dadoo and Naicker to attend the UN General Assembly meeting in Paris. Dadoo was actually taken off the plane after he had boarded it. Undaunted, he left South Africa by Mercury Airways, a private company, without a South African passport. Upon his return, the travel document he had used (made by himself) was seized. In 1977, our son Rashid would forge a passport and escape into exile. He would only return after the change of government.

The refusal of passports to Dadoo and Naicker provoked an international protest, with Gandhi adding his voice. The government relented and issued passports to the two leaders.

There was a massive attendance at Red Square on 9 February 1947 to bid them farewell, and among the speakers was Dr AB Xuma, president of the ANC, who had just returned from the UN, excited and satisfied with his trip. I wondered whether he had ever addressed such a large gathering. He made the right calls: 'Reject communal franchise. Don't sit on the Advisory Board.'

When plans were being made for Naicker and Dadoo to leave for India, I thought of my sister Amina – Gorie Bai, as I called her – who had married our uncle Mohamed Meer's son, Ahmed (Hajee Bhai), at the age of fourteen and never returned to South Africa. I thought of her wedding and the weddings of my two other sisters, Ayesha, who was only seven at the time, just a year older than me, and Fatima, or Budie, as we called her, thirteen years old. As I looked back on those marriages, I thought of the family politics that were involved. Cassim Meer, our father's nephew, wanted his somewhat errant son, Yusuf (YC), to marry Ayesha, who was bright and beautiful. YC was no match for her. In return Cassim Meer offered his sister's daughter, Khatija, to my oldest brother Hussain (HC), who at the time was accumulating his own negative marks. That seemed a fair exchange. My father thought that marriage would settle him down. Cassim, in addition, brought a proposal for Budie, offering his sister's son Salejee. The greatest worry for parents in those days was to settle their children in marriage, especially daughters. The prospect of settling four children in marriage in one go must have greatly appealed to my father.

Two of the four marriages contracted during those hectic, festive days in Waschbank failed miserably. Seven-year old Ayesha, delivered to her husband's home at the age of thirteen, never found any love there, and she eventually prevailed on my brother AC to 'rescue' her. My sister Äpa sold one of her gold bangles to raise the necessary train fares. Ayesha came to live with us in Pine Street and then moved with us and our parents to Baker Street, and then we all moved with AI and Äpa to Ritson Road. My oldest brother HC was not the home-making type. He took to drinking and he and Gorie Apa, as we called his wife, and their daughter Zohra moved in with MI.

But my sister Gorie Bai and Hajee Bhai were happy. Theirs had been a love marriage within the severe constraints of our home in Waschbank. Hajee Bhai, I was told, had been totally struck by Gorie Bai, and had written her love poems.

Now when Monty was about to leave for India, I persuaded him to include Surat in his itinerary and visit my sister, whom I had not seen for twenty years.

When Monty returned, apart from giving us a detailed account of his meetings with Nehru, Gandhi and Sarojini Naidoo, and of the mass meetings they had addressed and the heroes' receptions they had enjoyed, he also gave AI and me a report on Surat. They had been entertained at Rajawadi, the family home, to biryani and solo, a sweet rice dish, and they had met my sister who had spoken to Dadoo at great length, since they both spoke Gujarati. But Monty's conversation with her had been restricted to a few formalities they had managed in Zulu.

SEVEN

THE END OF INDIAN PASSIVE RESISTANCE AND THE BEGINNING OF APARTHEID

1946–1948

INDIANS AS PROHIBITED IMMIGRANTS IN THE TRANSVAAL

The Immigrants Regulation Act of 1913 had, by 1946, played havoc with the lives of Indians, making them foreigners in the land of their birth. White foreigners could move about freely in the country, Indian South Africans could not.

The Act denied Indians of one province the right to be in another. The provincial barriers were in fact harsher than the pass laws against Africans. We had to obtain permits to leave Durban for Johannesburg, and they were issued for only three months at a time, so that the permits had to be renewed in the province visited. If one defaulted, one could be deported. The same rules were applied to students enrolled at university. This law was applied stringently against Indians, and waiters employed in Cape Town and Johannesburg were deported in scores.

In 1948 I completed my LLB, and the office of the Commissioner for Asiatic Affairs promptly slapped me with an order to leave the Transvaal on the grounds that I was a prohibited immigrant. That office had resented my presence in the Transvaal all along.

The Natal Law Society had shut down law lectures offered to non-whites to prevent them from becoming lawyers; the Transvaal Law Society had followed suit using other tactics. It had refused to register my articles with AI Minty in 1944 on the grounds that I was a prohibited immigrant, even though I had not been declared as such. The Department of Asiatic Affairs co-operated with the Transvaal Law Society, ruling that serving articles was tantamount to employment, and since an Indian from Natal was prohibited from being employed in the Transvaal, my articles could not be registered. I was ordered to leave the Transvaal immediately.

Dadoo had retorted in anger, 'We are not going to take this lying down. We will fight it.' We engaged the leading silk in immigration laws, Advocate Attlinger, and Bram arranged for him to represent me pro deo. Attlinger threatened to take the matter to the Supreme Court, and both the Law Society and the Commissioner for Asiatic Affairs backed down, but the registering of my articles was delayed by nine months.

In 1946, JN was charged for failing to renew his permit. He was defended by Vernon Berrange, who had a reputation for being invincible. JN had a valid permit to be in the Transvaal and this was Berrange's cocksure defence. 'In keeping with the Act, Mr Singh has a valid permit to enter the Transvaal,' Berrange addressed the court. The magistrate studied the papers before him.

'Mr Berrange, according to the copy of the Act before me, an Indian from Natal is in breach of the law if he is *found* in the Transvaal. This is the amended Act. What Act have you before you?'

Berrange had the unamended copy, which said 'entered', not 'found'. He was put out and embarrassed that he had erred in not studying the Act conclusively. He left the court, leaving JN to deal with his own predicament!

JN was found guilty and sentenced to imprisonment without the option of a fine, and when he had served his sentence, he was deported. We knew the train by which he would be taken and arranged a reception at the station, giving him a hero's farewell.

In 1948, I left for Durban almost immediately after being served with a deportation notice, not wanting to risk a repeat performance of what had been meted out to JN.

BREACHING PROVINCIAL BORDERS

Gandhi's 1913 resistance had been focused on defying provincial barriers. We now planned to do the same in the second phase of our 1946 campaign. Our passive resistance struggle had been highly successful. Almost 2000 volunteers had been imprisoned with hard labour, but by the end of 1947 passive resistance showed disturbing signs of flagging. It became clear to us that to revive interest we would have to change the form of our struggle. We decided to attack provincial barriers. It would, we hoped, bring back memories of the 1913 Gandhian resistance against the 1913 Immigrants Regulation Act.

On Sunday, 25 January 1948, fifteen resisters, led by RA Pillay and R Mahabeer, set out in pouring rain in two cars, to begin the second phase of the passive resistance campaign. They travelled to Pietermaritzburg and from there to Ladysmith where, after refreshing themselves, they continued their journey to Charlestown.

THE END OF INDIAN PASSIVE RESISTANCE

I had travelled to Johannesburg at the time, waiting with Dr Dadoo on the Transvaal side of the border to monitor and take appropriate action when the resisters were arrested, as we expected them to be. However, there was no sign of the police. The resisters crossed over. Nothing happened. We had to think quickly of our next move. We decided that the resisters would go on to Fordsburg and occupy a plot of land on the corner of Lovers Walk and Avenue Road, and defy the Land Act there. I hurried to Fordsburg to put together a welcoming reception, over which I presided.

The Durban resisters pitched their tent at the identified plot. The authorities ignored them, instead arresting Doctors Naicker and Dadoo for aiding and abetting the resisters. They were sentenced to six months' imprisonment in Durban and Pietermaritzburg respectively. Undaunted, Dr Goonam led her batch across the border on 13 March and was likewise arrested and sentenced to six months' imprisonment.

Manilal Gandhi followed with his batch of resisters. On 11 April 1948, he and his resisters crossed the border; Gandhi, the leader, remained untouched, but his followers were arrested and sentenced to imprisonment. The resistance was not going according to plan. The government was playing its own game, and we did not know what it was.

In August, Monty Naicker, the NIC organiser, SV Reddy, the NIC recruiting officer, MD Naidoo and Green, the NIC clerk, were charged for aiding and abetting resisters. We advised Green to plead not guilty, expecting him to get off. We needed him in the office. The officials pleaded guilty. We thought for a moment that they were after the leaders. This time the magistrate let off the officials and sentenced our office clerk to four months' imprisonment!

The second phase of our resistance did not pick up steam, partly because the authorities refused to play our 'game' according to our rules. We were confused. It seemed that we were not in control of the campaign.

The Passive Resistance Council stated diplomatically that it was calling off the campaign in view of the new government and new opportunities that may exist. I liked neither the second phase nor the reason stated for its closure. Some argued that it was in true Gandhian tradition to give your enemy the opportunity to rethink. But we knew we had called off the campaign because we could not sustain it.

The 1946 resistance had continued for two years, at the end of which 1710 volunteers had been imprisoned and the foundation laid for sanctions against South Africa, which would prove to be a significant factor in the defeat of apartheid. The 1946 passive resistance campaign also moved South African's racism from a domestic problem to an international one, which continued to be debated annually at the UN.

But now it was time to end it. To our shame, the NIC executive announced its closure in a manner that many of us could not support.

In June 1948, DF Malan became the prime minister of South Africa. Verwoerd alone would exceed him in his maniacal notion of race superiority; internationally he was exceeded by Hitler alone. To the shock of many of us, the NIC executive sent Dr Malan a letter of congratulations, and informed him that we were calling off passive resistance. This message produced confusion and conflict, and was repudiated at a full working committee meeting.

THE ASSASSINATION OF GANDHI

In the midst of our problems we heard the shocking news of the assassination of Mahatma Gandhi. We were at the Congress office, Debi, JN and I, when the news came through. It was as if we had lost a personal mentor.

On that Friday all Indian shops closed, and at the huge assembly that gathered at Red Square to celebrate his life, Dr AB Xuma said, 'Gandhi was a man whom the whole world has accepted as an inspiration to those who fight for freedom.'

I had the feeling that with Gandhi's death the century itself had ended, although it was only halfway through. What remained of the century belonged to another era. We had lived in Gandhi's time. Now we would live in some other time. The social processes of humanity would never be the same again. We would blunder our way into the technological age where human values would fade in their impact on human relations.

The passing on of Gandhi, who had taken a personal interest in our liberation struggle, spurring us on with words of encouragement, dampened our spirit. We too came to the end of a phase. We concluded that we could not pursue passive resistance simply as Indians. If we were to succeed at all, we would have to work with our fellow disenfranchised South Africans and white democrats who were willing to join us.

I saw no successor to Gandhi on the world stage. In South Africa, we looked forward to Luthuli's leadership.

The Nats wanted to keep their parliament lily-white. They could not even tolerate an indirect black voice. So, out went the communal franchise Smuts had offered the Indians and at which, Smuts said, they had 'foolishly' tweaked their noses in his face. Out, too, went the Coloured and African representatives (albeit white people) in parliament.

I personally felt we lost nothing by this further 'disenfranchisement'. It accelerated the unity of the disenfranchised, for it brought us into line with each other, eliminating the petty differences in treatment that made one group feel favoured over the other, and which inhibited unity.

EIGHT

VIOLENCE AND UNITY

1948–1949

I left Johannesburg for good in mid-1948, and returned to my roots in Durban with an LLB degree and a treasure trove filled with memories of friends and political experiences that had contributed so richly to my life. It was in Johannesburg that I had grown close to Anton Lembede, Nelson Mandela, Walter Sisulu, Moses Kotane, the Cachalia brothers, Yusuf Dadoo, young Ahmed Kathrada, Bram Fischer, the Harmels, the Bernsteins, Joe Slovo and so many others with whom I had spent a significant part of my life in united opposition to apartheid.

I was loath to leave my flat. I thought of the many parties and the intense discussions I had there with Bajee, Kathy and Nelson, who had filled the flat with their intelligence, wit and laughter; my neighbours, who never complained; the housewives who sent me delicacies to enjoy. There was consolation in the fact that Kathy took over the flat, and its history would continue with him.

I was leaving Amina Bai Pahad, Chotie Bai Bhayat, Maryam Cachalia, Zainab Asvat and all those other magnificent women: Jamila Bhaba, Suryakala Patel and Mrs PK Naidoo. Also Salim Saleh, Molvi and Yusuf Cachalia, Yusuf Dadoo, Kathy, Goolam Pahad and so many others. I would miss them, their generosity and hospitality.

My sister Äpa was happy to have me back; AI and I were now working together in the NIC. Debi was pleased because I could help him with his many pressing responsibilities.

I had an LLB, but the articles I had served in the Transvaal were not acceptable in Natal. I had to re-register them in order to practise as an attorney.

I SERVE MY ARTICLES FOR A SECOND TIME
Ashwin Choudree, a Congress activist who had formed part of our lobbying team at the UN, and one of the first Indian lawyers to qualify in the country,

articled me, and I was grateful that he treated the articles as a formality, which they were. This left me free to spend as little time in his office as I wanted. I spent most of my time in the NIC office with Debi, and occasionally reporting for the *Guardian* and earning a little money.

I found the work at Choudree's office enlightening because of the interesting clients, one of them being ML Sultan.

ML SULTAN

I had met ML Sultan through MI. He was the kinsman of Charles Dickens's Scrooge, both in his miserliness and in his awakening to charitableness. The difference, I think, was that in Sultan charity and miserliness were his two sides. The knowledge that he should be charitable didn't come as a sudden revelation; that side was always there, though exercised cautiously. Sultan was a little man who wore a red fez and the traditional Muslim tailored long coat. He had a car, locked up in his garage, but he used the train on his daily forays into town. MI met him on one of those train journeys. MI took the train from Pinetown and was joined by ML Sultan in Escombe, about four stations later. They travelled together for four more stations before they reached Durban. Sultan would invariably be reading something in Tamil script, for he originated in Tamil Nadu, South India, and came to South Africa as an indentured labourer. He was still an adolescent when he was brought to the colony of Natal. It was rumoured that he became a millionaire by lending money (and charging interest) to his fellow indentured labourers – not a nice way of earning money, and decidedly haraam according to Islam, Sultan's religion.

Sultan took such a liking to MI that he did one of those rare things – he invited him, with his family, to his home for tea. I was included in the 'family' that MI took to that special tea.

The tea was neatly laid out by Sultan's daughter-in-law, who whispered to us that the old man was not talking to her. She was clearly distressed by this and was appealing to MI for help. MI tried. He asked Mr Sultan outright why he was not talking to his daughter-in-law. We could see he wasn't talking to her, he said, though we saw no such thing and would have been none the wiser if she had not drawn our attention to it. But MI was protecting her. Surprisingly, Mr Sultan took no objection to the question. He explained that she had broken a jug and hidden all the pieces away, out of sight. 'She did not report the matter to me. I don't like such dishonesty. She deserves her punishment.' MI did not interfere any further, save to say he hoped the punishment would end soon.

During our tea we were disturbed by a delegation that came to see Mr Sultan about a donation for a project in which they were involved. They emphasised that the project was for Muslims, thinking that would attract Sultan's money.

But Sultan said he did not support sectional causes. 'Allah is Rab-ul-á-lamen – Lord of the Universe. He is not Rab-ul Muslameen – Lord of Muslims. Show me anywhere in the Quran where Allah is described as sectional, favouring one group over another. Where does the Quran say Rab-ul-Muslameen?' He sent off the delegation, disappointed. Both MI and I were impressed with Sultan's universality, but knowing his parsimony we were left with a lurking suspicion that he may only have used it as an excuse to save his money.

But then, Sultan did bequeath his millions to the technical education of all races, not only Muslims or even just Indians. Africans make up the majority of students at the ML Sultan Technical College today.

At Ashwin Choudree's office I discovered another aspect of this venerable benefactor, and again I was left in a quandary. Was he just wily and parsimonious? He came in with a legal problem, which required the opinion of a senior counsel. We got the opinion and gave him the account.

'Strange,' he said. 'I brought you a legal problem of which you knew nothing. You were ignorant. Now you have become knowledgeable. You have learnt from the senior counsel. You expect me to pay you for your tutoring?' Ashwin did not want to argue against this logic. We paid the senior counsel.

At the NIC office we became thoroughly involved with the crisis in Indian education. The Indian people had built 165 schools for Indian pupils up till then, using their own resources. The Department of Education had so neglected Indian educational needs that, in 1948, there were 30 000 Indian children of school-going age seeking admission to schools. The worst was that for the first time in our history there was no accommodation in the one and only boy's high school: Sastri College turned away 250 pupils. Nine hundred and fifty-two Indian pupils had passed Standard Six that year.

THE CONGRESS HIGH SCHOOL

JN Singh, a former teacher and later a lawyer, headed the Congress Education Committee. I worked closely with him. Our first task was to research the extent of the shortages in accommodation, both at primary- and high-school level. Our findings received good publicity in the Indian newspapers. We organised a protest march and 800 schoolchildren participated.

We didn't leave the matter there; we established the Congress High School and admitted the students who could not get into Sastri College. Dr MB Naidoo, one of our best educators at the time, headed the school. The standard pursued was parallel to that at Sastri, for the same teachers taught at both schools. The teachers taught at Sastri in the mornings and at Congress High in the afternoons. Dr Naidoo was proud of the report he presented on the performance of the pupils at the end of the year.

THE 1949 RIOTS

On 13 January 1949, the peaceful, sunlit city of Durban suddenly exploded into flames. I was at home in Ritson Road when I had an urgent call from Debi Singh, summoning me immediately to the NIC office. There was alarm in his voice. All he said was that there was terrible rioting in town. I left immediately, walking briskly to Bewsey Grove to shortcut into Berea Road, where I took a tram to West Street. There was no quicker way of getting into town, and this was the route I usually took all the years that I lived in Ritson Road with AI.

I got off at the corner of West and Grey Streets and rushed to the NIC offices in Saville Street. I was the first to arrive. Debi had alerted the entire working committee, but this was not the time for protocol. There had to be instant action. Debi gave me a report as best he knew of what had happened. Rumours had spread like wildfire, and these in turn had heated passions to boiling point. Africans, armed with sticks, stones, knobkerries and whatever else they could lay their hands on, were attacking Indians and their property.

One rumour had it that an Indian adult had assaulted an African youth; another that the Indian adult had killed the youth; a third rumour placed the youth's decapitated head atop the dome of a temple or mosque; then it was confirmed that it was a mosque, identified as the Grey Street Mosque, except that there was no head atop its dome, or even on a minaret.

Within the hour the NIC office was teeming with committee members from all the branches. There were reports of trouble in most of the Indian areas. The office was tense with anxiety and fear as we discussed the reports and co-ordinated a plan of action. News came that African workers at the docks, many of whom lived in appalling conditions in the barracks, were marching towards Cato Manor armed with sticks, to take revenge.

The Grey Street complex was wild with panic. I contacted AWG Champion, president of the Natal ANC at the time, and asked him point-blank if he would help. His response was unhesitatingly positive. 'What do you have in mind?' he asked. I told him I had telephoned Leo Boyd, then mayor of Durban, requesting a van with a loudspeaker, and that it was on its way. I wanted him to join me in patrolling the areas, calling for calm, whatever the results. He said I should pick him up as soon as the van arrived.

We patrolled Victoria, Queen, Grey and Pine Streets, and then headed for Berea Road to intercept the dock workers. We tried addressing the gathering crowds and the marchers in Zulu and English, calling on them to return to their homes. The Grey Street complex was wild with panic. Laughing and smiling men carrying sticks were breaking shop windows, and crowds were rushing in to loot the exposed goods. The very remarkable thing was that there was not one policeman in sight. It was rumoured that the police had arrived in vans, distributed sticks to the rioters, and then disappeared.

We worked from the NIC office the whole of the night of 13 January, and among those who came to help were many who would later work closely with Chief Luthuli; prominent among them was Mangosuthu Buthelezi. He stopped his normal work and put in full-time duty with us in the ensuing days.

The marchers from the docks reached Cato Manor and targeted Indian homes and shops. Mayhem reigned the whole night of the 13th. The morning paper reported on the extensive damage done and the streams of Indian refugees that had collected at schools and religious institutions.

I went home for a wash and change of clothes in the morning. A lorry carrying some people was parked outside 62 Ritson Road. As I entered the house I bumped into Behn leaving, somewhat excited and intent on her mission, but as pleased to see me as I was to see her. She told me that there were many refugees at the school in Pinetown and also at her home. Among them was the family of her friend Jesse, whom they had rescued in their panel van from their home on the edge of Cato Manor, in 45th Cutting. She said she had come with members of the Pinetown Relief Committee to collect food, and she was going to the grocers in town. I didn't have time to speak to her for longer, but I was pleased that she was making herself useful.

Mr RT Chari from the Indian High Commissioner's office saw the rioting in Clairwood as he was returning from Port Shepstone. He came straight to the NIC office and gave what help he could. He kept India informed of developments.

The violence subsided only after the navy moved in. We looked at the damage: 142 dead − 1 European, 87 Africans, 50 Indians and 4 unclassifiable by race. A further 1087 were injured − 32 Europeans, 11 Coloureds, 541 Africans and 503 Indians.

Never before had South Africa seen so much carnage from race riots. But in the dark clouds there was a silver lining: the ANC and NIC united to present evidence before the riot commission, appointed by the government under Justice Van den Heever. We engaged senior advocate Dr Lowen to represent us jointly.

I was charged with preparing the brief for Dr Lowen. I planned to collect as many affidavits as I could to establish selective and pointed attacks on Indians, the collusion of the police with the 'rioters' and the instigation of whites. From newspaper reports it was becoming abundantly clear that there was an official conspiracy to paint Indians as black marketeers and dishonest traders exploiting Natives, and thus deserving of their wrath. The Natives were doing no more than teaching the Indians an overdue lesson.

I needed help to collect the necessary affidavits. I had worked with Molvi Cachalia in Johannesburg and I knew his competence in this field, so I telephoned him and asked him to come to Durban and help. Molvi came with Kathy, and they did a wonderful job. They stayed with George Singh.

THE ANC AND NIC WALK OUT OF COMMISSION HEARINGS
Our case was well prepared and we were confident that we would break the witnesses who would be brought to exonerate the government and make Indians the scapegoats. But the Van den Heever Commission ruled against the cross-examining of witnesses. We had solid evidence of how the riots had been influenced by racist incitement from cabinet level downwards, and Dr Lowen had planned to call in witnesses such as high-level government and police officials. But when the basic right of cross-examination was denied, the ANC and NIC, in unison, walked out of the Commission with their mutual counsel.

Liberal whites and Africans who gave evidence before the Commission vindicated the racist slur on Indians. The South African Institute of Race Relations, represented by Mr Maurice Webb, Dr Edgar Brookes and the Reverend Sibiya from Dannhauser, blamed the riots on the government's racist policies and its unrealistic plan to expatriate Indians.

Reverend Sibiya told the Commission that Indians were not the only black marketeers, there were also African and European black marketeers. Pending repatriation, Dr Brookes pointed out that a strategy of economic strangulation of Indians had been pursued, and Afrikaners had organised boycotts of Indian traders in the Transvaal. In Natal the Europeans had pursued a programme of antagonising Africans against Indians.

There were many whites among those convicted for looting, all of whom were without any fear of the police. One senior white police witness told the Commission that Senator Petterson had intervened and asked him, in the midst of the rioting, not to enforce law and order.

The Nationalist government was out to destroy any cordial Afro-Indian relations that existed and, in particular, to arrest any unity flowing from the Dadoo–Xuma–Naicker Pact of 1947. The Malan government was promoting its own Bantu National Congress in 1949. They hated Dr Xuma's lobbying at the world body against race discrimination, and hated the Indians all the more for supporting, even instigating him to do so, as they saw it.

The riots were a great test of the leadership of the NIC under Dr Naicker. The entire working committee gave diligent service in the refugee camps where Indians, fleeing from their homes, had gathered for refuge. The NIC offices became the hub of community activities. The staff from the Natal Indian Organisation[1] offices also moved into our offices because many of their leaders had sought refuge in Greytown during the riot.

We organised joint African–Indian nursing staff to help in the refugee camps

VIOLENCE AND UNITY

and joint African–Indian meetings so that Indians and Africans could face each other again, and see each other as people of a common God.

The Nats, in the meanwhile, saw an opportunity to pursue their diabolical plans. They began preparing ships to expatriate the desperate refugees, bereft of all their worldly goods, to India. They had already increased the stipends payable to Indians accepting expatriation. But this scheme was already in total disarray for a number of reasons, including the fact that in 1947, when India gained her independence, she was no longer prepared to be party to the ethnic cleansing that the Nats wanted to pursue.

But the riots unwittingly and unexpectedly had positive results, in that they provided a basis for Afro-Indian co-operation.

AFRICAN AND INDIAN LEADERS MEET TO HEAL THE RIFT

It is my view that it was the meeting of African and Indian leaders, convened at the Durban International Club on 6 February 1949, that laid the foundation for the united action that followed. It was the most representative meeting of Indian and African leaders ever. Among those present were Dr AB Xuma, Oliver Tambo, Professor DDT Jabavu, JB Marks and Selby Msimang. The Indian leaders who attended represented the whole political spectrum, radical and conservative, from Natal, the Transvaal and the Cape. There was unanimous agreement that meaningful action had to be taken at leadership level to inspire confidence among Africans and Indians; that despite the violence Africans and Indians were bonded by their common oppression; that the violence was, above all, an expression of the herrenvolk strategy to divide and rule, and there was overwhelming evidence to support this. This meeting led to the establishment of the Joint Council of the African and Indian Congresses, headed by the presidents of both Congresses, and which included AWG Champion, JB Marks and Moses Kotane. Very significantly, it included the former youth leader, Oliver Tambo, who, along with Nelson Mandela, had been resisting Afro-Indian unity. Both JN and I were on the Council. We had excellent allies in the former Youth Leaguers. They were in many respects like us. I had come to know Oliver, Nelson and Walter very well. I was convinced that together we could launch a very powerful passive resistance campaign.

The violence was a clear message to us that we could not work alone; we had to draw our people together and unite so that their suffering and anger could be positively focused on the source of their deprivations – the racist government – and not be manipulated against fellow victims.

We discussed the matter at great length. The urgency was felt more among members of the Indian Congress than the African Congress, but nonetheless three weeks after the 'riot' we set up a joint council of the African and Indian

Congresses. That was the forerunner of the Congress Alliance, which later launched the 1952 Defiance of Unjust Laws Campaign. We would triumph over adversity of the worst kind.

Those of us who had founded the Liberal Study Group and worked in the Non-European United Front had urged a decade ago – and Dr Abdurahman even earlier – that unity and united action of the disenfranchised were essential in defeating racism. The NIC reconfirmed its view that while the Indian passive resistance had contributed significantly to the liberation movement, the time for such ethnic movements was over. We had to mobilise the united force of the disenfranchised – in unity against racism to overcome racism.

Monty Naicker had called for a united democratic front to defeat apartheid in July 1948. Such a front could only become a reality if the ANC responded to the call.

THE ANC RESISTS WORKING WITH NON-AFRICANS

The ANC was not ready to work with other groups in 1947. Among those who had serious misgivings on the matter was Nelson Mandela. He was not impressed with the Doctors' Pact, and was very concerned that the leadership of the ANC was being compromised. I tried to convince him that nothing but good could come out of our organisational unity, that in order to defeat the Nationalists we had to unite against them. I knew the rising power of the ANC Youth League, of which Nelson was an important leader. We expected the Youth League to take over the ANC and steer it towards radicalism through leaders such as Luthuli, Sisulu, Tambo, JB Marks and Mandela. I hoped that such leadership would lead a militant movement of democrats and non-racists against apartheid and topple the Nationalist government.

Luthuli was the president of the Natal ANC at the time. He had defeated AWG Champion with the support of men such as Mangosuthu Buthelezi. Champion himself, in an interview with me, had pledged that so long as Luthuli was president, he would not oppose him, and he kept his word. I placed my faith in Luthuli's leadership as the national president of the ANC, and I never regretted it. Deeply religious, he was honest, strong, totally capable and very charismatic.

Nelson and I discussed our different approaches to conquering racism and I was confident that he would come round to my way of thinking. We had a good relationship, worked well together and enjoyed each other's company, sharing jokes and ideas. We talked intensely and frankly on political issues. Nelson had to overcome two barriers in accepting me as a friend: my communism and my Indianness. Communism was the easier barrier to overcome, for there were the non-Indian comrades – white and African – among whom were men like

Bram Fischer, Joe Slovo, Moses Kotane and JB Marks, towards whom Nelson had already softened and whom he admired. I assumed this included me in my communist role.

But there was a real problem vis-à-vis the image of Indians in African eyes in general, and it was reflected in his too. In many of the country areas the only shopkeepers were Indians with small shops, small stocks and small earnings. There were few large, wealthy merchants among them, but the stereotype was propagated of rich exploitative Indians, mainly by racist whites. Consequently, I suspect that my Indian part remained a problem for Nelson – not in our social relationship, where I was IC, neither communist nor Indian, just myself, his friend, whom he loved – but on a group level. Ultimately, our personal relationship and trust overcame prejudice and distrust, and paved the way for united action.

Smuts or Malan, United or National Party, both were white, both racist, both oppressive and tyrannical. But the Nationalists were worse – they institutionalised racism in order to secure white ascendancy forever, an impossible aspiration. They were legislating for their political security with such a vengeance that within a few years even the wearing of ANC colours would become a criminal offence, punishable by five years' imprisonment. The death penalty would be used with such impunity that it would make South Africa the foremost hanging country in the world.

The assumption of Nationalist power coincided with the radicalisation of the ANC. Within months of the Nationalist victory, the Youth League took control of the ANC. The youth leaders were Africanists; AP Mda was the firebrand who stood at the extreme right of this position; he would never change his position. Walter Sisulu, frank, open and likeable, stood at the opposite end, and was supported by JB Marks and David Bopape, who, like us, believed in non-European unity. But the die-hard Africanists held sway for a considerable length of time.

HIE DHLOMO'S SEMINAL ARTICLE

HIE Dhlomo and I had been good friends since as long ago as 1937, and he had addressed the Liberal Study Group. He was a poet and I admired his literary genius. We were in the Valley of a Thousand Hills one day when he was so overcome by the physical beauty of the landscape, that he, there and then, quite spontaneously composed a moving poem. He recited it later at a gathering in Stanger. There was great applause and he was asked to read it again. He turned to me and requested I read it for him, and I was honoured to do so.

In 1950, he wrote a seminal article in the *Forum*, a liberal journal, and a group of us, all members of the TIC, discussed it while relaxing in Goolam Pahad's flat. Dhlomo maintained that the Indian passive resistance campaign had made a significant impact on Africans. The Indians, he said, were turning to Africans as their fellow oppressed, and there were discussions in both Indian and African circles on the possibility of joint action in the near future. Young Kathy walked in on this discussion and his interest was aroused. Those of us who had worked towards non-European unity for the last ten years and who, through our passive resistance campaign had unleashed a powerful force, believed that we would not succeed against the racists until and unless Africans joined us. We were greatly encouraged by Dhlomo's statement: 'The present leaders of the Natal Indian Congress are young men and students of international politics who look not only to India for inspiration and help but to world opinion.' He was seeing Indians as represented by us and not as the hostile stereotypes manufactured by racist whites.

I wondered what effect Dhlomo's assessment of Indians was having on Nelson. He was part of the fraternity of exclusivist Africans who kept us at arm's length politically, and were not prepared to admit us into their circle. How could we break down their reserve? How could we convince them that we were genuinely concerned about the African people; that we sought to assist them in realising freedom for all South Africans; that we wanted to support and strengthen them and not usurp their leadership? I sympathised with Nelson's Africanism and did not see it as racism, but as a legitimate claim for African ascendancy in an African country. I could not, however, sympathise with his refusal to co-operate with us in strategic demonstrations for the elimination of pass laws, for freedom of speech and for the right to franchise, simply because the campaigns did not originate in the ANC.

I was more than prepared to realise non-European unity, to which I aspired, through the ANC. The ANC, however, was not prepared at that time to open its doors to non-Africans.

In the meanwhile, we of the Indian Congress continued to work with the CPSA and APO in order to realise unity against apartheid to the extent we could.

We organised a 'Free Speech Rally'. The ANC refused to participate but its president, Dr Moroka, presided over the rally, much to the chagrin of his executive.

THE ANC REFUSES TO SUPPORT FREEDOM DAY RALLY

Ten thousand people, predominantly African, filled Johannesburg's Market Square and enthusiastically supported the resolution calling for a general strike in May 1950, the Freedom Day strike. The ANC did not support it unequivocally; the Transvaal branch supported it unofficially.

Kathy was young, impulsive and impatient. Bumping into Nelson on the street by chance one mid-morning, he confronted him point-blank on his reservations about working with Indians, and with non-Africans in general. He was particularly angry because of the Youth League's refusal to support the planned Freedom Day strike. He told Nelson that he (Nelson) might be a big African leader, and he (Kathy) just an Indian youth, but he challenged him to a debate in any African township of his choice, and he could guarantee him the people would support him (Kathy) and the strike, and not him (Nelson) and his opposition to the strike. Kathy's manner must have been very rude, for Nelson brought up the matter at a meeting of the joint executives of the Indian and African Congresses and the Communist Party. I reasoned with Nelson to leave the matter with me, I would deal with it. 'He is young and impulsive, and admittedly he was rude and boastful and spoke out of turn, but his heart is in the right place. I will speak to him.' Nelson agreed, though the anger in his eyes did not dim.

I spoke to Kathy and counselled restraint and diplomacy. Kathy was not one to capitulate once he had taken a position, and he insisted that Nelson and company were wrong and had to be told so bluntly, 'not all this kid-glove business, which was a waste of time'. This was Kathy's strength, to stand by what he believed in, but at times it also resulted in immovable obstinacy.

ANC YOUTH LEAGUE AND INDIAN CONGRESSES HOLD DISCUSSIONS

We were encouraged when the new leadership of the ANC, the former Youth Leaguers, opened discussions with us of the TIC on the need for joint action. The talks were difficult and continued for months. We had practically exhausted all our arguments. It wasn't that they did not see the value of joint action – we had just come up against a recalcitrant attitude overlaying prejudice and insecurity from which the Youth Leaguers had to be liberated, in order to enable them to launch a united onslaught on apartheid.

We were going around in circles, revisiting points already covered. We struck notes of extreme tension; the Youth Leaguers insisted on recording every word in long hand – even the venue of our discussions became relevant. The TIC office was seen as compromising the ANC; the venue was shifted to JB Marks's office in Rosenberg Arcade in Market Street. That Marks was a communist was secondary; that he was African was primary, and hence his office was beyond reproach.

It was Walter who eventually broke the deadlock, saying, 'We have talked enough. These people are sincere. There is no reason to doubt them. Let us work together where we can.' But this was not to be for two more years.

When, years later, I met Walter after he had spent twenty-seven years in prison, he said to me, 'You know, after I moved for joint action, that night your friend (meaning Nelson) walked away from me when we were returning home and said I had sold out to Indians. He accused me of being a traitor.'

Traitor or no traitor, the fact was that we were drawing closer together, both politically and in our personal relations. And when the state passed the Suppression of Communism Act, banning the Communist Party and threatening other political parties with the same fate, the ANC realised it had to work with non-Africans if it was to succeed against the Nats.

THE COMMUNIST PARTY IS DISSOLVED, 1950

The Central Committee of the Communist Party, in anticipation of its banning, dissolved the Party in 1950. The ordinary members of the Party, like myself, had no part in that decision, just as we had no part in the Party's decision to support the war at a time when we were opposing it. We were merely informed of the dissolution. The Party had for years given me a non-racial home. I had enjoyed the camaraderie of whites, Africans and Coloureds. We could continue the personal relationships formed, but those too were not maintained because there was an underground, secret formation that selected 'reliable' or credible comrades, and by that act dissipated the former unity. Whoever did the selection, they created suspicion and tension between the chosen and the discarded. I fell in the discarded category; nonetheless I continued to help old colleagues when they came on their annual drive to canvass funds for the *Guardian* and the *New Age* in Durban, and they stayed with us on those occasions. These visits ended when the last vestige of the *Guardian* folded and that proud paper disappeared. I had worked as a reporter on it for years and Fathu had helped me before our marriage.

The resounding response to our Freedom Day strike demonstrated that the people would follow those who represented their concerns, and if the ANC was not part of that struggle, they would go ahead without it. That, I am sure, was an important factor in the ANC's ultimate decision to work with us. Though successful, the strike was marred by police shootings, which resulted in eighteen protestors being killed. While we succeeded in attracting overwhelming support for our Freedom Day strike, we were helpless against state violence. The police opened fire on an unarmed crowd and eighteen protestors lost their lives.

EMPLOYERS TRY TO DIVIDE AFRICAN AND INDIAN WORKERS

The ANC and SAIC called a national day of protest on 26 June 1950 in commemoration of those killed, and invited the APO, TIC, NIC and CPSA to support it. I felt a sense of triumph. We were at last uniting in action. We organised vigorously for the strike. Nelson had graduated to the executive of the ANC and as such was one of the key organisers of the strike. He came down to Durban with Diliza Mji, and I joined them in canvassing support in

Natal. I took them to Pinetown to meet Behn. I could see they were charmed by her and I felt very proud.

In Durban, Indian workers stayed away from work. The Durban City Council took the lead, focusing on Indian workers, and dismissed 334 Indian employees as against 80 African employees. This was deliberate, to divide the two groups. For weeks I sat in the NIC office with Debi Singh, attending to the hundreds of dismissed workers who came for assistance. We set up a centre at Merebank for the convenience of the workers, and for weeks I travelled out there daily by bus to attend to their unemployment and other benefits, and provide them with immediate relief.

The experience of working together sealed Afro-Indian unity; we established a joint executive committee and decided to launch a campaign of defiance against racist laws. This would not happen until 1952.

INDIA TABLES RACE DISCRIMINATION
AT THE UN AS AN INTERNATIONAL PROBLEM

India's freedom and her role as a founding member of the UN, and Pakistan's entry as a member of the UN General Assembly, brought us fresh hope. The Assembly, up till then overwhelmingly representing Euro-American interests, was opening up to the decolonised Asian and African nations as they won their independence after hard struggles, and paved the way for the voice of the so-called Third World to be heard. But the controlling role of the USA in the Security Council would dull the thrust of the democratic forces.

India, represented by Nehru's sister, Vijayalakshmi Pandit, had tabled the issue of racial discrimination in South Africa at the UN General Assembly in 1946, at the height of our passive resistance campaign. South Africa had opposed it on the grounds that it was a domestic issue. The General Assembly, however, had referred it to its First and Sixth Committees, who supported the Indian complaint and retained it on the UN agenda.

In 1959 the Sixth Committee of the General Assembly resounded with the eloquence and legal brilliance of the Indian and Pakistani delegates – Sir Benegal Narsing Rao, brother of Rama Rao, and Sir Mahomed Zafrullah Khan, respectively. India simultaneously prepared for her first general election, and Mrs Pandit returned home to participate in the largest poll ever – 175 million voters. In January 1952, the General Assembly called on Dr Malan's government not to proceed with the Group Areas Act, and set up a three-person commission to assist South Africa, India and Pakistan to resolve the conflict. The Malan government, as expected, rejected the resolution.

The Nationalists could reject as many UN resolutions as they wanted; South Africa's racism would become a perennial issue on the UN agenda, and opprobrium against it would continue to grow until racism in South Africa – institutionalised as apartheid – was destroyed. Racism would remain a political issue and objections would be raised in every area it was practised. South Africa would be excluded from the Olympics and many countries would refuse to compete against South African sports teams. A cultural boycott would also follow.

NINE

SETTLING DOWN TO FAMILY AND WORK

1950–1956

While the march to freedom continued and I remained a part of it, I took time off to establish my legal practice, marry and found my own family.

I COURT AND MARRY 'BEHN'
The men in my family married in their early twenties. In 1950, I was thirty-two years old and unmarried. I was considering proposing to Behn. I had never considered proposing marriage to any woman before. There was no doubt in my own mind that I wanted to marry Behn, but I had my doubts that she had romantic notions about me. Both my sisters, Ayesha and Äpa, were nudging me in her direction. We were at the station one evening. Behn's mothers, Ayesha and our cousin Amina Peer from Dundee were seeing Behn off, who was returning to Johannesburg after her mid-term recess. Ayesha came up to me and said, 'Just now when you were talking to Behn, Amina Boo said, "That is a pair made in heaven." One needs to heed the advice of one's elders.' I didn't say anything to her and she did not push me any further.

On another occasion, my sister Äpa, sensing the extra attention I was paying Behn, asked me, 'What do you think of Behn?' She obviously meant as a marriage partner. I brushed her off, saying Behn was too young. My feelings about Behn were very private and they were my own. The last thing I wanted was for my sisters to think they were arranging this relationship for me. I was falling in love with Behn, if I wasn't already in love with her. I didn't know what her feelings were for me. I had to declare myself to her first. It was a matter we had to settle between us.

We used to correspond with each other after I had left Johannesburg and she was still a student at Wits. In one letter she wrote that she had met Violaine

Junod at the Alexander Clinic where she was doing her practical in social science. 'Miss Junod told me she knew you and had visited you at Kholvad House,' and then quite innocently remarked, 'Ismail, what were you doing with all these young ladies visiting you?'

When I try to recall when my feelings towards her changed, I trace it back to an afternoon in my flat in Kholvad House in mid-1948. She came to see me on her way to writing a mid-term examination at Wits. I had received my orders to leave the Transvaal and return to Natal. She had come to wish me goodbye and had brought me a present of two comic musicians carved in wood. I was unwell and lying in bed. She walked into my flat, her face flushed from walking in the cold. I thought how beautiful she looked, and suddenly saw her as a woman. I was surprised to feel an impulse to take her in my arms. I stopped myself and reminded her that she would be late for the examination. She left, and my room had never felt so empty.

There was another time when we had not seen each other for some weeks because both of us had been consumed with relief work in different areas following the riots. That was in January 1949. I had just completed a telephone call and was putting down the receiver on the sideboard when I saw her entering the doorway of 62. She stopped on seeing me and stood at the opposite end of the sideboard. I said something to her like, 'It is a long time since I saw you. I missed you.' She replied, 'I missed you too,' out of politeness I thought. We looked at each other for a brief moment and then she dropped her eyes in embarrassment. I felt that same surge of emotions I had felt in my flat in Kholvad House a few months earlier.

I saw more and more of Behn after my return to Durban. She had given up studying at Wits and enrolled at the University of Natal, attending lectures at the non-European campus at Sastri College. On the days she had late lectures she stayed over at her paternal uncle AI's house. I had my own room there with my writing desk, and I put it at her disposal when I was not using it. I was reporting for the *Guardian* at the time, and sometimes I asked her to do some interviewing for me. I recall her arranging for Chief Luthuli to be photographed at Crown Studio. I also recall sending her to interview AWG Champion when the Nationalist government produced a 'national' African leader overnight in opposition to the ANC. Bhengu, an inyanga,[1] obligingly made all the desired rabid, anti-Indian statements. Behn returned with a refutation of the trumped-up Bhengu, and a pro-Indian statement from Champion.

At times Behn and I took the tram together from Ritson Road to town. Often when I returned home from work, I would find her working at my writing desk. I would interrupt her studies and we would talk. I enjoyed her intellect. She came up with some fascinating ideas. I also came to realise that she could be careless and forgetful, aspects that disturbed me, but I felt I could live with it.

On one occasion she sauntered in at 62, and said she had made a mistake about the venue of her exam – she had gone to Sastri, but the exam was being written at City Building. She was already some twenty minutes late. I was in a state of high panic but she was quite calm. I telephoned for a taxi and drove with her in my pyjamas to make sure she didn't lose any more time and was safely deposited at the door of her examination. Then I sighed with relief and began my own day's chores.

Fathu's lectures began at about 3 pm, and her last lecture ended at about 9 pm. This was in a subject called Native Administration, later renamed African Government and Law, which started at 8 pm. Behn was the only Indian student taking that subject, which impressed me. All the other students were African, among them Mangosuthu Buthelezi.

I used to walk Behn to her late evening lecture and fetch her at the end of it. It was during one of those walks that I communicated my romantic interest in her. I took her in my arms and kissed her. I saw that I had startled her. She had not expected that move from me. We completed our walk in silence. I gave her some time before I took the matter any further. I felt she needed to sort out her feelings about the new relationship I was offering her. She had always seen me as an uncle. After all, I was her father's first cousin; as such I was his 'brother' and her 'uncle'. She had always seen me and introduced me as such.

I confided to Behn that I had had two former relationships, but there had never been a question of marriage. I don't quite know how she took it. She had remained silent. Then, one afternoon when I returned from town, she asked me point-blank why, if my former affairs were over, I kept letters and photographs from them? It was a challenge I could not dismiss. The next day, while Fathu was away at lectures, I took the letters and photographs to AI's backyard, and when Behn returned later that afternoon, she found me making a bonfire.

I wanted to convince her by that act that she was the only woman in my life. I think I succeeded in doing so. It was after this that she accepted me as a suitor; our relationship grew and we found ourselves very much in love.

During our courtship I gave Behn an opal brooch we bought together at Payne Bros. It was my first legal earning of £1 14s. I also bought her a grey corduroy skirt and a red blouse. It gave me pleasure to do so. Our courtship was a quiet, uneventful affair. We just got to know each other – we took walks in the Botanic Gardens, or I met her in between her lectures at Sastri College, and when she began doing her practicals at the Durban Indian Child Welfare Society in Baker Street, I walked the few metres from Saville Street to meet her during the lunch hour. We wrote to each other when she went to Adam's Mission for a week during the July vacation, and she telephoned me in the mornings from a call-box. I waited for those calls before leaving for the NIC office and complained to her that she was spoiling me: I waited for her call and was late for work.

Our engagement was a private affair between the two of us, and totally unacceptable to her parents. I took her to a jewellery shop where I spent all of £13, the maximum I could afford on a ring, with perhaps the smallest diamond in Durban. Chota Motala, recently returned from Bombay with a medical degree, had acquired a new Baby Austin. We commandeered it and, with Chota driving, went to the beach where I put the ring on her finger. We sealed our engagement with milkshakes.

When Behn went home to Pinetown that day and excitedly showed her mothers her ring, they were aghast. They quickly took the ring off her finger and returned it to my sister Äpa. That was not the way a marriage proposal was made, or an engagement sealed. While we were all one family, her mothers were hurt. They felt that their daughter had not been accorded the respect due to her. She couldn't be betrothed over a milkshake. Äpa and AI put the matter right and went over with a formal proposal. Our engagement followed, but we were not part of it. The elders in our family, the men, met, read the fateha,[2] drank sherbet[3] and formally enquired the purpose of the occasion, then formally announced it was to mark the engagement of Fatima bin te Moosa Meer to Ismail bin te Chota Meer.[4]

Behn wanted to complete her degree, and I wanted to be admitted as an attorney and set up my office and home before we married. Living with either of our families was unthinkable. I could not dream of living with her parents, nor she with Äpa and AI. At any rate, my time of living with Äpa and AI was long overdue to end. They had done enough for me and I had to move on.

I was admitted as an attorney in 1950. Fathu and her mother accompanied me to the Supreme Court in Pietermaritzburg; Khan drove us there in MI's car. On our return journey we stopped at the new Midmar Dam where we picnicked, and I bought Behn a Zulu-bead love letter.

We arranged to marry after Behn's graduation. She graduated in absentia because of the colour discrimination that still prevailed.

We began looking for accommodation for our home and my office. There was an acute shortage of housing and office space in Durban during 1950–51. The Group Areas Act had taken its toll; the Grey Street Indian complex was frozen. Every available commercial and office space was filled. All extensions to existing buildings were forbidden. No new development was allowed without special authorisation, often involving bribery. I could not find an office in Durban and was becoming quite desperate when Roly Arenstein offered me a position as legal assistant in the branch office he was planning to set up in Verulam. I accepted Roly's offer and opened the Verulam office in 1951.

Roly had rented the old court-house building, old-fashioned and free-standing, with large grounds. In my initial quiet days when I waited for business to pick up, my first members of staff, Mr Nabie and young Aubrey and I grew vegetables in the backyard. The soil was good and we grew a fine crop.

Since Roly was unable to put any time into the Verulam office, he handed it over to me.

I ESTABLISH MY LEGAL PRACTICE IN VERULAM

The first Meer to emigrate to South Africa, my uncle Mohamed Meer, had started off in Verulam, and I had fond memories of working there with HA Naidoo in the Sugar Workers Union. It was a small, one-street sugar town with a close-knit Indian community, segregated from the African, white and Mauritian (Coloured) communities.

We had the greatest difficulty finding a house in Durban. It would have been easier to find one in Verulam, but we did not wish to centralise our lives there. I had all my political responsibilities in Durban. We eventually found a semi-detached cottage at 1197A Umgeni Road at £7 a month. Number 1197 was occupied by Benny and Myna Mungal and their children, Pam and Anil.

I prepared an antenuptial contract to establish Behn's independence, but she rejected it angrily and said we could not begin our marriage on a divisive note. So the antenuptial contract was never signed and Behn elected to be my 'ward'.

We set our wedding date for 11 March 1951. Fathu organised a concert for the family on the night before the wedding. The only outsiders were my friends JN and Radhi Singh. Fathu produced an 'operetta' in Urdu, featuring the family children as indentured Indians on their departure from India and their arrival in South Africa. JN was so impressed with it that he thought it should be presented by the NIC to raise funds. Years later, Fathu produced *Ahimsa-Ubuntu* on that theme. It was a success and toured India and Sri Lanka.

OUR WEDDING DAY

Our wedding day was bright and beautiful. Everyone from 62 Ritson Road had left for Pinetown; I was waiting for Ebrahim Goga, who had offered to take me in style in his new open sports car. He arrived and I sat down on the passenger seat beside the driver in my first tailor-made suit in fawn terylene, the fashion of the time for Indian grooms. Ebrahim inserted the key into the ignition, turned it and pressed the accelerator, but there was no sound. The engine wouldn't start. Try as much as he would, the engine remained stubbornly silent. I was in a state of panic. I feared I wouldn't make it to my wedding on time. There was no other transport in sight. Just then Dr Goonam arrived and pulled up alongside us. Seeing me, she asked, 'Ismail, how do I get to 68 Bamboo Lane?' My panic subsided; I told her with enthusiasm, 'I'll take you there if you take me with you.' I got into her car and we sped to Pinetown, leaving Ebrahim to deal with his beautiful, but errant, sports car.

As we approached the poinsettia-lined driveway, we were stopped by Behn's youngest sister, Baby, as we called her. She was playing her part.

'You can't come in,' she said, somewhat uncertain of her ground. 'I want money!'

I suddenly remembered the custom, but I had forgotten to carry any money! I borrowed £5 from Goonam, who found it all very amusing. The money paid, Baby allowed us to proceed.

My best men, MB Yengwa and JN, were waiting for me. Molvi Bashir was ready to perform the nikah ceremony. Unused to wearing a fez, I had placed it on the table instead of my head. To my acute embarrassment, Molvi Bashir's voice resounded over the public address system. 'Bhai Ismail, put on your topee.' He didn't know the microphone was on. Topee on head, he performed the very brief nikah ceremony. Fathu's proxies – I do not remember who they were – testified to her agreement to marry me, and I recited in Arabic after the Molvi Sahib that I was taking Fatima bin te Moosa Meer as my wife. We were married. The registration in terms of the state law followed.

The reception in MI's vast beautiful garden was just about the most multi-racial I had known. The guests were served high tea instead of the traditional lunch. The bride sat on a stage in the women's section, and I didn't see her until the evening when it was time for us to leave for our new home. There was a great deal of weeping. Behn's two mothers apologised profusely for not having trained her in the culinary arts.

'She has been involved in studies all the time. She does not know how to cook,' they sobbed.

'If you had told me this earlier, I would have reconsidered marrying her,' I teased, and put smiles on their faces.

Chief Mangosuthu Buthelezi, who attended our wedding, referred to it in later years when addressing Indian audiences. He said it was the first Indian wedding he had attended and he had been surprised that a Meer could marry a Meer, for Zulus practised exogamy, and a Buthelezi could never marry a Buthelezi.

SETTLING DOWN TO MARRIED LIFE

Omar Khan drove us to our new home in Umgeni Road. I carried my wife across the threshold; Khan left and within minutes Behn was the forgetful person I knew. 'I forgot my suitcase in the car,' she said. I settled her in our spanking new bedroom, with its Swedish bedroom suite – a present from her parents – new chintz curtains and new wall-to-wall linos, all put together by Neocraft at £6 a month, and also a present from her parents. There was a light drizzle outside but I rushed to the garage at the corner and telephoned my sister. After all, Behn couldn't very well sleep in her fluffy pink chiffon wedding dress. I knew that Khan would make a stop at 62 before proceeding to Pinetown. Khan returned with Behn's suitcase and we began our married life.

In the morning our neighbour, Myna Mungal, brought us bhajee and roti and we added that to the bhaj pod.[5] Later in the day the Mungal children, Pam and Anil, visited us, and they became our constant companions from then on, becoming sort of older siblings to our children when they were born.

Our house had just two rooms and a kitchen. The toilet-cum-bathroom was outside. There were two tiny gardening plots, one in front and one at the back. MI's gardener planted snapdragons in the front plot and they grew magnificently. I planted beans in the back plot, and since I came home late from my office, Behn watered them with a watering can. I had a healthy crop, but alas the monkeys who lived in Burman Bush at the back of our house harvested them. One morning I caught one fat fellow red-handed as he ran off with my beans clutched in both hands.

I returned to work on the second day after our marriage, which was a Monday. Behn came to see me off at the station, which was almost on our doorstep, and I boarded the train with the lunch Behn had prepared for me.

Three days after our marriage I came home to find my wedding suit, of which I was so proud, hanging on the clothes line, water dripping. I shouted in shock, 'You have ruined my suit! I'll never be able to wear it again! Suits must be dry-cleaned, not washed. How stupid can you be?' Her response was that she knew we had very little money and she was economising! My anger continued unabated for more than a day and I refused to talk to her. I knew she was afraid and hurt, but I felt she had to learn and make amends, and it was she who eventually broke the coldness between us.

I found it a good story to tell at parties. Friends found it amusing and thought it was at Behn's expense; she never seemed to mind since I told it with affection.

I didn't fancy her male student friends visiting her. She had bought a pair of black slacks to work in the garden, she said, and I had laughed at her. One day I returned home to find her in those slacks, in conversation with young Soni outside our house. I am afraid I wasn't polite to Soni. I made it quite clear without saying a word that his time was up. He got the message and left. Behn was upset but she had not yet learnt to stand up to me. That would come much, much later.

On another occasion I returned home from work and found her missing. Phoowa, who had become our housekeeper and cook, told me she had gone to the market. 'Had she gone by bus?' I asked. Phoowa said she had gone by bicycle. I exploded. 'This wouldn't do! She was a married woman, the wife of a lawyer; how could she cycle around?' The distance from our house to the market was a good five miles. I waited for her outside the house, my anxiety mounting by the minute. I look back on that afternoon and am amazed that my blood pressure hadn't done a somersault. She eventually came into view, vigorously pedalling up Umgeni Road. She came up to the house, applied the brakes, got off her cycle, and leaning it against the wall, smiled up at me expectantly. Hanging from the handlebar was her basket of vegetables. I was flabbergasted when I realised she was expecting to be complimented for her efforts. 'What do you mean, cycling to the market? Can you see how silly you look? Do you think it's a proper thing for you to go cycling?' I demanded. The brightness left her face and it darkened with confusion. She was close to tears. 'I was saving on bus fare,' she said. The bus fare to town was only a ticky, so I didn't see much saving. We agreed that she would not ride her bicycle in Durban; she would do so in Pinetown and I had it sent there.

But apart from these eruptions we were happy together, enjoying simple pleasures. We went to the cinema in the evenings, usually to the Avalon, taking the tram. We loved Hindi movies. I always said that there was no such thing as a bad Hindi movie; one could always count on a few good dances and a few good songs. On occasional evenings we took the tram to the City Hall and walked around in its vicinity, or went window-shopping on West Street. We invariably spent our weekends at 84 Ritson Road. Once or twice, we walked from Umgeni Road to Ritson Road.

SHAMIM

Shamim's birth was a very special event. We had longed for a child, and Shamim was born on 11 May 1953, two years after our marriage. I recall when Behn was pregnant with her. I had a dream about this precious child I was holding in my arms, and it was saying 'liminade please'. I used to say 'liminade' for 'lemonade' as a child; I was seeing myself in our unborn child. I related my dream to Behn; she wanted to know if it was a girl or a boy and what it looked like. I told her very pretty, with black hair, but I didn't see the sex of the baby. We treated the dream as a sort of reality.

Behn's gynaecologist was Dr Mohamed Mayat, who was also our close friend. Before our marriage Behn had attended his marriage with Julu Bismillah in Potchefstroom. Behn had one or two false alarms and he was called out at unearthly hours. But he said that the tea I made him was worth the call. Finally she was due. I drove her to St Aidan's Hospital. Dr Mayat and Dr Goonam were there and I left her with them while I attended to her admission. When I returned, I saw the two doctors walking with her, one on either side. Goonam said, 'Look how brave she is, and she is in her final stage.' Behn beamed with pleasure. Behn's mothers arrived from Pinetown. She was admitted into a private ward and the three of us kept her company. They moved her into the delivery room at about 5 pm. I couldn't kiss her in the presence of her mothers. She would have been very embarrassed if had, so I just held her hand reassuringly.

I saw Dr Mayat leave the delivery ward at about 6 pm, and I became alarmed. 'What's going on?' I asked.

'The baby won't be born for an hour or so. I am going home for a bite.'

He invited me to join him. I was in no mood to eat; I was sick with anxiety. I declined angrily. I felt he should remain at Behn's side. I caught a twinkle in his eye and realised he was teasing me and taking advantage of my nervous state. That irritated me all the more. He had hardly been gone half an hour when I saw him rushing into the delivery room. Soon thereafter one of the nurses emerged from the room and announced, 'It's a baby girl.' My two mothers-in-law beamed happily and began congratulating me. I was overcome with relief that Behn's ordeal was over, and overpowered by the sense of fatherhood that I had suddenly acquired.

The nurse brought the baby. Bhaboo held her in her arms. We gazed on the little mite, prettier than in my dream. The nurse took the baby to the nursery and said she would return with her shortly. Behn was wheeled into the ward soon thereafter, weak, pale, in pain and drugged. Bhaboo had arranged to sleep with her and take care of her. The nurse brought my little daughter for a few minutes. I held her in my arms, somewhat nervous, bemused, but totally charmed and overwhelmed with pride, while the two grandmothers looked on approvingly.

Then the nurse took her away to settle her in the nursery. There was no point in my hanging around. I celebrated the birth of my daughter by going to the cinema and seeing *The Student Prince*. I returned to the hospital early the next morning. Fathu looked well and the baby was with her. Her mother left, the nurse took away the baby, and Behn and I enjoyed some quality time alone together, wondering at our new status. I told her the story of *The Student Prince*, and she listened in rapt attention, as she did to all my stories.

Fathu's ward was full of flowers, sent by friends. YC's mother, Bhabi, came to visit, looked around and remarked proudly, 'Behn is in a flower garden.' But some weeks later Bhabi came to our home, and sitting cross-legged on our bed took the baby on her lap, examined her very carefully and pronounced, 'This one ear is twisted.' She never realised how deeply she wounded me. Our baby was perfect, and what nonsense was Bhabi talking! Behn's mothers comforted me later. 'There's nothing wrong with the baby's ears. They are perfect.'

It was Bhabi who had got me to call Behn, Fathu. We were in Pinetown one day, entering the house. Bhabi was just behind me, Behn before me, rushing ahead. 'Behn!' I called. 'Let us go together.' Bhabi turned towards me and gave me a resounding slap.

'How dare you call your wife "sister"! You should be ashamed of yourself!'

I accepted the slap in good humour.

'What should I call her then?' I asked.

'Call her Fathu.'

I don't think Behn was pleased with this, but from that day on I called her Fathu and not Behn, which indeed means sister.

I wanted Fathu and the baby to go home with me. Fathu had prepared the nursery in the little space of the room leading off from our bedroom where I had initially put my writing desk. She had covered the wicker crib in white satin that she had scalloped, trimmed with lace and embroidered. She had painted the large wall with an African Peter surrounded by pumpkins, and the two smaller walls with Little Miss Muffet and Mary and her lamb. But the new mother had to spend her confinement with her mother. Custom extended that honour to my mothers-in-law, and they expected to take Fathu and the baby to Pinetown, to care for them until they were truly well and strong. I would have liked Bhaboo to move in with us and care for Fathu and the baby in our home, but I couldn't interfere with custom. However, I complained daily to Fathu over the telephone about how lonely I was, and how Phoowa was not cooking the right food, and so on, and eventually persuaded her to cut short her stay with her mothers, much to their disappointment. So mother and baby returned home earlier than expected.

The whole family participated in naming our daughter. MI made a list of appropriate names and wrote them out neatly in English and Urdu. Everybody was happy with the name 'Shamim', which translated into fragrant breeze, except for Violaine, who became her godmother. She said it would be something of a tongue-twister for Shamim to stand before the magistrate and say, 'My name is Shamim Meer.' The Ms coming together will tongue-tie her. She saw Shamim as a passive resister. I said there would be no need for passive resistance by the time Shamim grew into a young woman, and she needn't worry about the 'Ms' coming together.

WE BUY A FRIDGE AND A CAR

We made two major purchases for Shamim's arrival: a car and a fridge. Cars were in very short supply during and after the war and there was a very long wait on delivery. The only car we could get was a Volkswagen. A lot of doubts were expressed about this car since it was new on the market. I think we were the first Indians to buy a Volkswagen. It was not as beautiful as the conventional cars of that time. The first day I took it to Verulam and parked it outside my office, my landlady's young daughter stopped by to look at it and, after examining it carefully, pulled her face and announced, 'Flat-nosed!'

The fridge was bought before the car. The salesman made many trips to our house, sitting on the couch in our front room and talking us into buying it. We eventually bought his fridge and wondered how we had lived without it. I was against buying anything on hire purchase. I had to save all the money to pay for it in cash. I think this was instilled in me by my father.

The beach and Mitchell Park were the special places to which we took Shamim. I sang a special song to her while she looked at the moon: 'Oh, my mama, look at the moon. It is round like a balloon.' Not much of a song and I was hardly a singer, but Shamim liked it. At Mitchell Park we made the acquaintance of a white cockatoo, who danced for Shamim as I clapped my hands. We made many visits to the cockatoo.

SHEHNAZ

Shehnaz followed on the heels of Shamim, two years later. Fathu insisted on giving birth at home. Our friends Leo and Hilda Kuper had introduced us to Dr Davidson and we were very happy with him. He agreed to deliver Shehnaz at home. A very pretty nurse from the Mother's Hospital came to help. And of course Bhaboo was there when the time came.

Dr Davidson examined Fathu and estimated that there was enough time for him to make one emergency call. But Shehnaz was in a hurry and she arrived sooner than expected, on 28 June 1955, and the midwife from the Mother's Hospital delivered her competently. Dr Davidson, Fathu said later, was in time to deliver the afterbirth. The nurse came regularly for six days, and each afternoon I left her at the nurse's home. Äpa came to see our new daughter and pronounced her beautiful.

We wanted to name our second daughter Yasmin, but MI preferred Shehnaz, so we gave her both names, Yasmin Shehnaz. But MI won, for we all began calling her Shehnaz.

RASHID

Rashid came within fifteen months of Shehnaz, on 2 September 1956. He was born breach, a walloping eleven-pounder. The girls were five pounds each. We were not to have any more children. We didn't plan it that way – nature did. We never practised birth control.

The five of us filled our twin beds; the children insisted on sleeping with us. We were a happy family, though I was an anxious father and husband, which weighed on the others.

FAMILY LIFE

When the girls grew a little older we bought them tricycles. Shamim was the first to get a tricycle. We would go window-shopping in West Street and the girls enjoyed cycling along.

Our weekends were spent with the extended family at MI's residence in Ritson Road, to which he had returned, being forced to sell his estate in Pinetown because it fell in a white area. He spent a considerable amount of money, remodelling and extending 84 Ritson Road to meet the family's requirements. But the Group Areas Act put paid to that and his home was expropriated, as were the other Meer homes at numbers 62 and 26. Most of the family moved to Reservoir Hills, where MI was the first to buy a property. His son Ismail ('small' Ismail) and his family occupied it. Then EM's son, Unus, who had qualified as a doctor in Madras, and MI's third son, Ahmed, who had qualified in medicine at Lahore, built houses there. More recently, MI's grandson Munir purchased a property there.

The weekends at 84 overflowed with MI's generosity and bubbled with the noise and laughter of the entire clan of some forty members. There were three generations under one roof and each enjoyed the company of contemporaries.

We, as a small family unit, also did our own things, apart from the 'clan'. We took the children to parks where they played on swings and to the beach where they played in the sand. On rare weekends friends in Tongaat gave us the use of their beach cottage, and we took the entire clan there and had great picnics.

I travelled each day by train to Verulam until we had the car; then I drove there, taking with me two large pots of lunch Phoowa cooked, one of curry and the other of rice, for my entire staff. They looked forward to that lunch because it was tasty and the menu was varied.

Fathu began wearing a sari when she was pregnant with Shamim and she continued wearing a sari thereafter. Once we were in Tongaat visiting Gopalal Hurbans. One of my Muslim clients said to Gopalal, 'We respect Mr Meer, he is such a good man, but why is he going about with a Hindu girl?' Gopalal told him, 'She is his wife, very much a Muslim, and her name is Fatima.'

My time was absorbed by the family, the office and my political activities, organising conferences, writing reports and issuing the necessary press statements on behalf of the NIC. Aubrey Naraidu had joined us. His father was a school principal and we travelled together to Verulam by train. He approached me to take his son in, and I was happy to do so. I became very fond of Aubrey, who I hoped would study law and serve his articles with me. At the time he was my private secretary. I dictated my thoughts to young Aubrey, who wrote in a clear long hand while I paced the floor and smoked cigarette after cigarette – I was a chain-smoker at the time. The statements and reports were then typed and taken to the media. The media did not pay us much attention, but we persisted nonetheless.

We visited the Naraidus in their hilltop home in Canelands, with the river flowing below. Shamim, two or so years old, was with us, happy throughout the visit.

Eid approached and we decided to hold a party for our entire 'clan' in our small house, in the Christmas tradition. We put up a tree and hung it with gifts for the forty-odd members of our extended family – my nephew Haroon, AC's son, became Pappa Eid. We found a red gown and made up a beard of cotton wool for him. He played his role with humour and with the grace and generosity it required. Everyone, from my venerated elder cousins, AI and MI, my brothers and sisters and their children, and Fathu's brothers and sisters, joined in the fun. It was a party the family never forgot.

We celebrated Shamim's first birthday. We borrowed boxes from Ballims, our corner shop, and covered these with crêpe paper. We moved out the furniture from the front room, hung balloons and streamers, and invited the children of our friends, the Gumedes, Kupers, Arensteins, Bhagwans and Mungals, as well as the children of the family. Shamim was agog with happiness, but I didn't know who enjoyed the party more, she or her mother.

Shamim was not yet a year old when Fathu was offered an appointment as Dr Hilda Kuper's research assistant. I knew how much research meant to Fathu. We decided she should take the job. Shamim watched pensively, uncomplaining on her nursemaid's arm as one parent after the other went off to work. Fathu was away for half the day. Dr Jacobson, who worked at the health clinic, gave her a lift each morning. The clinic was run by Dr Sydney Kark as a new experiment in community health, and the research was part of that project.

On 24 August 1954, Bertha Mkhize and Fathu, president and secretary respectively of the Durban and District Women's League, held a meeting in association with the Indian Child Welfare Society, headed by Gadija Christopher, on the issue of discriminatory prison sentences. Over a hundred women representing sixteen political, social and welfare organisations met to discuss the sentences passed in the Cape Province – a European was sentenced to nine months' jail for raping a twelve-year-old Indian girl, and a Coloured man was sentenced to death for raping an adult European woman. The Indian girl bore a child following the rape.

The meeting condemned the inequality of the sentences and unanimously adopted a resolution, which ended with the observation:

> In the administration of justice there can be no room for inequality based on racial consideration, and when such unequal sentences are imposed, they are bound to increase the already mounting tension in our multi-racial society. We express our further concern at the comments made by the learned judge in the East London

case of rape to the effect that it was 'within the knowledge of the court that Indian children married at an early age'. This statement, if correctly reported, seems most irrelevant for it has no bearing on the offence committed and it creates the impression that the judge did not regard the Indian girl concerned giving birth to a child at the age of 12 as an aggravating factor.

Fathu loved her work with Hilda; she made many friends and their talents intruded into our home. On my third birthday after our marriage, she presented me with a jersey knitted by a new-found Newlands friend, and a surprise party. Both were failures. The jersey was so large that two of me could have fitted into it; and the party was Cassim Amra's, not mine. She had consulted Cassim, thinking he knew my friends and tastes. Cassim's idea of a party was Cape Town-based: music, dancing and drinking, which were not my pleasures. He invited some of my friends, but more of his.

After everyone had left, I told Fathu she was never again to arrange a surprise party for me. She kept to my instruction until I turned eighty, but of that later.

TEN

THE DEFIANCE CAMPAIGN

1952

By 1947, eighty-seven years had lapsed since the arrival of Indians in South Africa, fifty-three years since the founding of the NIC and thirty-five since the birth of the ANC. Indians and Africans had never united to challenge the racists. They now prepared to do so and the credit, ironically, at least in part, was due to the Nationalists – they provoked Afro-Indian unity. The 1949 riots, dreadful as they were, forced the leaderships to rethink their political strategy.

The violence, the emergent tension and the realisation that the power of the racists was fuelled by the inter-racial conflicts of subordinate groups, all combined to motivate the historic declaration by the African and Indian Congresses that they would jointly launch the Defiance of Unjust Laws Campaign.

The support was not even in all four provinces.

THE EASTERN CAPE

There was unprecedented support from the Eastern Cape, which brought forward a new leader in Dr Jongwe, young, strident and a powerful orator. Accordingly, the planning meeting was held in New Brighton, Port Elizabeth's African location. The press conference was held there too.

I attended the planning committee meeting. We announced 6 April 1952 as the National Day of Protest (the Gandhian Hartal), preceding passive resistance; 22 June was declared the Day of Volunteers and 26 June the launch of Defiance. Also, 6 April was the day on which the master race had scheduled to celebrate the tercentennial of the arrival of Jan van Riebeeck and the colonisation of the country.

While in Port Elizabeth, in between our briefings, Reverend BTE Sigamoney persuaded me to accompany him to visit a friend. The township of small houses on sandy roads was dominated by a veritable palace-like mansion.

'What is that?' I asked the reverend.

'That is where my friend lives.'

'Your friend?' I repeated, somewhat in disbelief. 'What does your friend do?'

'He is a bishop,' he said.

'An African bishop?' I asked in disbelief. I never knew there was such a thing. The reverend ignored my remark.

'Let's go in and see him. He is Bishop Ndungane.'

We were at the door of the 'palace' and were taken inside by an attendant, who announced us to the large and jovial bishop. He welcomed us and very soon refreshments were placed before us.

The bishop laughed at Reverend Sigamoney. 'You are still a bloody fool working for the white man. Look at me. I have a fleet of cars. I am an independent person. Those whites would never let me progress. They wanted me to be part of them when they would never be a part of me. Can you be a bishop? I am a bishop. My congregation brings me the money. They don't take it to a white bishop who pays me a pittance of a salary from it.'

This was a new experience for me, but the self-appointed bishop made no dent in Reverend Sigamoney's commitment to his church.

THE PRESS CONFERENCE

There was considerable interest, both national and international, in our proposed campaign. We decided to hold a press conference. Oliver Tambo and Nelson Mandela asked me to chair the press conference. They had no faith in the ability of President Moroka to answer the questions put by foreign correspondents.

'You answer them,' Oliver said, 'and Dr Moroka can follow in agreement.'

Among the correspondents was Robert Stimpson of the BBC. He had just covered the transfer of power in India.

'What is the ANC's policy on land?' Stimpson asked. 'Does it favour collective farming or individual land rights?'

The doctor had no answer. He hesitated and began mumbling.

'Before the doctor answers,' I broke in, 'let me explain. This is a matter still under discussion in the ANC.'

'Will you compromise on the franchise? It is most unlikely that the Nationalists will concede to universal adult franchise.'

I looked meaningfully at Dr Moroka and he waited for my reply. 'That is non-negotiable. We insist on universal adult franchise.'

Dr Moroka followed: 'We must have one man, one vote.'

'And what about the women?' Stimpson addressed the question directly to Moroka, who repeated, 'women?' in confusion.

I stepped in. 'The ANC does not discriminate between men and women.'

Stimpson was an astute correspondent. He saw what was happening. He invited me to take a walk with him that evening.

'Why are you propping up this doddering old fool?' he asked, referring to Moroka. 'Have you been to his surgery?'

I said I hadn't.

'Well, for your information, he segregates his patients in his waiting room; special facilities for Europeans, not so special for non-Europeans.'

I assured Stimpson in strict confidence that at the coming elections in December 1952, Moroka would be replaced by Chief Albert Luthuli. He promised to keep the information confidential, which he did.

The resolution to launch the Defiance Campaign was passed. The signature of the president general was required. The ANC possessed no car at the time. The secretary to the Head of the Indian High Commission, Mr RT Chari, placed his car at our disposal, and Walter Sisulu set off, Indian flag waving in front of him on the bonnet of the car, to get Moroka's signature.

THE DAY OF VOLUNTEERS AND MANDELA'S FIRST SPEECH IN DURBAN

The Day of Volunteers was successfully launched in Durban on 22 June, as planned. The keynote speaker was Nelson Mandela. To the best of my knowledge, this was his first speech in Durban. He was bowled over by the large turnout, over 10 000 strong, almost equally made up of Indians and Africans. The others on the platform with him were Chief AJ Luthuli, Monty Naicker, Debi Singh and MB Yengwa.

We discussed the meeting as we drove home. Nelson was exhilarated. He said he had never seen so many Indians at a political meeting. I told him that eighty per cent of the national Indian population lived in Durban, and most of the Indians were workers. This was all very new to him, the Indian profile being so different in the Transvaal.

The form of the Defiance Campaign closely followed the Gandhian model, though it did not incorporate his philosophy of Satyagraha. Molvi Cachalia had worked out the strategy for the fifth passive resistance campaign in Urdu, the language he knew best. It was translated into English by Yusuf Cachalia.

Following the Gandhian procedure, the ANC wrote to the head of the white state requesting him to repeal the six unjust laws,[1] failing which the Defiance Campaign would be launched. The SAIC followed with a similar communication. Dr Malan ignored the SAIC communication; he responded to the ANC with a threat.

The Defiance Campaign was accordingly launched, as planned, on 26 June 1952. Port Elizabeth led the way in the early morning with thirty-three defiers. Johannesburg followed in the afternoon with 106 defiers. There was a hiccup in

Johannesburg when Reverend Tsantsi, selected to lead the first batch of resisters, failed to turn up. He telephoned to say his doctor had advised him against going to jail.

The national volunteer-in-chief, Mandela, then turned to Nana Sita, who was suffering from bad arthritis and probably in worse health than the reverend. But he was a seasoned resister and agreed without hesitation to replace Tsantsi. He proved to be an inspired and inspiring leader. Another disappointment was the non-appearance of the secretary of the Transvaal ANC, who was to be second-in-command. Walter Sisulu stepped into his place.

The first batch of twenty-five resisters in Johannesburg, including four Indian women, set off for the location in Boksburg; Walter Sisulu followed with his batch of twenty-five. In keeping with the Gandhian formula, the magistrate was informed in advance by the chief volunteers of the two organisations leading the campaign, Nelson Mandela (ANC) and Molvi Cachalia (SAIC) respectively, that the resisters would enter the location in Benoni. After some hesitation on the part of the police the location gates were opened, the resisters surged in, and the police arrested them and locked them up in police cells.

NELSON MANDELA AND YUSUF CACHALIA ARRESTED

A second batch set out at night to breach the curfew regulations. The police not only arrested them, but also arrested Mandela and Yusuf Cachalia, whom they found on the scene. If the government felt that that would put a spoke in our organisation's wheels, it was sadly mistaken. The volunteer-in-chief had a great deal of work ahead of him, but we had planned for all contingencies and the campaign continued without further hitches.

There were 250 resisters on the first day, collectively in Johannesburg and Port Elizabeth. They inspired such enthusiasm that in the months that followed, the number of volunteers increased and spread to all parts of the country.

DURBAN JOINS DEFIANCE ON 31 AUGUST 1952

Durban sent her first defiance batch into action on Sunday, 31 August 1952, two months and five days after the campaign was launched in Johannesburg and Port Elizabeth. Organisational problems both in the Natal ANC and the NIC were responsible for the delay. Chief Luthuli, the newly elected president of the Natal ANC, was moving cautiously. He was not yet ready to unite with the NIC. While in the Transvaal the ANC and TIC organised joint meetings, in Natal the two Congresses held separate meetings on 6 April, the National Day of Protest. The ANC held its meeting in the Bantu Social Centre, as it was called then; the NIC meeting, convened at Red Square, had by far the larger attendance. The NIC

The Defiance Campaign, 1952. I am leading my batch,
at the Berea Road Station, Durban, just before our arrest

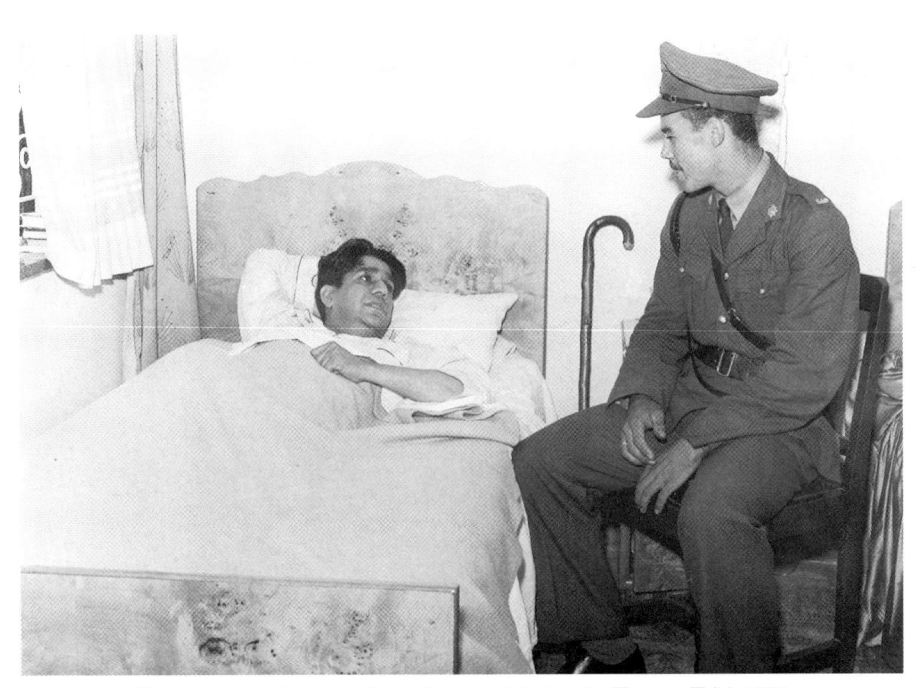

Recuperating at home under police guard during the Treason Trial, 1956

My family, 1956

My favourite picture of Shamim, 1956

Yusuf Cachalia, Solly Nathie, Debi Singh, Shamim and Rashid

Alan Paton plants a tree in our garden. Dr Gumede looks on.
Burnwood Road, Sydenham, circa 1957

Our house warming. Hilda Kuper, the Gumede children,
JN Singh, his daughters and Fathu

My family, 1957

Eid 1960. The photograph of my family I hung
on the wall of my cell and talked to when I got low

My siblings and I, circa 1960

Fathu and I with Monty Naicker, MN Pather, and George Singh, at the opening performance of Alan Paton's *Mkhumbaan*, 1960. We were arrested under the state of emergency the next morning

Fathu and I, 22 May 1971, Nqutu, Zululand

With Dr Monty Naicker, 1974

Rashid and I before his departure for London to be admitted into high school, 1976

Family photo taken after Fathu's release from prison in 1976

attracted as many, if not more, Africans than the ANC meeting. Chief Luthuli soon realised the wisdom of organising together and the first defiance batch, led by Dr Naicker and Stalwart Simelane, was made up equally of African and Indian resisters.

DR MONTY NAICKER LEADS THE FIRST BATCH

Though late in starting, the Durban launch was impressive. Four thousand people assembled at Red Square. Dr Monty Naicker and Chief Luthuli addressed the rally; Monty handed over his presidency temporarily to the veteran VL Lawrence, who had served as Gandhi's secretary. Both Luthuli and Naicker were in top form. Chief Luthuli declared, 'We begin today, in this province, to take on the government head on. The time for talking is over. We will now deliberately break their fascist laws; let them do whatever they will.' Monty supported him, stating, 'We are determined to defy discrimination and unjust laws, to save our souls, our honour and our future. Fascism is being strongly implemented in South Africa. Only the people can uproot this threatening menace.'

The speaking done, the first batch of twenty-one resisters – among whom was my brother AC, along with AKM Docrat, Mannie Naidoo, Reverend JM Sibiya, Theresa Mofokeng, A Vadival, Fatima Seedat, Billy Nair and Jay Singh – marched from Red Square with thousands of supporters, along Pine Street, turning into Grey Street and then into West to the Berea Road Station. There they separated from their supporters who had accompanied them. The supporters waited at the top of the station, where a huge battery of intimidating policemen was already in attendance. I kept close to the resisters for it was my job to publicise the official communiqué. The resisters descended the steps and entered the 'Whites Only' waiting room. The resisters sat down and looked at each other; AKM defiant, Billy Nair resigned, AC calm, Monty composed, Fatima Seedat and Jay Singh chatting away in somewhat subdued tones, and Stalwart his usual smiling self.

The police moved in and the chief walked straight to Monty. He knew him well because of his numerous arrests. He warned Monty that he and his followers were breaking the law. Under Act so and so, section so and so, this waiting room was reserved for Europeans only. He told them that they would be arrested if they did not leave. Monty replied, 'We are defying that law. We refuse to leave. You may arrest us if you will!' The sergeant said, 'You leave me no alternative!' and turning to his men, commanded, 'Arrest them!' Some eight or nine other policemen charged in and arrested them. The resisters followed the police outside. It was all very peaceful and civilised. They walked up the steps, following the police, and at the top of the stairs were ordered into the waiting police vans while we applauded, sang and exchanged thumbs-up signs.

Monty, Stalwart and the rest of the resisters spent that night in the police cells, separated by race and gender, though they had defied the law together. The next day they were brought to court. My nephews, Iqbal, Salim and Shafique, cried to see their father a prisoner. I took them aside and consoled them. Dr Naicker addressed the court, which was packed to capacity. They heard him in silence, in deference to the rules of the court, but their hearts were filled with his stirring words and they suppressed their cries of support.

They were sentenced to fines of £7 10s each, or one month's hard labour. As expected, they chose the latter.

I LEAD A BATCH OF RESISTERS

I followed my brother to prison a few weeks later, leading my batch on 29 November 1952. We, however, were not taken into custody. After being held at the 'Whites Only' waiting room of the Berea Railway Station where our names were taken, we were allowed to go home. The authorities had changed their tactics and resisters were being summonsed to appear in court. I was happy to have this respite and spend more time with my family. We appeared before Magistrate Russell on 6 January 1953, were found guilty of breaking the apartheid laws and sentenced to the usual three weeks' hard labour.

The hard labour imposed on us was really hard. A part of the bay towards the Bluff and Salisbury Island was being reclaimed, and we were ordered to join the labour gang. We were driven there from Durban Central jail each day at the crack of dawn, and returned towards the evening. We worked with wheelbarrows and spades, digging, loading, depositing. Mercifully, it was August and the weather cool. Nonetheless, it left our hands blistered and our backs sunburnt. Relief came at the end of the day when we showered and cooled down.

A prison is a place where one's values are tested. Reduced to practically nothing, can you share that nothing, or do you curl selfishly into yourself? We survived the test. We fared well and came out of prison strengthened.

Though I was only in prison for a month, it seemed much longer because of missing Fathu and worrying about the office. But imprisonment also gave me time for contemplation, taking stock of my life, and planning. Prison time was also discussion time. In the evenings, after a day of sweat-work, we relaxed on our mats and discussed the political situation. Unfortunately racial separation continued to prevail even in prison, and we Indian resisters were separated from the Africans. Our discussions would have been far more fruitful if we had been locked up together.

We discussed how the laws that applied to us separately as Indians and Africans made our joint participation in political campaigns difficult. When the curfew laws were defied, the resisters were exclusively African.

In later years when I was listed and banned for life from all political organisations, we established the Combined Ratepayers Association and ended up being an exclusively Indian association because of our residential segregation.

Later, in the seventies, Fathu, with her colleagues, formed a federation of residents rather than ratepayers, and managed to cut across race and class. They concentrated on common housing problems in the townships where the communities, regardless of race, were all tenants of the Durban municipality.

PETER ABRAHAMS PROVOKES CRITICISM

While we were in prison, *Drum* magazine published an article by our former Liberal Study Group colleague Peter Abrahams, who had emigrated from South Africa and was visiting our country. He contended that all blacks in South Africa should accept 'Africanism' as the basis of their struggle. He criticised Indians and Coloureds because he charged they did not identify with Africans, not even the leadership, among whom sharp prejudice existed. How did he know? we wondered. He had spent a few days in South Africa, contacted none of us, and had gone to town on his observations.

We could not deny that Indians and Africans entertained deep prejudices against each other. There had to be attitudinal changes. We activists deemed ourselves freed from prejudice, but we knew this was not shared by our respective peoples. We were nonetheless critical of Abrahams as someone who had 'run away from the challenges of racism and from the struggle', and who thus had little right to criticise us.

BANNING ORDERS AND VIOLENCE END DEFIANCE

The government was intent on snuffing out the Defiance Campaign. It banned a number of members of the Communist Party, among them Dr Dadoo, JB Marks, Moses Kotane, JW Bopape and SM Ngwevela, under the Suppression of Communism Act. It defined communism as practically any opposition to the government, and more bans followed.

The banned defied their bans and continued with the Defiance Campaign. They were arrested and sentenced to four months' imprisonment, all except Dr Dadoo, who was sentenced to six months on account of his previous conviction.

While the bans continued, the Defiance Campaign flourished as resisters swelled the ranks. The strength of the campaign lay in its non-violence. The government saw this and tried to destroy it by provoking violence. It gave permission to resisters to hold a rally in the Eastern Cape, and when the ground filled with people they moved in and opened fire, killing seven people and injuring scores. An inflamed mob attacked symbols of white power and two whites were killed, one of them a nun whose body was mutilated. Urgent legislation banned all demonstrations against the government, including passive resistance. In addition, practically every organiser was banned. The ANC was forced to call off the campaign.

Starting off with 139 resisters on the first day in two centres, the campaign had spread throughout the country like wildfire. Factory and office workers, doctors, lawyers, teachers, students and clergy; Africans, Coloureds, Indians and even some Europeans, old and young, had rallied to the national call and defied the pass laws, curfew regulations and apartheid on railway stations. At the end of the year, more than eight thousand people of all races had defied various laws and suffered prison sentences.

THE DEEPENING OF APARTHEID

Even as the ANC prepared new offensives, the Nationalists extended the frontiers of oppression. In 1953 the Bantu Education Act was passed to keep Africans underdeveloped, and the Bantu Authorities Act intensified the government's administrative control. At the same time the pass laws were extended to include African women. This was only the beginning; as time went on, the racists came up with more repressive inventions.

An important spin-off of the Defiance Campaign was the impact it had on some white capitalists. Boris Wilson was a fellow member of the Students Representative Council on which JN and I had served. He qualified in medicine but went on to become a business magnate. In 1952, ahead of his time, he spelled out the interdependence between 'white' businesses and 'Native' South Africans. His thesis was simple: 'We need the Native, we need his buying power, the Native needs us, needs our capital. Let us exchange equitably and live in peace.'

OTHER LIBERATION ORGANISATIONS

As the campaign proceeded, fears of non-African domination declined in the ANC. It was clear by 1952 that Mandela had moved from the Mda–Africanist position to the Sisulu–integrationist one. An Africanist tendency, however, remained. This sector resented non-African influences in the struggle and the fact that the leadership in the Defiance Campaign was shared almost equally by Indians and Africans. The vast body of resisters were Africans – seventy-one per cent of the resisters in 1952 coming from the Eastern Cape alone, which had a handful of Indians. This unequal distribution of resisters was bitterly resented and it contributed to the formation of the sectionalist Pan African Congress (PAC). We did not calculate the numbers of resisters into respective percentages of the total Indian and African populations. Had we done so, the Afro-Indian imbalance would not have looked so uneven.

While the ANC suffered dissension from the Africanists, the NIC suffered dissension from the Non-European Unity Movement (NEUM). This Trotskyite organisation criticised us for concentrating on Indians and not being sufficiently concerned about other non-Europeans. The challenge was led by Dr AI Limbada, known to his friends as Limbs, a handsome and charming young doctor who had been my contemporary at Wits, though a good seven or eight years my junior. I had joined the law faculty before he joined the medical. He was present at our wedding and had worked hard at putting up the stage for the bride. I knew him from Dundee where, on its rural hinterland, his father ran a country store. He had begun his university career at Fort Hare. At some stage he became attracted to the Non-European Unity Movement and became one of its prominent activists.

While the members of the NEUM were very critical of us, they had no action strategy of their own, unless one called their policy of non-collaboration with the government, action. They rejected the ANC as collaborationist because some of its members had served on the Native Representative Council (NRC). They did not distinguish between the ANC and its members, and tarred the ANC with the same brush as it did its 'collaborative' members on the NRC. They regarded passive resistance, and indeed all NIC/ANC mobilisations of the people against the government, as useless, meaningless, opportunistic and exploitative of the masses, serving the ends of the 'leaders' and not the people. They believed that the way to liberation was through intensive education or 'conscientisation' of the people, the fundamental primer of that education being the Ten Point Programme. Action against the government could only be undertaken after the people had been politically educated.

To my mind, the whole process of engaging in action was meaningful education. We dismissed the NEUM rhetoric as puerile. Unlike me, Fathu respected the NEUM, and I found this painful.

Fathu had become attracted to the NEUM during her first year at Wits. She had been drawn into what one might describe as an NEUM cell, run by Seymour Pappet. I should have given this episode in her life greater attention, but I was too involved with my own affairs at the time to spare her attention. She found one subject, statistics, difficult, and I arranged with Harold Wolpe to help her, half thinking that he might also nudge her towards the Party. But he spent very little time with her and the subject remained confined to the statistics she never mastered.

Her interest in the NEUM coincided with the withdrawal of the Cape Coloured vote and segregation of Coloureds on trains. The NEUM organised a protest meeting in Johannesburg and, I think, to put her to the test, directed her to put up posters in the Indian area advertising the meeting, with Seymour Pappet. They stood out like a sore thumbs in the Indian community, and there were telephone calls to her father about his daughter walking around with a white man. So when she came home that December, the family tactfully advised that she enrol at the University of Natal. She herself was finding boarding difficult, so she agreed. She never returned to Wits after coming home at the end of 1948, which was also the year I was extradited to Natal.

Limbada visited us once, soon after our marriage, bringing us a magnificent rooster from his farm, and sleeping the night on our ottoman in the front room. I wondered at his sudden unannounced visit, though on the other hand I thought he could just have been returning our visit to his family, which took place soon after our marriage. But then Limbs was a passionate member of the NEUM, which sought non-European unity just as we did, with this difference: our orientation was Leninist, his Trotskyite. I suspected he was trying his luck at enlisting us.

In July 1951 the Dundee branch of the NIC held a meeting chaired by VG Naidoo, who accused Dr Naicker of betrayal. He criticised the plan of action of the NIC as adventurism, which, he argued, could never lead to non-European unity. That could only be achieved through a process of education based on the NEUM's Ten Point Programme.

A month or so later, the Cape NEUM leadership, while visiting Natal, tried to 'seduce' Fathu to join them. I was most upset when Dr Goolam Gool, his wife Halima – the 'Muslim Girl' of the *Indian Views* fame – and IA Tabata visited her deliberately during my absence. My suspicion in this respect was confirmed when they declined our invitation to dine with us. Fathu, however, was far too actively involved with the NIC to join the NEUM, which in any case had no branch in Durban. I put down her sympathy with that movement as a reflection of her fair-mindedness and political tolerance. She did not agree with my rejection of the NEUM, holding that it had a role to play in the liberation struggle and that it should be recognised and respected.

While I continued to resent her penchant for the NEUM, which could have threatened our marriage had our love not been as strong as it was, I knew that she was far too strong-minded and could never be brainwashed. Most importantly, she would not commit herself to their Ten Point Programme as a precondition of membership. She was not one to commit herself to a 'doctrine', and she placed the Ten Point Programme in that category; she wanted to keep a free mind.

We had formed the Anti-Segregation Council within the NIC to overthrow the conservatives, and committed ourselves to non-European unity. The Limbada group was now seeing itself as the radical force within the NIC and us as the conservatives – a ridiculous proposition, but there it was.

We took their opposition seriously. We had come far in the process of united action with the ANC, and we were intent on protecting it. We had every faith in the goal we were pursuing. Limbada's attempt to affiliate the NIC to the NEUM was not restricted to Dundee; it was spreading to other northern Natal areas. We decided to confront this threat head on and eliminate it. The NIC Conference was due to be held in September, and Chief Albert Luthuli had been invited to open it. The NEUM considered him a collaborationist, despite the fact that he had resigned from the Native Representative Council. We held meetings in Newcastle, Dundee and Ladysmith to reaffirm branch allegiance to the Dadoo–Naicker policy. Debi, Monty and I set out for the meetings; Fathu joined us. We were newly married at the time and she did not want to be left alone at home. The trip was both tiring and enjoyable, tense and exhilarating.

Our first meeting was in Ladysmith. Our contingent was strengthened by Dadoo, who had travelled from Johannesburg with a supporting group. Dr Sader took the chair. Dr Limbada and VG Naidoo were given guest speaker status. A vigorous debate followed, at the end of which a clear majority reaffirmed their dedication to Dadoo and Naicker.

We went on to Newcastle where the branch had laid out a splendid lunch. The Limbada group was there in full force. They expected to recruit the branch into the NEUM, but their hopes were dashed after Monty, Debi and I addressed the large meeting. There was resounding reaffirmation of support for us. Dadoo and his group returned to Johannesburg. We went on to Dundee, Limbada's stronghold. We faced a tough challenge: the house was divided between our supporters and Limbada's. The fact, however, that Limbada did not have a clear victory, as he had anticipated, encouraged us. We knew we had to work harder in Dundee. It remained Limbada's stronghold and the branch eventually affiliated with the NEUM. We left Dundee late that night, thoroughly exhausted and cold. Fathu and I curled up in each other's arms on the back seat to keep warm and ignored Monty's teasing.

We expected boisterous opposition at conference, and it came. There was a demonstration against Chief Luthuli, who was called a quisling, but the Chief took it in his stride. Limbs had organised and rehearsed a battery of speakers and they attacked the NIC and ANC. They demanded that the NIC disassociate itself from the ANC; they dismissed passive resistance as a stunt. There were angry, emotion-charged exchanges, but Gopalal Hurbans was a strong and meticulously fair chairman and he kept the meetings under perfect control, so much so that Dr Limbada congratulated him.

DR LIMBADA'S DUNDEE BRANCH IS EXPELLED

Conference resolved that if a branch affiliated with the NEUM, it could face disciplinary action. Once the Defiance Campaign began, the Limbada group could no longer be tolerated, as it rejected the ANC as the key organisational partner and wanted it to be replaced by the All Africa Convention (AAC), which was untenable. Dr Limbada's Dundee branch was brought before a disciplinary committee of the NIC and was expelled after a full hearing. The Limbada group did not survive; it petered out as the Defiance Campaign grew in strength.

FUNDING FOR OUR CAMPAIGNS

Up to the time of the Treason Trial we depended entirely on local monies raised from our members and supporters of our campaigns. The 1946 passive resistance campaign was run on funds collected from the local Indian community, and had cost approximately £100 000 in the first year; probably £200 000 in the two years. The Defiance of Unjust Laws Campaign was similarly run with monies raised by the two Congresses. We went out canvassing for donations. The moneyed section of the Indian community was the conservative section, which had formed its own organisation, the Natal Indian Organisation. Its most influential leader in Durban, in the fifties, was AM Moola, his distinctive mark being his black fez worn somewhat cockily at an angle, but beyond that he was as strait-laced as they come; he contributed to the NIC coffers.

The Gujarati Hindus were our first donors in Durban, but the other communities also came in generously. Monty kept an open line of communication with the Muslim and emerging South Indian business communities, and this paid off well. The Women's and Youth committees were powerful fundraisers, organising dances, concerts and bazaars. Fathu was very active in these activities. During the Treason Trial she raised considerable amounts by taking a bus-full of performers and holding concerts on the Natal North Coast and in Johannesburg.

The rank-and-file membership was an invaluable resource – they maintained the resisters through private hospitality and contributed in cash through membership fees.

There was no outside funding during both the 1946 and 1952 campaigns, and virtually nothing from the white sector in those days. Overseas funding started coming in during the Treason Trial, when the Defence and Aid Fund was set up. It was also then that the Church began raising its voice against apartheid atrocities.

There were enormous travelling expenses, but these were borne by the activists themselves. Those with cars shared with those without. Rarely, if ever, did organisers travel by aeroplane, though they covered vast distances; bus and train were the more usual modes of transport. The telephone, especially long distance, was used sparingly. Money was required, above all, for full-time organisers, and they served on minimal salaries. The campaigns were sustained primarily by the enthusiasm and commitment of leaders and followers, rather than by cash.

The dependence on local funding also kept us more bonded, more united than we may otherwise have been. Capital in those days was, as now, more or less a white monopoly. Among non-whites, Indians alone had developed a business class and had a source of capital; this was the key factor for the anti-Indianism generated by whites in the country. But Indian capital was the main source of funding for both the 1946 and 1952 campaigns. The Indian community also had an infrastructure of halls, chairs and public address systems that could be hired, but more often than not were acquired as 'donations'; printers were prepared to give long-term credit.

The main fund-raisers in the Transvaal were Narainsamy Naidoo, Molvis Saloojee and Cachalia, Nana Sita, Manilal Galal Patel, Solly Nathie and Ismail Jada. One of our most generous donors was Ebrahim Laher.

I recall accompanying Molvi Cachalia at the initial stage of our fund-raising drive in the Transvaal.

We started off our drive with Gardee, knowing he was both wealthy and miserly, but the hopeful factor was that he had supported Gandhi. Gardee's reaction was, 'You know I am a hard nut when it comes to giving, yet you have come to me?' Molvi said, 'Yes, and with good reason too. You worked with Gandhi. You believe in passive resistance. You are as against this new law as any Indian. Why should you not support the campaign?'

Gardee gave us £1000, a fortune in those days. We then went to Bákie, another over-solvent merchant who specialised in selling fezzes. Bákie, as we expected, told us first to go to Gardee, assuming that Gardee wouldn't give, and thus he would be absolved of his responsibility. Molvi asked Bákie to get into the car with us and we drove him to Gardee. We told Gardee we had brought Bákie to him because he doubted that he, Gardee, had donated money to us. Gardee assailed Bákie with a string of choice Gujarati swear words, and said, 'I have given this cause £1000. Now see if you can match that.' Bákie gave us £500. The money came in generously after that.

We had very little access to the media. The white media virtually ignored us. The ANC had started *Abantu Batho* in 1912, but the circulation was small and the paper died in its second year. During the fifties, the liberation movement relied on the *Guardian*, renamed *New Age* after its banning, the *Leader*, the *Indian Views* and *Indian Opinion*. We also distributed our own handbills, pamphlets and newsletters.

FATHU AND I ARE BANNED

In November 1954 the government banned both Fathu and me from all gatherings. To her pride, she was banned a day ahead of me and other NIC officials. She had been washing her hair at the time and took her time drying it before answering the door. Fathu had long, thick, brown hair and it took a long time to dry. We did not have a hair-dryer in those days and she was very prone to catching colds if she did not dry her hair thoroughly. Her hair was still wet, so she wound a towel around it turban-like and opened the door, to her surprise, to two members of the Special Branch. They served her with a two-year banning order! She told me later that she had been bowled over by the attention, and had felt as if a medal had been pinned on her. She telephoned me excitedly and I in turn telephoned Monty, who decided to tease her. He telephoned her and pretended to be the chief of the Special Branch. Assuming a deep voice, he asked, 'Have my men served you with your banning order? Do you understand it?' and then his voice suddenly returned to normal, 'Oh, Fatima, sorry, they have come for me as well.' Fathu was three months pregnant with Shehnaz at the time.

The next day, I too was honoured with a banning order.

Fathu's banning followed exactly a month after she was dismissed from her job as Hilda Kuper's research assistant, a government appointment. The dismissal had upset us very much, Hilda perhaps even more so. She assured us that she had submitted positive reports about her assistant and could not understand the dismissal. We could only assume that the government had not wanted the embarrassment of having a banned employee, so her dismissal preceded her banning.

Both Fathu and I were on the executive of the NIC, and in terms of our banning we had to resign our positions. Nonetheless, we continued to make our contributions as best we could, though it was difficult as we were also banned from all social gatherings.

The banning order prevented fellow banned persons from communicating with each other. So, technically, Fathu and I couldn't communicate with each other. We of course ignored that, but we had to be careful about attending our usual family gatherings.

Fathu became the first woman to be banned in South Africa, and Fathu and I were the first couple to be banned in Natal. Her banning was a recognition of her work in the Durban and District Women's League, which operated a healing programme between Indians and Africans, whose relations had been ruptured by the 1949 violence. The League, financed mainly by Indian bus owners, ran a nursery school and distributed free milk to African children, apart from fund-raising for our political work.

The whole purpose of the banning orders at that point was to sabotage the Congress of the People (COP). But that didn't happen, though many among those responsible for the Charter were not able to attend the conference.

By the end of 1954, a very large number of Congress leaders in all the provinces of South Africa were banned under the Suppression of Communism Act.

Dr Naicker and Fathu – both not 'listed' (in the government's list of members of the banned Communist Party) – were entitled to reasons for their banning. These reasons came almost fifteen months after the two-year bans. The minister said that they had associated with listed persons, and that for the safety of the state he was not prepared to disclose the other reasons for banning them.

AI MEER

In the first week of 1955 came the first five-year banning order in the whole of South Africa. The honour of receiving it went to my cousin, AI Meer, who had held the post of secretary of the NIC in 1945 and 1947 and of the SAIC in 1948 and 1949. He had served a term of imprisonment during the passive resistance campaign in 1946, and had represented us at the United Nations in 1947.

CR Swart, the Minister of Justice, said that action was taken against AI because he was promoting feelings of hostility between whites and blacks, and because he was furthering the objects of communism, though he was not listed as a communist.

AI Meer, South Africa and the world knew he was doing nothing of the sort. He was preaching the fellowship of all South Africans, white and black. The minister had failed in his attempt to make AI a 'listed person', thus tacitly admitting that AI Meer was not furthering the objects of communism.

My listing, compounded with my banning, changed my life. I was cut off from practically all my former activities. I was forced to resign from a number of organisations in which I was active, above all the NIC. I tried pursuing my political ideals through other channels, but in vain. One needed a historically established structure and its credibility. We held a very successful conference on franchise under the Ratepayers Association, and we strove to develop that organisation as an alternative to the NIC, but it didn't work.

The banning did not crush the spirit of freedom. We decided that we wouldn't play into the hands of the authorities by defying our bans and thereby completely removing ourselves from the community.

ELEVEN

THE VERULAM PRACTICE AND SOME CASES

My banning order restricted my practice. I had by then accumulated an appreciable number of clients in rural Ndwedwe, but was not allowed to go there. My practice suffered even more the following year when I was arrested for treason, and it suffered again during the 1960 emergency. I appeared in court whenever I could. I had developed something of a reputation as a criminal lawyer. I also did some conveyancing. I enjoyed my work very much, whether it was applying for a licence or defending someone charged with a crime. Each case was unique and a new learning experience. The clients brought their anxiety, pain, insecurity and sense of injustice; everyone was innocent. But innocent or guilty, they were in trouble and troubled, and this demanded sympathy and understanding. I strove to give them that to the best of my ability, but always bearing in mind that justice depended on truth.

I once defended three prison warders. The prosecutor was very surprised at my knowledge of conditions in prison.

'You must have done a lot of research preparing for this case!'

'No,' I said. 'I know from personal experience. I've been there.'

He didn't believe me and I didn't think it worth explaining to him that I had been there as a political prisoner, not a criminal.

THE IMMORALITY ACT

One of the worst Acts passed by the Nationalist government was the Immorality Act. It reflected both their depravity and lunacy. As with so many racist Acts, the Act itself, not its infringement, was immoral. Everyone brought before the court under the Immorality Act was a victim of the Act. My sympathy was always with the victim.

Sex was certainly not immoral, as the Church sanctified it in marriage, and if it was immoral then it was immoral in itself, regardless of who practised it, and certainly not only when the partners were of different races.

An Afrikaans firm in Pretoria, looking through the directory of attorneys, came upon my name. Assuming that I was European – Meer can also be Dutch – they engaged me to represent their client who was arrested under the Immorality Act.

Although the 'immorality' occurred in union, the partners were tried separately. Invariably, although the 'crime' was one and common to both partners, the sentences differed, the white partner getting off lightly, and the court coming down heavily on the black.

I appeared for Mr Cross and he was sentenced to six months, suspended. His co-accused, an African woman named Angelina Shabalala, had no legal representation. When she came up for trial I asked the magistrate if he would adjourn the matter for a short while so that I could see him in his office before he tried her. He agreed. It was common practice for the white person charged with contravening the Immorality Act to be given a suspended sentence, and their partner in the same 'crime' to be sent to prison. I told the magistrate that I would be appearing for her, and that I wanted him to give her the same sentence. 'It is the same crime. It would be absurd if you gave her a different sentence, and if you did, I would take it on appeal.' He saw the logic and concurred with me. I then went to the young woman, who was taken aback when I told her I wanted to represent her, and that I would do so free of charge. Duly engaged by her, I pleaded guilty on her behalf and pointed out that Angelina was guilty of one and the same crime as the accused, whom he had given a six-month suspended sentence. Her sentence should be no different from his. The magistrate passed the same sentence on Angelina Shabalala as he had on Cross.

This was ground-breaking – it was the first time that both accused in an Immorality Act infringement received the same sentence in the Verulam Court.

In another case the police produced a bed sheet, which they alleged was stained with seminal discharge, as evidence that an immoral act had been committed. The couple had been found on the beach. My clients told me they had been picnicking. The police had not bothered to carry out a forensic test on the evidence.

I cross-examined: had tinned milk also been found among the items collected as evidence? The police admitted it had. 'Would you,' I questioned, 'be able to distinguish condensed milk from seminal discharge?' They could not. My client got off.

An Indian musician was charged along with an Afrikaans girl under the Immorality Act. The young girl was alone, with no one from among her people to give her moral or any other support. She was brought to me by the musician for whom I was appearing. I told her I would defend her pro bono and telephoned her father, who was an elder in the Dutch Reformed Church. The case received considerable publicity and I was hard-pressed to protect her from being hounded by the press. The father was very angry on the telephone. He made it quite clear that he would have nothing to do with the case or his daughter. As far as he was concerned, she was dead.

His behaviour was disgraceful and beyond redemption. I spoke to Alan Paton about it. He had written *Too Late the Phalarope* before the South African classic, *Cry, the Beloved Country*, but *Cry* had been published first. I told Alan the reality was very different from his fiction, where the white community gathered in forgiveness and support around the erring son. He listened intently in his characteristic way, brow puckered, his face squeezed as if it were a rubber ball. He considered my comment but made no reference to his book, which was a successful novel and had its own reality.

The most tragic case I had relating to the Immorality Act was one that involved the treasurer of Stanger. He had been arrested with an Indian girl. I got them both out on bail. The girl was very young, and I arranged with Goonam, a sort of quasi-social worker who accompanied prisoners when they were moved from one centre to another, to take her in until we could find a permanent solution for her. I ought to have shown greater concern for the white treasurer. His social status was an aggravating factor. He was too overcome with shame and recrimination to live with himself. When the trial began, he didn't present himself. The court was told he had committed suicide!

The young girl, however, had a happy ending. Goonam reminded me one day that I had undertaken to be her 'father', so I had to perform my duty accordingly. A young man was interested in her and his parents were due at her house to ask for her hand in marriage. She was duly married and I hope she is happy. I never heard from her again.

PORRIDGE PRAYER, HOLY COMMUNION, MECCA AND CANE SPIRIT
Another racist law involved the consumption of liquor.

Non-Europeans were not allowed to purchase or possess liquor during my years in legal practice. Porridge prayers, as they were called, were popular among South Indians. Not only was porridge served at these prayers, but to pep them up also dagga and cane spirit. There was a police raid at one of these ceremonies and the householder was arrested. The accused engaged me. He insisted that this was an injustice since the use of cane spirit was made obligatory by the prayer. His arrest was a violation of his religious freedom. He, of course, was wrong, since no Bill of Rights existed at the time. I did not get him off as he had hoped I would; neither did I get him an exemption from the court allowing him the use of liquor in religious ceremonies. We had one of the most unimaginative magistrates with tunnel vision. He considered only two factors – liquor and Indian, and according to the law these two did not connect. My client was found guilty and fined.

Reverend Giyana, also arrested for possessing liquor, asked me to offer the court a rather far-fetched explanation as to how he came to be in possession of cane spirit. His defence was that he usually purchased wine for Holy Communion from a certain bar. On the said occasion he had, as usual, taken his bottle and asked for wine to be poured into it. It turned out that the barman had poured in cane spirit instead. The reverend did not know that the bottle contained cane spirit and not wine.

The magistrate said it was a story that stretched his imagination, but he would give Reverend Giyana the benefit of the doubt, and discharged the case against him. My guess is that the magistrate was impressed with the reverend's very dignified appearance and his collar.

Mr Vanker came to see me one afternoon, very worried. I knew Mr Vanker very well. He worked closely with Mr Deedat, a distant cousin of mine, in the Islamic Propagation Centre. While I did not agree with Mr Deedat's approach to propagating Islam, I admired his skill in drawing large audiences. I objected to his attacking other religions as inferior in order to prove Islam superior. I followed the Quranic Surah, which stated all religions to be equal, and different paths leading to a common salvation, 'For each we have appointed a diverse law and traced out a way. Had Allah willed, He could have made you one community. But that He may try you by that which He hath given you (He hath made ye as you are). So vie one with another in good works. Unto Allah ye will all return and He will then inform you of that wherein you differ.' [V48, S5]

I particularly liked Mr Vanker, who was very modest and amiable. He unrolled the rather large scroll he was carrying under his arm and spread it on my desk. It was a calendar put out by Fraser's Hotel in Tongaat. It displayed two rather good pictures of the holy cities of Islam, Mecca and Medina, and between them, the very prominent message, 'Drink Cane Spirit'.

Mr Vanker was pained and angry. 'This is a desecration of the holy cities. How can they exploit Islam to advertise cane spirit when Islam specifically declares the taking of alcohol as haraam?'

He wanted me to take immediate action. I telephoned Mr Cohen, the owner of the hotel, whom I knew well. He was surprised that his calendar had evoked such a negative response from Muslims. He said he had intended to pay tribute to the two cities. 'Most of my customers are Muslims. I thought that this year I would express my gratitude to them by giving them a calendar depicting something close to their hearts!'

I asked Mr Cohen how many calendars he had distributed. He said he had just received his first consignment of a hundred, and he had distributed about five. I asked him not to distribute any more. I telephoned the printer, Mr NV Mehta, and told him not to print any more calendars. Mr Vanker would pay him for the cost he had incurred. So the matter was amicably resolved.

ILLEGAL IMMIGRANTS

Another law with which I had no sympathy was the one dealing with the rights of aliens. The definition of 'alien' was such that families could be divided and destroyed.

I had a deportation case. The man was a Mozambican. He had three children, all born in South Africa, where he had worked for seven years. I appeared before an Afrikaner magistrate. I pointed out that he had discretion; if he bent the rules a bit, he could save my client from deportation and save a family from being uprooted. The magistrate considered that. He said the law was cruel and he was not going to be a party to inflicting cruelty. He would exercise his discretion. He ordered that the family should continue living in South Africa.

The Afrikaner magistrate had a sense of responsibility about a law passed by his own people, and if he was convinced of its injustice he was prepared to deal with it. This was not the case with English magistrates, whom I found to be invariably timid and prone to applying the law to the letter.

I presented a similar case to an English magistrate. He propounded on democracy and human rights and how the principles should be honoured, but how it was not always possible to do so. The law was the law, was his attitude. It had to be respected. My client was deported and his family split up.

STOCK THEFT

Ever since the days of colonisation, the strictest laws prevailed with regard to stock theft. Blacks were 'naturally' stock thieves, a prejudice crystallised in the nineteenth century with the border conflicts in the Eastern Cape, when the Xhosa, resenting European intrusion on their land, 'confiscated' the whites' cattle that they found grazing on their land. European law dealt stringently with the Xhosa miscreants.

I had a case of stock theft. It involved fowls, not cattle, but fowls were small stock, so the same law applied. Lotchi Cho Cho was charged with stealing Mahabeer's fowls. The Mahabeers presented their case. I asked one question to all three witnesses in the box: 'How did Lotchi Cho Cho carry away the stolen fowls?' Mr Mahabeer said he held them by their necks, Mrs Mahabeer saw him carry them under his arms and her son said he carried them by the legs.

The magistrate listened and then turned to the prosecutor. 'You've heard enough?' he asked. 'There are so many contradictions here that I must find the

A FORTUNATE MAN

accused not guilty and discharge him.' Then he turned to me and said, 'Mr Meer, will you tell us what is the true story behind these contradictions?'

'Your honour, the star witness is missing in this case. It's a love story. It has nothing to do with stock theft. Lotchi Cho Cho and the Mahabeer daughter are in love. They had an arrangement to meet each evening at a chosen spot. Lotchi Cho Cho would flash his torch. Savithree would come and sit on a bench. Then Lotchi would arrive, put his arms around her from behind and close her eyes with his hands. Then they would kiss and spend some amorous quality time. The parents suspected something was going on. So, on the said evening, they set a trap. Mrs Mahabeer put on Savithree's sari and impersonated her daughter. When the torch flashed, she occupied Savithree's customary perch. The rest is history. Lotchi made his amorous advance on Mrs Mahabeer. Father and son pounced on him, dragged him into the fowl pen, tied him up, slaughtered two of their hens, then called the police and charged him with stock theft, to punish him for interfering with their daughter and to get him out of the way. They don't consider him suitable for their daughter.'

LICENCE APPLICATIONS

One of the most lucrative legal businesses in my days was licence applications. I would go to court with fifteen to twenty files. I had gained a reputation for winning licence applications.

Licensing laws were instituted in Natal to protect the European trader, particularly from the Indian. Every mining centre had a concession store, reserved for whites. Twenty-five per cent of the wages of miners were paid in concession money, which the miners could only spend in the concession stores. Miners were thus forced to take their custom to these stores.

One morning I had a telephone call from a leading QC.

'IC, are you appearing in Stanger?'

'Yes, I am.'

'I have an application for a wholesale business. All the shopkeepers in the area are objecting.'

I told him there was no such thing as wholesale in the area, since the retailers were allowed to have unlimited stock. Apart from this, each area specified its own distance between shops. In Indwedwe there couldn't be two shops within a two-mile radius of each other. The licensing laws were finicky. I had become familiar with all their intricacies, which bowled over the QC. I just had more practice in licensing matters. One didn't expect a QC to be well versed in such local issues.

My success in licensing matters had spread to a group of five Muslim venerables, and they came to my office one fine day suitably attired in fezzes, long

THE VERULAM PRACTICE AND SOME CASES

kurtas [long shirts] and flourishing beards 'attesting' to their piety. They wanted to extend their businesses to Inanda.

'You know Mr Polkinghorn.' It was put to me more as a statement than a question.

'And Mr Becket,' they continued. 'And Mr Smith, etc., etc.' They were all magistrates and members of the Licensing Board. All of them were well known to me, and I replied in the affirmative. The group's spokesman then told me their business. They wanted to apply for a licence to establish a business on the border of KwaMashu. They asked me my fee. I said it would cost them £75. He placed a wad of notes on my desk. 'Here is £1000. You will know how to distribute this money.'

I was enraged. 'You are Muslims,' I said. 'You come here making an exhibition of your piety and you propose something that violates the basic tenet of Islam: bribery and corruption.' The spokesman of the group proceeded to calm me down. He said he knew that I was lecturing on the Quran, but I was missing its key sentiment. 'You agree with me that the Quran wants all of us to be happy?' I conceded that, though somewhat guardedly, because I was sure there was a sting in the tail. 'We want to spread happiness all around. Mr Polkinghorn will be happy, Mr Becket will be happy, Mr Smith will be happy. You will be happy, and we will be happy when we get our licence.'

I got up and walked to the door of my office, 'Please go,' I said, 'before you corrupt me.' I saw five beards shaking incredulously as they left my office.

DAGGA

The possession and consumption of dagga were illegal. Dagga has always been regarded as a dangerous drug by the authorities, and its possession and consumption serious offences. Rural Africans cultivate dagga, and it forms a very important product in their capital accumulation. There is a viewpoint that it is pretty harmless and the authorities are knocking it to protect the tobacco industry. Whatever the fact of the matter is, Sooku cultivated and consumed dagga, and he got away with it.

One morning I arrived in Tongaat and found a great cleaning operation in progress. I asked the foreman, 'What's going on?'

'Mr Watson has ordered the town to be spick and span. An important sociologist, Fatima Meer, is coming,' replied the foreman.

'That's my wife,' I said. 'I have come here so often. No such cleaning has ever been done for me.'

The foreman explained that she was coming to do some research.

Fathu was researching the relation between crime and living conditions. Mr Watson attributed the relatively low crime rate in Tongaat to the garden-like

163

surroundings of the town. Company houses, emulating Cape Dutch architecture, were nestled in their individual gardens. One of them belonged to Mr Sooku. Fathu, reporting on her day in Tongaat that evening, gave me an enthusiastic account of his garden, in which she had found Sooku and his son, Ramlall, relaxing after work.

The next morning I found Sooku's garden an exhibit in court. Sooku was charged with cultivating dagga. He engaged me to defend him. I told him this was a very serious offence, carrying a maximum sentence of five years and a £1000 fine. He sent off his son to come to court with the money.

I put Sooku in the box. The prosecutor put the charge before him and asked 'Guilty or not guilty?' Sooku's voice had dropped to a low-pitched whisper, apparently because he was having difficulty breathing. I had to repeat the question to him before I got a barely audible 'guilty', which I relayed to the court. I then presented his case. 'Your Worship, Mr Sooku suffers from asthma.' Mr Plowright raised his head in interest. He suffered from asthma and I could see he was struggling for breath. I continued: 'Mr Sooku's defence is that he was told that if he grew this plant, which he did not know was dagga, and he dried the leaves and powdered them and then ingested them mixed with water, his asthma would be cured. Your Worship, as yet he has not had the leaves!'

Mr Plowright appeared sympathetic. 'I am going to be lenient with you. I find you guilty and I fine you £5.'

Sooku was so elated at having saved £995 from the £1000 he had brought to court in expectation of the fine, that he forgot his simulated asthma and called out in a robust voice, 'Ramlall, bring £5 and pay the fine!'

PERMISSION FOR BANNED CHIEF ALBERT LUTHULI
TO LEAVE FOR DURBAN FOR URGENT HOSPITALISATION

Dr MV Gumede was Chief Luthuli's doctor. He was a most likeable man and our families had developed a close relationship. One day I got a call from MV that the Chief was very ill and needed to be hospitalised. He wanted to admit him to McCords Hospital in Durban. Since the Chief was banned and restricted to Groutville, he wanted me to get the necessary permission from the magistrate. I promised MV I would telephone him within minutes with the permission. This was an emergency. The Chief, the only Nobel Prize recipient on the continent at the time, was a very important person and no risk dare be taken with his health.

I tried to get hold of the magistrate, Mr Francis, but I could not reach him. He was away in Stanger. In those days one had to get through to the exchange to telephone from Verulam to Stanger, and I couldn't get a call through. In desperation I decided to give Chief Luthuli the necessary permission on behalf of the magistrate. In the circumstances, granting permission was a mere formality, I rationalised. I telephoned Dr Gumede and instructed him, 'Take down the following: "Chief AJ Luthuli is hereby granted permission to leave the magisterial area of Inanda for the purpose of admission to the McCords Hospital in Durban."' MV took the Chief to Durban and hospitalised him. He was diagnosed as suffering from lead poisoning, and the source was later traced to his water tank, which had been newly painted.

When I eventually reached Mr Francis several hours later, I reported to him that Chief Luthuli had to be taken to hospital in an emergency. 'You were not available and I did not want you to suffer any recriminations, so I authorised his doctor to take him to Durban for hospitalisation.' Mr Francis thanked me for having done him a favour.

Later, we visited the Chief at McCords Hospital. He expressed a desire for big black prunes. I bought some and Fathu fussed around decorating them in a basket with flowers and leaves before we took them to him.

The Chief recovered and I visited him at his home on a special mission. Thulani Gcabashe was my articled clerk and he was courting the Chief's second daughter, Hilda. I acted as his 'umkhongi' [marriage co-ordinator] and took his proposal of marriage to the Chief. I participated in the negotiations about how many heads of cattle the young bridegroom should give to marry the daughter of the Chief. I forget now the number we arrived at, but I was intrigued by the Chief's adherence to traditional custom.

We resumed our work in our respective Congresses.

TWELVE

FREEDOM CHARTER

1953–1955

In 1953, when Shamim's arrival made us parents, Professor ZK Matthews proposed that we should draw up a blueprint for a democratic South Africa. The proposal captured our imagination. We rejected the apartheid state in which we lived. What then was the kind of state in which we would like to live? We decided that we would go to the people and canvass their views, and from these structure a blueprint for our South Africa.

CANVASSING THE PEOPLE
July and August saw the Congress movement – comprising the ANC, SAIC, the newly formed Congress of Democrats (made up largely of former white members of the banned Communist Party), the African People's Organisation and the South African Congress of Trade Unions (SACTU) – energetically combing the cities, towns and villages, streets and factories of our country, popularising the concept of the Congress of the People and recording the people's response.

We held secret meetings at Dr Sader's farm in Ladysmith and at Gopalal Hurbans's in Fairbreeze near Tongaat. Our Fairbreeze meeting, chaired by Chief Luthuli, was raided and the police went off with our discussion documents. The raid shocked us and we realised that we had been infiltrated by spies.

Regional conferences were held at which delegates submitted the demands tabled in their respective areas. The thousands of responses were sifted, coded and counted, and from these a national draft was drawn up and discussed at regional Congresses of the People.

NATIONALIST RETALIATION – LISTINGS AND BANS
In October 1951, in the midst of our mobilisation of support for the Defiance Campaign, I was listed as a communist, along with Dr Naicker, Debi Singh, Nana Sita and Yusuf Cachalia of the NIC and TIC. My practice was just beginning

to take off; the listing, apart from prohibiting me from being associated with the NIC, which had become my life, and threatening to strike me off the attorney's roll, ended my work as a journalist.

We were keen to bring as large a spectrum of the South African society as we could to the Congress of the People. I found myself addressing a number of meetings called by the Liberal Party. Fathu accompanied me to all these meetings. They were interesting because of the very lively discussions they stimulated. We found that while the white members were attracted to the idea of the Congress, the African and Indian members opposed it, arguing they had joined the Liberal Party to escape the radicalism of the Indian and African Congresses, and here they were back to square one.

ALAN PATON

Alan Paton telephoned me and said he would like to meet me and have a one-on-one discussion. I invited him to our home in Umgeni Road. He had read commentaries on communists and communism. He wanted to understand the Party and its members in South Africa through first-hand discussions.

I knew Alan Paton; we had met at parties and exchanged ideas in general company. He had spoken from our platform against the Group Areas Act. He had read Arthur Koestler[1] and was influenced by him, but he wanted to separate prejudice from fact. He wanted, he said, to understand communists and had selected me as one from whom he could learn.

I had admired Paton; now I took a liking to him. As I found out later, the feeling was mutual. He wrote an article, if I recall correctly, in the *Forum*, where he claimed me as a fellow liberal. I wasn't sure that this redefinition of me was a compliment. I knew that by defining me as a 'liberal' he sought to draw me closer to him.

We talked long, holding nothing back. I explained to him that as a young non-white I had been in search of an organisation that was open to all races and that was against racism and fascism; one that saw democracy as the right of all men and women to be equally entitled to share in government, and all God-given and socially created resources. I told him that I had joined the Communist Party because I found that it pursued these values. I also told him that I found no conflict between communism and Islam apart from the attitude to God, which was a personal matter. He inclined his head, knitted his brow and contorted his face into a tight knot. It was Paton in deep thought, Paton in challenge, as I realised as I came to know him better. I summed up my beliefs by stating that I had joined the Party because it was anti-poverty and anti-racism.

Alan Paton's birthday was celebrated each year with a hundred or so friends, mostly members of the Liberal Party, but including Africans and Indians.

Among them were Chief Luthuli, Chief Mangosuthu Buthelezi, Archbishop Hurley, JN and Radhi Singh, Devi and Denis Bhagwan, Pat and Sakunthalay Poovalingam, Joe Thorpe and many, many others. Fathu and I also became included in this select list. Each year some prominent person was invited to be the key speaker. One had the distinct feeling that it was a great honour to be asked to speak on his birthday. His wife Dorrie was homely and hospitable. The parties were great fun and the repartee and exchange of ideas scintillating.

The Liberal Party did not join the Congress of the People, but many of its members, such as Leo and Hilda Kuper, became our close, lifelong friends. Alan and I served on the Phoenix Settlement Working Committee – I as chairman for years. Alan's contribution was wise and dedicated. Later, Alan, Peter Brown and I looked after Nelson's daughter-in-law Rennie, paying her fees at Inanda Seminary and visiting her at Nelson's request.

Professors Leo and Hilda Kuper arrived in South Africa during the Defiance Campaign. Both of them took a keen interest in the campaign, attending our mass meetings and accompanying resistance batches as they defied the racial laws. Leo made a study of the campaign and his work on the subject was banned in South Africa. The whole second volume of *The Oxford History of South Africa* was likewise banned in South Africa on account of the chapter on African nationalism.

I AM LISTED AS A COMMUNIST

The government listed communists in 1951, thereby threatening serious intrusion on their freedom, but it was not until July 1962 that the Department of Justice published in the *Government Gazette Extraordinary* the 102 persons whose speeches and writings could not be published: fifty-two whites, thirty-five Africans, nine Coloureds and six Indians. I was one of the 102. We were allowed to object to our listing, and I was among those who applied to do so.

The *Government Gazette Extraordinary* of 16 November 1962 listed me as Meer Ismail Chota, alias Meer Ismail Cassim. I was not alias Meer Ismail Cassim. I was Meer Ismail Chota. The list also gave my residential address as 15 Market Building, Etna Lane, Durban, an address at which I had never resided. The doubt was thus raised whether the person listed was indeed me. More importantly, I argued, no good cause had been shown for the removal of my name from the attorney's list and none existed. I 'scrupulously observed the meticulous standards of honesty and accuracy' required by members of my profession, and I had a string of testimonials from fellow practitioners and magistrates to testify to this.

I believed I had legitimate grounds for objecting, and these did not concern my political affiliations or my ideological commitments; they were technical and concerned my identity. The name published in the list was arguably not mine.

I engaged Rafesath as my attorney and John Milne as my counsel. We pointed out that there were such serious errors in one paragraph of the *Government Gazette* that we doubted the accuracy of the full text of the evidence against me, and requested the entire record.

The department asked for time, but we never heard from them again. I met John Milne several years later at a political trial. John Milne was the judge president of the province by then. He asked me what was happening about our case. I said he as judge president would be the person to know.

As a listed person I could not prepare anything for publication; this included speeches, but if the speech was not prepared it was impromptu, so I made 'impromptu' speeches and was never troubled by the police.

While prohibition from our usual political activities and from publishing came into effect immediately, the clause striking us from the attorney's roll was held in abeyance and we continued to practise, at their mercy, not knowing when the axe might fall and we might be struck off.

The Nationalists, out to smash the campaign for the Freedom Charter, carried out raids on the offices of the *Advance* (the *Guardian* before its banning) in Cape Town, Johannesburg and Durban. We held our meetings in secret, knowing that we were being watched and the police would not hesitate to arrest us. In addition, the government began their own campaign of banning key leaders in our movement. But this did not deter us from our work.

The better part of Sunday, 5 June 1955 was spent at the working committee meeting of the NIC. It was a most democratic and representative meeting, despite the fact that many top officials and executive members had been banned by the Minister of Justice. Every NIC branch was adequately represented, proving the oft-declared statement by the NIC that for every NIC leader banned, two or more rise to fill the vacancy.

This was our last working committee meeting before the historic Congress of the People at Kliptown. The committee stressed the importance of the Congress and heard with satisfaction the progress made in all parts of South Africa for the Kliptown meeting, set for 25 and 26 June 1955.

The final Natal meeting to approve the national draft took place in the surgery of Dr GM Naicker. The government's banning did not prevent those banned from being fully involved in the discussion of the draft, which was eventually read out clause by clause at the Congress of the People before being adopted.

After the October and November bans, Pietermaritzburg held its regional conference of the Congress of the People on 5 December 1954, attended by 197 delegates. In February 1955 the NIC branch held its well-attended annual general meeting, at which Dr MM Motala was re-elected chairman, with SB Mungal and AS Chetty as joint secretaries.

All our Pietermaritzburg Congress leaders were subsequently banned, but this did not prevent Pietermaritzburg and the rest of South Africa from continuing to work openly and courageously for the Congress of the People.

The COP Natal regional conference in December 1954 was opened by Robert Resha of the ANC's national executive. Before the delegates made their valuable contributions, they were addressed by Dr GM Naicker of the NIC, John Hoogendyk of the Congress of Democrats, Violaine Junod of the Liberal Party and Mannie Naidoo of the Trade Union Action Committee.

NT Naicker, the NIC's acting secretary, read out Dr Naicker's message, which emphasised non-violence: 'Whatever we do, we must not veer from the path of non-violence.'

In the years to come people would be asked who gave us the Freedom Charter. The answer is, the people gave us the Charter.

The government, in a bid to prevent the Congress of the People, had banned key activists so that many of those responsible for the drawing up of the Charter were unable to attend the Congress on 25 and 26 June.

By the time the Congress of the People was held, Yusuf Dadoo, Monty Naicker, Albert Luthuli and many other top leaders, including Yusuf Cachalia, Nelson Mandela, Oliver Tambo and Kathy Kathrada, were prevented by banning orders from attending the launch of the Charter. Fathu and I were also absent because of our banning orders. EV Mohamed of Stanger, who was Chief Luthuli's unofficial personal secretary, registered at the ANC desk as the Chief's official representative.

THE CONGRESS OF THE PEOPLE

Saturday and Sunday, 25 and 26 June 1955, occupy a very special place in the history of the freedom struggle in South Africa. The Congress of the People met on those two days at Kliptown in the Transvaal on a site identified by IM Jada, a prominent member of the TIC. The Freedom Charter was unanimously adopted by nearly 3000 delegates from all parts of South Africa and 3000 members of the public – over 6000 people.

Among the large number of messages that came to the conference were messages from the President of the Indian National Congress, from Chou En-lai, prime minister of China, world-renowned American singer Paul Robeson, the prime minister of Sudan, and numerous world bodies of workers, women and youth.

MANILAL GANDHI'S ACCOUNT OF THE CONGRESS OF THE PEOPLE

Manilal Gandhi, who attended the Congress of the People, has left us a record of what happened at Kliptown on those two historical days. Since I myself was not there, I give you the report as it appeared in the *Indian Opinion* of 1 July 1955:

> The Congress of the People to formulate the Charter of Freedom for all democratically-minded and freedom-loving people of South Africa, which was held in a privately-owned sports ground at Kliptown, about eleven miles away from the City of Johannesburg, began its session at 3.30 p.m. on Saturday, June 25 and concluded on Sunday at 5 p.m.
>
> Its grand success was beyond all expectations. It would not be amiss to say that never in recent history of South Africa has such a representative meeting of the oppressed people known to have been held. And it was under the most difficult circumstances imaginable.
>
> Under the Suppression of Communism Act and the Riotous Assemblies Act it banned the movements of all the Congress leaders that count when the proposal for such a meeting was made known a year ago. It banned many public meetings called for the legitimate purpose of airing the grievances of the people.
>
> One cannot but bow one's head to and very heartily congratulate the organisers of the meeting for the magnificent work they did.
>
> There were two thousand eight hundred and eighty four delegates from throughout the Union of South Africa present at the meeting despite the fact that about two hundred were prevented by the authorities at Beaufort West in the Cape Province and at Standerton in the Transvaal Province from proceeding to the meeting, under the pretext of not being in possession of permits required under the Immigration Laws or passes under the African Pass Laws.
>
> It was all done, quite obviously, for the purpose of frustrating the holding of this meeting.
>
> Besides these delegates, there had assembled at this meeting over three thousand of the public.
>
> The police, both European and African, and a squad from the Special Branch were present at the meeting from the beginning to the end.
>
> Notwithstanding that provocative act, it must be said to the credit of the public that they were not sullen and angry but were happy and gay during the whole session.
>
> The weather, too, had been exceptionally kind.
>
> But on the day of the meeting it was like a beautiful clear summer day which testifies that God had showered His blessings on the meeting.
>
> After the preliminary work had been done, the draft Freedom Charter was taken clause by clause and speeches were made on it and each clause was then put to the vote and passed unanimously.
>
> There was justifiable emotion in the speeches made. It was a demonstration of the physical, mental and spiritual torture suffered by a vast majority of this so-called democratic country.

Mothers spoke feelingly about the future of their children; pass laws which were causing the Africans untold suffering and humiliation were condemned; the Bantu Education Act was described as slave education act; the living conditions of the Africans were condemned; their economic conditions under the industrial laws affecting them adversely were strongly criticised.

Some unsavory things were quite justifiably said about the policy of the Prime Minister, Mr JG Strydom and the Minister of Native Affairs, Dr Verwoerd.

Things went very smoothly until after lunch which was served to all the delegates between 2 and 3 p.m. during which period the whole crowd was entertained with songs and music.

Then half an hour after the afternoon session commenced, between 3.30 and 4 p.m., all of a sudden it was announced from the platform that armed police were coming towards the platform and that the people should remain calm.

There was some excitement and the people were on their feet to look at what was happening.

About twenty to thirty police, armed with sten guns surrounded the platform while higher officials walked on to it, and then it was announced that the police had presented a search warrant to the chairman of the meeting, Mr P Beyleveld, which said that they were investigating a charge of treason, and that they had come to look for 'inflammatory and subversive literature.'

There was surely no need for all this military display since there was no secrecy on the part of the organisers of the meeting.

It was held in the open and the police had access to all the documents they desired.

But, of course, it would be a wonder if the South African Police would practise a little grace. To be graceful is evidently not in their dictionary.

There was surely no occasion to tear down the peoples' national flags and to tear off the delegates' badges. But, nevertheless, that was the first thing they did.

Then while the delegates on the platform were being searched, the police stood by below with sten guns just ready for orders to shoot. They had a wild look on their faces.

Some jeered at the delegates and while the delegates were shouting 'Africa' with their thumbs up some of the police were responding with their thumbs down.

They apparently thought they were courageous standing with guns facing an assembly of six thousand unarmed people.

That was of course not all. There was an army of fully armed police, both Europeans and Africans, and over thirty mounted police surrounding the whole area in which the public had gathered.

Their number is said to have been about two hundred but it appeared to be much more.

Once again it was to the credit of the organisers and to the vast assembly that they refused to be intimidated and kept their heads and proceeded with the remaining work.

Due credit must also be given to the police for having allowed the remaining work of the meeting to be concluded whilst the delegates were being searched on the platform.

There were just a few more clauses in the Charter remaining to be discussed; the last one, just when the police came on the scene, was on Peace and Friendship.

The whole draft Freedom Charter was then passed with acclamation and with the singing of the African National Congress anthem 'Nkosi Sikelele,' with the government being present on the platform as though to bear witness to it. It was all an act of God.

And then the searching of the three thousand delegates began. The police had already taken all of the papers referring to the meeting – thousands of copies of the agenda, the draft Freedom Charter, the messages received from distinguished personalities from throughout the world.

Every delegate was searched and his or her name and address were taken and all the papers connected with the proceedings of the meeting were taken away.

Every European, in addition, was photographed. Searching went on till a little after 8 p.m. and the scene was then removed to the police station.

Scores of Africans and some Indians were arrested for not being in possession of the required permits or passes. The sum of about £60, I was told authoritatively, was paid in admission of guilt and all of them were released.

On their way to the police station the Africans were roughly handled both by the European and African police. There were instances in which men were beaten up and kicked and spat on by the police.

This is quite a common thing with the police in dealing with Africans, in particular. It is nothing to be surprised at when, at times, some Europeans are not spared. There is no remedy for it. The only remedy is a firm determination not to yield to the tyrant no matter whatever happens; not to lose one's own head and start retaliating by the same methods ...

Manilal continues to record his own philosophy: 'There can be no compromise where reason is completely absent and unreasonableness, stark injustice and tyranny is the order of the day.' With these words Manilal Gandhi ended his article on the historic Congress of the People, which gave us the Freedom Charter. And in the *Indian Opinion* of 8 July 1955, the full text of the Charter was given, with the following opening words:

> We the people of South Africa declare for all our country and the world to know:
> That South Africa belongs to all who live in it, black and white, and that no government can justly claim authority unless it is based on the will of all the people ...

Indeed, history was made in South Africa. The Freedom Charter took its rightful place with the other human documents including the Rights of Man of France, the American Declaration of Independence and the declarations that came from freed Afro-Asian countries.

The written report to the NIC by its delegates to the Congress of the People described the conference as 'the most epoch-making event that has ever taken place on South African soil and on the South African political scene'.

It recorded that 'at the Kliptown Conference the fundamental achievement was the spontaneous assertion of unity in thought, action and spirit for a free and better South Africa'.

The report recorded that of the 2884 delegates attending the conference, 360 were Indian, 320 Coloured and 112 white.

The working committee of the NIC, at its meeting held at the Bharat Hall, Durban, on 28 August 1955, noted with approval the formation of the National Joint Consultative Committee to popularise the Freedom Charter, and the contemplated formation of regional committees. The joint committee consisted of two representatives each from the ANC, the SAIC, the Coloured People's Organisation and the Congress of Democrats – the four national liberation organisations.

The working committee was informed that regional committees had been formed in the Natal Midlands and in northern Natal.

It noted that one million signatures in support of the Freedom Charter would be canvassed for, and that of this figure the Natal allocation was 150 000. Meetings were to be held throughout South Africa and the Freedom Charter fully explained, so that every home in the country knew what the Charter meant.

The government had done everything in its power to prevent the COP, but it failed. It had raided offices, drawn a blanket of intimidation over the people, banned practically all activists and leaders. But the COP happened on a scale beyond the imagination of the banned leaders, leaving the Nationalist government helpless and defeated.

The Nationalist government then resorted to a new tactic – it pinpointed 156 key organisers of the COP and charged them with treason.

THIRTEEN

THE TREASON TRIAL AND THE FAMILY

1956–61

THE ARREST

5 December 1956 was a historic day. The early, pre-dawn sleep of 156 South Africans throughout the country was disturbed as the police swooped down and arrested them for treason. I was recuperating from an appendectomy operation at MI's, my cousin-cum-father-in-law's house in 84 Ritson Road. My doctor, Dr Davidson, declared me unfit to travel and was emphatic that if the police wanted to remove me from my bed, it would be at their peril. This restrained them, and they compromised by placing a full-time guard over me; two young policemen who took turns to watch over me day and night. They sat stiffly at our bedroom door, which was kept ajar so that they could observe us – Fathu and I, and our three children.

It was a most uncomfortable experience not only for us, but for her parents' entire extended family, which comprised some fifteen members. The young policemen, not used to large families, appeared bemused and nervous. They saw me as a terrorist and wondered how many more in the family were terrorists like me. But after a few days they relaxed and began to see us as ordinary people, or as rather special people because they were impressed with our white callers, the Kupers, the Arensteins and especially Violaine Junod, whose irrepressible spirit could not be contained. She insisted on them seeing the baby and playing with the girls, which froze them up. She was trying to 'humanise' them. The girls were not co-operative either; they preferred to keep their distance.

When I was considered fit enough to travel, the police came to remove me. The whole extended family gathered to see me off. Rashid was too young to know what was going on, but Shehnaz, a toddler, clung to me and cried frantically. I could not understand what she thought was happening, but clearly she found the situation more traumatic than any of us. Shamim was withdrawn and taut with fear, perhaps comprehending more than we gave her credit for. Fathu had to forcibly wrench the girls away from me as the police prepared to take me. She remained stoic. She was not one to break down in front of others. I worried about her and wondered how she would cope. I did all the household shopping. She would now have to do that herself and care for the children and keep an eye on my office. The comforting thought was that she had the support of her large family.

My first stop with the police was at the magistrate's office in Durban. The formalities done, I was taken to the railway station – they had, up to then, kept our mode of transport secret. The family had thought I would be going by car. I was escorted by three security policemen, one Indian and two whites, and we boarded the train to Johannesburg. The white guards were in the European section, several coaches away from mine. They appeared quite happy to leave guard duty to the Indian policeman, Freddy Moorges. Freddy was a good sort. He had joined the police force but kept his soul to himself. He showed me great respect. He had tipped off someone in the NIC office that I would be travelling by train, and the NIC branches were alerted to be on standby and greet me suitably in the towns where we halted.

Freddie said to me, 'I'll be in the toilet each time your people come to greet you. You can talk to them at ease. The two European policemen are six coaches away from us. They will be sound asleep. They won't bother you.' And it was as he said. There were crowds to greet me at Pietermaritzburg, Ladysmith and Newcastle.

Later, Fathu thanked me for the telegram I had sent her. I had sent her no telegram, but I recalled Freddie asking me my residential address. He had sent her the telegram, which had simply stated, 'Arrived safely. Ismail.'

THE FORT PRISON

All three policemen were on guard at Johannesburg Station and more came with a police van. I was taken to the Fort, processed into a prisoner and taken to my fellow treason trialists. They gave me a joyous welcome. I was happy to see friends from Durban, Cape Town and Johannesburg, some of whom I had not seen for a long time.

Chota Motala,[1] Debi Singh, Gopalal Hurbans, Chief Luthuli and Nelson Mandela, to name a few, embraced me and explained the procedure in prison. They were behaving like seasoned old-timers, and well they could, since they had preceded me to the Fort by a whole six days.

Unlike the Defiance Campaign, when we were separated in prison according to race, during the Treason Trial all the non-European men were kept together, but European men were separated from the non-European.

We were 120 African, Coloured and Indian men, imprisoned in two large halls, one on the ground floor and the second on the first floor. We named them 'Upper House' and 'Lower House'. By pure coincidence, the total number of the treason accused was about the same as the number of members in the House of Assembly of the South African parliament. But there the similarity ended. We were all brain; they were all brawn.

The women accused were not imprisoned together as we were. The ten African women were separated from the two Coloured, one Indian and six European women, and they from each other.

Where the others spent fourteen days at the Fort before being released on bail, I spent eight. I would not have missed a single one of those days for anything; not because they were so pleasant, but because of the solidarity they inspired.

The common complaint was lice. They crawled over us from the blankets in which they were embedded. They made sleep well-nigh impossible. Most of us spent more time killing the lice with our hands than sleeping. Our complaints led to our cells being fumigated and the situation improved somewhat.

Conditions, as were to be expected, were better in the European cells; the food was better and they had mattresses for sleeping on; the non-Europeans had felt mats. Indians and Coloureds were given bread for supper; Africans were given mealie meal. We shared whatever we were given. The African prisoners qualified for meat twice a week, the others more often.

There were water-borne toilets in the two 'houses', and six showers and eight water-borne toilets in the yard, which we shared with other prisoners during exercise time.

Our day began at 6.30 am with breakfast; lunch was served at 11.30 am, supper at 3.30 pm. From 12 noon to 2 pm, all 120 of us were locked together in the 'Lower House', enabling us to have a 'Joint Session'. We were locked up for the night at 4 pm.

Lock-up time was always a misery for the warders. They could never get their counting right. Their work was complicated by the fact that they were required not just to count prisoners, but to count them by race. Until all the prisoners were accounted for, the warders could not leave. One evening the counting went on endlessly. Then they pronounced in utter puzzlement, 'The total number is right. But the number by race is wrong. There is one Indian short and one African too many.' Then their eyes settled on Joe Matthews with his longish hair. 'You there, you are the missing Indian!' And so they solved their problem for that night.

The same performance began the next evening. Dr Naicker could take it no longer. 'You mind if one of us did the counting?' he asked. The warders discussed this among themselves. I am sure they were not allowed to delegate the counting to prisoners. But the warders, anxious to join their families for supper, gratefully accepted the proposal. Monty called on Nelson to do the counting. He got it right the first time round in some ten to fifteen minutes. 'You see,' said Monty, 'if he can get the counting right here, he will one day get the whole country right!' Monty never realised how prophetic his words were. The warders were very grateful and their wives happy, since they had not kept supper waiting.

We were released on bail two days before Christmas, and were accommodated in Johannesburg in the homes of friends. Most of us could not afford to pay for accommodation and we wanted to rely as little as possible on the Defence and Aid Fund. In any case, the Fund could not pay for accommodation. None of the treason accused from the NIC drew any money from it.

Chota and I stayed with the Pahads. They could not have been more hospitable. They only had two bedrooms in their house, the one occupied by their young sons – Ismail, Nasim, Aziz and Essop, and the other by Goolam and Amina Bai. They insisted we take their bedroom while they slept on the convertible couch in the living room. They won out on the first two nights, but on the third night I forcibly moved into the boys' room and Chota into the lounge, and we reinstalled Goolam and Amina Bai in their bedroom. The custom was to give visitors the best. But we argued that we were not visitors, we were there indefinitely, for as long as the trial lasted. Eventually the Pahad's neighbour, OH Mohamed, offered us a spare room in his apartment, and we were all comfortable. It was such kindness and hospitality that sustained us through those harsh days.

We had our evening meals with the Pahads, and while we felt we were imposing on them they assured and reassured us that they enjoyed our company and appreciated the honour of having us. We were happy with the Pahads. Goolam was great company and Amina Bai was always cheerful, responding happily to my light-hearted banter and teasing.

It was the time spent in the Drill Hall that got to us. I built up anxieties about my office and about the children and Fathu. She was careless. Did she close the doors at night? Switch off the stove? Would I hear of some accident? Would there be sufficient taking of fees at the end of the month to keep the office going, the home fires burning? My anxiety erupted in ulcers in my mouth. I could not eat, and when Ramadaan came I could not fast. I wrote to Fathu of these things and her replies were full of concern and comfort.

THE PREPATORY EXAMINATION

The preparatory examination to test whether there was sufficient evidence to try us began at the Drill Hall in Johannesburg on 19 December 1956. We were led into a huge wire cage; someone had hung up a sign: 'Dangerous, do not feed'. Our lawyers fulminated in indignation at their clients' inhumane treatment. The cage was removed. The 156 accused were seated alphabetically, without apartheid, according to their province of residence: the Transvaal, followed by the Cape, Natal and the Orange Free State, in that order. TIC member Paul Joseph sat next to Helen Joseph of the Congress of Democrats; I found myself with the Ms, close to Professor Matthews, Nelson Mandela and Chota Motala.

Of the 156 accused, 105 were African, 23 European, 21 Indian and seven Coloured. There were 137 men and 19 women. Ten of the women were African, six European, two Coloured and one Indian. They represented almost all the different ethnic and language groups in the country.

There were two married couples, Errol and Dorothy Shanley of Durban and Advocate Joe Slovo and his journalist wife, Ruth First, of Johannesburg. There was one father-and-son pair, Professor ZK Matthews, acting principal of Fort Hare, and his candidate attorney son, the ever-smiling Joe. There were three priests, the Reverend DC Thompson, the Reverend JA Calata and the Reverend WS Gawe. There were six doctors, seven legal practitioners and two architects. The largest number of accused were workers, and they included a number of trade unionists.

The Drill Hall was large and bare with absolutely no character, no ventilation and hard seats. It could have been a barn, or an enclosed space for military exercises. Its most oppressive feature was its roof, of corrugated iron, most of it without any ceiling, a small part covered crudely with hessian. It covered almost a quarter of an acre. The elements, sun and rain, beat down on it and through it onto us. It was a wonderful conductor of heat, so we steamed on hot summer days and got wet on rainy days, with some of us opening our umbrellas to protect ourselves from the rain that leaked through the roof. A great deal of court time was lost because of the thunderous rumbling of rain, which stopped the inaudible proceedings. Our defence lawyers were Rosenburg QC (who later withdrew because of differences in the handling of the trial), Berrange and Coaker, with Joe Slovo appearing for himself. There were other lawyers engaged by individuals.

The court commenced at 9.30 am; the accused took their seats at 9 am to enable the court orderly to take the roll call. The magistrate, Mr Wessels, who had served as Chief Magistrate of Bloemfontein, and who would go on to become the chairman of the Group Areas Board, bowed impressively each morning and afternoon as he made his entry and exit.

There was a tea break at 11 am and a lunch break at 12.45 pm. The prison authorities supplied lunch at the Drill Hall, but we were not dependent on that food. The women in Fordsburg got together daily and lovingly cooked our lunch from a carefully prepared menu. Zainab Asvat usually delivered it in a small truck, enough food not only for us, the treason accused, but also for our guests and the journalists who gathered daily.

The afternoon session commenced at 2.15 pm, often with a five-minute tea break at 3 pm. There was a postal service; one of the orderlies took our letters and posted them for us. I made full use of this service and broke the boredom by casting my thoughts homeward, to Fathu and the children, and penning them on paper. At 3.45 pm the proceedings closed for the day. I rushed 'home' to the Pahads; Amina Bai knew that the first thing I would do was look for my daily letter from Fathu. Her letters were my lifeline. Throughout our separation during the Treason Trial, Fathu and I wrote two letters a day to ensure that we received at least one a day from each other. I read that letter over and over again. It restored me and prepared me to face the next day. I needed to be reassured that I was loved and missed, that I wasn't forgotten. It was a great comfort that Fathu and I shared mutual feelings for each other. Fathu wrote: 'Each day I open the mailbox, I find a letter from you; on the one day, there were two and each day I receive the letters with a feeling of surprise.'

There was one period when, for three successive days, I received no letters. On each of those days I wrote to Fathu about the missing letters. On each of those afternoons I rushed home to disappointment. Then on the third day (6 April 1957), I received three letters. Amina Bai gave them to me with relief; she had grown tired of my moodiness following my disappointments. I took the letters expectantly. Amina Bai told me she had had to pay a six-pence surcharge. I gave her the six pence. I examined the envelopes carefully. There was no sign of any stamps having been put on two of them; on the third I could give Fathu the benefit of doubt; the stamp could have come off. I was fed up and in no mood to read the letters for which I had waited for three days, as Amina Bai put it, 'like water in a desert'. I settled down and wrote to Fathu about the pain she had caused me by her carelessness. 'I didn't get the letters on time because you forgot to stamp them. The one envelope looks like the stamp came off, but it is quite clear that you did not stamp the others. I told you to put the date below the air mail label, just 5-4-57. Instead you wrote at the back of the envelope 5th of April 1957. All you needed to write was 5-4 in front, below the air mail label, not at the back.'

Then I thought perhaps I had been too hard on her, so I added, 'I am not criticising you. I love you very much. I do not want to upset you OK? That's understood.' On another occasion she had addressed the letters incorrectly, and there was a two-day wait before I received my letter.

THE TREASON TRIAL AND THE FAMILY

But there were times when Fathu also complained. 'A week has gone by and I have received no letter from you. It is as if you don't exist.' I took immediate action and sent off a letter with Chief Luthuli, who was leaving for Durban that afternoon. He promised to give it to her personally, which he did. Fathu wrote:

> I was deep in sleep. The whole house, added to by [nieces] Zeenith and Farieda, was equally in sleep. I heard a knock on the door. There were voices and the shadows of men. My heart stood still for a moment. Was it you? I was in my pyjamas, so I opened the door slightly and looked out. It was Chief; Albertina [Chief Luthuli's daughter] was with him. They brought me your letter, short and hurried, but very welcome and very precious. You say you received two letters from me, you should have received three I posted, two before your last visit and one on Tuesday morning. There are two more letters on the way, one posted on Friday and another yesterday, Saturday.

During one lunch break, Nelson asked me to accompany him to the telephone booth. We got into the booth; he dialled a number and spoke very softly, gently, I'd say amorously, to someone at the other end. He then handed the telephone to me, saying there was somebody he wanted me to meet. I said, 'Hello, who is speaking?' And the reply came, 'This is Winnie Madikizela.' And she added, 'I know all about you from your brother Nelson and he will tell you about me.'

I learnt from Nelson that he was deeply in love with Winnie. 'What of Eveline?' I wondered, but that was his problem.

THE PROSECUTION'S CASE

The prosecution began its case on the thirteenth day of the preparatory examination. The state had to establish that we were all communists bent on overthrowing the apartheid state through violence. The state depended on the evidence of its witnesses, mainly police spies who had infiltrated some of our organisations and had attended our public meetings to establish a case. They had made copious notes on our speeches.

The Crown began leading evidence on the documents seized during their raids. The first twelve days were taken up by evidence dealing with documents seized from offices of the Congresses, the *New Age* and other organisations in Durban and Johannesburg.

I wrote to Fathu that Berrange's opening address was brilliant:

> Two days have passed and we have had only one witness, submitting document after document and reading into the records only the names of the organisations and individuals they referred to. After all the documents were put in as exhibits,

we were told that the Crown would call expert witnesses to prove that those charged were intending to overthrow the state by violent means in order to set up a Communist People's Democracy.

The Defence has not had an opportunity as yet to go into details of any of the documents. We have now been told that in all some twenty-one thousand documents will be introduced by the Crown, a grim thought, enough to depress the bravest soul.

As the exhibits mounted and books joined documents, it became clear to us that the police had raided the homes of individual accused and offices of organisations and newspaper offices indiscriminately, and had taken away sacks full of stuff of which they could make neither head nor tail. It reminded me of the Gujarati proverb Budie[2] often quoted: they had stuffed their mouths with such big ladoos [sweetmeat balls] that they could neither swallow them nor spit them out.

The state was overwhelmed by its mountain of papers and did not know how to sort out the relevant from the irrelevant, how to analyse, make sense of, and impute meaning to the bales of stuff it had gathered. The fact of the matter was that there was nothing treasonable about the Freedom Charter or the Congress of the People. The state was hopelessly hoping to concoct treason in the course of the trial, and it would spend four years trying to do so. It would scrape the bottom of the barrel of its deluge of documents and statements of witnesses and come up with absolutely nothing to prove its case. Its own court would find all 156 accused not guilty and discharge them on 29 March 1961.

Judge Rumpff would say that after considering all the evidence, his court concluded that the ANC was not a communist organisation, and that the Freedom Charter did not envisage a communist state.

After a month of sitting in the preparatory examination and being dulled by its tedium and stupidity, I came to the conclusion that the worst punishment one could suffer was to have one's own speeches, delivered years back and recorded by near-illiterate policemen, read back to one by equally illiterate readers, who made gibberish of the original statements.

I have summarised proceedings for a few days in a few lines. The actual presentation took many hours, the time being doubled owing to poor voice projection, unintelligible pronunciation, and in many cases inaccurate translation from one language to another. The brief lines skim over the excruciating fatigue and the unbearable boredom the delivery provoked.

Friday, 25 January 1957
Six police witnesses gave evidence dealing with documents seized from the offices of the *New Age*, (Durban), the Natal Indian Congress and from Accused No. 1, Farid Adam.

Monday, 28 January 1957
Twelve police witnesses gave evidence dealing with documents seized from ten accused, including Farid Adam and Mohamed Asmal.

Tuesday, 29 January 1957
Sixteen police witnesses gave evidence on documents seized from ten different accused, including Paul Joseph and AM Kathrada, and other banned members of the Transvaal Indian Congress and the Transvaal Indian Youth Congress. Exhibit No. AMK 75 was a letter from AM Kathrada declining an invitation to attend a cocktail party at the Soviet Consulate because of his banning order.

Wednesday, 30 January 1957
Fourteen police witnesses gave evidence dealing with documents seized from nine of the accused. For the first time a non-European Crown witness, Detective Sergeant Tabete, gave evidence. Hearing was then adjourned to Monday, 4 February 1957.

We all sighed with relief. It gave us four days to return home and spend time with our families and in our offices.

Towards the end of February I received a letter from Fathu, which plunged me into waves of agony. I had heard from Chota, whose sister Gori Apa was married to my eldest brother HC, about Rashid's accident and subsequent convulsions. But Fathu, who wrote to me about all sorts of things, even matters that concerned her friends, hadn't written one word about my son. I telephoned her. I was livid with anger. She froze at the other end and told me little apart from repeating that she was sorry and that Rashid was well, and she would explain all in her letter.

Her letter didn't just come out with the facts; it couldn't, since it sought simultaneously to exonerate.

She wrote that she was shocked, shaken and confused for three days. She knew her anxiety and gauged how much worse mine would be, far away from home. 'I am generally optimistic and if I was so shaken and so distraught, how much worse would be the effect on you.'

She said she had needed to share her anxiety with me: 'It was horrible keeping it all to myself,' but she had wanted to spare me the pain.

> I wanted to save you the anxiety. I know how much you go through as it is. I could not bear to add to that. I lived days of terror and could not move away from Rashid despite the doctor's assurances, lest there was a recurrence of the convulsions he had suffered. I wrote you three letters, long and detailed, describing the incident

but I did not post them to you. I wanted to be certain of Rashid's condition and to spare you any unnecessary anxiety. I understand the nature of convulsions now. I did not then. I was, for almost the whole of last week, a victim of the maxim 'a little knowledge is dangerous'. It was dangerous for me; how much more dangerous would it have been for you, who are always anxious?

It took some time for her to get to the point and even then there were unnecessary diversions: 'It was a lovely day.' She had taken the children to Reservoir Hills, 'and that was a very right thing to do. Had you seen them before the accident you would have agreed. They were so wonderfully happy, sitting in the grass, eating the gulab jamboo and sev you had bought me.

'I played with the children all the time,' she continued.

We then went into the kitchen. I gave Rashid some tea and he drank it all. He wanted to play on the floor. I did not want him to play outside, and I had good reason for that. He got into the sand and kept picking up stones and I did not want him to be frustrated by my continuously stopping him. Then he kept wanting to clamber up the steps to the veranda and I was afraid he might fall. I took him into the house and put him on the floor of the lounge and closed the door. All the children were with me playing happily. My thoughts turned to the curtains, looking old and drab. I left the room to suggest to Fafa[3] that she should get new curtains. I had hardly left Rashid when I heard him cry. It wasn't an alarming cry. I rushed to him. He had hurt the front of his head. Above the left eyebrow, there was a spot of blood. I picked him up. He made grunting noises, nothing otherwise. I took him to the bathroom and wiped his eyebrow. He was fine apart from the bruise. I laid him on the bed. He was quiet. I had the feeling that he had suddenly become too quiet. I noticed his pupils travelling to the corners of his eyes. I thought that the pattern on the quilt had caught his attention and then I felt a tremor through his body. I was alarmed. I called to Fafa. Rashid began vomiting. I picked him up and held him over the bed. Fafa was now kneeling beside him, looking into his face. His body began trembling. Fafa said he was having convulsions. He changed colour, his eyes were white and his tongue seemed as if it would drop out. It was terrible Ismail. I was frightened as never before in my life. Fafa applied some eau-de-Cologne. He seemed to revive. I was frantic. Fafa wrapped him in a blanket and held him. I put the girls beside her in the car and drove as fast as I could to town, through Quarry Road. Ismail you can imagine what I went through in those 15 minutes. I didn't understand what was happening to him. I kept asking Fafa if he was breathing and she listened to his heart and reassured me. The first doctor we reached was Nad Pillay, but I didn't see his car so I drove on. I stopped at Dr Chetty's surgery in Umgeni Road and I rushed in, leaving Fafa with the children. I hurried through the congested waiting room to the dispensary. The dispenser recognised me. I asked if the doctor was in. He said yes and then Ismail, I could not speak. I was completely exhausted. I turned away, muttering something like going to the car. The man followed me in alarm. 'Are you ill Mrs Meer?' he asked. I had the feeling that I was agitating the entire surgery. He followed me outside, across the road to the car, saw the sick baby and went ahead of me to tell Dr Chetty. I took Rashid from Fafa and followed him, the girls came up behind me with Fafa. Dr Chetty was very calm, Ashwin Chowdree was there for some reason. Even before seeing Rashid, or asking me, he said 'convulsions'. I just nodded. I could not speak. Rashid, for the first time since he had vomited, began to cry. He had developed a temperature, Dr Chetty gave him an injection and inserted a sleeping tablet in his rectum. We returned home. I telephoned Dr Davidson immediately. He came soon, examined Rashid thoroughly and said he was fine. In fact, when Dr Davidson arrived, Rashid gave him one of his loveliest smiles and pulled his tie and began playing with his stethoscope and his pad, and charmingly waved ta ta. Dr Davidson was so impressed that he told Hilda[4] what a beautiful boy Rashid was. She said he very rarely commented on the beauty of his patients. Dr Davidson kept Rashid on sleeping tablets for three days, one-quarter grain twice a day. Rashid's temperature rose again on the second day. Dr Davidson examined all his muscular movements for any signs of brain impairment and reconfirmed that Rashid was fine. He explained that convulsions are common in infants; their control over the nerves of their brain is not well developed and therefore very often the slightest reaction, like fever, can bring on convulsions. He is convinced that the fall had nothing to do with the convulsion. It was coincidental. He feels Rashid was heading for a temperature and the knock on his head broke down his resistance to a greater degree than it would have normally, leading to his convulsion. He is certain that Rashid did not suffer a concussion and reassured me that even a concussion is nothing to worry about. I called him three times because I kept having doubts. He confirmed his opinion each time. I asked about a brain test. He said that it was complicated and not without discomfort, and in his opinion, entirely uncalled for. He said that had there been any brain damage, there would have been physical symptoms in the course of the week. He was convinced that there was nothing to worry about.

I had X-rays done despite his opinion that that was unnecessary. Ahmed[5] arranged this at McCords. They took two plates. Rashid was in great form and very popular with the nurses. The plates show no damage to the cranial structure. Dr Gumede saw them and said they were lovely plates, the reading quite clear. The little skull was perfect, revealing a spate of teeth ready to emerge. 'It's his teeth,' Dr Gumede concluded. Dr Gumede has had his third daughter (fourth child).

I put the letter aside and shook my head, concluding that Fathu had kept this away from me because she was afraid of my temper. But I couldn't shake off the feeling that, all said and done, Fathu was careless.

I wrote to her frankly and told her about my misgivings. I told her I pointed out these things because I loved her, that she should worry when I didn't open my heart to her. Fathu was receptive and contrite, but defensive. 'You consider me as lacking in responsibility. Unlike you, I am not very ordered. I am untidy, but I am not irresponsible.'

She gave me the benefit of her wisdom: 'mishaps, troubles will happen. It is for the two of us to share them and be sufficiently brave to bear them. Since when has your life been smooth sailing and happy? Since when is our life or anyone's life without its turmoil? Take today for instance …'

The letter did not dispel my anxiety.

Minnie, MI's cousin's daughter, was living with us at the time, and there was Sharda who helped with Rashid, and Phoowa who did the housework and cooking. So Fathu had sufficient home support; and always there was her family, a pillar of strength.

Yet I worried because I am by nature the worrying type. When away from home I was anxious about the home. Fathu was the more relaxed of the two of us, but I worried about that too. I thought her too relaxed, and as a result inclined to be careless and forgetful. The difference in our temperaments only aggravated my anxiety. I wanted her to be more like me, I suppose, anxious and careful, but in retrospect I realise that we worked well together because of our complementary temperaments. I probably would not have been able to cope with her had she been like me, and it was because she was as she was that she coped with me.

By September, Fathu and I had lived apart for nine months, excluding the fortnightly weekends. The separation impressed on us the preciousness of the time we spent together. We had begun to take each other for granted; the separation underlined our need and dependence on each other.

As our sixth wedding anniversary approached, I thought of what my marriage meant to me and I summed up my feelings in my letter to Fathu: 'I greet you, my wife, on this day of our anniversary. The eleventh day of March is the most important day in my life, for on this day, the most beautiful woman in the world became my wife. Without her, this world and everything in it becomes meaningless. I love you. Thank you for being so patient with me. I who am such a difficult person (11.3.57).'

And to ensure that my feelings were communicated to her on that precious day, I sent her a telegram with a shorter version of that message: 'With love and adoration, I greet you on this anniversary of our wedding.'

She reminded me of the day she received her certificate of merit in political science. 'You were in the hall, I was so pleased to see you.'

And then she recalled, 'Six years today, we pledged to preserve our love and that love grew into something we never dreamed of, our beautiful children. There was one, then two, then three and now there are five of us.'

She concluded: 'I was a young, immature girl when you first kindled feelings of love in me and now that love has grown into a fire that death alone can extinguish. I love you more today than ever before.'

The prosecution witness is droning on and on, in Zulu, the translator struggling and faltering. I turn to the photographs Fathu sent me taken by Ranjith Kally, a celebrated photographer. There is Shamim in a bathing suit with a parasol, a smile lighting up her face; there is Fathu in her white sari, the colour I like best on her, looking like a fairy; and another of Fathu seated on the lawn in Botanic Gardens with Shamim, Shehnaz and Rashid beside her, a beautiful mother with lovely children. There is Shehnaz in a pretty dress, shoes and socks, laughing happily, and one of Fatso, hand in mouth, so chubby, his eyes deep-set in the fat of his cheeks, soft and beautiful. Fathu describes him as plump and contented, perpetually smiling. The smile remained to the end of his life.

The Treason Trial challenged family morale. The absence of husbands and fathers told on the wives and children. We worried about our businesses. Some feared they would have no business to return to. I was fortunate that I had Fathu to help me with my office. She and my loyal staff, Aubrey Naraidu, Puran Maharaj, Mr Sithole, Mr Shahadat Naby and Cassim Amra (ostensibly doing his articles with me), kept the office intact and saw to it that no case was turned away because of the absence of the attorney. Aubrey and Mr Sithole sent me reports on the office, and once or twice Aubrey took lifts to Johannesburg and reported to me personally on the office. On one occasion I took Aubrey to a party at the home of the Harmels, but he felt uncomfortable and did not enjoy himself.

The takings at the office averaged £258 a month. To keep the practice going, the staff and Fathu engaged attorneys and advocates. Two of the advocates, Hassan Mall and John Didcot, went on to become judges. The company of Vahed, later joined by Pat Poovalingam, was particularly helpful. The firm of Burne, Swart, Hudson and Rindle had an office in Verulam and they were very supportive.

Most of the treason accused could not afford the cost of long-distance travel, and would have found it difficult to survive without the subsidy from the Defence and Aid Fund, which helped only with the barest essentials, and transport was not one of these.

The preparatory examination was conducted in Johannesburg. The accused who lived outside Johannesburg, in Durban, Cape Town and elsewhere, had the added problem of travelling to be with their families and attending to their work. I managed to return to Durban, on average, once a fortnight, taking lifts by car or travelling by train and hardly ever by plane, because of the expense. Monty,

Chota, Debi, Gopalal Hurbans, Debi Singh and NT Naicker usually motored together. More often than not we travelled to Pietermaritzburg in Chota's small Volkswagen, travelling the short distance between Durban and Pietermaritzburg in Hurbans's car, sharing the expenses. The weekend visits home were fleeting. There were also recesses when I would have more time, which I allocated between home and office.

We spent those long motoring hours discussing many things. Hurbans usually came up with interesting theories. One of these was that since the world was revolving, the time would come when we wouldn't travel at all, but wait for the world to move to the point of our destination and we would then shoot down. I found this theory innovative and intriguing. Chota, as it turned out, had a stomach full of Hurbans's theorising. We were driving alongside fields of sunflowers for several miles and Hurbans was holding forth that the sunflower always faced the sun, moving with it. Chota suddenly stopped the car, got out and demanded Hurbans get out too.

'Look at your sunflowers. Are they facing the sun?' he challenged.

They had their backs to the setting sun, if sunflowers have backs. We heard no more theories from Hurbans for the rest of the journey.

I travelled as often by train as by car, but I preferred to travel by car because it was quicker and cheaper. One never knew what to expect on the train. I made one trip by train with Monty and his wife Marie. I wrote to Fathu, 'The train was over-full. The compartments and passages were packed and Monty and Marie had no privacy at all. It was just as well you didn't come. We reached Heidelberg at 7.40 pm and travelled by car and we reached the Pahads at 8.30 am.'

On occasions when I arrived home late at night, hoping to spend some quality time with my wife, I found strangers in my small house. On one occasion I found myself stepping on sleeping bodies, spread out on the floor of our all-purpose front room. Mercifully, my place in our bed was secured. Fathu explained that her friend Nana and her husband and their friends had come to Durban but couldn't find accommodation. They were there just for the night.

On another occasion I arrived home to find Zainab Reddy and her daughter ensconced in our front room. If I had not restrained Fathu, she would probably have stuffed our two rooms with people she considered in need. Zainab, a talented artist, had married Venget Reddy, who was completing his medical studies in Bombay. The South African government passed a law in 1955 against the entry of wives from India after a fixed date that year. A number of our students studying in India had married there, as was the case with Venget Reddy. To beat the ban, his wife Zainab and their fifteen-month-old daughter arrived in Durban while Venget Reddy remained in India to complete his studies. The Reddys lived in Stanger. Zainab found living in Durban more congenial, so she and her daughter were in our house. I don't recall how long they stayed with us. Zainab eventually found a lectureship at the University of Durban-Westville (UDW) when it was still housed on Salisbury Island, and caused some waves because she defied the rule confining her to the non-Europeans' toilet and 'polluted' the one marked 'Europeans Only'. She became quite a celebrated artist in the short time she spent in Durban. The Reddys eventually settled in the UK and we lost touch with them.

MARY LOUISE HOOPER

The ANC acquired a fairy godmother in Mary Louise Hooper, an American of means who was in love with everything African. She adored the Chief, whom she referred to as Boss, or Albert. I do not recall anyone else calling the Chief, Albert. He had such a commanding presence, reflective of a biblical patriarch, that we could not conceive of addressing him with any sense of familiarity.

Louise's large, black Ford came to be known as the 'Congress Special', since it was at the disposal of the ANC. The Chief, Dr Conco (Zamie) and Yengwa (Bonnie) usually travelled with Louise, but when one of them, for some reason or other, dropped out, then someone outside of this group would be offered a lift. On a few occasions I got a lift in the 'Congress Special'. Louise was also a source of financial assistance to the Natal ANC and certain ANC accused.

Louise was a fun lady, generous to a fault and very good company. One evening Gopalal Hurbans arranged a dinner party at the flat in Johannesburg where he was staying. Louise was the guest of honour. After dinner we sat around talking and joking. Louise asked NT to guess her age. 'If you get it right, I'll give the ANC a donation,' she said. We saw NT studying her very seriously. I could see he was going to lose us the donation. He actually wanted to evaluate her correct age when all Mary Louise was looking for was reassurance that she looked younger than her years. NT did the opposite; he guessed her age a good four years older and not only lost the bet, but also a good friend. We tried to cover up by saying, 'Ridiculous, Louise is much younger,' but the damage had been done.

At times, Louise took us on picnics, and while in Durban invited us to her house overlooking the Valley of a Thousand Hills. One party she gave remains inscribed in my memory. It was such a jolly party. There was JN and Radhi, Monty and Marie, Chief and Nokukhanye and their daughter Albertina, MB Yengwa, Stalwart Simelane, Dr Wilson Conco, his wife Shiemie, Steven Dlamini, Archie Gumede, Leo and Hilda Kuper, Violaine Junod, Alan and Dorrie Paton, and more whose names I forget.

We were all friends; white liberals and Indian and African Congress members. We were bonded in our opposition to apartheid. Our common political interest had expanded into the social. We met at each other's homes and supported each other. The Patons and Kupers and Violaine Junod joined us in our placard demonstrations and raised funds for Defence and Aid.

We danced around Louise's dining room table, round and round and round, the Chief leading, us following, the spirit of togetherness drawing us in its embrace, as we sang Zulu freedom songs of the day. A favourite was, 'Vula Malan siya qonqota' ['Open the door Malan, we are knocking'].

We would continue knocking until the end of our political time, and the door would be forced open by another generation that would make the townships and the country ungovernable. It would be after Malan was long gone and FW de Klerk would be head of state. It would not happen until 1992, and we were in 1956, thirty-six years away from freedom.

Louise's party celebrated several birthdays, hers, the Chief's and Chief's son's. It reminded me of our birthdays.

Fathu and I had not spent either of our birthdays together for two years. She wrote to me on my birthday, 5 September 1957:

> Today is your birthday. I hailed it early as the day broke. I would have telephoned then, but I thought I might disturb your hosts. I did not want to begin the day with a selfish act. The number of days of personal significance in our family have grown from two to five. For me, your birthday is the most significant in my life. I love today because it brought you to me and with it all the joy in my life. Last year, on your birthday, I was in hospital, so we couldn't do much together. Next year, perhaps we will be in our new home, relaxing on our terrace, enjoying cool drinks.

My present from her was a set of colour slides of the children and a viewer through which to see them. It was the first time I experienced that technology. Martin Russell had taken the slides. Fathu went to enormous trouble to ensure that I got them on my birthday, per Bobby Harrypersadh and *Drum*.

On Fathu's birthday I sent her gladioli and roses, and she wrote:

> I have had a very pleasant day because you have been close to me. I have felt you near and that nearness has been very reassuring. Thank you for your card, telegram, flowers and the beautiful pyjamas. They fit me perfectly. Most of all, thank you for your thoughts and your love. I tried on the pyjamas and Shamim watched and said, 'You look lovely Mummy.' I have put them away for now and will wear them when you come. Shamim does not understand a birthday. To her a party is a birthday, so she kept asking when the birthday would begin.

Fathu recalled her birthday the previous year. 'I was very pregnant with Rashid and in Ritson Road, nursing Shehnaz who wasn't well. You brought presents in colourful wrappings, a cake for all of us, handkerchiefs and a sewing basket with a £5 note for me.'

The baby I left behind turned one and I wasn't there. Rashid and I were born in the same month – in September, I on the fifth, he on the second. I longed to be with my family and celebrate his first birthday. Fathu wrote to say they had an impromptu party.

> Rashid was feeling so happy and so very bright that we had a little party. We bought a cake from Ballim's [our corner shop] and some minerals and we lit the solitary candle that heralded the completion of our son's first year on earth. Rashid was aware that he was the centre of attention and he looked up at all the faces that surrounded him and smiled at them in turn as we sang 'Happy Birthday' and cheered him, little Shehnaz coming in each time after the rest. Then we played games – Pam, Anil, Myna, Benny, Anushka [our immediate neighbours], Shamim, Shehnaz and I. We all enjoyed the party. I was so proud of him, this one-year-old son of ours, so happy. But we missed you. It is very lonely now and the children are sleeping all around me. Just last night, you were lying next to me and it was the same the night before and tonight, there is this loneliness.

THE TRIAL CONTINUES

The evidence of the Crown witness drones on, stumbling over words like 'petit bourgeoisie' and 'Busman's holiday', which he pronounces 'Boesman's holiday'. The transcription is often erroneous and one has to be attentive to pick this up.

I am far from the Drill Hall, in Durban, with my family. I am thinking of Fathu, of how dependent I have become on her, even before our marriage when she was a slip of a girl. I think of the time I introduced her to Wahajar Rasool and he responded insultingly: 'She looks like a victim from the Bengali famine.' I was deeply hurt. Behn was on the thin side, but I was proud of her. Rasool was a Bengali who had been allowed into the country as a special concession to the Muslim community as an Arabic teacher. He had a keen intellect and sharp tongue.

At the end of the sixteenth day of the prosecution's submissions, 4067 documents had been presented, of which 2702 were seized from the offices of organisations and 1365 from individual accused. By this time forty-five witnesses, all members of the South African Police force, had given evidence.

The books seized from the libraries of individual accused included books by or on Marx, Engels, Lenin and Stalin. Other writers included in the raid were Professor Julian Huxley, Harold Laski and GDH Cole. We wondered whether the police had been given some elementary instructions on 'dangerous' authors, or whether they had taken the books mindlessly and the sorting out of the dangerous from the benign had been the work of some rare intelligence. They had jubilantly seized Anna Sewell's *Black Beauty* from our home, the title probably conjuring some violation of the Immorality Act in their myopic minds, or something secretively political, simply because the book was found in our home. That book did not appear among the exhibits, which made me think that they did employ some intelligence to sort out the 'offensive' from the inoffensive. Unfortunately, that intelligence appeared incapable of dealing with anything beyond the obvious.

We tried to break down the tedium of the proceedings by converting the evidence into cricket scores. We were keenly following the bulletins on the match between South Africa and the visiting MCC touring the country. We adopted cricket terminology as the documents piled up against the individual accused. The first accused, Farid Adam, easily reached his century with 118 exhibits. He was followed by the highest scorer, Lionel Bernstein, with 179 exhibits. Among the century scorers were Paul Joseph (134), Helen Joseph (145) and Aron Mhlongo (127). TX Makiwane missed his century by only one exhibit. The lowest individual scorer was B Hlapane with only five exhibits.

When a heavy downpour forced the court to adjourn, the bulletin announced, 'Heavy rain stopped play.'

We used the telephone sparingly because it was expensive – Fathu usually telephoned me after eight at night when the rate was cheaper. At times she telephoned earlier so that the girls could speak to me, Shamim in intelligible sentences, Shehnaz in words she was just beginning to form, and Rashid just making gurgling sounds. I would wait for those calls. I did not telephone. I didn't want to burden my hosts any further. They were already exceedingly kind in giving me free board and lodging.

At times I waited for a call and it did not come, leaving me desolate, frustrated. Then Fathu's letter would complain of the frustration at her end:

> It is early, very early; outside there is just half light, deep dark blue; the milkman has not yet come, and a few early workers can be seen making their way to factories. The little boy is next to me gurgling happily and big sister Shamim has just got up. It is not yet 6 am. I ask the exchange if I can still put a call through at half rate. He says I can. He dials your number, your phone gives a strange ringing tone for quite a while. Shamim waits expectantly. I know you are near the phone, dozing or thinking of us, but your phone is out of order. My grip on the receiver tightens as if that would put the telephone right, but the telephone does not connect. Shamim smiles at me expectantly; but the phone is a case of 'ek nadie kê daw kunare, mil nê sê majboor' ['One river has two banks, but it is impossible

THE TREASON TRIAL AND THE FAMILY

for them to meet']. I live from fortnight to fortnight. There are just two periods in the month – your coming and your going. Shamim thinks you are in the phone and is upset when you don't talk.

I agonised when I expected a call and it did not come. I wrote to Fathu:

> Why have I to be punished this way? I have not slept a wink last night and now I can feel the usual nasty headache coming on. Last night Chota received two telephone calls from Pietermaritzburg, but I, the unfortunate one, none. Since Monday night, I have been waiting each night for your call and when it does not come, I console myself by saying, 'Fathu will perhaps phone me tomorrow' and the next night the same happens, now a whole week has passed with no letters and no phone calls. The trial itself is a big strain on me.
>
> The fact that my office cannot continue as usual is a source of constant worry. I miss you and the children so very, very much and then I don't even get a letter. Why should I have to suffer so much? Indeed, if I have done anything wrong please let me know, but don't punish me like this.

Then Fathu wrote and explained her own telephoning problems.

> My Ismail, I'm sorry I phoned so late last night. Obviously you were missing the children and wanted to hear their little voices as well. I thought of phoning you at 8.30 pm, but the operator said there was a two hour delay, so I thought I might as well phone you at 12.00 pm and save some money. The alarm was not working and I had taken it to Ritson Road to be fixed, so I remained in a half-sitting position with the light off, for fear that I might otherwise fall asleep and not be awake at 12.00 pm to ring you. I thought I'd make a fixed time call and have the operator wake me. I was told that would cost full rate plus fifty per cent. I am sorry about your pain. Try not to miss us too much.

Both Fathu and I kept an eye on our finances. Fathu was all for cutting down on household expenses, which averaged about £35 a month. She sent me regular accounts of her expenditure, even of money spent on odds and ends for the children. In March 1957, she listed: 'Food £14.2.2d, Clothing for self £4.0.0, Clothing for Children £2.3.0, Household Help £6.0.0, Petrol £3.1.0, Rent £7.0.0, Electricity £1.0.0, Telephone £1.0.0: Total Household Expenditure: £38.6.2d.'

MI, her father, enquired if the office was managing and if she had an adequate allowance. He offered to help. MI was once again coming to my rescue.

I was satisfied with Fathu's frugality, but she had ideas for further cuts. She sent me several proposals, the most drastic being that we give up the house and move in with her parents. As far as I was concerned that was unthinkable and entirely unnecessary. I wanted both office and home to be left intact when I returned.

She proposed selling our car and actually went around to garages getting quotes, but they were so low it depressed her; she also suggested retrenching some of the domestic help. I assured her that we had not reached anything near destitution, that we would continue our household as I had left it on my arrest. She, however, reduced the office staff by two, on the advice of Mr Hudson, and gave me the reasons for doing so. I agreed with her.

Fathu then started looking for employment. She went to the extent of offering to teach in a madressa, which worried me very much. Fortunately Leo Kuper offered her a job and, in the process, carved out a career for her in sociology. He offered her tutorials. The department had taken on five tutors that year, both white and non-white. She wrote to me happily: 'I have started my tutorials, seven a week, three at Sastri in the afternoons and four at City Buildings in the mornings. It boosted my ego considerably when students indicated their strong preference for me – 21 August 1957.' In the year that followed, she was the only one retained as a tutor and was later promoted to lecturer. But that was some time after the charge of treason had been withdrawn against me.

Fathu also wrote a woman's page in the *Graphic* but the owner, Kanabaran Pillay, never paid her, though he had undertaken to do so. He never paid me either for the reports I sent him on the trial. He replaced Fathu with Zainab Reddy. I was upset about this, but Fathu wrote to me that Zainab would contribute something new and different. I could not accept that Zainab would be better than Fathu. I thought she was being over-generous.

I advised her to concentrate more on creative writing.

The accused from the Cape gasped when Amos Nhlapo, a familiar comrade, took the witness stand. He had served in the ANC office in Kimberley and had been elected by the branch as a delegate to the annual conference in Bloemfontein. For all the trouble the prosecution took, Amos did not produce any incriminating evidence against anyone.

Solomon Ngubase was presented to the court with great expectation. The Crown prosecutor informed the court that the Crown would lead evidence of violence committed during the Defiance Campaign in 1952 in the Eastern Cape.

Ngubase testified that while the ANC leaders pretended to advocate non-violence, the volunteers in the Defiance Campaign were told to resist arrest and engage in violence. He claimed he had perpetrated violence as a volunteer and had taken part in burning down a cinema in Port Elizabeth. He further testified that the ANC had planned to obtain arms and ammunition from Russia, China,

India and the Gold Coast; that Messrs Sisulu and Bopape were to be sent to Russia to obtain ammunition and gunpowder; that the ammunition and the gunpowder were to be stored in the Transkei; and that all the Europeans in the Transkei were to be murdered in Mau Mau fashion. He also testified for good measure that the ANC conference had discussed the parentage of Dr Malan, and concluded that his father was a European and his mother a Hottentot! He claimed he had participated in writing the Freedom Charter together with Advocate Mall, Dr Letele and Dr Mji. He also claimed that he had the original draft in his possession. He accused Professor ZK Matthews of being a spy in the ANC who instructed him to commit violence.

Under cross-examination, Ngubase admitted that he had written to the magistrate of Kimberley and volunteered to give evidence. He also admitted that he had referred to Dr Letele a number of times because he was keen on getting his own back on Mrs Letele, who had testified against him in a fraud case in Kimberley. He further admitted he had asked Advocate Mall to appear for him when he was facing a charge in Durban, but Mall had declined to do so.

It was clear that Ngubase was motivated by revenge against members of the Congress movement. When asked to identify Dr GM Naicker, whom the witness said he knew well, Ngubase, after a careful scrutiny of all the accused, pointed out Accused No. 149, Mr Debi Singh.

'I am going to ask the Court to hold that all your evidence is a deliberate falsehood,' retorted Mr VC Berrange, counsel for the defence. Crown witness Solomon Ngubase had come from prison where he was serving three years' imprisonment for fraud to testify at the treason inquiry. He admitted that he had been a thief and a liar.

Under cross-examination, Ngubase admitted that he had lived a large part of his life in lies, that he had served a number of prison terms for criminal offences, and that he had committed other crimes for which he had not been convicted.

Ngubase had claimed to be a BA graduate of Fort Hare, but under cross-examination admitted that he did not have such a degree. He also admitted that in the past he had claimed to be a Bachelor of Science graduate and that he had practised illegally as an advocate, and had been imprisoned for doing so.

Ngubase burst Mr Liebenberg's bubble. He was the most absurd and unbelievable of all the state witnesses. There was no way his testimony could hold up in court, and the fact that the state used him as a witness was indicative of its bankruptcy in establishing its case.

The treason accused drew world attention; we found heavy demands made on our time by British, European and American visitors who wanted to see for themselves that we were normal human beings, not demented terrorists. Those of us chosen to satisfy such curiosity found ourselves working overtime. During the day we sat through the trial, in the evenings we attended the 'parade'. Debi Singh, Gopalal Hurbans, Chota Motala and I were often called up on this duty, but Chief Luthuli and Professor Matthews bore the brunt of it. They were worked the hardest. Yet those evening sessions were very important. They gave us an opportunity to meet interesting and influential people. Our input was also important to draw monies for our Defence and Aid Fund. It was during those meetings that we discovered the change that was taking place in Afrikaner thinking, led by such Afrikaner intellectuals as Professor Pistorious.

I met Anthony Sampson at one of those meetings. He wrote *The Treason Cage*, profiling eight of the treason accused and selecting me as one of them. It was also at one of these sessions that I had the opportunity of pointing out to the American ambassador that non-whites were never invited to their Fourth of July celebrations. 'I know why too,' I told him. 'If you invited Chief Luthuli or Dr Naicker, then your government guests would not come. But then you go on record as supporting apartheid.' The ambassador said he had never looked at it that way. I do not know how soon thereafter they changed their policy, but Fathu and I were included on their guest list after my discharge, and we enjoyed Consular hospitality both on big occasions and at small intimate dinners.

The tedium and the heat in the Drill Hall often had some of us nodding and dosing off, and day-dreaming. On one such occasion, I was picturing Fathu's promise – 'I'll close the door on everyone, put away the key on your briefcase, send the children away, put your head on my lap and run my fingers through your thick black hair' – when I was rudely pulled out of my reverie into reality by a statement that intruded into my subconscious.

'I read from my notebook from notes taken on 13 June 1952. "The time has come to shoot Malan."' The statement was attributed to Dr Naicker.

I was all attention. Dr Naicker usually read out his speeches; I often wrote them. Those were not words I could ever have written. They were not words Dr Naicker could ever have spoken. I moved to the front, to Berrange. I whispered to him that Dr Naicker could never have said those words and that he should examine the policeman's notes.

Berrange did just that and underlined the verb the police constable had used. He asked him to spell 'shoot'. He spelt it 'CHECK', as it was written in his notebook.

'So,' Berrange said. 'What you wrote here is not "The time has come to shoot Malan," but "The time has come to *check* Malan." That's what you wrote on 13 June 1952. Isn't that so?' The constable agreed. Who had doctored 'check' into 'shoot'? Could we accept that as just a mistake, or was there something very sinister here? Was the prosecution resorting to falsehoods in order to present us as a violent group in the absence of any evidence at hand to establish this?

We realised that if we were to be guaranteed accuracy and if we were to save the court time and speed up the legal process, we would have to pre-check and correct, if necessary, all documents submitted as exhibits. Berrange called on all the lawyers among the 156 accused to check the evidence. So we joined the forty-odd state attorneys and prosecutors to help them prepare their reports against us. Ironic as this sounds, if we had left the prosecution to blunder along helplessly, we would have been sitting in the Drill Hall forever.

My mind drifts from the trial to the pen-pictures Fathu paints of the children in words. In 1957 we had been married for six years and had three children. At the time of my arrest, Shamim, the eldest, was not yet three, Shehnaz had just begun to walk and Rashid was three months old. They were growing up without me. Fathu reminded me that Rashid had spent three-quarters of his life without me, Shehnaz half and Shamim a quarter. For herself? It was infinity. She was anxious that I should not miss out on their development. So she kept me abreast with their words and play.

I see them on the beach having their breakfast – Shehnaz and Shamim splashing in the water, Rashid playing boisterously in the sand; Shamim at her first ballet lesson, breaking out of her shell as she dances as a fairy and laughs up at the elves.

If I was not physically present to watch the children play their games, Fathu took me to them.

> Shamim put on shorts this morning and doffed an old hat and announced, 'I am the Pappa, Anushka is my wife.' 'And me?' Shehnaz asked. 'You are our child.' I went to teach and when I returned I found that Shehnaz had had enough of step-parenting. She rushed to me with all her complaints. 'Anchuchu punch me, I'm not Anchuchu's child. I am your baby.' Later while we played on the bed she said, ever so sweetly, 'Anchuchu my friend,' and when Anushka came she made amends for Anushka's failure to say sorry to her. 'Anchuchu, you my fliend. You punch me that time, you say sorry.'

Shehnaz begins to speak during my absence. Fathu wrote in May:

> Shehnaz is beginning to talk. She smiles and her cheeks plump up, and her two front teeth peep out as she pushes out the words, 'My Pappa say how you Shehnaz? You all right? Bring you lucky packet,' and she nods her head vigorously

in confirmation of the lucky packet and in celebration of her speech. She is now Shenoo, not Shehnaz.

She is grown up now. She accepts that I have to leave her to go to work. That crying and clinging is over. I don't have to perform the disappearing trick. She now says, 'Mummy go teach. Sheyna say Mummy goobye.'

She saw a photograph of you in which you appear. She said, 'Ook! (look) My Pappa moking (smoking) ieglet (cigarette).'

I see Shehnaz at her first visit to the bioscope through Fathu's words, spellbound as she watches the Three Ring Circus, and pleased with her new bioscope-going status.

Shehnaz appears to be the most demanding of our three children. Fathu writes that her personality is already imprinted.

On our journey back from Dundee, she wouldn't allow Shamim near me; when after a great deal of patience Shamim protested, Shehnaz complained. 'Tamim (as she calls Shamim) mookow (her word for scold) me.' She lies on the bed next to me thinking of you and turns the thoughts into a song, 'pup-pa, pup-pa', then her mind turns to Rashid and she sings, 'Sid (Rashid) pity (pretty) boy.' Then she rolls over onto the sleeping Shamim and transferring the offence to Shamim complains, 'Tamim kick.' Shamim accidentally pushes the door and Shehnaz suffers a slight injury. She retaliates by biting Shamim's finger. Shamim cries and threatens to tell Pappa and Shehnaz adamantly declares, 'Minch (my) Pappa! Not yours! Minch, minch, minch Pappa!' and stamps her little feet and claws Shamim's face. If you ask Shehnaz whose baby she is, she says, 'Haf (half) Mummy, haf Pappa.' I take her in my arms and cradle and sing to her. She commands, 'Don't sing, talk!'

Another witness takes the stand. There is nothing significant in his testimony. I am engrossed in another letter:

The girls are beside me, scratching on paper. I offer to write for them. Shamim declines the offer and says she will write her own letter; Shehnaz copies big sister and says, 'Me lite my own self,' and the two of them scratch away. So while I write, they 'write' alongside me, on the bed, their writing paper on their bags, their pencils making big scraping noises. Shamim is drawing you a man. She says she is making funny people. Shehnaz just scratches and then complains, 'Me can't do like Tamim. Tamim draw funny people.'

Shehnaz is finding life very trying at the moment because she wants to do everything Shamim does but can't and is frustrated. Her moment comes when Minnie 'borrows' the Hansa baby, Farida, fat and placid. She sits quietly on

Shehnaz's lap, her face bigger than Shehnaz's and for the first time in her life, Shehnaz has someone she can control and mother, unlike Rashid who pulls her hair, makes big noises and is forever rolling and crawling. 'I like you Fatieda,' she says. Shamim observes, 'Farida is white like you mummy and I am like Pappa.'

Close to me is a silent, very small, very pretty little girl who looks at me with big unblinking, brown eyes and in those pools, I see you. In her own room, fast asleep, an independent soul cuddles in her Basuto blanket we gave her on her birthday. In the front room, fat and firm, with restless arms and restless legs, is your son.

I come home and Shamim asks me how I have come. I tell her in Pappa's car and she is all excited. I tell her my Pappa's car, not your Pappa's, and she loses interest.

I am cuddling and kissing Shehnaz. Shamim objects. 'Why you people doing that?' 'Don't you like me to kiss Shehnaz?' I ask.

'But you must kiss me too,' Shamim demands. It took her a long time to complain that I only carried Shehnaz who monopolises me. I was waiting for this complaint. For all Shehnaz's helplessness and innocence, she knows how to get all the attention she desires.

Rashid at six months competes with Shehnaz to be carried by me, and when Phoowa or Sharda calls him and he is in my arms, he turns his back on them.

Shamim adores Rashid and often mothers him. She fondles him and is very patient with him when he pulls her hair.

I wish you were here to help. I am trying to write to you. I have Rashid and Shehnaz, both demanding my attention simultaneously. Rashid is crying. Shehnaz is demanding. I hand over Rashid to Sharda and take her outside. She points to the star filled sky. 'Ditch all starch' (This all stars). Then she thinks of you. 'How Pappa dive (drive) mococar (motor car)?' And she laughs happily.

Fathu takes them to the bioscope and returns exhausted, vowing never to take them again. 'They gave me such a hard time, especially Shehnaz who has learnt to be a big nuisance.'

In July I am cold and sick and I write to Fathu: 'It does not matter how many warm clothes one wears, nothing seems to help.'

Fathu reminds me that Eid is around the corner, and she wants to know my plans. I write to her that I want her to join me in Johannesburg since I cannot come to Durban. I had thought Violaine could drive her up in the Volkswagen. 'But our darlings must have you on Eid. They must not be left without both of us. How will the farishtas [angels] come? And who will report to me their expressions in the morning when they see what the farishtas have brought them? Then I want you to take the plane to Johannesburg in the afternoon so we can be together. Don't worry about the expenses, we can afford them on an occasion like this.'

MI had introduced farishtas in lieu of Santa Claus in his and AI's families, and the children – Fathu and her siblings – had looked forward to the presents they brought on the two Eids. We continued the custom in our family.

Fathu spends a few days with me in Johannesburg. She attends the Treason Trial. We lunch at Plantos, on food Solly Nathie has brought from Evaton. That evening we are invited to dinner at Nelson's home in Orlando. His mother has cooked a special dinner. She is our host, the head of the household, and she serves us with gracious and loving care. We retire to talk on the convertible couch, below a portrait of Lenin, all fiery against a waving red flag. We discuss the trial, laugh at some of the prosecution's faux pas. There is a serenity about the evening. We are happy.

Fathu returns. Her letters continue.

> Violaine insisted I take the girls to see John and Julie but Shehnaz fell asleep, so I took Shamim, Myna and Pam. We returned home to a very angry Shehnaz. Why had we left her out of the party? Why had we not awakened her, or taken her, sleeping!
>
> Shamim learnt today that a dream is not reality and she was disappointed. When she got up this morning, beside me, I told her that I had dreamt about you. 'Your Pappa came in my dream last night and he brought a parcel.'
>
> 'What was inside?'
>
> 'An umbrella for you.'
>
> 'Where is it?'
>
> 'The umbrella is not here, it was in the dream.'
>
> She looked at me for a while, thinking it over in her little mind. Then a smile of enlightenment broke on her face and she said, 'We will write to Pappa to bring the umbrella here.'
>
> On Sunday night after Shamim fell asleep, I put her on the other bed, leaving Shehnaz next to me. She was most cross in the morning and refused to come to me on my bed and kept up a silent obstinacy for almost fifteen minutes. She had a case. She had told me expressly before sleeping that she wanted to sleep next to me. She says when you come she'll sleep in her bed but when you are away she wants to be next to me.

Fathu rarely complains, but in one letter in May she apologised for not writing, 'but this is not due to negligence, it is a reflection of my rather occupied state'.

> On Monday I found the children in a state where they wanted more attention from me. They were missing you and so my whole day was spent in fussing over them

and playing with them. And you know our children, Ismail, they're not a lot to sleep early. I was so exhausted, I would have fallen asleep before them had they let me.

Tuesday was a long day for me. I had my tutorials and there was an extra one I had to do.

Wednesday, I worked on the car. I cleaned it and then made the best arrangement I could for compounding and polishing. It has to look good if we are to get a good price for it. There is also some touching-up of the upholstery. Apart from the car, the lounge is in a mess. Wednesday being my only free day, I also concentrated on the lounge. The afternoon found me busy again with an extra tutorial and then I had to come home and put in a lot of time preparing a lecture. Today I have a lecture at 6 pm, a favour to Mr Njesane and after opening my fast at Ritson Road, I'll be off to City Building; I will leave the children with my mothers for an hour and then we'll all go home.

Shamim got up this morning and wanted to know if I would buy her her teddy bear today. I tell her yes. She asks which shop will we buy it from. I tell her Stillers.

'Which shop is that?' she wants to know.

'You know where your Pappa's station is? You know where they sell flowers?'

She knows the shop and there is a happy smile on her face. She wants to know what kind of teddy bears there are in the shop. I say I don't know what kind.

'But you said you knew the teddy bears there.'

I told her that that was a long time ago.

'Yes, but what kind of teddy bears? How big?'

I tell her she should choose a teddy bear she could carry. She indicates with her arms. It seems big to me, bigger than she can manage. I tell her she should choose a smaller one. She says she wants a teddy bear as big as Yakub.[6] Yakub is huge, almost as big as herself.

At Stillers, there were two huge teddy bears lying on their backs on a top shelf. I thought she would never see them and tried to direct her attention to smaller ones near at hand. She wasn't interested. She knew exactly what she wanted. She looked around, about and up, and spied the two fellows on the top shelf and her face lit up and she pointed to them excitedly. The shop assistant smiled and took down one of the big fellows and held him up against Shamim.

Shamim clapped her hands and said, 'This is the one I want Mummy!' and tried to carry him. He growled as he bent over and after that, there was no getting him away from her. So I ordered him, and parted with all of £2.6s.3d.

The assistant took away the teddy for wrapping. What anxiety when Teddy was not returned immediately. She was convinced we hadn't bought him.

'You said we are buying it from Stillers. Now you are not buying it!'

I reassured her that we had indeed bought her teddy and she should just be a little patient, but she went up the stairs to see if the teddy was still there. Just then, the attendant brought the big fellow.

And now Shamim wanted to go to Ritson Road as quickly as she could to show off her teddy bear. What excitement from the children there. Teddy was shown to all the grown ups. Teddy was taken next door to the Asmals.

'When will Baby and Farida come?' Shamim clammered. She couldn't wait to show them her teddy; and 'When will Gorie come?' She stayed over at 84 that night in the hope that Ahmed would come from Kranskop in the morning and she would show him the teddy.

I told Shamim our house had white ants. She corrected me, 'This is not our house. You said we borrowed it. You said you'll give it back when we have our own house.'

The house plans were ready. Alan Lipman, our architect, has given her six sets of specifications and working drawings. The first contractor has quoted £4500. He thinks we could get a cheaper quote.

The house we were renting had grown too small for us. We had bought a plot of land and had encouraged the Bhugwans to buy a plot adjacent to ours. We had engaged Alan to design both the houses, but Alan had concluded that only one house could be built on the two plots since the frontages were too small. The Bhugwans had graciously offered us their plot. Fortunately they found another plot of land and Alan designed their house as well. Indians did not get building society loans in those days. We succeeded in getting a loan, but when the society learnt of my treason charge, they withdrew it. The loan was reinstituted after Leo Kuper stood guarantor for the treason trialist.

The house building was progressing. Fathu was attending to everything herself. She was working closely with Alan Lipman, seeing to the passing of the plans, supervising the digging of a hole to find out if there was sufficient seepage for a septic tank and attending to building society deposits. The specifications for the house were ready, and she had given out the plans on tender to several builders.

> Two-thirds of our children are not well; the one-third behaves reasonably but scolds Sharda because she restrained Anushka, 'Eh, why you hit my fliend?'
>
> Rashid is irritable. He appears to be on the brink of putting out a lot of teeth. Poor, good, big daughter has been running very high temperatures, she smiles up at me. Teddy bear, big and yellow, sleeps next to her. We are expecting Dr Davidson. She complains now and again. 'Doctor is taking so long.' She is such a good child. She asked for jelly and custard and ate it all. Rashid is off food and milk. Rashid had his anti-diphtheria and tetanus and whooping cough injections. He was wonderfully behaved, never cried, smiled all the time. He is a lovely baby. We exchange quiet looks, then he smiles ever so sweetly, a bit serious when

confronted with strange things, but otherwise wonderful, so like you. He had his first visit to the barber. Ahmed took him to the family barber, Sulieman. We discussed the style. Ahmed suggested a Yul Brynner, teasingly. The barber gave him a Tony Curtis.

More letters, more news of the goings-on at home. Violaine and the Kupers are keeping close contact.

> Hilda insisted on cooking me a birthday lunch despite my protests. Violaine took the children to see the Rag procession and joined us at a picnic.
> Violaine came on Friday evening at about 8 pm, frisky and drunk from a cocktail party at the American Consulate. She looked lovely in a white dress and matching hat, but for a while quite unmanageable and unpredictable. Then she settled down and talked about John, how she had been waiting for him for the last six months; she couldn't make him out, did she look sexy in her white ensemble? I reassured her she did, which was true. I had seen John earlier that evening. He had gone to Verulam and taken the car. He had come to return it and said he had been very hurt by Violaine because she had not phoned him for four days. I told her this. She said they had gone to a party together and danced through to the wee hours of the morning. Violaine is in love and wants to know if I experience being in love the same way as she does. I don't know how she feels but I know how I feel. When I think of you I overflow with warmth and feel tender and good towards everyone, pure and honest in myself and extend those feelings to all around me.

This is the first time I have had being in love defined to me, though her letters often brim with her love for me. 'Loving is not a habit,' she writes, 'it rejuvenates.

'Martin [Russell] came to see me. He was all in a knot about his wife and Margo. He feels happy and free with Margo. He no longer loves his wife. He loves Margo but he is overcome with guilt at depriving his son of a father.'

She writes about a meeting of Defence and Aid and the tension between the Congress of Democrats and the Liberal Party: 'Violaine read out names on the Natal Working Committee. Margaret Hawthorne[7] walked out in protest because no members of the COD were included in the list. Vera [Ponnen] joined her in loyalty, but Michael [Margaret's husband] remained and listened to Violaine who, almost in tears, explained the difficulty she had in getting even the ANC and NIC represented on the committee.'

Fathu attended a party at Violaine's, where John commented, 'Fatima looks so beautiful tonight, like a film star stepping out of a film magazine.' I felt so proud to read that. I wish I was there accompanying her.

Fathu went to Perumal's school with Shamim and Shehnaz. 'Mr Perumal telephoned early in the morning and asked if I could please address his pupils on courtesy, it was courtesy week. He said something like he had forgotten and this had to be done in terms of the syllabus. I told him it was impossible. I had a tutorial at 10 am. He said I would be finished long before that. He sounded as if he was in real trouble and wanted me to save him at the eleventh hour.'

I think of paunchy Mr Perumal, walking his dog in the morning. His bulldog was also paunchy. I remembered remarking to Fathu, 'Dog owners and dogs look alike; they take on each other's appearance after a while.' Fathu had laughed and at the same time rebuked me for making fun of Mr Perumal.

I suppose she was making amends for laughing at Mr Perumal, and so dressed Shamim and Shehnaz and drove to Umgeni Primary School with Sharda.

> Mr Perumal came to receive us at the car and suggested the children join me. Chairs were put out for them alongside mine on the veranda, which is on a higher level overlooking the ground where the children were assembled, fresh-faced and neatly clad in their uniforms. I was speaking through a hand mike. Shamim sat demurely, respectful of the proceedings. Shehnaz started off well, but as I was developing my theme and had the pupils' attention, she started, 'Cally me Mummy, cally me!' I tried ignoring her but her demand persisted, increasing in volume. I picked her up with my free hand and rested her on my hips. 'There's no courtesy here,' I quipped, trying to make a joke of the disturbance, and the children laughed appreciatively. 'You are older, you understand the need to be courteous. She will do so too when she gets a little older.' The children clapped. Shehnaz had succeeded in intruding into my speech.

Now how can one attribute motivation to a two-year-old?

They had a family gathering at Reservoir Hills. Fathu writes:

> The night is cold, the fires warm and little flames sparkle gently in the grates laid out in a row on the lawn. The sky is clear, slightly flaked with fleece clouds. No moon looks down, no stars peep through. The sky is black and cold. But we sit snug in the hollow of the rock garden, our cheeks aglow with the tender heat of the smouldering coals, our appetites growing keen as the smoke gently wafts the fresh crisp smell of sizzling meat. The children are warm in their pyjamas and gowns, Rashid looking like Henry VIII, is passed on from arms to arms. He is much in demand.
>
> AI, EM, AM, AC, my father are all here. Someone says Ismail is not here. Someone adds, 'He is especially fond of family occasions,' and another voice

adds, 'We miss his spirited organisation.' But you are here in your wife and your children.

It is teatime at the Drill Hall. The international press coverage on the accused: they want to know how we feel, how we see the future. Those who speak, speak for all of us when they say, 'We see the treason arrests and the court proceedings as a challenge to democracy. We are not intimidated. We believe our cause to be just. We are winning more and more friends, even among the Afrikaner *volk* [nation], and we believe we are influencing both blacks and whites with the justness of our cause.'

I don't think that any treason trial anywhere in the world has had the volume of coverage ours has. Barbara Castle, a columnist for a British journal, who was later promoted to a cabinet post in the Labour government, has come to get a first-hand account of the treason proceedings. She wants to give her readers an intimate, first-hand account of the trial and of racism in South Africa. On the advice of the accused she books two seats over a Friday and Saturday at the theatre and cinema; then, accompanied by an African accused, she sets out to take up the bookings. As expected, her companion is refused admission. They also visit a night club and church on Sunday, and are barred entry there as well.

There are streams of journalists and they ask all sorts of questions. I send reports to the *New Age*, the *Indian Opinion*, the *Indian Views*, the *Graphic* and the *Leader* on a weekly basis. Though the latter two promised to pay for my columns, they never did. I was out of pocket for the postage paid, but my satisfaction was in the coverage given to the trial.

I am friendly with one of the prosecutors, appropriately named Van der Merwe. He bad-mouths the state because he has heard that the state has employed the former MP Oswald Pirow at R30 000 per month. Rumour or fact, there is considerable tension among the attorneys and prosecutors who are being paid a fraction of that. Van der Merwe asks me to point out 'JB Marx'.

I point out JB Marks, secretary of the Mineworkers Union. 'Why are you so interested in him?' I ask.

'All the books we confiscated are written by him,' he said. 'He must be a very clever man.' Marks and Marx had become one in Van der Merwe's mind.

We drew our amusement from simple events and simple statements.

The Natal treason accused made good progress in Afrikaans. But it took some time for them to realise that the signboard 'Hou Links' [Keep Left] was not the name of a street. Dr Motala returned to the Drill Hall one lunch hour after his shopping, sporting a new pair of 'goggles'. He looked most impressive. The 'goggles' caught our president Dr Naicker's fancy. He asked Dr Motala where he had purchased them. Dr Motala, in all seriousness, told Monty he had made his purchase in a shop on 'Hou Links' Street. The next day Monty was still without goggles – he could not find 'Hou Links' Street as every street in Johannesburg bore the sign 'Hou Links', beckoning the motorist to 'Keep Left!'

It was during the Treason Trial that I discovered that Chief Albert Luthuli was not only a national and international hero, but also an underworld hero.

One day, while walking to the back of the Drill Hall, I spied Mac the Master in comfortable attendance. I had got him off once on a charge of receiving stolen goods. I was curious to know what he was doing at the Drill Hall. He said he had become a changed character. He was a great supporter of Chief Luthuli.

'For whom has he written his book *Let My People Go*?' asked Mac.

'For the people,' I said.

'Exactly!' he replied. 'And how are they to buy the book at £2.2.0d at the CNA?'

I agreed they could not afford the price.

'We have 600 copies, Mac said gleefully, 'and we are selling these to our people at two shillings and six pence. Good, eh!'

I could see how impressed he was with his own contribution to the freedom struggle! He proceeded to tell me how his organisation had changed.

'You remember the Chinese shop at 88 Orlando? I was arrested for the stolen goods there. You know I was innocent.'

I had no such knowledge, but I did not contest the point.

'Now we are very clever.' Then, lowering his voice and assuming a conspiratorial tone, he said, 'Look, this trial is going to go on for a long time. I have some unwrought gold. You need the money. How about it?'

I thought, here I am charged with treason; I am being asked to add a charge for dealing in illegal gold. I smiled and shook my head.

'What about other things?' he persisted. 'We have everything for you at very much lowered prices. You want radios, come to shop so and so in Orlando. You can get furniture at a quarter of the price in shop XYZ. Here, we have a catalogue.'

Mac produced catalogues listing a whole range of furniture at greatly reduced prices. Mac the Master said they no longer stole and then tried to get rid of the goods – they now stole on order!

The firm of Mandela and Tambo, or the other way round, had opened their offices in Chancellor House. The Pahads lived in Orient House close by. The two partners deposited their daily earnings in the safekeeping of Amina Bai Pahad before banking it the following morning. Pride of place in the Pahad home was a huge portrait of Chief Luthuli. One day while Amina Bai was alone at home, some burglars raided her flat. They tied her up and went about their business. Then their eyes fell on the portrait of Luthuli.

'Who is that?' they asked.

With local qawalis (singers) at the Jama Masjid, Delhi

Getting to know Indians in India, 1979

Nelson Mandela and I, 1991

With Joe Slovo and Alfred Nzo at our home, 1991

At home, in Burnwood Road, 1991

With Fathu, circa 1991

With our daughter Shehnaz and our grandchildren in Cape Town.
Nadia is on Fathu's lap, Khiyara on sister-in-law Zubie's Lap

Family picture, 1994. Back row: Rashid, Nadia (Shehnaz's daughter), Shehnaz and Maia (Shamim's daughter). Front row: Zen (Shamim's son), myself, Shamim, Fathu with Shehnaz's daughter Ayesha on her lap, and Khiyara (Shehnaz's daughter)

Members of the Sastri College Alumni

Inauguration of Resistance Park, Durban, 1996

With JN Singh, Dr Goonam, Kathy and TS Maharaj, 1996

Being hooded on receipt of honorary doctorate in law (LLD)
at the University of Natal, 1998

Fathu and I with Shamim and Shehnaz in our living room, Burnwood Road

Waiting in the VIP room with guests – including Dr and Mrs Beyers Naudé – during Nelson Mandela's eightieth birthday, July 1998

My eightieth birthday celebration, 5 September 1998. Fathu helps me blow out the candles. Shehnaz and our grandchildren, Nadia and Zen, look on

With Michael Sutcliffe at home, September 1998

'My father,' she replied.

The burglars did an about-turn. They untied Amina Bai.

'This is the wrong address,' they said, and left.

THE STAR WITNESS

The state was setting great store by expert witness Dr Andrew Murray, professor of philosophy at the University of Cape Town. He attracted a lot of attention. The public gallery was full to bursting point on the day he began his evidence. Apart from the usual media personalities there was Dr Dadoo, Professor Hansie Pollak, Dr Ellen Hellman and other academic and political notables. All were in expectation of the wisdom he would impart to help the state, once and for all, prove its case and put all of us hopefully to death, or at least behind bars for life.

Professor Murray was in the witness stand for ten hours. He claimed that he was an expert on Marx, Lenin, Stalin and Mao Tse-tung. His key theory was that communist rhetoric was characterised by such words as 'fascism', 'oppression', 'democracy' and 'militant'. He further said that communist structures included youth and women sectors, and that the ANC constitution was shot through and through with communist rhetoric. His stock response to extracts presented to him from statements and speeches made by the accused were 'out and out communistic', 'straight-from-the-shoulder communist'.

Professor Murray propounded on the concept of 'aesopism', which, he claimed, had been developed by Lenin, in terms of which everything communists said had the opposite meaning. When communists talked of non-violence they meant violence. Several speeches were presented to him, one of them being mine.

Monty Naicker had issued a press release of the keynote address I had given at the Natal Congress of the People in 1954. The Special Branch had found a copy of that press release while raiding the Congress of Democrats' office in Johannesburg. The prosecution now used this speech as incriminating evidence and placed it before the expert witness for analysis and interpretation. I was all ears and attention.

Detective Sergeant G van Papendorf, of the Johannesburg Security Police, took his stand in the witness box to hand in documents confiscated by the police in the raid on the Johannesburg offices of the Congress of Democrats.

PAPENDORF: Your Worship I confiscated this document in the Johannesburg office of the Congress of Democrats.
PROSECUTOR: Your Worship will note that this document will be marked and referred to as Exhibit C93 and will the witness further identify the document?
PAPENDORF: It deals with the Natal Congress of the People held in 1954 and it bears the name of accused MP Naicker as having issued it in his capacity as

the Organising Secretary of the Natal Indian Congress. It is headed 'Speech delivered by IC Meer – the keynote address on the Freedom Charter to be adopted in 1955'.

I recalled that meeting. The hall was flooded with the Special Branch. Berrange was on his toes.

BERRANGE: The defence requires the entire document to be read into the record and not merely handed in.
PROSECUTOR: Sergeant Papendorf will you read the contents of Exhibit C93 into the record.
PAPENDORF: Mr Meer said that the leadership had repeatedly stressed two cardinal points in their campaign. They were that non-violence was the basis of all campaigns and that there was to be no hatred towards the whites.

In his address Mr Meer said: 'When we are launching another great campaign, let me stress that we are not advocating any form of violence. Anyone who talks of or engages in violence is the enemy of the people. Even if we are provoked then too, there must be no violence on our part, because those who engage in violence will be harming our cause and they can have no place in the peaceful campaign we are initiating.

'I have to stress this point, not because I have any doubts on how our people will behave, but because of the sinister propaganda which people in high places in the government of the country are carrying out and will carry out against the freedom movement in South Africa.'

Mr Meer continued: 'It is our task to enshrine the hopes and aspirations of the people of South Africa into this Charter of Freedom. That is the objective of the Congress of the People – a specific and well-defined objective.'

He added that there was always the danger of nationalism taking a narrow and bigoted path, as Afrikaner nationalism had done in South Africa. One would have to guard against a black nationalism preaching in the reverse what the Nationalists were preaching today.

'Fortunately,' said Mr Meer, 'the ANC was not narrow and bigoted; it had called on South Africans of all races and colours to come together in formulating a Freedom Charter, a charter which would prevent the emergence of bigoted nationalism on the part of the liberation movement of the oppressed people of the country.'

Professor Murray analysed my Kajee Hall speech as a typical example of Marxist double-talk to say one thing but to mean the opposite. 'Meer was exhorting his audience to violence though he focussed on non-violence. The repeated use of non-violence, was the repeated exhortation to violence!'

Berrange was brilliant in his cross-examination. After listening to a score or so of other extracts and Professor Murray's standard response to them, Berrange read out a passage from a book. Murray's interpretation, as expected, was 'out and out communistic'. When asked if he recognised the author, he said he couldn't be sure. Berrange said, 'I am sure. It is an extract from your own book. The communist author is you yourself.' That took the wind out of Professor Murray's sails.

His evidence did untold harm to his academic reputation. I didn't follow his career, but if I had been the principal of the university, I would have ended his appointment there and then. There was, in our time, a tremendous aura about professors. Murray contributed towards dimming that aura.

I wrote to Fathu:

> I am thoroughly fed up and tired with this lousy Johannesburg. The Drill Hall is getting on my nerves. There is this fantastic nonsense of the cheesa army. The whole day was spent on this cheesa cheesa business. I don't know why the crown should have decided to lead this evidence. I'll do anything in the world to have you with me. I have never missed you as much as I miss you now.

The seriousness and dullness of the proceedings were temporarily replaced with uncontrollable laughter when a detective sergeant handed in two placards seized at the Conference of the Congress of the People at Kliptown as incriminating evidence: 'Soup with Meat' and 'Soup without Meat'. The police, with their exceptional thoroughness when it came to suspicions of insurgence, had even raided the kitchen of the Congress of the People!

The prosecutor, Van Niekerk, contributed to the entertainment when he produced an exhibit entitled 'The Hydrogen Bomb' with the kind of gusto that suggested he had actually pulled out a hydrogen bomb from the police raids. The magistrate calmly pointed out to him that it was only a documentary heading.

I turn to Fathu's letter. I am reading it for the third time. She writes: 'The children were very excited with my cards. They flashed them around. They are very pretty. I couldn't get them away from them to put them away carefully.' I'm so glad they liked them.

As I have stated before, until the Treason Trial we depended on our own people and our own local resources for funding. Even during the Treason Trial, the first monies were collected from local sources.

The Defence and Aid Fund indeed played a vital role by providing for the defence of the accused. If I remember clearly it gave a monthly grant of £11 or

R22,00 to each needy accused. Almost all the NIC and TIC members refused to take any money for themselves.

In Durban our women formed a committee headed by Marie Naicker, Fathu and others to raise funds, and Alan Paton was making the rounds among white advocates in the city for donations. Our women's group in Pietermaritzburg – consisting of Mrs D Bundhoo, Mrs Choti Motala and Mrs SRR Naidoo, among others – did magnificent work to raise funds.

The Defence and Aid Fund, headed by the Anglican Archbishop of Cape Town, Dr Geoffrey Clayton, was indispensable to our Treason Trial. Thus, though the 156 treason trialists never came to know the archbishop personally, they gave him glowing tribute when he died in March 1957. We were more au fait with Bishop Ambrose Reeves of Johannesburg, who had secured the services of Mary Benson as the secretary of the Fund. For a conservative like Clayton it was indeed a bold step to identify himself with the Defence and Aid Fund.

While our people were taking a keen interest in the welfare of the accused and their families, the work done overseas was equally impressive.

From London came the news that Canon Collins alone had raised the magnificent amount of £13 000, and in the United States of America, Mrs Eleanor Roosevelt had agreed to act as one of the sponsors.

Accused No. 84, Ike Horwich, found time to make the bust of our Monty Naicker. It was produced in bronze after a sitting of almost sixteen hours in all. Horwich came from Cape Town where he was an architect. Since the treason inquiry commenced at the Drill Hall, he had produced many interesting court sketches, which appeared in numerous journals in South Africa.

South Africa and the rest of the world were becoming familiar with our leaders.

The preparatory examination had commenced at the Drill Hall, Johannesburg, on 9 January 1957, and went on until 17 December 1957, when the charges against sixty-one of the accused were withdrawn.

The hearing resumed on 13 January 1958, and on 22 January the Crown called its last witness and closed its case. The Attorney-General added four more names to the list of those against whom the charge was withdrawn. Mine was one of the four.

I was particularly distressed about Chota, my constant companion and second cousin, with whom I had travelled to and from Johannesburg, often in his car, sometimes by train, and on rare occasions by plane. Now I left him, and my happiness was subdued by that thought and the fact that many of my comrades were still trapped in the case.

Ninety-two accused were left to appear in the Palace of Justice in Pretoria when the court reconvened in August. While I was greatly relieved not to be included in that prestigious list, I was sorry that the travail had not ended for the others, all of whom were as innocent as I, as the Palace of Justice in Pretoria would ultimately find in March 1961 when all of them would be discharged. Nor was the ANC proved to be a communist organisation, or the Freedom Charter a blueprint for a communist state.

The trial had continued for five years with enormous costs to the state and defence, and incalculable losses in the lives of the accused; some quite apparent, the greater part hidden, unobservable.

Having lost in their own law court – failing in their conspiracy to put 156 of us away for life for mobilising democrats against them to end their racist domination – the Nationalists now turned to legislative powers to emasculate and destroy us, but this too did not succeed. We were ultimately destined to overcome, but it would require far greater effort and greater sacrifices than we had envisaged. Both Fathu and I, though looking forward to being a family together, realised that we could not do so in isolation of the political struggle, and that struggle would be part of our family life. We had barely settled into our marriage when the Defiance of Unjust Laws Campaign was upon us.

POST-TREASON TRIAL

My relief and happiness at being reunited with my family was boundless, but short-lived.

After the Treason Trial a new spate of banning orders was issued, and I was once again banned. That, combined with my listing, affected my practice significantly. I was confined to the magisterial district of Inanda and Durban. I had a large practice in Indwedwe, and I had to sacrifice that.

The assault on my freedom of expression and movement changed my life. I was cut off from practically all my former activities. I was forced to resign from a number of organisations in which I was active, above all the NIC. I tried pursuing my political ideals through other channels, but in vain. One needed the historically established structures and their credibility. We held a very successful conference on franchise under the Ratepayers Association and we strove to develop that organisation as an alternative to the NIC, but it didn't work. The government did not have to ban the SAIC or any of its constituents: it had successfully rusticated its leaders and activists.

I turned my mind to other pursuits. Debarred from politics, I began to study religion and became particularly knowledgeable in Islam and Hinduism. I studied the Quran and the Vedas. I became much in demand as a lecturer in these scriptures. I gave a series of lectures to the Arabic Study Circle and became close to the Arya Samaj, a reformist Hindu group. Fathu, AI and I began studying the Quran. We sat with the major translations, Assad, Mohamed Ali and Yusuf Ali, and discussed the translations and commentaries of each. Fathu and I also developed a common interest in the religions of the world, and we concurred in our views. This gave us great pleasure, particularly because we so often differed in our political views.

I cultivated a keen interest in gardening and became a rosarian. I ordered rose trees from nurseries and travelled long distances to purchase them. I pruned them in season and fed them with compost and fertiliser. Zwelinye, our gardener, partnered me and became a rosarian himself.

As a listed person I could not prepare anything for publication; this included speeches. But the banning said nothing about impromptu speeches. I considered all my speeches as falling in the latter category.

With my 'rustication', Fathu became the prominent and active member of the family. She could publish, I could not. I supported her in her work and was both glad and proud that she threw herself into human rights causes and took up community issues. She established the Black Women's Federation in 1975, and was elected its first president. She founded the Institute for Black Research at her university. As my involvement in public affairs receded, Fathu moved more and more into the limelight, and soon I found myself being referred to as Fatima Meer's husband.

CULTURAL AND SPORTS BOYCOTT

The cultural and sports boycotts began in 1957. George Singh, Cassim Bassa and Dennis Brutus were some of the initiators. Fathu was among the earliest agitators against discrimination in the performing arts. She organised protests to pre-empt a cultural boycott, working closely with the NIC Youth Congress. Hassan Mall was secretary at the time. They wrote to artists intending to perform to 'Whites Only' audiences, and picketed them when they came, despite representations asking them not to.

Local producers, regardless of their political affiliation, also came under attack. Cecil Williams was attacked for staging his production at the Alhambra, which was for whites only, when he could have exercised the option of staging his play in a hall open to all, such as the Bolton Hall.

Ian Bernhardt of African Artists brought the musical *King Kong* to Durban and left the booking to the City Hall administration, which practised segregated seating arrangements for blacks and whites. He was very co-operative when the issue was raised with him, and all subsequent performances were at open venues.

FOURTEEN

SHARPEVILLE, THE STATE OF EMERGENCY AND THE BIRTH OF UMKHONTO WE SIZWE

1960s

State repression never subsided, for repression was the only means the state had to cope with the rising tide against apartheid and the mounting demands for democracy and equality.

The 1960s and 1970s stand out as decades of intensified state oppression. We as a family suffered refusal of passports, banning orders, detentions and bomb attacks. The inflictions were not confined to Fathu and me; they were also visited on our children. They were refused passports to travel and study abroad. Our youngest child, Rashid, was in addition banned, detained and excluded from enrolling at every educational institution in South Africa, even at UNISA, which is long-distance learning.

While state harassment and violence affected black people in general, it targeted some families more than others. We were just one among hundreds picked out for special attention.

SHARPEVILLE AND THE 1960 STATE OF EMERGENCY

In 1959, the ANC planned a massive anti-pass campaign, to begin on 31 March 1960 and climax on 26 June. The PAC pre-empted the ANC when it began its own passive resistance campaign against passes on 21 March. Pass-bearing Africans were asked to dump their passes at the nearest police station and defy arrest.

In Cape Town, the PAC had branches in Langa and Nyanga, where the conditions of Africans were worse than in other townships. On 21 March 1960,

2000 people marched to the police station and handed in their passes, stating that they would not carry them any more. By evening the defiers had swollen to 10 000 at Langa.

On the same day, in Sharpeville, Evaton and Vanderbijlpark, almost 30 000 demonstrators marched to police stations and dumped their passes. At Sharpeville the police opened fire, and within minutes sixty-nine people, including women and children, lay dead, 180 of them having been shot in the back while running from the shooting.

We were stunned by this barbarism; shock waves ran through the country and the world. It seemed to us that the Nationalists had gone mad and dug their own grave; they would not be able to withstand the international revulsion that gathered against them. But the Nats lived to see another day and another massacre, this time of children in Soweto in 1976, and it was not until 1990 that they were forced to call it a day.

Following the Sharpeville massacre, Chief Luthuli, Nelson Mandela and other executive members of the ANC made a bonfire of their passes, and followed this with a call for a national day of mourning and stayaway from work on 28 March. There was a resounding response to this call.

In Durban, the police carried out a beer raid in the largely shack settlement of Cato Manor. An enraged crowd retaliated and nine policemen lost their lives.

The Nats declared a state of emergency in the entire country, and mass detentions followed.

MY DETENTION

Fathu and I were disturbed in our sleep by the sound of cars pulling up in our driveway. I had developed a sixth sense about invading police. I opened the door of our bedroom leading to the balcony and, looking out of it, saw armed police running towards our house. I called out, 'Don't panic, I am here!' I went down the stairs, hoping to reach the door before they started banging and disturbing the children, but it seemed that banging on doors had become an involuntary reflex with them. The captain in charge announced they were taking me in, in terms of the emergency regulation. I was given time to pack some clothes. Fathu ran around helping me and at the same time reassuring the children. They were now older: four, five and seven. They were bemused and scared. Though the experience of police invading our house was not new to them – they had gone through my former arrest – this in no way protected them against the trauma of each new assault. The trauma remained the same, if not worse, from the knowledge of the previous assault. They did not cry, but I could see the panic on their faces. I kissed my family goodbye, not knowing when I would see them again. Fathu was, as usual, stoic, as she was expected to be.

We were taken to the Durban Central Prison where I joined Chief Luthuli, Monty Naicker, Dawood Seedat and others too many to mention. We didn't know at this stage how long we were going to be there. We knew that Roly Arenstein was bringing an urgent application for our release on the grounds that the emergency regulations had not yet been gazetted. We knew he would succeed and we would get a very short reprieve, but it would be sufficient to allow us to plan our strategy. We stood around tense in the bare cell.

As darkness settled in, we heard the guards approach by the clanging of their keys. Our cell door was opened and we were told we were free.

We decided that the rest of us would give ourselves up the next day, by which time nothing would prevent the government from detaining us.

We held hurried discussions and decided that Steven Dlamini, JN Singh, Monty Naicker, Kay Munsamy, Billy Nair and Roly Arenstein would not hand themselves in on the following morning as the rest of us would. They would go 'underground' and work; a tough task, but they accepted it unhesitatingly with a sense of duty and did not look back.

Fathu was waiting for me in our Volkswagen. She ran towards me, but even as I was getting into the car she saw Bertha Mkhize emerge from the women's prison, and impulsively ran back to embrace and greet her. I shouted after her agitatedly, 'We have to leave! They will arrest us!' and even as I spoke and she got into the car, Bertha was rearrested. They would have done better had they both got into the car than wasted time being chummy. Fathu and I spent the night with friends in Reservoir Hills. Her mother Bhaboo stayed with the children at our home. We did not risk using the telephone, certain it was tapped.

We returned home in the morning. Bhaboo informed us that, as expected, the police had come at dawn, interrogated her about our whereabouts, and when she claimed she did not know, they told her she was lying and shouted at her, frightening both her and the children.

I now had the task of telling the children that I would be going away for a while. They wanted to know where, and whether Mummy was going as well. I assured them Mummy would stay with them, that I was going to be in prison. 'You know the government is bad. They don't like me. They are afraid of me, so they will keep me in prison for a while, but it won't be for long.'

'And Mummy? They are not afraid of Mummy?' It was Shehnaz who asked the question. I brushed the question aside. 'Mummy has to look after you!' But Shehnaz made 'Mummy' feel that she had somehow betrayed the cause for not being arrested alongside me. We joked about it.

I made some hurried arrangements about my office, and then Fathu and I went to Attorney Abe Goldberg, requesting him to accompany us to the police station, where I would give myself up. Fathu looked at me somewhat despairingly as we said our goodbyes in the car; then both of us went into the police station, where I handed myself in and Fathu drove home.

The most distasteful part of imprisonment was the search for contraband hidden on one's body. They made you jump and dance naked as they probed your private parts in their search. I hated this assault on my person, which was also an assault on my personality.

I settled into a common cell with my fellow detainees. As during the Treason Trial, African and Indian detainees were imprisoned together in one cell, but our detained white comrades were separated from us. We slept on mats, on the floor. The mats and blankets had their portions of lice. We picked them off our bodies at night, and during the day put out our blankets and mats in the sun, hoping the lice might crawl into the light and stay there, but that is not the way of lice.

We were detained in a new block, in a general hospital ward, while new cells were under construction. The conditions were better; there was water-borne sewerage and showers. There were 100 prisoners in the cell, but the political detainees were a handful – Chief Luthuli, Ismail Gangat, NT Naicker and his brother MC, MB Yengwa and Stalwart Simelane. Billy Nair joined us some weeks later. He had gone underground but was picked up by Captain Swanepoel at Himalaya House.

Our families organised themselves into a 'Detainees Care Group'. MI sent us a crate of detective novels, and we were allowed to order food from the Goodwill Lounge. Fathu arranged with the owners, Pumpy and Namy, two utterly round, large-hearted brothers, to deliver the delicacies prepared by the families. Fathu took the food to the cafe and they delivered it to the prison, returning with the money the detainees paid for the food. During the sardine run we were served freshly fried sardines. Mrs Christopher – her son-in-law, Enver Hashim, was one of the detainees – sent us the most delicious chicken pies. Dawood Seedat's mother sent us purie pattas and samoosas. So each day we had some delicacy or other.

We were all in very good cheer. We organised our days so that there was time for serious discussion and for joking and laughing. Chief Luthuli presided over our formal discussions and debates. These were wide-ranging in subject matter. We discussed lobola and found the older men, the 'fathers' and potential recipients of lobola, in favour, and the younger men, the payees, in opposition. We presented papers on political ideologies and strategies – Marxism, liberalism, Satyagraha and capitalism. We discussed different religions and analysed our political struggles and histories. MP ran a wall newspaper and each day mapped out both internal and external happenings.

The warders, at first aloof, relaxed and grew friendly. They told us that our wives were demonstrating outside the prison, and that the colonel was getting very agitated. I learnt later that our wives had organised prayer meetings outside the prison on Saturday afternoons.

We were allowed two visits a week, and Fathu took every visit throughout my detention. Fathu wrote after our first visit:

> It was wonderful seeing you on Wednesday. You looked well and it did me good to know this. It was nice to hear you complain a little about the pillow and blanket. I came home last night to find your letter. It was such a surprise, the best I have had in memory. We have reached a position where we expect so little and so when little things like this happen, we really get jubilantly happy. Perhaps there is something in what the chief warder has been saying that it is good to be parted for a while.

She gave me news of the home front: 'Rishi [our dog] is growing. Baba [our part-time gardener] is helping me with the garden. The cannas have flowered vigorously. It would do your heart good to see the cassias. The mauve of the petra and yellow of the canary creeper frame our living room window prettily, but the flower beds below are empty. I will have them filled and blooming for your return.' She went on to report on her brother Ahmed's wedding. 'The new couple look very happy. All families seem very proud and satisfied, particularly at 84.' Shamim, now educated enough to write her own letter, gave me more news about the wedding. 'Shehnaz and I had on our off-shoulder dresses yesterday and took photos with the bride. And Rashid wore his long trousers and a white shirt and took photos, and in one of the photos, I was giving the bride the bouquet. On Saturday, we all went to Brighton Beach. There was a pool and no waves in it. Even Shehnaz was bathing in it. From your daughter, Shamim.'

I wrote to Fathu:

> I am getting down to study Zulu and have been finding it most interesting. I also attend classes in Afrikaans and perhaps soon I will write to you, at least a few sentences, in Afrikaans. We have made an attractive bookcase with apple boxes, two-tiered, and placed a potted plant at the centre of the top tier. It picks up our cell. Just above the bookcase, on the wall, is your sketch of the children ransacking the 'shop' – a top compartment of the wall-to-wall cupboard in our bedroom. On the opposite wall is my lovely girlfriend with her three admirers – Shamim, Shehnaz and Rashid. We are deeply grateful to all those outside who are helping us to make life bearable.

Each time Fathu came, I presented her with a list of our requirements. We saw her as the chief officer in charge of our comforts. We expected our orders to be executed promptly, and I am afraid I gave her a dressing-down when they weren't. Her other responsibility was to keep my office in Verulam running, and submit written reports on the cases coming in, the lawyers engaged and the fees collected.

We had a barber among us, and he ordered a complete set of barber's 'tools' so he could dress our hair expertly. I passed on the order to Fathu, and when she delivered the very professional-looking instruments, I accepted them quite casually and demanded, 'Where is the barber's coat?' She gave me an exasperated look, but said nothing. Much, much later, after our release, I heard her tell friends: 'I got those tools with great difficulty. I got no thanks. Instead I was asked, "Where is the barber's coat?" They really got very fancy in that prison.' It was said in good humour. But when I think of it in retrospect, I am ashamed of the demands I made on her and amazed that she so conscientiously responded to them.

Outside, Roly, Monty and JN decided that a week-long prayer meeting should be organised at Phoenix, during which Sushila Behn Gandhi should be asked to fast and a mammoth rally organised at the end of it. Fathu was directed to implement this, and she did so with the help of her women's group. The event was a huge success. I recall one visit when I blew my top off at her. I had been anticipating the visit the whole morning. Afternoon came. My colleagues were called up for their visits. I waited. I became anxious, wondering why Fathu had not come. Would she come? Had something happened to one of the children? Eventually I was called. By now my anxiety had reached its limits. It exploded on her. Fathu listened, not saying anything. I later received a letter from her in which she explained why she had been late, and I felt ashamed.

> I was very disturbed after seeing you yesterday. I'm terribly sorry for being late. Hassan Mall had to clarify certain matters with Mr Vahed about your Inanda case. I couldn't leave Mr Vahed in Verulam and rush to you. He had to be in Durban by 3.30, since he was leaving for Newcastle. Thus my delay. I know this is very trying for you. You have had more than your share of suffering. I understand it to some extent, but you alone experience its magnitude. This is a time when I should not add to your anxiety and I can hardly forgive myself for having failed you like this. If it is any consolation to you, on practically every other occasion I have been the first person outside the prison gate, often waiting an hour for the officials to arrange our visits.

I apologised to her for my bad temper. 'I am fully aware of my shortcomings and I can only say with all my heart that I love you very, very much, and that I will do my best to be a good and considerate husband.'

During one visit Fathu was accompanied by a beautiful young white woman, Brenda Magid. I don't know how Fathu came to befriend her. Fathu was running around in our Volkswagen at that point, and she had complained about the brakes, but was not doing anything about them. She drove to university daily on a steeply undulating road. Brenda assured me she would see to it that the brakes were secured, and she was as good as her word.

One of the warders was preparing for his exams and came to me for help. In exchange he said he would pass on letters from Fathu directly to me, and censor them after I had read them.

One day I got a distressing letter from Fathu. It had a familiar ring. It began with profuse apologies, holding me in suspense, and then dropped the bomb that she and her companions had been arrested!

The wives and children of the detainees had marched through Grey Street and turned into West Street en route to the City Hall, where they had planned to hand the mayor a memorandum asking for the release of their husbands. They were all arrested, detained for a few hours at the Smith Street police station, charged and then released. She had wanted our children to march with her, but they had been brought too late by her mothers. The other women had marched with their children and were arrested with them. She half-suspected her mothers had purposely delayed in bringing the children. I thought so too, and complimented them for their good sense. A police station was hardly the place for children. Fathu wrote that they were being defended by Advocate Shearer; Roly Arenstein had made the arrangements.

I pictured the march as she described it; I read out the letter to the other detainees. They were pleased that the women had protested. They heard more about the march from their wives when they came to visit them. Chief Luthuli said the women had to be commended for raising their voices and not sitting at home helplessly. Fathu need not have apologised so profusely. I could see her relief when I met her with a broad smile during her next visit, and not a grim face set to scold her for heaping more political trouble on the family. The other detainees complimented her and their visiting wives. I was so proud of her. I wrote to her, 'I don't think we have ever been as close to each other as now, nor has our love been so deep. I wish I had the capacity to tell you how deeply I feel for you, how proud I am of you, my beautiful wife.'

We were detained together with the prisoners arrested in Cato Manor following a beer raid and the killing of nine policemen. There was an altercation between a warder and one of the prisoners. The warder alleged that the prisoner had struck him and broken his spectacles. Our cell decided I should adjudicate the matter. The superintendent in charge accepted my offer to mediate. He was keen to settle the dispute and prevent it from going any further. The 'hearing' took about fifteen minutes. The prisoner alleged that the warder had kicked him and he had struck him in retaliation. The warder insisted that he had not kicked him deliberately; he had done so accidentally. The two men eventually accepted each other's explanation and apologised, and the matter was settled.

Children were not allowed in the prison, but an exception was made on Eid Day. Shamim, Shehnaz and Rashid came with Fathu and Bhaboo, all of them in their Eid fineries. Their lovely smiles disappeared momentarily when they saw me behind the grille. I think they had expected to run into my arms, all three together. But I joked about the grille, and they saw Dawood Seedat's children talking to their father and Fathu talking to me as if the grille was normal, and they relaxed and were soon prattling away, telling me lots of stories about the goings-on at Ritson Road – about Mota Pappa, as they called their grandfather, and their grannies, Nullie Ma and Amina Ma, about their new shoes and the Edie [money] in their pockets, and the film show they were going to in the afternoon. The time was over all too soon and we parted, they to go home, I to return to my cell, where I turned from the real to its representation. I looked at the phtograph of my family, engrossed in a book, and I was overwhelmed with a desire to hold and embrace them.

I wrote to Fathu:

> It was great seeing you with the children, but I must admit I felt very alone, and somewhat depressed after you left. I consoled myself with the photograph you left me. It is a charming photograph. Thank Ranjith Kally for it. I will again be at the grille during our next visit. Do not worry about me. I am adjusting to this situation. What else can this lover of yours say except that he loves you deeply and waits for the day when he returns home to all of you.

My cell mates helped me out of my depression. They teased, 'Ismail had a small meeting, but Dawood had a mass meeting with so many children.'

Fathu wrote how happy the children had been to see me:

> Their only complaint was that there were two bars. If there had been one bar they could have held your hand and perhaps even kissed you and hugged you. Phoowa asked Rashid if he felt sorry for you and he said no because you had told him that you were happy inside. They loved your letters and made me read their part again and again, all except your fat boy who said, 'Hopeless part. I don't like my part!' He has asked me to write and tell you that he is a good boy. You called him naughty. Shehnaz simply loved her part and grew shyer as she asked me to read it again and again.

We were released after three months. Before my detention I was fond of cowpeas, but cowpeas were standard fare in prison and I had lost my appetite for them. I arrived home to cowpeas curry. Fathu, in her innocence, was serving my favourite dish, or so she thought. I was enraged: 'I get back after spending three months in prison eating cowpeas and you give me cowpeas!' Fathu did not know what to do or say.

Later in the afternoon we went to Ritson Road, and my mothers-in-law noted my weight loss. I said I had lost 20 lbs in prison. As we were leaving, Shehnaz wanted to know whether I was going to the prison to find the £20 I had lost there!

THE TURN TO ORGANISED VIOLENCE

In the meantime the marathon Treason Trial lumbered on. By now the state had decided to proceed with the trial of thirty of the original accused; the rest would be tried later. Even while the trial proceeded, the thirty were detained under the state of emergency and brought to court while being held as detainees.

After more than four years, on 29 March 1961, one year and eight days after the Sharpeville massacre, the court delivered its judgment. The accused were *not guilty*. The prosecution had failed to prove that the ANC was a communist organisation, that the Freedom Charter envisioned a communist state or that the ANC had conspired to violently overthrow the state.

But the apartheid rulers were determined to hang on to power. The world's condemnation of the Sharpeville massacre and the collapse of the Treason Trial would not deter them from their course of more and greater repression. On 8 April 1960 the ANC and PAC were banned under the Suppression of Communism Act.

South Africa was trapped in a cycle of increasing repression by the state and a rising tide of militancy among the oppressed. This brought about a debate among us about the methods by which we could attain freedom. The matter began to be discussed in the different organisations that made up the Congress movement. Around August/September 1961, the national executive of the banned ANC met secretly on a farm in Groutville, Natal, under the chairmanship of Chief Albert Luthuli.

On the same night the Indian Congresses met in Tongaat. We were preparing for the issue to be discussed at the joint executives of the Congresses to be held the next evening.

Chief Luthuli had raised the matter with me and was deeply concerned as to whether we had exhausted all means of non-violent struggle. There were tense moments when the matter was discussed at the Indian Congress. Many of us had grown up under the strong influence of Gandhi with a deep commitment to non-violence. Others felt strongly that we had to shift to organised violence, while seeking to preserve the little space left for open protest by virtue of the fact that the Indian Congresses were not banned. Tempers frayed when those who expressed a commitment to non-violence were accused of being afraid to go to jail. Finally we agreed that we would go to the joint meeting with the ANC, as we felt that there was still the possibility of using non-violent methods of struggle, but that we would not stand in the way of the ANC if it decided otherwise.

The joint meeting took place at 8 pm at the beach house of the Bodasinghs, near Stanger. The debate continued through the night. Chief Luthuli, the president general of the ANC, presided. He opened the meeting by informing us that the executive of the ANC had met and decided to allow the formation of an organisation that would engage in violent forms of struggle. Despite this decision, he requested that members of the ANC executive feel free to participate and express their own individual views in the debate. This agitated some of those who were in favour of the turn to violence. One of them, from the Indian Congress, accused Chief Luthuli of being a pacifist, to which the Chief responded sharply: 'You steal my chicken in my yard and you will see whether I am a pacifist!'

The issues before the meeting were stark. Were we contemplating a shift to violence as an easy way out of the hard task of mobilising the people in the face of repression? Would resorting to violence lead to the neglect of the orthodox forms of mobilisation? JN Singh put the matter crisply: 'Non-violence has not failed us; we have failed non-violence.' It was a vigorous debate. By turning to violence would we not be giving the regime the excuse to come down on us even more heavily? Would we not be sacrificing the legal space that the Indian Congress, SACTU and the CPC still enjoyed? On the other hand, if we did not shift to violent means, would we not be failing our people by not harnessing their rising militancy and providing them with the leadership needed?

Nelson Mandela was unrelenting in championing the turn to violence. As dawn crept on us, we wrapped up the debate and endorsed the decision that the ANC had taken the night before. We had placed an enormous responsibility on Nelson Mandela. Our decision led to the birth of Umkhonto we Sizwe, which announced its existence in the midst of explosions that rocked South Africa on 16 December 1961. I felt we were moving into unknown territory, and could not help a feeling of disquiet in spite of the optimism of so many others. Little did I know that it would take more than three decades of struggle and twenty-seven years of imprisonment for Nelson Mandela before the birth of democracy in South Africa.

FIFTEEN

STUDENTS TAKE OVER

1970s

BLACK CONSCIOUSNESS

The period following the 1960 emergency and the banning of anti-apartheid political organisations had the effect of subduing black political activism for at least five years. Black Power and Black Consciousness then erupted on the South African scene, and the youth in particular were charged with a militancy that we had not known before. Our children, now university students, were heavily influenced by this militancy, and we as parents found for the first time that they no longer accepted our definition of their lives.

OUR CHILDREN

We had planned their education up to that point and guided them through the obstacles set up by the apartheid system. In 1957, when Shamim was ready for school, Fathu had the greatest difficulty finding a school that would admit her. I was in Johannesburg at the time as a treason accused. She wrote to me and told me how she and our small daughter trudged dusty roads going from school to school, seeking admission and suffering rejection after rejection. Mrs Morel, the principal of Dartnel Crescent, visited us at the Drill Hall and wanted to know if there was any way in which she could help. I mentioned Shamim's schooling problem. There was a small pause, then she said, 'Ask Fatima to bring her along and I'll see what I can do.' Fathu had already been to her and had come away with a rejection. I wrote a very tactful letter to Fathu. Mrs Morel was far from being her favourite person. Mrs Morel had tried to teach her mathematics and dismissed her as a 'cabbage'. I told her that she should go and see Mrs Morel for Shamim's sake. But she didn't have to. Shamim was offered a place at St Anthony's, which was our first choice anyway. In time all three of our children attended St Anthony's.

I took the children to school. The usual routine when I settled in with the family was for all of us to leave the house together each morning. I first dropped Fathu at the university where she was teaching at the time, and then the children at school, before driving off to Verulam. In the afternoon the children took the bus home. It took a while before I was able to buy Fathu her own car.

The girls enrolled at Durban Indian Girls High School, Fathu's old school, after completing their primary education. We wanted Rashid to attend Waterford School in Swaziland. He was given a passport to travel to the school and write the entrance exam. Neither Fathu nor I had a passport, so Val Brown, a close family friend, took him to Swaziland. He succeeded in gaining admission to the school, but was refused a passport to study in Swaziland. We then applied for a passport to Britain, and surprisingly he was given a passport for a year, restricted to the United Kingdom. He enrolled as a day scholar at King Alfred School and lived with Fathu's brother, Bhai. He returned at the end of the year to holiday and renew his passport. To our great disappointment, they refused to renew it. Rashid could not continue his studies in the UK. He enrolled at Sastri College, my old school. He matriculated there and went on to enrol in Fine Arts at the University of Durban-Westville (UDW). However, after his banning he was prevented from continuing his studies there, and instead he worked with Andrew Verster, who inspired him greatly.

By the time Shamim passed her matric and was ready for university, the Nats had completed their plan to establish segregated universities for each race group. Black students were prohibited from attending 'white' universities, except by special permission, in disciplines not available on the black campuses. Not wanting Shamim to go to the Indian university, we obtained ministerial permission to enrol her in architecture. That was a mistake. Shamim wanted to study social science. Fathu tried to have her transferred from architecture to social science, but the university chose to remain true to the government and, though already at the university, they declined to transfer her from one faculty to another. Excluded from Natal, Shamim enrolled at the University of Durban-Westville, but spent only one year there owing to student troubles. She completed her first degree at UNISA through correspondence, working at the same time as a social worker at the Durban Indian Child Welfare Society, and then with the aged.

Shehnaz wanted to study overseas but her passport application was refused. She completed her first degree, in law, at the University of Durban-Westville, and her LLB at the University of Cape Town, then went on to Warwick University in the UK where she obtained her master's degree in law.

Shamim, Shehnaz and Rashid were at UDW during a politically volatile period, and all three were strongly influenced by Black Consciousness.

Shamim and Shehnaz pursued their postgraduate studies at the University of Cape Town. Rashid pursued his postgraduate studies at Sussex University in Britain during his exile, where he obtained his master's degree in philosophy, and then went on to graduate in journalism.

The children lived with us almost to the end of their teenage years. We guided them as best we could, but left them to decide their own careers. Our home bubbled with young people while our children were with us. They came to party and some even to stay. The children rarely asked permission for the arrangements they made; it was their home.

I saw Black Consciousness as a radical movement, but I did not support its exclusion of whites; neither did Fathu, but as elected president of the Black Women's Federation, she abided by the democratic decision.

Steve Biko emerged as the most important black leader outside of system institutions. He came to see me and invited me to serve on the panel of honorary lawyers he was setting up for his South African Students' Organisation (SASO). I readily agreed to serve on the panel. Fathu was more involved with Steve Biko than I was. He had been her student at medical school and she shared political platforms with him.

Our whole family was devastated when he was killed during his detention.

TIN TOWN FLOODS

Nineteen seventy-six was a climatic year for the country and for my family. It began with the Umgeni River bursting its banks following heavy rains, and making the little community of 'Tin Town' homeless. Wet and desperate, they sought refuge at a school in Springfield. Fathu and I went out there and organised relief. We housed them first in community halls, then moved them into tents and finally prevailed on the government to provide them with permanent housing in Phoenix. Fathu headed the relief committee that was set up. Prior to the floods, she had been very active organising a national conference for women at which the Black Women's Federation was founded. She was elected its first president. The Black Women's Federation became very involved with the students, with Winnie Mandela, an executive member, playing a prominent role on the Parents' Committee set up in Soweto in defence of the pupils. In Durban, Fathu organised a protest rally. She was clearly too active for the comfort of the Nationalist government, so she was served with another banning order in 1976, this time for five years. She was forced to resign from the presidency of the Federation of Black Women and chairmanship of the Tin Town Relief Committee.

THE SOWETO PUPILS' REVOLT, 1976

The students' revolt burst onto our political panorama at about the same time as the Umgeni floods. In Soweto, high-school pupils revolted against the introduction of Afrikaans as the medium of instruction; the government opened fire on pupils marching peacefully. The racist army was taking on children: a child, Hector Peterson, was shot dead. His comrade, also a child, picked up his dead body as bullets rained around them.

Apartheid began its war on the black youth. Student demonstrations became the order of the day on black campuses, and students began to be rounded up and placed in detention. Our son Rashid was one of them.

RASHID, FATHU AND BOBBY ARE ARRESTED

They came, as usual, at dawn on a July morning in 1976; not for me this time, but for our son. I congratulated him. 'I am proud of you,' I said, as they bundled him into their car. For that he received a few extra kicks, he told me later.

For a fortnight we went through the agony of not knowing where he was. Then we were told he was being detained at the Wentworth police cells. We could see him and take him pre-packed food. We visited him and found him cheerful, and that comforted us. When we retired to bed that night I said to Fathu she had escaped detention because of her banning order. We missed Rashid, but I comforted myself that Fathu was safe beside me in our bed. I dreaded being separated from her again as I was in 1957 during the Treason Trial, but separation was inevitable.

The very next day, while at work in Verulam, I had a telephone call from her. The police were there – she was being detained. I realised she would be taken before I reached Durban. I asked my brother AC to go to the house immediately and telephoned her sister Baby. As I had suspected when I reached home, they had already taken her. George Sewpersadh[1] and I went to the headquarters of the Special Branch in Fisher Street. She was there, quite calm and resigned to whatever was to follow. We said our goodbyes and she was moved to the cells. I did not know where she was taken, but then discovered that she had forgotten to take her medication. She had been diagnosed a diabetic just a month earlier. I telephoned the head of the Special Branch, Colonel Steenkamp, who actually apologised for her detention. To my surprise, he told me where she was being detained and gave me permission to take the medication to her. I took her two sisters, Baby and Gorie, and her brother Farouk with me. Her cell was not too bad, and she had settled into her 'bed' on the floor. She was pleasantly surprised to see us.

Shamim's husband Bobby Marie, then secretary of the Institute for Black Research, was detained almost immediately after Fathu. Both Shamim and Shehnaz were studying at the University of Cape Town at the time.

Fathu was moved to the Fort in Johannesburg, and Rashid and Bobby to Benoni. They were in detention for five months. I flew to Johannesburg every week, staying over for two nights to take the two visits allowed. I usually stayed with Yusuf Cachalia; Fathu's friend Nana Weinberg fetched me from the airport and drove me to the Fort. When she was unable to fetch me, Hemant, Fathu's friend and Jessie's cousin, helped out. Irene, our housekeeper and cook, prepared large hampers of food, usually beans, rotis and kebaabs, which I took to both prisons. I used to buy two sets of roses, for Winnie and Fathu. I smuggled out her paintings on visiting days, Thursday and Friday. Three weeks later, flowers were prohibited.

All three of our detainees were released at the end of the year, and I hoped that we would be allowed to settle down to a quiet family life, but that was not to be. All three of them were banned, and this created problems.

While Fathu was in prison the Wildlife Society published their fund-raising book. They had invited Fathu to contribute a drawing. I recall other contributors included the Minister of Justice, who had banned her. Since she could not be published, the society was forced to tear out the page on which her drawing of an aloe was printed. It was a pity that the drawing on the reverse of hers also suffered censorship.

Ahmed Bawa, George Sewpersadh and Fathu's brother, Dr Farouk Meer, were detained in 1980. I visited them as their attorney. I telephoned Dr Cachalia in Benoni and asked him to keep eight dozen samoosas ready, to be fried when I got there. Dr Cachalia didn't question the request; he got the ladies in the family to make the samoosas and I put them in a special bag I had brought. I arrived at the prison with the piping hot, crisp samoosas, and was conducted into the visiting room. I opened my bag, called the warder and gave him a samoosa. 'Taste,' I said. He did, and looked at me. 'Tasty, heh!'

'Very tasty!' he concurred. I gave him four more. 'Now close the door and see no one disturbs us.' My 'clients' were waiting for me. I placed the samoosas before them. I never saw eight dozen samoosas disappear so fast.

I asked them to write messages to their families in my book since I was sure the room was bugged. They were not allowed to send out any uncensored writing. I gave them an opportunity to do so. Young Bawa, later Deputy Vice-Chancellor of the University of Natal, wrote long, loving words to his grandmother; others wrote to their wives and children. They requested light reading material, all except Sewpersadh who ordered Volume 5 of *Krishnamurthi*.

RASHID'S ESCAPE

A banning order is bad for every banned person; it is excruciating for a lively teenager. Rashid was practically under house arrest after his discharge from prison. He lived in isolation. He was very frustrated and we saw this, but didn't know how to help. I do not know at what point he decided to leave the country – he was always closer to Fathu than to me. Andrew Verster put his graphic skills to good use and made him a passport. Rashid permed his hair as some sort of disguise, and he left the country quietly, without saying goodbye, through Johannesburg airport on a South African Airways flight. We heard later that he had arrived in London, and we sighed with relief. He was eighteen years old.

He enrolled at Sussex University and completed his master's degree there. He made many friends and was popular, being active in students affairs, and after his graduation, supporting community causes. He had a very good position with the Greater London Council, but he hankered to work with the BBC, and so did a degree in journalism and achieved his ambition.

THE STUDENT SCENE POST-1976

The student scene in the post-1976 period continued to be volatile. They were literally making the townships ungovernable, as called for by Oliver Tambo. While I appreciated their impact on the Nationalists, I was anxious about the violence erupting all around us, as Inkatha and the United Democratic Front (UDF) grappled for power and the police played the one against the other and went much, much further. They attacked the homes of activists and they killed.

Black universities, Black Consciousness and the students; all of these components went together. The explosion that occurred in Soweto did not remain contained in Soweto; it affected every campus. At UDW, the students boycotted lectures in sympathy; they went on an indefinite strike. Their leaders came to see Fathu, who advised them that a strike was a negotiating strategy. It had to be related to demands and called off when the demands were met. There couldn't be an indefinite strike. If not goal-focused, the strike would peter out. But the students had minds of their own. The university responded to the strike by writing letters to parents, warning them that their sons and daughters would be expelled if they didn't attend lectures. We formed a Parents' Committee to help the students. The committee comprised Fathu and I, Mohammed and Julu Mayat and Mr and Mrs Maistry, and I think Hassan Mall and Chota Motala. We held meetings with the Students' Committee in a back room at Shifa Hospital in the evenings and tried to come to some agreement between ourselves and them, which we could take to the university authorities to end the impasse. Habib Rajab, the chairperson of the South African Indian Council and also of the University Council, was called by the rector to join the discussions. We discussed hard and long and eventually got the rector to concede to the students' demands, which included the right to an SRC.

The Students' Committee was to have waited for us outside the rector's office to be informed of the outcome of our meeting, but there were no students there. Instead, they organised a meeting at the Alan Taylor Residence at Wentworth, where SASO members branded the Parents' Committee a sell-out.

The students had not abided by our arrangements, and as far as I was concerned had acted without integrity. They had gone back to their former, unrealistic position of an indefinite boycott.

The next day – as I recall, a Monday – the students gathered on the soccer field at UDW, and both the Parents' Committee and SASO leaders addressed them, following which the general student body took a vote on the boycott. The students divided into two groups, those for and those against the boycott. The students appeared to be about equally divided on the issue. We suggested that the votes should be counted, but the Students' Committee refused. They declared that the majority wanted to continue the boycott. We pointed out that a considerable body of students had supported the strike but were now attending lectures. Their vote should be included in the vote being taken, but SASO refused this. The boycott continued, but each day the numbers of the supporting students dwindled. Ultimately neither the Students' Committee nor SASO made any gains. The boycott failed, unity dissipated and the students returned to classes in dribs and drabs on the university administration's terms. The students had gained nothing.

That episode left a bad taste in our mouths vis-à-vis student politics. In the days of my youth issues were clear, and grey areas few and far between. In the new, emerging political scenario, strategies and principles were confused.

OUR HOUSE IS BOMBED

Unfortunately the matter did not end there. Frustrated by their failure, members of SASO instigated an attack on our home. We had some visitors and were in our living room, talking, when a petrol bomb crashed through our very large picture window, shattering the plate glass. We were instantly on our feet and I was outside hoping to pin down our attacker, but all I could see was the back of a speeding car. The veranda was gutted with petrol, spilled from the bottles that contained them – unsuccessful 'bombs'. I thought of what would have happened if the crimson sateen curtains had caught fire. The ceiling of the house is timber.

That was the one bomb attack where an arrest was made. It emerged at the trial that Harry, the son of Debi Singh's friend, Jay, and his accomplice, one Chetty, had set our house alight 'to teach Mrs Meer a lesson'. I had known Harry as a young boy and now he was a young man. The police charged him. I had not seen him at our house. Harry's accomplice, who had thrown the bomb, was sentenced to five years' imprisonment, reduced to the option of a fine on appeal. The extenuating circumstances were that he was influenced by greater minds, Strini Moodley and Saths Cooper.

I didn't want him punished, whether guilty or not. I was called as a witness at the trial. I testified to what had happened. I couldn't testify as to who was responsible for the attack. That was police work. Young Harry's life ended in tragedy. He committed suicide a year or so later. Debi had treated him as a son, and that made him my son also. None of us really knew the boy or the man. He must have lived his life within himself.

In December 1977, soon after Fathu's release from prison following five months of detention without trial, we suffered another bomb attack. We were all upstairs, and Fathu and I were in bed with our three young nieces, her sister Baby's daughters, who were living with us while their parents were visiting India. We were all totally absorbed in my stories drawn from my childhood. All the children in our extended family were brought up on these stories. A hot favourite was the one about my friends Jeebhai and Baboo going fishing on the Busi River, much of it invented. 'I cast my line and felt something biting at the end of it. I pulled it, and there, at the end of the line, was a shimmering silver fish. My mother was so pleased; my father made a fire and we braaied the fish and had a delicious meal. Baboo said he would also catch a fish. He cast his line and his father made a fire and his mother prepared the masala. Baboo cast his line in the river and after a little while shouted, "I've caught a fish, a big fish, it is heavy!" He struggled and panted and pulled and at last brought out his catch – a big black boot!' This always evoked uncontrollable peals of laughter from the children. 'Baboo caught a stinking shoe! His mother braaied a stinking shoe, your mother braaied a lovely fish!' they would chant at the end of it.

And the next story had them trembling with fear.

'We were travelling to Waschbank. It was a very black night. There was no moon in the sky to light our way. We were driving at a good speed. Suddenly, the driver slammed on the brakes, and brought the car to a sudden stop.

'"What's the matter?" we asked.

'"There! There!" he said, pointing to a spot on the road, his face white with fear.

'"There is a child sitting in the middle of the road," the driver said in agitation. We looked and saw the child, but as we looked, the child grew and grew and grew.'

My storytelling was interrupted by a sudden scream from the next room, where Shehnaz was studying for her matric examination. 'The garage is on fire!'

Fathu was off the bed and racing down the stairs. I was following fast behind her when I heard gunshots. We reached the door. Zwelinye, our former gardener who was visiting us, was on the floor near the door, shot and bleeding. He was gasping for breath and simultaneously warning Fathu, 'Get away from the door! They are swearing at you! They want to kill you!'

I helped Zwelinye get up and guided him to a chair; Fathu got some cotton wool and Dettol to give him emergency first aid. I telephoned the police and ambulance. I heard cars revving and speeding away. Our attackers had fled. The police and ambulance were not long in coming. Zwelinye was removed to hospital. I went out to examine the situation. A number of gunmen had been involved. They had poured petrol on our driveway and set it alight; the glass in our garage door had a neat bullet hole, and the glass in the entrance door was shattered. We retrieved a number of rifle shells. There was gunpowder in the bougainvillaea bush in front of our door, and some branches were burnt. We reconstructed the attack: petrol had been poured on our driveway, right up to the garage to set it on fire. For good measure a pistol had been fired to urge on the flames. Simultaneously two men armed with rifles had taken their position in the bougainvillaea bush to shoot at anyone who burst out of the house to attend to the fire. Zwelinye was the first one out, and he had been shot in the shoulder. Had Fathu preceded him, she would have been shot in the head, her head reaching Zwelinye's shoulder, and that would have been the end of her. I thanked Allah for her life.

Three weeks later, three cars similar in description to those involved in the attack on our house were seen outside the house of Rick Turner.[2] There was a ring of the doorbell. Rick Turner went to open the door and was shot dead. A young life, a brilliant mind, a compassionate and great heart all extinguished because a crazed government had sent a crazed gunman to still his voice of reason, which sought to end discrimination and racism and bring South Africans together.

We lived through one more attack.

In the mid-1980s our province became riddled with violence as 'war' broke out between the UDF and Inkatha, which were caught in a power struggle. I was excluded from the political stage in terms of my listing. Fathu participated for both of us. I thought she did too much. I wished desperately that she would calm down and do less.

People trapped in the crossfire turned to Fathu for assistance because she was just about the only person fearless enough or foolish enough to help. Nobody was prepared to join her because the situation was too explosive. She called a meeting of the activists she knew; they advised caution and non-intervention, but she persisted. I was afraid for her, but there was no stopping Fathu when she was convinced she was doing the right thing. People in danger, or threatened in any way, telephoned her, and she would telephone the police and try to get them to assist. When the police did not respond or said that both sides were equally guilty and they were not interested, she turned to the media, or to the Progressive Party, which, being white, had a better rapport with the police. Whether her interventions helped, I don't know. Helpful or otherwise, I would have preferred her paying more attention to the household, and to me.

The Residents Association in Umlazi called a memorial meeting in protest of Mrs Mxenge's assassination.[3] Fathu was one of the speakers. She left home at about 6 pm, driving herself to the meeting in our Volkswagen. When some hours had passed and she had not returned, I grew anxious and paced the floor, stopping expectantly at the sound of every approaching car. I should have laid down the law, I said to myself, and she would have listened to me as she usually did, even though against her will.

Somewhat close to 12 pm she drove in; I was ready to give her a tongue-lashing, but when I saw she was close to tears, frightened, her sari ripped, I could only comfort her, enquire if she had eaten, and offer to make her tea. When she declined these, I led her to bed and she recounted her ordeal. An Inkatha impi had broken up the meeting, and people had jumped down from the gallery in the hall. A young comrade had led her out of the hall, and they had fled and crawled underneath barbed-wire fencing and criss-crossed through an open field while flares lit up the darkness and exposed them. However, they safely reached her car, parked in front of the cinema. They found a man lying there. They put him on the back seat of the car and drove madly through blockades of burning tyres, eventually reaching the hospital, only to be told that he was dead, and they should take the body to the mortuary. Fathu broke down and cried, and all I could do was comfort her. But the constant thought in my mind was, 'Why does she not listen and stay at home like other wives?' And I had to acknowledge that it was precisely because she was not like other wives that she was my wife and I loved her.

The following night we had our third bomb attack.

Both Fathu and I were in bed, reading, when we heard a terrible explosion. I ran down and slipped on petrol. I shouted to Fathu, who was following me, to be careful. As I looked out, it seemed as if our house was engulfed in fire. I opened our front door and found a petrol bomb on our doorstep about to explode. I took it in my hands and threw it, as far as I could. It exploded as it touched the ground. If more bombs had exploded, the ground floor of our house would have been gutted and we would have been trapped in our bedroom upstairs.

Our neighbours came out to help; somebody telephoned the fire brigade, but by the time it arrived the bombs had been extinguished. Several bombs were later retrieved from the garden around the house.

Nobody saw our attackers, but our shrewd guess pointed to Inkatha. Fathu had addressed a meeting at the UDW earlier that day and had verbally attacked Inkatha.

FATHU AND BOBBY ARE CHARGED FOR ATTENDING A DINNER PARTY

Fathu's five-year banning order expired in 1981, a day before another five-year banning order was clamped on her.

Fathu was not one to be constrained by the law. She knew that I would stop her if I had wind of any movements that violated the conditions of her banning order. I was careful; she was not only careless, but took deliberate chances and did the things she thought she ought to do regardless of her banning order. I wasn't aware of all these activities because she kept them away from me. She knew that I would come down on her like a ton of bricks if I ever found out, so why would she risk that?

However, I knew about the Christmas dinner at Andrew Verster's, because I was also invited. I declined the invitation and warned Fathu that she should not be going either. Rashid's friend Piushi, a young Kenyan woman living in Britain, was visiting us at the time. They all piled into our Volkswagen and drove off, leaving me grumbling. A little later Dr Goonam arrived, her usual cheerful self. She wanted to know Andrew Verster's address and offered me a lift. I told her I wasn't going and neither should she. 'They've been discussing this party the whole day on the telephone. They are going to be arrested and I'm not going to be a part of it.' Goonam left. Later that evening, Shamim, Fathu and Bobby returned with very worried faces and reported what had happened. As they were about to begin dinner at Andrew's house, a whole contingent of police had barged into the dining room and begun taking photographs. Then they announced that they were charging Bobby and Fathu for breaching their banning orders.

If they expected me to say, 'I told you so,' I disappointed them. Instead I busied myself organising their defence. I called Sewpersadh, and we telephoned Ismail Mohamed and engaged him as senior counsel. I saw the case as an opportunity to expose the vindictiveness of the banning order and the pettiness of a government that spied on private social gatherings, arresting people whose only crime was being together, in this instance at an innocent Christmas dinner. It intruded on people's privacy under the subterfuge of securing the safety of the state.

I more or less took over the organising of the hearing. I saw to it that the case was covered by the press, and there was a good turnout at the court. The public gallery was packed to capacity on the day of the hearing, leaving even standing room at a premium. Alan Paton was among those who had to stand throughout the trial. There was a good turnout of students. I commandeered a witness room and used it as a tea room for counsel, serving them biscuits and tea during the short recess. I had brought flasks of tea and milk from home. The only mistake I made was to ask Sew to get a water tumbler for counsel. I thought he'd get it from an orderly, but he drove into town to purchase it, and returned just in time to hear the magistrate adjourn the case.

The prosecutor, fat and ginger-haired, especially brought out from the Transvaal, began his case. Sergeant van der Merwe was the first witness. Led by the prosecutor, he informed the court of how he had kept watch outside 125 Essenwood Road, and how, at about 6.30 pm, a Volkswagen had driven up, parked outside the house, and an Asiatic male and four Asiatic females had got out and entered the house. How, a little later, a second car had arrived, and a European couple alighted, and how later still a third car had arrived and an Asiatic female had entered the house. He testified that at this point the police had changed their position and kept watch through a window. They saw the accused eating, drinking and talking to the guests. They had then entered the house, all twelve of them, and one of them had started taking photographs. At one point Mrs Meer had said, 'I am guilty. Why continue with the photographs?'

Ismail Mohamed cross-examined him. First, he wanted to establish that Mrs Meer, a good Muslim, was not drinking alcohol. 'Mrs Meer was drinking grape juice,' he stated as a matter of fact. 'There was grape juice on the table?'

The sergeant agreed.

'My information is that you did not announce yourself. You jumped a wall and broke into the house. You believed that the accused would be breaking their banning orders and thereby breaking a law.'

The sergeant said words to the effect that he had wanted 'to catch them in the act', which is what defence counsel wanted him to say. If he knew that the accused were about to break the law, why did he not warn them and prevent a breach of the law? Why did he allow a crime to be committed? Did he not have a duty to prevent crime? He had no reply!

Witness No. 2 was the captain who had served the banning order on Fathu. He gave his evidence in Afrikaans. The court asked if we wanted an interpreter. Our counsel said he was proficient in both languages. The captain testified that he had served Mrs Meer with her banning order, and that her son Rashid had read it out to her. Mrs Meer had said that she would get her lawyer to clarify the order to her. Ismail Mohamed briefly consulted Fathu and then cross-examined witness No. 2.

'Did Mrs Meer tell you she would consult a lawyer or did you tell her to do so?' The captain admitted that he had asked her to do so.

Witness No. 3 was Sergeant Perumal. He had served the banning order on Bobby. Ismail Mohamed cross-examined him in Afrikaans. Perumal looked helplessly at the magistrate, who said he would be provided with an interpreter.

Ismail Mohamed, who was clearly playing games, chided the sergeant. 'You are a member of the police and you do not speak Afrikaans?' He then informed the court that there was no need for an interpreter; he would cross-examine the sergeant in English. He asked the sergeant if he knew the definition of a 'gathering'. The prosecutor objected. Our counsel insisted the question was very relevant to the whole case. Argument sustained. Perumal explained that if two or more people went to a billiard saloon and paid for it, it wasn't a gathering. Likewise, if they went to a restaurant and paid for the meal, it wasn't a gathering.

Our counsel said how ridiculous his understanding was. 'If a sergeant in the police force does not know what a gathering is, how are my poor clients to know?' Even Perumal's white colleagues sniggered at his discomfort.

Witness No. 4 was a guest at the dinner party. Peter Noel-Barham, a restaurateur who ran the British Middle East Sporting and Dining Club in Durban and the Persian Garden in Johannesburg, portly with an impressive beard and double-breasted blazer, looked like a ship's captain. His wife was in the gallery.

Led by the prosecution, he confirmed the arrival of the accused and the fact that they sat and talked and dined together. Defence cross-examined:

DEFENCE: Did the police announce their arrival?
PETER NOEL-BARHAM: No, we were taken by surprise. In fact, I thought the photographer was a friend of Mr Walsh.[5]
DEFENCE: When did the police identify themselves?
PETER NOEL-BARHAM: It must have been after the second (pause) or first photograph. I think it was after the first.
DEFENCE: What did Mrs Meer say?
PETER NOEL-BARHAM: Words to the effect that she was there, present. She was not denying it. She said, 'Okay, Okay. Why take more photographs? I am here.'
DEFENCE: Was anything political discussed?
PETER NOEL-BARHAM: Come to think of it, I made the only political remark. I said to my young companion from England, 'You see how well we get on here, for all the contrary things you may hear.'

Our counsel continued cross-examination and his argument right into the late afternoon. The magistrate frowned that the matter was far too complex, and he needed time to consider the implications. He adjourned the case to 12 May.

On 12 May he found both Fathu and Bobby guilty, and gave them suspended sentences. We appealed against these sentences. Ismail Mohamed strongly felt that his arguments challenging the vagueness of the banning order needed to be placed before judges. Judges Didcott and Shearer presided in the Supreme Court, and they upheld our counsel's argument that the definition of a gathering under the law was void for vagueness. This set a precedent and put the state on the defence, sending it to the drawing board to amend its legislation.

That was not the only time Fathu was in court for breaking her banning order. She was building extensions to the Ohlange High School in Inanda, outside the limit of her confinement. She was visiting the building site almost daily to supervise the operations, evading both me and the security police. However, when she set up a craft centre at the Phoenix Settlement and went to work there, the Special Branch caught up with her and she was arrested. Fathu feared my rage more than the arrest, but again I surprised her by taking a philosophical attitude and setting about planning her defence.

Again Ismail Mohamed came to our rescue. He took enormous trouble studying the sea tides in order to build an argument that there was no consistency in the boundary. But he had an unexpected bonanza when the prosecution's expert witness, asked by the prosecutor to define the boundary between Durban and Inanda, pointed out that the boundary was not continuous, that there were gaps. Ismail Mohamed used that to get her off. If there was no continuous boundary, how could she be contained within it?

SIXTEEN

TRAVELLING ABROAD

1979–1990s

Fathu began getting invitations to attend conferences and present papers. The government picked and chose the conferences it allowed her to attend. Well motivated applications were made for passports and repeated enquiries were made as to the state of the applications. While we waited anxiously, replies only came close to the time of the flight, or even after the flight had left. In 1975, Fathu was allowed to take up an invitation to the Delhi School of Economics as a visiting lecturer at the invitation of Professor Srinivassan, through the intervention of her principal, Owen Horwood, who later became Minister of Finance in the National Party cabinet. In 1972, she was allowed to take up an invitation from the US State Department to the United States. I had no such invitations as motivation for a passport. No matter how much I missed Fathu or found her absence from home inconvenient, I never dissuaded her from going abroad when she had the opportunity; I always encouraged her.

The children got passports to accompany her to India. I was left with the household help, Irene, Sheila, her young son Preggie and our gardener Zwelinye.

Fathu was given passports for a specific academic engagement, for the duration of the engagement. She was invited as the Cornell Professor at Swarthmore in 1984 and the Carlton Savage Professor in International Relations and Peace at Oregon University in 1990. In that year, I was given a passport to attend a conference on Islam and Apartheid in Washington. She too was invited to the conference, where we were jointly awarded the Imaam Abdulla Haroon Award for Struggle Against Oppression and Racial Discrimination in South Africa. We spent a very pleasant weekend together. Fathu had to return to Oregon on the Monday to continue her lectures.

We had an arrangement while she was in Oregon that I would ring her daily to remind her to take her medication. The telephone would ring thrice at her end and she would know I was reminding her and thinking of her. In this way I was sure she took her medicine, something I always worried about because she was prone to forget. She was not expected to and did not pick up the receiver; that would have left us with a telephone bill beyond our means. When we needed to speak, we spoke.

BRITAIN

I was issued my first passport on 17 October 1978, restricted to Britain. I arrived at Heathrow Airport on 23 June 1979.

I stayed with Bhai, Fathu's brother, and Zubie, his wife. They treated me like a VIP. Rashid came to meet me. There was not much change in him. He was the same lanky youth, full of energy, throwing himself into causes he believed in and running from one to the other. He was affectionate and wanted to show me around London, familiarise me with the Underground and take me to the theatre and his university. We travelled by train to Brighton, where he lived while studying at Sussex. It was peak hour and we had to stand part of the way. It was graduation time and the campus was full of students in gowns and caps hired for the occasion. Rashid's accommodation was the typical student pad, untidy and uncomfortable. I found Brighton's beach too stony.

Rashid had many friends and he appeared to be very popular. As in Durban, he was involved in student politics. I was comforted by the manner in which he had adapted to his new environment and by his cheerful, happy disposition. But I missed Zubie's pampering and decided to return to London, having more or less exhausted the sights of Brighton.

This was my first visit to this great city of Charles Dickens. Fathu's brothers, Bhai and Siddiek, were all for showing me around the Old Curiosity Shop, the Inns of Court, London Bridge and Trafalgar Square; they took me to Bath and to Shakespeare's country.

I loved London. I explored the tube and wandered around the city. I became quite familiar with the transport system. I made a very interesting trip to the Houses of Parliament. From Bhai's house in Dorchester Gardens, I walked across to Mutton Brook to the bus stop on the High Street, where I took a tram to Golders Green. From there I took the tube to Embankment, where I changed from the Northern Line to the Central, to Westminster – all for 70 pence return. I visited Westminster Abbey and pondered over the graves of the great and famous who had made it to that very exclusive burial ground. I walked around that part of London and after a good lunch at a very good restaurant, I walked to Parliament in time for the afternoon session. There was a long queue of people wanting to purchase tickets to the House of Commons. Fortunately I had been given a ticket by an MP, so I was spared the queue. Fifteen minutes before the Commons began its deliberation, I presented my ticket and was directed along with other visitors to the concourse to witness the Speaker's procession enter the House – very sombre, very impressive. I then followed the group to the entrance of the East Gallery, where we entered the British parliament that, for centuries, had ruled the Empire. I watched the proceedings and wondered if the debates had changed very much in their ponderousness from the time when Britannia had ruled the waves.

At 2.30 pm question-time began, with the MP representing Lord Carrington answering the written and many supplementary questions from both sides of the House dealing with foreign affairs. The outreach of the British parliament had diminished substantially since the last World War, and so Ireland and Irish violence consumed all the time.

Just after 3 pm Margaret Thatcher took her seat, and there was an audible stir among the visitors who, up till then, had been fairly quiet. She began answering questions directed to the prime minister with great skill and humour, living up to her reputation as the belle of the House.

I left the debate at about 4.30 pm and traced my way back from Westminster to Embankment, to Golders Green and to Dorchester Gardens, where I found Shehnaz waiting for me. She had been backpacking in Europe before enrolling at university. She was bubbling with accounts of her travels and kept us entertained for the best part of the evening.

I had a nostalgic meeting with Michael Scott. We talked about the 1946 passive resistance campaign. I was surprised that he had not met Zainab Asvat, since they had both settled in London. Zubie organised a dinner party bringing together a number of old comrades – Yusuf Dadoo, Michael Scott, Zainab, Brian and Sonia Bunting and the Yengwas. It was a very happy party. Oliver Tambo came to meet me and we embraced like old-time friends, which we were.

Yusuf Dadoo took me to a mushaira, a gathering of Urdu poets. He was very keen to show off his travel card for pensioners. He told me with childlike enthusiasm, 'Watch,' and went from tube to tube, showing his card and not paying a penny, while I bought my tickets.

After the mushaira, which I enjoyed thoroughly, Yusuf said, 'We will now go and eat.'

'At this hour!' I exclaimed. 'Will there be a restaurant open to serve us?'

There was a twinkle in his eye as he said, 'Watch,' and we walked through some London gullies, coming to a small Indian restaurant, quite full and aromatic with the kind of food we liked. I was as always deeply touched by Yusuf's humility and simplicity, and his pleasure in the little things that he could do for his friends. Fathu had told me how, during her first visit to London, he had invited her to supper and prepared delicious grilled chicken.

Even in London one could not get away from the problems of the struggle at home. Yusuf keenly sought my assessment on developments in South Africa. In particular, he was concerned about divisions that had opened up in the Indian community. The apartheid government was seeking to co-opt the Indians and eventually promised to hold an election for the South African Indian Council, which it had created as a separate institution. Leaders and activists in the struggle were divided about how to approach the election. They were of one mind in rejecting any separate institution, but they differed sharply about the tactics we should employ. One group insisted that the only honourable path was to mobilise the Indian community to boycott the election. The other wanted to exploit the opportunity provided by the election by getting candidates to stand for election, getting the public to vote for them and paralysing the institution from within once elected.

Yusuf invited me to a meeting at which representatives from home espousing both viewpoints were present. They had travelled to London under all sorts of excuses to consult Dr Dadoo and the ANC with a view to resolving their differences. They were Thumba Pillay, Pravin Gordhan and Roy Padayachee. Yusuf brought along with him Mac Maharaj, who had served twelve years' imprisonment on Robben Island, and was now in exile in Zambia, and Aziz Pahad, who was based in London. The meeting was preceded by days of discussion held separately by Mac with representatives of both viewpoints. That night Yusuf brought us together in order to commit the different viewpoints to uniting the people in action.

I never saw Yusuf again. After his death, I was told by Joe Slovo that he had requested that I should write his biography. However, Fathu brought the instruction from Brian Bunting that the biography would have to go through the Russian Politburo. This inhibited me from attempting to write it.

My last trip to London, in September 1996, was in the company of my KwaZulu-Natal parliamentary colleagues, en route to the US to gain insight into the institutions of American government.

In Washington I took a great liking to the hotel porter, a Pakistani. While he was placing my luggage in my room, he quoted an Urdu couplet with a broad smile: 'It is said we come into the world empty-handed and we leave empty-handed, but I am a poor man and I have to live. Place something in my palm now and when you leave, don't forget to do the same again.' I laughed and gave him a generous tip. I looked out for him when I left the hotel and gave him another generous tip.

Our KwaZulu-Natal contingent had a long wait at Heathrow airport on our return journey – almost a whole day. I commandeered my nephew Iqbal and my brother-in-law Bhai, and they came with transport and took care of our delegation, showing us the sights and resting and refreshing us with food and drink.

INDIA

My comrade of long standing, Cassim Amra, and I flew into Bombay Airport on Saturday, 9 December 1978. We filed out of the plane and queued at the immigration desks. It was a nuisance, but it pleased me when the official refused to accept and stamp our passports, because it testified that the sanctions we had requested some thirty years ago were in place. We were told that we would have to fill in special forms, and these would be stamped in lieu of our passports. 'But,' said the official, 'we have run short of those forms and you will have to wait for the forms to arrive.' How long would that take? The official did not know. I asked if he had at least one form and offered to copy the necessary number by hand. The official hesitated for the shortest while, and then agreed that it was a good solution. He gave me pens, sheets of paper and two of the five forms he had at hand. Cassim and I got busy processing some thirty forms and cleared the queue of South African visitors. The official thanked me and we were on our way out of the airport, and on Indian soil. We hailed a taxi and were soon making our way to the Ambassador Hotel, passing vast informal settlements sprouting, it seemed, from the water-logged ground.

Both Cassim and I were overwhelmed by the congestion of vehicles, ranging from donkey carts to bicycles, scooters, trucks and buses, all filled with people.

Our hotel was centrally located. We walked to the famous India Gate and looked up at the giant cinema hoardings. I felt a sense of wonder and affection as I contemplated the land of my forefathers.

We visited Goolam Pahad's comfortable apartment on Peddar Road. Goolam Bhai was contemplating a second marriage. Molvi Cachalia had arranged a wife for him. Amina Bai had died several years ago in a motor accident. Her relatives were present in the apartment and they were raising objections. They attempted to draw in our support.

We spent four enjoyable days in Bombay and then left by the famous Flying Rani to Surat, from where the Meers had emigrated to South Africa towards the end of the nineteenth century. My cousin Kader came to meet us and took us to Kimberley House, built in South African architectural style by MI's maternal uncle, Ahmed Mohamed Vania. It was a beautiful house with a floral mosaic floor, mahogany wood panelling and Victorian mahogany furniture. Our hostesses were MI's maternal cousins, three spinsters, who welcomed us very formally in beautiful English and then relaxed into Gujarati. They explained that their maternal aunt, MI's mother and her three children, MI, AI and their sister, had lived there with their grandmother. Next to Kimberley House was a narrow vacant strip of land on which goats grazed. It was the land on which the original home of my grandfather Ahmed Meer had stood. It was also the house in which my father and his brothers had been born. Close by stood the imposing mansion of Mohamed

Meer, built with money earned in South Africa. I was making contact with my roots and it gave me great pleasure.

We spent almost five weeks in India and each day was rich and enjoyable. India was poverty and India was splendour, but above all it was a country of pride and dignity. We found the country enchanting, everything our elders had told us and more, for we saw far more of the country in the seven weeks we spent there than our elders had in all their lives. They had not gone beyond Bombay and Surat. We enjoyed the hotels, the Clerk Shiraz in Agra, De Paris in Varanasi, Fort Aquador in Goa. I did not miss home a single day. It was as if I was at home.

We saw sculptural and artistic wonders at Ajanta and Ellora, and met a guide who gave us a lesson in fine art that I am sure would have taken university lecturers a semester to instil in our unartistic minds.

On a relaxed morning at the Hotel Sudarshan in Madras, I called room service and asked for a pot of tea and three slices of toast.

'Not possible, sir,' said the voice on the phone.

'Not possible?' I repeated.

'Not possible, Saab,' the voice confirmed.

I noted that from 'sir' I had become 'Saab', and wondered whether it was a promotion or demotion.

'Why is that not possible?'

'Saab, you can have two toast, four toast, six toast, eight toast, ten toast …'

'Stop, stop, sir!' I said. 'You have made the point, you can count in twos.'

'I am not "sir",' he said. 'You are sir! I am your humble servant, sir.'

'Right. Now that you have defined the relationship, may I have one cup of tea and three toasts. I don't want more. I don't want less.'

'Saab, I am sorry to repeat, but repeat I must. You may have two toasts, or four toasts, or eight toasts, or ten…'

'Stop, stop,' I said. 'I get the idea. Now I'll tell you what you will do. You send me four toasts and I'll return one. Then I'll have my three toasts and you will have sent the four.'

'No, Saab, you may not do that. That will be against the rule. You may have two toasts, four toasts, six toasts …'

'Look,' I said. 'Suppose I change the order and you send me one pot of tea – it must be hot, very hot, and one roll.'

'That is possible. I will immediately send you one pot of piping hot tea and one roll.'

'Now that we have completed the order, will you tell me why this endless counting in twos?'

'Sir, our toaster toasts in twos. We can't be wasting one toast each time an order comes.'

'And apart from serving rolls, what else do you do?' I asked.

'Your humble servant is a student at the university studying for my master's degree in history. I work at the hotel part time and during holidays.'

We saw the Taj and the Kutub Minar and the magnificence of Moghul architecture, and were dumbstruck by their splendour; and we saw the devotees at the Ganges as it flowed through Varanasi and washed its shores. In Delhi, I watched Cassim at the famous restaurant, Moti Mahal, as he walked to the podium with great flourish, and showered the singer with rupee notes, returning to his seat with equal flourish. He did so some five or six times, enjoying himself immensely, and I enjoyed watching him. At Hyderabad, the stationmaster filled in the forms in triplicate.

'To what purpose?' I asked.

'When the memsahibs travelled by train, we had to keep perfect records in the event of an accident.'

'But the memsahibs are long gone,' I said.

'But not the rules; they remain,' he said.

India is free of the British, I thought, but British domination remains.

On the flight to Delhi, the very attractive air hostess caught our attention and I was flattered when she came towards me.

'You are Mr Meer? I see Mr Meer written on your luggage.'

I said I was. She wanted to know if I was related to Fatima Meer. I was surprised. I told her I was married to her and asked her how she knew my wife. She said she was a former student and that Fathu had once lectured her.

HAJ

My father had never gone on Haj,[1] and neither had his two younger brothers and my cousins, MI and AI, because, I think, of financial difficulties. My eldest uncle, Mohamed Meer, had gone on Haj, taking his children with him. Budie remembered that trip and often talked about it. It had been a hard trip, travelling on camels through the desert sands from Jiddah to Mecca and Medina.

In 1984, Fathu and I made our Haj. Mecca and Medina had changed dramatically; there was neither sand nor camel and we sped along macadamised highways, neon lights heralding the cities as we emerged from the darkness. We were accompanied by my brother AC and the Fakroodeens, father and daughter, both doctors, and Mrs Fakroodeen. Sarah had arranged our board and lodging in Mecca with a Gulambhai.[2] We arrived in Jiddah, travel weary, having had to spend the night sitting on a bench in Nairobi Airport, where we had changed into our ehram, the seamless white cloth draped around our loins and half across our chests. It was in itself a statement of our unity, knowing neither wealth nor race: 'Allah Humma Labbaika' ['Here we surrender to thee, Oh Lord, a single humanity, in equality, equal before you'].

We had taken our connecting flight at dawn. There was no Gulambhai to receive us at Jiddah. We sat on the pavement outside the airport with nothing to do but look at bunches of fresh dates for which we had no stomach, anxious about our immediate future. We were feeling very sorry for ourselves when we were rescued by Hafez Saab, who offered us board and lodging and to conduct us through our ritual – be our muallim.[3]

My sister Ayesha, niece Zohra, and Choti Mamie (Mrs EM Meer), her son Nash (who had served his articles with me) and his wife Anisa, had arrived in Mecca ahead of us. We contacted them by telephone and learnt that Gulambhai had been arrested and was in prison. They said we did well in contracting with Hafez Saab. We travelled from Jiddah to Mecca by bus, arriving at night. We deposited our luggage at the hotel and went to the great mosque where we made our namaaz [prayer]. As I raised my head from my Sijda [prostration] I saw the Kaaba.

I had heard so much about it since childhood. I had seen so many pictures of it reverently hung on people's walls. I had never been impressed by the nondescript black cube. Now I was overcome by its splendour. The reality was nothing like its representations. I nudged Fathu, still in her Sijda, and said in subdued excitement, as if sharing a charmed secret: 'See the Kaaba! See!' She lifted her head and gazed on it and was moved to tears. It was an inspirational moment for both of us. We found ourselves quite unexpectedly sharing a mutual ecstasy. Set on the vast white marble floor against the black sky, the Kaaba was a black gem of ethereal beauty. We made our tawaaf [ambulations]; AC was not in a condition to walk the rounds so he was carried in a sedan chair.

We proceeded to perform our sai,[4] walking seven times to and fro between Safa and Marwa, the two hillocks between which Bibi Hazra had run in desperation calling on Allah to save her baby, the infant Ishmael, the son of Hazrat Ebrahim (Abraham), who was on the verge of death for want of water. And even as she had run and prayed, her baby had struck his little feet in the sand and the water had sprung forth from 'Zam Zam', an eternal spring in the desert for all humanity. We drank of this water from the very same spring, piped into tanks in the mosque.

We were at the confluence of faith and mythology, where the evidential is both myth and reality. It is not Mohamed (Peace Be Upon Him) we meet at the Kaaba, it is Abraham and the Egyptian bondswoman, Bibi Hazra, who bore him the son Ishmael, the progenitor of half the Arab nation. Was Hazrat Ebrahim a myth or fact? Was Bibi Hazra a myth or fact? And the infant Ishmael who fathered half the Arab nation, a myth? And the Arabs a myth?

We retired to our rooms after the dawn prayer, worn out by the aeroplane journey from Nairobi, the bus from Jiddah and the performance of our rituals. We spent the major part of the following day in our rooms. Fathu brought out some halwa prepared, she said, by AC's daughter-in-law's family. She passed around the choice goodies, praising all the while the Bassa ladies' cooking, until Mrs Fakroodeen, unable to bear it any longer, said very gently, 'We brought this naan kathai and halwa. My sister-in-law made them.' I didn't allow Fathu to live down this faux pas. It was one of the jokes I told against her. She took it in good humour as she did my other jokes against her.

Our hotel, more like a boarding house, was within the boundary of the haram, and within walking distance of the Great Mosque. We had two rooms, very humble; the women, Fathu, Dr Sarah Fakroodeen and her mother, occupied the one, and we three men, Dr Fakroodeen (senior), AC and I, occupied the other.

The food was tolerable; Fathu took special care of AC, who was frail and stayed in bed most of the time. She kept him supplied with canned fruit juices for which he had developed a liking.

I took Fathu to the first floor of the Haram Sharif, remembering what Essop Ba Kathrada, a friend in Verulam, had told me. 'From that floor, where there is not such a crowd, look down on the Kaaba and see the pilgrims whirl around as if impelled by some mechanism – it is such a glorious sight.'

And we experienced that glorious sight as we stood at the wall where the first floor Jamat Khana [prayer space] ended, looking across and down. We stood there for half an hour or so, mesmerised by that divine whirling, overpowered by its spirituality and tranquillity.

We walked back to our 'hotel'. Fathu said it was close to prayer time and we should go after performing our Zohar Namaaz,[5] but I insisted on leaving. I thought we'd take a brisk walk and reach our room where we could pray together. We were still on the road when we heard the Azaan.[6] The shopkeepers rolled out their mats to make their namaaz. We did not have prayer mats, so we prostrated before Allah on the bare pavement.

We were about to set out for Mina when AC had a blackout. Fathu ran up into the kitchen and brought some sugared water, and mercifully AC revived. He had given us quite a shock. We never knew why he had that brief blackout, but thankfully it did not recur.

We had gone on excursion to Mina a few days before the Haj period, and the silence in the valley matched that of the three Satans[7] positioned under the bridge. The valley was now transformed with the hubbub of thousands of families settled under the roof of the winding bridge with their utensils, cooking pots and gas burners. At a convenient distance, rows of toilets and washrooms were assembled. Those who knew warned us that by the end of the day the crowds would swell to such numbers that there wouldn't be standing room.

We retired to our residence, an upstairs apartment with a number of rooms, all of them allocated separately for men and women, in dormitory fashion. Mats were laid out on the floor and we settled onto these after our prayers and a simple supper.

We left for Arafat by bus at dawn. The thousands of families squatting under the bridge had left earlier on foot.

The Plain of Arafat, only sand and rocks a few days ago, was now clad in tents as far as the eye could see. We arrived at our tent, large, decorated in colourful appliquéd designs and equipped with a number of air conditioners. The money we had paid entitled us to such comfort. I had expected to stand on the plain, facing the Kaaba, meditating on Jabal-e-Rahmat, the Monument of Mercy, from sunrise to sunset as the Prophet had done at the dawn of Islam. Instead we were sitting in comfort, away from the heat of the sun. I found this disappointing. I left the tent and stood outside for a while, trying to capture a meditative mood. I thought of the Prophet's last pilgrimage, centuries ago, when he had stood on Jabal-e-Rahmat and gave his last message to humanity: 'No Arab is superior to a non-Arab and no non-Arab has superiority over an Arab.'

The lunch was served in a style befitting the tent – rice and meat in large platters. We sat around them on the floor, five to a platter, and relished the fare.

I discovered that neither Mecca nor Medina were at the heart of the four days of Haj, but Mina. The first day of Haj began at Mina. The pilgrim came from Mecca to Mina, and from Mina left for Arafat and returned to Mina from Muzdalefa. About a million pilgrims traced that circuit in an approximate twelve-mile radius.

We made our noon and mid-afternoon prayers at Arafat as the Prophet had done, and at sunset we boarded our buses and left for Muzdalefa.

We made our Magrib and Esha Namaaz[8] at Muzdalefa, collected our pebbles with which to pelt the Satans the next day, and retired for the night on the sand, contemplating the stars in the black night and conversing softly. We were awakened by the Azaan and assembled for the dawn prayer, then left for Mina in our bus.

Driving to Mina was an excruciating experience. There were maybe a million pedestrians milling on the road, pushing and crushing each other. They had already broken the fences bordering the road; now some desperate persons tried to seek safety in our bus. Our fellow passengers and the driver swore at them and pushed them off. Quite unexpectedly, and without any warning, Fathu shouted, 'Are you Muslims or not? Why can't you share your space with your fellow Muslims, many of whom are clearly in danger of being crushed to death!'

AC and I sat quietly. Our fellow pilgrims were angry with her. She had been injudicious, but we agreed with her. Yet how many could our bus take and, had we allowed a few, a stampede would have followed. Fathu, impulsive as always, had not considered the situation and its consequences. We never discussed the issue. We had no answers. We had the impression that we were not as popular with our fellow pilgrims after that.

We literally took our lives in our hands when we went to pelt the Satans, standing unashamed and defiant at their stations under the bridge. Seven of us held each other tightly by the waist, and pushed our way through the crowds to reach the Satans. I had the feeling that the Satans were taking their own revenge on us.

We spent two days in Medina, and from Medina travelled by taxi to Jiddah. Fathu took the flight to South Africa, and AC and I flew to London to spend time with our respective sons.

TUNISIA AND EGYPT

In November 1992, both Fathu and I got passports to Tunis, Egypt and the UK. Fathu had been invited to a UNESCO conference. This was our first trip abroad together. We arrived in Rome early in the morning and took a connecting flight to Tunis.

We enjoyed our stay in Tunis; we enjoyed the hotel, our evening walks on the streets secured by patrolling police, and the sumptuous dinners with accompanying musical entertainment. I watched Fathu chair a plenary session and felt proud when one of the organisers said to me, 'She's made for the job.'

We took time off from the conference and I arranged for a taxi and guide to take us to the Roman ruins, a beautiful village and other city sites.

We went shopping in the Medina. Fathu became unrestrainable in her excitement at the vast array of goods. She bought a carpet and some beautiful ceramics, and they adorn our home.

After the conference we went to London to see our exiled son. We stayed with him in his house in Finsbury Park. He gave us his bedroom and made a bed for himself on the convertible in the lounge. It is my habit to be up very early, before anyone else. Throughout our married life I made our morning tea, and took it to our bedroom where Fathu and I had it in bed. In London I went shopping in Finsbury Park, enjoying the Indian shops and the small talk of the owners. I returned with freshly baked bread and Rashid made us a large breakfast.

We were routed to return via Cairo. Rashid arranged a trip down the Nile for us and paid for the tickets.

In Cairo we booked into the Ramesis Hotel, and our room on the ninth floor had a panoramic view of Cairo with the magic Nile flowing below us.

A FORTUNATE MAN

We began our excursion into Egyptology with the Egyptian Museum, then visited the silent pyramids and stayed until the evening to listen to the broken-nosed Sphinx recount his version of Egypt's history in a heavy British accent, from a British perspective. We visited a carpet school and watched the nimble fingers of little girls flying through the deft and warp as they knotted silken threads into beautiful designs.

Then we flew to Luxor and boarded a luxury cruiser down the Nile, stopping at historical points to admire the genius of the pharaohs. We disembarked at Aswan and called it a day. We did not fly on to Abu Simbel, though booked to do so. We were tired, and so we returned to Cairo and then home.

TRAVELLING WITH NELSON MANDELA

Travelling with Nelson, the world's most distinguished and popular former prisoner, was perhaps the highlight of all my travels abroad; but it was also very demanding and incredibly tiring. I, who had always had the greatest problems getting a passport, got one in eight minutes flat. I then had to obtain a visa for the US. I was required to state in the application form whether I had ever been charged for security infringements. I filled in 'many times', and this caused the clerk a problem. I asked to speak to the Consul General and told him I was issued my passport in eight minutes flat, and now I was going to see how many minutes it would take to get an American visa. It took one minute. This was my first experience of the Mandela magic.

We made two trips in 1990 – the first between 4 June and 6 July; the second from 13 October to mid-November. Before these trips, Nelson had travelled to various countries in Africa as well as Canada.

Our missions took us to the European capitals, the UK, US, Asia and Australia.

We set out on our intercontinental mission by public transport, for Mandela was yet to become president, when he would have a private jet at his disposal.

I watched Nelson in wonder. He was truly phenomenal. Within months of his release from almost three decades of incarceration, he stepped into the world as if he had never been isolated from it. Wherever he went he was met with rapturous applause, and he warmed to the millions as if he knew every single one of them. He was at perfect ease with world leaders who had spent years in office, and he towered over them in stature, both physically and otherwise. He managed his punishing schedule with no sign of fatigue and charmed all those he met. He seemed to enjoy the crowds as much as they did him. In the mornings he went out jogging whenever he could, to the delight of those who saw him.

Nelson was a world statesman at eighty. My mind turned to the Nelson I had first met at the age of twenty-five as a fellow student at Wits – handsome, debonair, with a penchant for designer clothes, a conservative Africanist who protected the African National Congress jealously from intrusion by non-Africans. I recalled my fellow detainee at the Fort, my fellow accused during the Treason Trial, the youth leader who, in 1944, had founded the ANC Youth League with Walter Sisulu, Oliver Tambo, AP Mda, William Nkomo and the brilliant Anton Lembede.

I recalled the Black Pimpernel on the run, who had spent a few days hiding at our house in Burnwood Road and regaled us with stories of his African adventure. He never tired of recalling how our children, concerned about his threadbare face-cloth, had clubbed together their pennies and bought him a new one. I recalled the regal figure in karos in the Nationalists' court, who had committed his life to the struggle. And now this new Mandela, an amalgam of all the old images of our past, present and future, incarnated in him, the most inspiring leader in the world.

The night before Madiba's arrest outside Howick in Natal, Fathu and I had been at the much talked-about party in Asherville, the last he had attended before his arrest.

During Madiba's imprisonment we had kept in touch with him through letters, and Fathu, his first authorised biographer, had been granted a 'family visit' to Robben Island in the 1970s through Winnie.

Fathu had also been allowed to see him at his request at Victor Verster prison, to revise the biography, and Fathu and I had visited him socially after his release from prison. I had linked up with him after a break of over twenty-six years. I found him elegant in an immaculate suit, looking like a senior statesman.

Perhaps his greatest development had taken place in prison itself. Mandela had fully conquered his restrictive environment and spent every minute of his prison time improving his God-given talents to the utmost. That was his greatest triumph in adversity.

During his long imprisonment the seed had grown into an acorn, and the acorn into a mighty oak, admired by the whole of humanity. Now I was with him as his speech writer in a delegation of fourteen, making a fleeting world tour to enable him personally to thank the countries that had supported the ANC during his internment, and to canvass their support for his Party, which would contest the election and form the first non-racial democratic government in South Africa.

Everywhere we went, the leaders of the five continents greeted him with admiration and awe. The less technologically advanced Third World's leaders were mesmerised and could not take their eyes off him. Often they looked at him with tears rolling down their cheeks. The First World was no less in its admiration, but its leaders, while shaking hands with him, simultaneously looked at the cameras to ensure that their meeting with the exceptional dignitary was publicly recorded.

There were huge audience turnouts in Europe, and I noted with apprehension the unhealthy adulation the people centred on him. It was reminiscent of the discredited cult of the individual – of Hitler, Mussolini and Stalin.

In Germany, Willy Brandt presided over an open-air plenary session. A second plenary followed in an august hall. Nelson made a brief comment and then took me by surprise when he announced, 'My friend Ismail Meer will speak on my behalf.' In the course of my address I articulated my concern. 'You in Europe are doing it again, repeating the cult of the individual – you created Hitler, Mussolini and Stalin. That should have taught you something. Everywhere in Europe, Mandela has been lionised, and no credit has been given to the long struggle of the South African people to win our freedom. Mandela is Mandela because he personifies the freedom-loving people of South Africa.' These words were met with tremendous applause.

One of our highlights in Europe was Mandela's meeting with Pope John Paul II at the Vatican. The ANC leader was given a private audience. It is clear that he made a profound impression on the Pope, for later, while on a brisk walk in the Alps where he was vacationing, the Pope all of a sudden stopped in his stride. His attendants rushed to him to enquire the reason for his sudden halt, and the Catholic leader said, 'Today is Mandela's birthday!'

On part of our European tour, two Afrikaner journalists were allowed to travel with us. The one journalist, a man, was based in London, and he kept repeating that he wished his people in the Free State could have seen how tens of thousands of whites in Rome had looked at Mandela with such great respect and admiration. The other journalist, a woman, said she had known FW de Klerk for many years, and she was surprised that Mandela had said that the South African president was a person of integrity. Mandela's response was that unless he accepted De Klerk as a person of integrity, he could not negotiate with him. I saw her eyes widen in wonder and veneration.

The Indian High Commissioner in Zimbabwe had complained to Fathu that the visit to India was too short, and begged for more days. Fathu had added her own words to the plea, and told Nelson, 'They are saying that they were the first to apply sanctions against South Africa's racist government, that they had placed racism on the UN agenda, and so they are deserving of a longer visit.' Nelson, bearing the burden of raising funds for the ANC to contest the first non-racial democratic election, said he would if they gave him $8 million. The High Commissioner's response was that they would gladly do so.

In Kenya, our group kept the Air India aeroplane-full of passengers waiting for over half an hour before we took our seats. I don't think the fact that they were flying with such august company made up for their frustration.

We were in India in mid-October 1990. On 15 October we experienced something of the splendour of the Raj at Rashtrapati Bhavan. The colonised, on liberation, had taken over all the pomp and ceremony of the colonisers. It occurred to me that we would probably do the same in South Africa.

The Indian welcome was stupendous. The ANC was accorded full diplomatic status and Mr Nphutu Mphele, the ANC's chief representative, was given the status of a fully fledged ambassador. Besides $8 million in cash, the Indian government provided a further Rs20 million to enable the ANC to obtain essential equipment in India.

The Indian National Congress offered a similar amount. Rajiv Gandhi consulted me on a project to which they could contribute in South Africa. I thought immediately of the NIC properties bought by Gandhi in Prince Edward Street and Umgeni Road that remained undeveloped. I discussed the matter with Nelson, who said money was urgently required to purchase Shell House in Johannesburg for the ANC headquarters, and so Rajiv's Party paid for Shell House, later re-christened Luthuli House.

The first award ever received by Mandela was from India, and this had followed Fathu's representation to Indira Gandhi, whom she had met in the early 1970s while she had been a visiting professor at the Delhi School of Economics. Fathu had continued a relationship with the Indian prime minister through correspondence, and she had used her influence to have the award bestowed on Nelson.

I travelled with Nelson to many cities, but the Calcutta reception was unparalleled. Our aeroplane landed in Calcutta in October. That city paid the highest tribute to Mandela; the entire city and its environs turned out to welcome this international hero. It seemed to me that millions lined the road a hundred deep all the way from the airport to the vast open meeting ground. Mandela acknowledged the reception with the words, 'I greet this city of revolution.' His words were met with a delighted roar from the crowds waving thousands of red flags. He went on to recount how, in 1913, Moulana Abdul Kalam Azad had sent Gandhi a telegram of support in South Africa, and went on to outline the contributions of Subhash Chandra Bose and other Bengali heroes.

His speech went down exceedingly well. Rajmohan Gandhi, a grandson of the Mahatma, who along with his younger brother, Gopal from Delhi, had travelled with us, remarked to me, 'He knows our history better than us.' I smiled and accepted the compliment.

The historic Hindu University in Varanasi, the world's oldest living city, conferred an honorary doctorate on our leader at a glittering ceremony, attended by India's leading academics.

From India we flew to Canberra in Australia. On 23 October our group, including Thomas Nkobi, Stanley Mabizela, Laloo Chiba, Barbara Masekela,

Eddie Funde, the ANC representative in Canberra and I, led by Mandela, held a lengthy meeting with the full Australian cabinet.

The deputy president of the ANC, in his comprehensive briefing, thanked the government and people of Australia for their support against apartheid, which had included economic, sport and cultural boycotts.

We next visited Japan, which was gracious, but Nelson drew a blank when it came to financial support. Yet he persisted. Barbara and I were deeply embarrassed and pained that our great leader should have to 'beg' for money, and we said as much to him.

Nelson told his own story about that visit when he invited my family to lunch at the presidential residence in Cape Town, over biryani and fruit served in the china and silverware that had stamped the style in government residences from colonial days. He wove the incident into a joke against himself.

'When I was in Japan,' he began, 'I met the Japanese prime minister. I told the prime minister about our country and about our coming election, and that we needed money to fight the election. He said nothing; he remained silent for a while. Then he said, "We don't give donations to political parties!" I persisted nonetheless, using every argument at my command as to why his government should make an exception in our case. He listened patiently, even graciously. Then he got up and left the room. I thought I had finally got through to him and he had gone to get the money. I waited and waited, but he did not return. Then the truth dawned on me. He was not returning with money, or returning at all, even to bid me goodbye. I was left alone to find my way out. But how to do that? I didn't know my way out. I left the room to see if I could find an attendant, and found one. I asked him, "How do I get out of this place?" Instead of guiding me, he asked, "How did you get in?" It took some time to convince him that I was a guest of the prime minister. He eventually led me out.'

On Thursday, 1 November, our Japan Airlines flight touched down on Malaysian soil. Waiting for us on the tarmac at Kuala Lumpur were Prime Minister Dr Mahathir Mohamed, the Minister of Foreign Affairs, Mr Abu Hassan bin Haji Omar, other dignitaries and press and television cameras. Nelson was brilliant in his interviews.

Throughout Kuala Lumpur, the city was decorated with huge billboards boldly proclaiming, 'MAHATHIR-MANDELA – FIGHTERS FOR HUMAN RIGHTS'.

Our trip was primarily a thanksgiving mission for the role played by Malaysia at the Commonwealth and the United Nations, in particular. Mahathir had made a special visit to Lusaka to meet Nelson soon after his release in February; now Nelson thanked the people and the government of Malaysia for their support.

Dr Mahathir Mohamed, a medico by profession, shared very many of

Mandela's concerns, and hence profitable discussions followed on reconstruction and development.

On our second day in Kuala Lumpur, four of us, led by Mandela, met the prime minister in his office. We were impressed with Mahathir's financial knowledge. He listened intently to the ANC's financial needs and promised generous support, but placed greater emphasis on the provision of housing and technical training, which his country could contribute. In respect of housing, the prime minister said that Malaysia had assisted other states and was exporting building components such as doors and windows, even to Western countries. He offered trained personnel to South Africa to help erect homes for the returning political exiles. He donated $5 million to the ANC's election campaign.

Our delegation also had an audience with His Majesty King Yang di-Pertuan Agong, a qualified barrister. The king is elected from among the nine traditional kings for a period of five years.

Malaysia was opening wide its technology doors to the victims of apartheid and Bantu Education. She was ready to train us in many fields, including electronics and the construction of motor vehicles. We kept learning more and more about how much the East has to offer, and how much of this remains hidden from us.

In Brunei, the chambermaid was rather talkative. She also eavesdropped on our conversations. I was telling our Zulu typist about my children.

'The daughters are married but not the son. We still have to find the lobola,' I told her in jest. The young typist said she would make herself available.

'And how many cows would your father require?' I asked.

'About twenty heads would do,' she said.

The chambermaid chipped in. 'Please sir,' she said. 'You could come to my father. He will only want a few fowls, two or three for me!'

The chambermaid's humility was charming; the rituals of being presented to royalty were trying. Waiting to meet the Sultan of Brunei in an antechamber, we were instructed on how we should conduct ourselves upon meeting His Majesty. 'See that when you sit your legs are not crossed, nor your knees separated; they should touch each other.' There were also instructions as to how we should present the gifts we had brought. We politely told the attendant that he need not bother. We hadn't brought any gifts.

Next was the United States. While Calcutta outdid New York in her public welcome, the University of Atlanta scored the highest marks for singing our national anthem, *Nkosi Sikelel' iAfrika*. Many of us agreed their rendering was better than anything we had heard in South Africa.

Fathu was in Washington a few days before our arrival. She had returned from a conference in Trinidad and was the guest of the Smithsonian Natural Science Museum, which she had addressed. She told me about that address.

Several ANC representatives in Washington were in the audience, and during question time one of them had asked, to her surprise, whether Mandela would identify with the expatriates. She said that she had assured them that neither Mandela nor people in South Africa saw any difference between those who had been forced into exile and those who had remained in South Africa. Mandela was the leader of all South Africans, regardless of where they resided.

She also reported that she had been invited to the senators' breakfast meeting, where she had been quizzed about the thinking of Mandela. One of the participants, Congressman Howard Wolpe, requested a private meeting with her after breakfast, when he asked whether she would be seeing Mandela before he arrived in Washington. He then instructed her to caution Mandela that, while in the States, if he so much as breathed the names Arafat or Gaddafi, he would lose all support in the country. 'Damn cheek,' Fathu commented, and I concurred. Nelson's reaction was similar when I communicated the conversation to him. The famous interview followed when Nelson asked the interviewer whether he was referring to 'our friends, Gaddafi and Arafat', and commented that 'America's enemies are not necessarily our enemies and America's friends not necessarily our friends', or words to that effect.

Travelling with Mandela was very tiring. In every city there was the motorcade and accompanying protocol. Our delegation was sorted into various cars to sit with the appropriate local dignitaries. Nelson's car led the motorcade, and when he alighted we had to run to catch up with him. It depended on your position in the motorcade how far you had to run.

One of Mandela's followers remarked that Mandela was probably treated with greater consideration for his person by his jail warders in the last phase of his imprisonment than by his colleagues in the first phase of his release.

There was a great deal of excitement over the New York reception. Historian Tom Karis had informed Fathu that it was very rare for the city to give a ticker-tape welcome. She was very keen for me to accompany Nelson to New York, but I was by then too exhausted and needed a break from the punishing schedule. Fathu said that if Nelson could take it, why not I? I told her Nelson had been resting for the last twenty-seven years; I had not. She laughed and did not pursue the subject any further.

I was too exhausted by the end of our visit to Rome to continue any further with the delegation. I had had enough of getting out of cars and running after our leader in order to catch up with him, before the lift took off to deposit us on the floor of our next meeting. Thabo Mbeki was leaving the entourage and going to London. I decided to join him. We left on the Italian aircraft that was transporting our delegation to Amsterdam. The crew offered to drop us off at Heathrow. I arranged to catch up with the delegation in Washington.

Thabo was met by his wife Zanele. I telephoned Bhai, Fathu's brother, who collected me, and I spent a few quiet days, happy for the relief and to eat familiar food, expertly cooked by Zubie. Most importantly, I could spend some time with Rashid.

On our return to South Africa from the US, we again stopped in London. I telephoned Bhai, Siddiek and their wives and invited them to the hotel where we were staying, and they had the opportunity to meet Nelson. I could see their pleasure and I was happy that I had managed to do this for them.

SEVENTEEN

MOVING INTO NON-RACIAL SOUTH AFRICAN DEMOCRACY

1989 ONWARDS

THE END OF APARTHEID

The year 1989 is crucial to our history. The power of the Nationalist state was waning. It had worn out the limits of its oppressive control. The security laws through which it governed began to be flouted with impunity, and the disenfranchised ignored segregation notices. Oppression can only continue for as long as the oppressed allow it to. At last this wisdom had come to us.

Crucially, in the face of that situation, the international banking concerns that had supported apartheid got cold feet about their loans to the Nationalist government, and called them in. That was the last straw. The apartheid government had the army but could not risk a civil war, not in defence of racism, which was akin to Nazism, and not in the face of economic bankruptcy.

The anti-apartheid forces, on the other hand, were unable to take over the state by sheer mass mobilisation or by the gun, or by a combination of both. The contending parties were forced to the negotiation table.

MANDELA'S PRISON CONDITIONS RELAXED, 1989

The one clear sign that apartheid was facing its demise was the relaxation of Mandela's prison conditions in 1989. In May of that year, Nelson invited Fathu and me to visit him in Victor Verster prison. We flew to Cape Town and drove to the prison. We found him in excellent form and were surprised to see how comfortably he had been set up. He enjoyed taking us around his 'house' – to his bedroom with its queen-size bed. He opened a cupboard and displayed his wardrobe, befitting a gentleman of presidential rank. He showed us his exercise room. We sat down to lunch, served by his warder, who also acted as his butler. Nelson indicated that he was having talks with government ministers. I came away convinced that his release was imminent, and negotiations on the cards. To facilitate negotiations, the National Party cabinet replaced the intransigent PW Botha with the far-sighted FW de Klerk in July 1989.

During our visit, Fathu brought up the matter of the publication of his biography, *Higher than Hope*, which she had written. She told him she was passing all the royalties to him. He suggested that they share the royalties between them. I said to Fathu perhaps she should consider that, but Fathu said if the book had any value at all, it was because it was his life. He was thus entitled to all the royalties; she would take no part of it, and she remained true to her word. She did not want Nelson to bear any expenses incurred in the writing of the manuscript – the typing, travelling, negotiating with publishers, etc. I, of course, paid for that. The book sold well and was published in several languages. All the royalties went to Nelson at a time when he was short of funds and needed money, among other things to furnish the house Winnie had built for him.

Nelson's release was announced while Fathu was in London, where she was spending a few days with Rashid before going on to Iran as a state guest. I telephoned her there and told her that Nelson would be released the next day.

The launch of Fathu's biography of Nelson in London coincided with his release, and her publishers took full advantage of this. She found herself in great demand by both the print and electronic media. Rashid became her PRO and helped her to sift through the large number of requests and make the right choices.

CODESA

While previously banned people were 'unbanned' and exiles returned from foreign countries, the government prepared to set up the negotiation table that would usher in our new democracy.

The negotiations began on 20 December 1991 in the vast World Trade Centre in Johannesburg, and delegates from nineteen organisations participated in discussions in the presence of the media and international observers. I was a participant on behalf of the NIC at some of the sessions. I did not find it an inspiring experience, owing to the dominance of delegates who had participated in the apartheid structures and who were now striving to retain their power.

The fundamental issue at CODESA was who should have power – the majority of the electorate, as favoured by the ANC – or whether it should be shared between the majority and minority parties – a government of national unity. The majority/minority problem remains an ethnic issue to the present day, with Indians and Coloureds feeling marginalised and vulnerable.

Negotiations and violence went hand in hand as certain structures, fearing that they would not gain at the ballot box or the negotiation table, attempted to derail CODESA in the hopeless belief that they would retain power.

Eventually there was agreement on the constitution, but it was burdened with the Sunset Clauses, which protected the vested interests of the Nationalists, and this hampered our new democracy.

THE FIRST NON-RACIAL, DEMOCRATIC ELECTION

South Africa held its first non-racial, democratic election on 27 April 1994. Fathu and I went together to the polling station at Springfield Model Primary School, taking our places in the long queue and waiting our turn to draw our crosses in support of the ANC.

I was nominated to the KwaZulu-Natal Legislative Assembly. Rashid's fellow detainee, Yunus Carrim, informed me that Fathu's nomination was high up on the provincial list. Later Winnie informed her that her name was also high on the parliamentary list, but when the ANC lists were published, Fathu's name was absent from both lists. We raised this matter with Kathy during one of his visits to us, and he confirmed that Fathu's name was on both lists. The ANC executive, however, had placed priority on her work on the board of the South African Broadcasting Corporation (SABC). If she entered government she would have to resign her position on the board; consequently her nominations were cancelled without consulting her.

Fathu was not one to push herself into any position, but her exclusion from the nomination lists upset me. I saw in it the victory of manipulative mischief over the will of the people.

I took my seat in the KwaZulu-Natal Legislative Assembly and contributed to that chamber as best I could. I was elected for a second term in 1999. Fathu supported me on the Provincial Legislature at all times and encouraged me in every way. She, however, never attended any of our meetings, and I did not ask her to.

MY ACTIVISM IN A NON-RACIAL DEMOCRACY

The departure of the Nationalist government and the ringing in of our new democracy breathed new life into me. I was suddenly free to speak my mind, to engage in whatever activity I chose; the heavy hand that had gagged my freedom of thought, expression and action was removed. I began forming a number of organisations. With JN Singh's return to Durban, we set about reviving the Sastri College Alumni Association. JN was elected president. We organised lectures and an annual dinner. The dinners are well attended and bring together many old friends and their wives. At the first dinner, JN and I stood at the door and I quipped, 'We didn't know when we married that we would be marrying grandmothers!' Fathu smiled as she usually does at my jokes, but Radhi retorted, 'Nor we that we would be marrying grandfathers!' The meetings of the Old Boys and their spouses – grandmothers and grandfathers – continue to be fun events.

I renewed my interest in education and established the Liberation History Foundation and the Democratic Education Advancement League (DEAL). I had been contributing a column in the *Leader* for forty-five years, recalling the involvement of Indians in the social and political life of the country. I now extended my interest in this field through the Liberation History Foundation. This body has been making a significant contribution in bringing political bodies and personalities together, and has provided a platform for celebrating our past heroes and politically significant days, which are now entrenched in our non-racial, democratic calendar. I have been putting out bulletins since 1997, recording the historical events celebrated at our meetings, and these are compiled into four volumes.

JN passed away a year after we had started working together. My world was shrinking. I had seen so many deaths. The family/clan had lost so many members. Only two of my sisters and I survive today from Chota Meer's eight children. Four of us siblings lost children during our lifetimes; my brother AC and I and my sister Budie lost sons, and Gorie Bai her daughter, Zainab. Fathu has lost her parents and two brothers. We keep in close contact with her two sisters and her surviving three brothers. None of the children of my father's brothers survive, though there are grandchildren and great-grandchildren.

The clan, as I knew it for most of my life, has been sorrowfully reduced. The Group Areas Act was the first assault. The Meer Fariya opposite the Botanic Gardens in Ritson Road, nearby Mansfield Road and Etna Lane, was swept away by the racist broom. We ceased to gather as we used to – then death took its toll. I am the only surviving son of the three Meer pioneers in South Africa – Mohamed Meer, Ismail Meer and Chota Meer. I am grateful for my life.

RASHID'S RETURN AND FATAL ACCIDENT

Rashid returned to South Africa in 1994, soon after the Nationalist government had taken the necessary steps to legalise the return of exiles. While we now had all the members of our family in South Africa, the time for reconstituting our family under one roof had long passed. That was never to be – Shehnaz was settled in Cape Town, Shamim in Johannesburg, and Rashid, after spending a few brief weeks with us, also settled in Johannesburg, the prospects for pursuing his career in radio being better there. He was, however, disappointed with the

SABC's offer to him. He had held a fairly senior position at the BBC, but the SABC offered him a fairly junior position, which he declined as he saw that it would cramp his style. He started his own company and was settling into it very successfully when tragedy struck. There was a motor accident. Rashid was driving the car; his companion was literally unscathed, but Rashid died on the spot.

Fathu had just been discharged from hospital after spending some two weeks in intensive care. She had collapsed at home, having suffered a severe heart attack, and had been removed to hospital. I was in Ulundi in the Legislative Assembly when I received the news that Rashid had been involved in an accident. I telephoned Shamim and found her in a very distraught state. While she did not say anything, I thought the worst, but I put it at the back of my mind. I couldn't be sure; I did not want it to be that. Yusuf Bhamjee drove me to Durban. Those two hours I spent driving to Durban were the hardest in my life. Yusuf tried to keep me occupied, asking me questions about our political past. I kept on answering, perhaps to get away from that gnawing intelligence that the worst may have happened to Rashid. We eventually reached Burnwood Road where Yusuf Bhamjee confirmed my worst thought – that Rashid was dead. It was confirmation rather than new information. I withdrew into myself. I saw the dozens of cars outside our home. I got out in a daze. Fathu met me at the door. I didn't expect her to be there. She was muttering, 'What will we do now? How will we live now?' I could not help her because I could not help myself. I led her to her bed and left her in the care of her sister, Baby. The house was full of people and I had to attend to them. Fathu and I needed time to ourselves, alone, but we did not get the time that evening. Dr Tayob, the cardiologist, attended to Fathu and sedated her, to keep her calm.

Rashid and I had become close during the last months of his life. I was in great pain, but I suppressed my feelings. I had to take care of Fathu, still fragile from her heart ailment.

The hearse with Rashid's body arrived very early in the morning, with Shamim, who, with Bobby and their children, had followed in their car. The floor of our living room was spread with blankets, and the women of our family and close friends had taken position there. Fathu sat with them. Rashid, in his white shroud, was laid out close to her. Shamim, Shehnaz and our granddaughters were beside her.

When the burial was over and the crowds had left, save for the very close relatives who were helping around the house, and when Fathu seemed calmer, I told her about the burial, for women do not go to burials in our community. I told her that our grandson Zen, my nephew Salim and her brother Farouk had descended into the grave. They had received Rashid's body and laid it to rest. Then Fathu and I held and comforted each other.

MY EIGHTIETH BIRTHDAY

I cannot lay the story of my life to rest without commenting on my eightieth birthday. I turned eighty on 5 September 1998. The day was like any other, except that Fathu wished me many happy returns early in the morning, as she had done on all the birthdays since our engagement, and she gave me a very handsome watch. The grandchildren followed with 'Happy birthday to you', 'For he's a jolly good fellow' and 'Hip, hip hurrah!'

Fathu said that we would go out for supper that evening, and that Dr Mike Sutcliffe and TS Maharaj would join us. Although I do not like eating out, I didn't object since she had made the arrangements. I'm not one for eating out. I was pleased she had invited Mike Sutcliffe. I had grown fond of him, and he had written a glowing tribute to me, published in the *Daily News*, commemorating my eightieth year.

Fathu disappeared in the late afternoon. She said she had a television interview at the University of Natal. When she hadn't returned by 6 pm, I got very agitated. 'She should be spending her time with me, not with a television crew!' I grumbled. TS Maharaj arrived with a white Nehru suit, his present to me. He insisted I put it on for dinner. I did so to please him. Shamim and her daughter Maia were with me, and their presence calmed me somewhat. Shehnaz's daughters were getting ready to go with us but Shehnaz was not around either, and when I asked about that I got some vague reply. I remained anxious about Fathu's absence. Then Mike Sutcliffe came and said he would drive me to the dinner and we would pick Fathu up at the university. I shook my head. 'She should have been here!' I said. We drove to the university and the Sutcliffes guided me through the side door of the Students' Union Hall. I had expected Fathu to join us in the car, but Mike insisted we should go down and meet her in the studio. 'Let us see what is going on there. It might take a few minutes.' I again shook my head and reluctantly entered the hall, where I was greeted with the loud singing of 'Happy Birthday' and the splendid sight of a full hall. Tables were laid for dinner and Fathu met me at the entrance, guiding me through the large congregation of friends and relatives to the stage. Shehnaz was the MC. Chief Buthelezi and Kathy represented Nelson, who had intended to come but at the last minute was ordered to bed. He had overdone things at the Commonwealth conference and had almost collapsed. I thought of the surprise birthday party Fathu had organised forty-two years ago, when I had ordered her never again to spring a surprise party on me. I had mixed feelings about this one, but I complimented Fathu on her perfect arrangements.

Shehnaz was much admired as the MC, and all my granddaughters made short presentations, Maia moving the vote of thanks.

Fathu's brothers and their families, their sons and daughters and their sons-in-law, had flown in from London. Ismail Mohamed paid glowing tribute to both Fathu and me. The Moosas produced a second cake and announced that they were also celebrating Fathu's seventieth birthday, which had passed a month before.

Soon after my eightieth birthday, I began having trouble with my leg. Fathu and I were driving to the airport. I tried stopping at the robot and found I couldn't engage the brake and clutch simultaneously. I began walking with difficulty.

At the time I was serving on the board of M-Net, besides being a member of the KwaZulu-Natal parliament. I took the necessary flights for as long as I could. Fathu has redesigned much of the house, and has installed supports to help me move around.

I still go to my office and have attended a KwaZulu-Natal government session, but I find myself keeping to my bed more and more. Fathu had a triple bypass in 1998. I was reasonably mobile at the time, and, with my daughters, kept at her side as much as the hospital would allow. She had to be hospitalised for diabetes, and I dropped her off and fetched her, though walking had already become a strain. The doctors cannot find the cause of the problem in my leg, but they reassure me all the time that I am in sound health – my heart good, my blood pressure normal, free from diabetes. Fathu's mild stroke in 2000 left me very anxious and highly disturbed, but she seems strong now. I am grateful that we are together.

EPILOGUE

Today we have four granddaughters and one grandson. We are doting grandparents and all five grandchildren were brought up on Waschbank stories. Fathu invariably joined us during those storytelling sessions, sitting on the side of the bed, as most of it was occupied by the grandchildren. Our eldest grandchild is Zen, Shamim's son, twenty years old, a handsome, tall lad who chauffeurs me at times and who is studying Fine Arts at the Michaelis School of Art in Cape Town; he is also a photographer who has already had his work published. We were exceedingly proud of eighteen-year-old Maia when she passed matric with six A symbols. She is an undergraduate student, also at the University of Cape Town. Shehnaz has three daughters: the eldest is fifteen-year-old Nadia, with obvious talent in music and art, and a lovely, helpful teenager; her sister Khiyara is thirteen and she brings me little ceramic figures she makes herself. Ayesha, aged nine, is the youngest of our grandchildren. She partners me in performing Jack and the Beanstalk. When I, as the excited Jack, call to her, 'Mother, Mother, come and see the beanstalk,' she gives her punchline: 'You silly boy, beans don't talk!'

Shamim is a writer and researcher, focusing on the issues of women and land, and women's rights in general. She was offered an ambassadorship by Nelson and given a choice of two countries, Indonesia or Hong Kong, but she declined, placing priority on her work on women. She has several publications to her credit, and is much in demand as a consultant on gender affairs in South Africa and abroad.

Shehnaz is a judge of the Land Claims Court. She too has several publications to her credit.

And I am very proud of Fathu and her accomplishments, which go on and on.

I thank Allah for my life and the people who have enriched it, both in the family and from the large network of friends and companions who have walked with me at different stages of my life and, in particular, those who have kept my mind and heart fixed on the goal of human equality and achieving peace in our lifetime.

APPENDIX 1

AN ADDRESS AT MR IC MEER'S EIGHTIETH BIRTHDAY CELEBRATIONS BY CHIEF JUSTICE ISMAIL MAHOMED

The end of the war saw the pitiless brutality of Hiroshima and Nagasaki, but it also saw wave upon wave of fresh idealism as good, decent men and women began to sing a resonating song of beauty and brotherhood, love and protest across the oceans that physically divided their ancient lands, and where there was sometimes so much intoxicating natural beauty mixed with grotesque human cruelty.

There was a state of creative restlessness everywhere as humanity appeared to seek a new mutation. Within a relatively brief period of potential drama, the movement towards colonial emancipation for millions became irresistible. Racial bigotry in key areas was challenged, and the United Nations was established, offering to some dreamers the first glimpses of an incremental progression towards the vision of a world government of equals.

South Africa was not insulated from this turmoil. Indeed, it was destined, in many ways, to become its centrepiece, as a new and energetic generation of young men and women, with the exuberance of youth and the energy of a pristine idealism, sought to confront the very economic and political foundations upon which the official policies of the South African state were premised. It was this turmoil that produced the young Nelson Mandela, whose eightieth birthday we celebrated with such justifiable triumph six weeks ago. It was the same challenge that also produced the incredibly energetic Ismail Meer, who is eighty today.

Ismail Meer was only nineteen years old when the youthful spirit that had been sparked within him in Natal propelled him to the editorial board of progressive magazines, such as the *New Outlook* and the *Call*. In the following year, he joined the Non-European United Front to give expression to the increasingly restless spirit within him, which rebelled against injustice. His later experiences in Johannesburg intensified that spirit, and what began as a nascent and exciting spark soon became a raging divine fire within his soul, matched in its intensity only by the ferocity of the evil with which it was confronted. He began what was to become a very deep, intimate and sustained friendship with Nelson Mandela. He grew and sparkled as a man, as a leader and as an orator with a compelling charisma. Even his legal studies became a temporary casualty as he was propelled into the passive resistance movement against arbitrary racial laws. He soon had his first experience of incarceration in a South African prison.

Ismail found himself within the very crucible of a deep conflict with racial injustice. It took him to the very heart of the resistance against apartheid. His moral universe expanded and soared. He was in and out of jail, continuously harassed, confined, persecuted, charged with high treason in a trial of epic dimensions, and banned for some thirty-eight years from writing, speaking or giving expression to his rich reservoir of sensitive idealism and his alluring vision of a durable civilisation, premised on the stable foundations of a constitutional democracy.

The voice of Ismail Chota Meer in all its colourful glory, in the expression of his rich skills as a lawyer of vast experience, a historian of great depth, and a versatile thinker of nimble insight, is now part of the feast that this nation enjoys: through his speeches in the Provincial Legislature of KwaZulu-Natal; through his diligent, sustained and objective inputs outside its formal corridors; through his rich and prolific writings in diverse media; through the profound jurisprudential and philosophical perspectives that he shares with his many thousands of readers; through the irresistible magic of his formidable personality; and through his superb oratorical skills at the many public and significant occasions that mediate the continuing maturation and destiny of a nation, now in a state of unprecedented transformation.

Eighty not out! It has been an innings of rare beauty and power, which has inspired legitimate awe, even veneration, among those privileged to share in its great thrill.

Ismail confronted and sustained hostile bowling in detention, cunning spins from banning orders and deceptive googlies in security surveillance, most of the time in failing moral light and on uneven ethical pitches, with a skill that was classically graceful, a sense of anticipation that was consistently unerring, a confidence that was demonstrably infectious, and a courage that was totally inspiring in its majestic magnificence. Keep on batting Ismail! Do not ever stop the magic! We will applaud you all the way to your century, because your heroism legitimises our own humanity.

Ismail Meer was very young indeed when he was so attractively – but in retrospect perhaps so inexorably – propelled into the struggle against racial injustice in South Africa, inspired in crucial areas by the great struggle of the children of his forefathers from India for their own emancipation from colonial rule.

May you have very, very many more happy years in this great land of your first and last love, giving expression to that wondrously creative restlessness within your soul, which reaches to the heavens beyond. Enjoy the laughter and the sweet innocence of your young grandchildren. Enjoy also those wonderfully rich opportunities for quiet conversations with your sensitive soul, offered by the incredible beauty of the deep blue waters of the Indian Ocean in mystical dialogue with the lush green vegetation and the golden sands of the North Coast, which have for so long and in so many different ways been so intimately a part of your exciting life.

APPENDIX 2

IC MEER IN THE KWAZULU-NATAL LEGISLATURE BY DR MICHAEL SUTCLIFFE

Like his close friend and political colleague, Nelson Mandela, IC Meer inspired many of us in our pursuit of peace, democracy and a better life for all. South Africa owes IC a special debt of gratitude for his unrelenting fight against evil and his principled stand against injustice, no matter where it came from.

IC, by birth, was a country bumpkin, growing up in Waschbank. While forced out of school through economic difficulties, he continued studying part time, and was rewarded with a matric from Sastri College. Whilst working as a trade unionist, he studied for a BA degree at the University of Natal, but the same university's racist policies denied him the chance of studying law in Natal, and so he left for the University of the Witwatersrand. There he studied law, and also shared a flat with the young Nelson Mandela.

IC was charged for treason in 1956, and for the life of the National Party government was banned from writing or speaking in public. He was detained without trial, banned, listed as a communist, suffered terrorist attacks on his home, but through all of this his determination to outlast and defeat the National Party regime never wavered.

Fortunately for the ANC, as we moved towards the election in 1994, Nelson Mandela reminded us of the importance of stalwarts like IC Meer. While not known for their toyi-toying prowess, or even widely known at branch level, such veterans as IC Meer brought into the legislatures of our country a deep well of wisdom from which we have all drunk. In IC's case, he found additional energy to continue his more than sixty years of struggle against apartheid from the days when he was a founder of the Liberal Study Group in 1934, to his founding the Liberation History Foundation in 1996.

The province of KwaZulu-Natal as a whole benefited enormously from having had IC Meer in its legislature. Without fear of contradiction, I can say that IC was probably the person most popular across all party lines in the provincial legislature, and he stands out as the pre-eminent debater listened to by all, from presidents and premiers to traditional leaders and us juniors.

IC Meer's art was to continually trace the trinities in our religious and secular lives. There are few people around who were as knowledgeable on the unity of religious life as IC. But he would often talk of those unities that guided our liberation struggle against colonialism and racism. Whilst Shaka left a legacy of unity in action, and Dube emphasised the need for Africans to reassert themselves, it was Chief Albert Luthuli who left a singular message that no matter what race you were, unite against apartheid. Of course, when you were dealing with IC Meer, it was almost as if he not only grew up with Chief Luthuli, but with King Shaka and Dr Dube as well!

IC brought together all those who fought for liberation. He counted among his personal friends not only Nelson Mandela and many other ANC leaders, but also Dr Mangosuthu Buthelezi and members of other political parties. However, he reserved his fondest admiration for our former president, and loved telling stories about who was actually the more handsome beau of the two! After all, Nelson Mandela was unable to recite love poems in Urdu and Gujarati, so could there have been any competition for IC Meer?

The deeply philosophical underpinnings that spurred IC on to even greater writings and speeches are contained in his oft-quoted trinity of Tawhid (the unity of our maker), Ahimsa (that without peace there can be no unity) and Ubuntu (the powerful tradition of tolerance).

Personally, I am deeply privileged to frequently have had as my passenger IC Meer, when we drove to meetings in the legislature. Of course, I would not admit to members of the IFP that one of the advantages of a dual capital (Ulundi and Pietermaritzburg) is that I had the opportunity to be educated by IC Meer in our travels. We shared the terrible loss of his son, and the way in which he and Fatima found peace through their weekly visits to Rashid's gravesite. We shared his reminiscences of his student days with Nelson Mandela, and the lonely dark years of his trials, bannings and restrictions. And we shared his deep pride in the accomplishments of not only Fatima, but also of his children Shehnaz, Shamim and Rashid. IC remained one of the most optimistic people in the world, always able to turn adversity into victory.

To have had leaders of his stature once more able to talk publicly, organise locally and negotiate with our enemies, gave us all great inspiration. The joy of the unbannings in 1990 often led to despair, such as that associated with the security force slayings in Boipatong. However, having the likes of Nelson Mandela, Oliver Tambo and IC Meer around, meant that for us there was no going back.

The ANC in 1993 and early 1994 had to organise its party lists for the various legislatures. Given the ongoing political violence in KwaZulu-Natal, it was decided that Jacob Zuma would 'remain' on the provincial list and be the ANC's candidate for premier. A process of popular selection interspersed with strategic deployment led to the list for the ANC in KwaZulu-Natal being finalised. IC was number thirteen on the list, and while many activists had not had the privilege to work with him because of his long years of banning, we soon realised what a giant of an intellectual he was.

Once elected, he was deployed on the Portfolio Committees of Education, Finance and Public Accounts, although there were very few areas in which IC did not have something significant to say. He was always delighted to speak, and throughout his speeches in the committees and assembly and in the motions he prepared, he balanced a historical analysis with a focus on the issues confronting us post-1994. But never did he allow us to become complacent. And the word 'hegemonic' did not exist for him, because while the ANC may have enjoyed great majorities throughout the country, all leaders had to be reminded that no one is truly free until the poor are freed from the shackles of racism, capitalism and sexism.

Ismail Meer served two terms in parliament, and he used those terms not only to scrutinise the bills to ensure their legality and grace of language, but also to engage on their moral correctness and their consistency with the Constitution and human rights.

IC never hesitated to criticise his Party, the ANC, when criticism was due. He brought a richness to the deliberations through his knowledge of world religions, cultures and history. He never demurred when the opportunity presented itself to introduce Indian languages and proverbs. He also used the provincial parliamentary platform to celebrate South African historical events and personalities. IC did this in conjunction with the Liberation History Foundation, which he had established. He was an overwhelming moral force, and never compromised his position to party loyalty or prejudices against his opposition.

IC's addresses reflected his personal history, his cultural background, his strong sense of religion and his commitment to democracy and to the Constitution. He manifested a dignity and authority born out of his years of action. His speeches reflected his obvious enjoyment of them, due, to some extent, to his sudden freedom to address audiences. He loved to illustrate points with Indian proverbs, which he introduced in the Indian languages without being self-conscious.

Selected speeches by Ismail Meer are available on the Internet at www.zebrapress.co.za

NOTES

FOREWORD

1. Winnie Madikizela-Mandela

CHAPTER ONE

1. Ghalib is an Urdu poet. His original poem in translation is, 'I know the state of affairs in heaven, but to indulge my heart, Ghalib, I entertain happy thoughts.'
2. Overseer of the workforce.
3. 'Indentured Indian' referred to those Indians who were brought from India, either by contract or shanghaied, as contract labour to work on the newly established sugar cane farms. At the end of the period of indenture a person was permitted to extend the contract for one more period, or be repatriated back to India or to remain in Natal. 'Passenger Indian' referred to Indians from India or Mauritius who paid their ship fares and came to South Africa as craftsmen, traders or priests and teachers.
4. Zulu word for reverend or teacher.
5. Islamic scholar and teacher.
6. Islamic theological school for the training of Moulanas, the Muslim clergy.
7. The struggle to maintain the autonomy of Muslims under the jurisdiction of the Caliph in the face of British domination.
8. Alternative Islamic medical practice.
9. Islamic school.
10. Teacher at a Madressa.
11. Teacher.
12. Mohamed Meer's youngest son.
13. The first of the five Islamic prayers. The Fijr Namaaz is performed at dawn.
14. On 13 April 1919, General Dyer ordered a brutal massacre of protesting crowds at Jalianwala Bagh in Amritsar. Over a thousand adults and children were killed or wounded.

CHAPTER TWO

1. Seth means trader.
2. Albert West assisted Gandhi on the *Indian Opinion*.
3. Satyagraha is non-violent resistance.
4. The highest award given by the Indian government in recognition of exceptional talent or contribution to society, for example cultural, military, social welfare or community service.
5. Gandhi's hut.

CHAPTER THREE

1. An educationist and one of the first Indian intellectuals to be appointed as a researcher at the University of Natal.
2. Gujarati-speaking Muslims from Surat and its environs.

EPILOGUE

3 Minister of the Interior and later deputy prime minister in the Smuts government.
4 The Durban municipality.
5 This was the name of the organisation formed by Gandhi after he left the NIC in 1913.
6 The group in Natal was known as the National Bloc, while those in the Transvaal called themselves the National Group.
7 Prime Minister Winston Churchill of the United Kingdom and President Franklin D Roosevelt of the United States signed the Atlantic Charter in 1941, characterising their countries' participation in World War II as a defence of democracy. They committed their countries to respect the rights of people to choose the form of government under which they will live. In order to advance the cause of African democracy and independence, the ANC set up a committee in 1943 under the chairmanship of Professor ZK Matthews. They produced a document titled *African Claims in South Africa*.
8 Marriage ceremony.

CHAPTER FOUR

1 Student fund-raising drive for charity, incorporating, among other things, a street procession with floats.
2 John Vorster was detained in the early 1940s for belonging to the Ossewa Brandwag organisation, which aligned itself with the Nazi ideology. He was pro-Hitler.

CHAPTER FIVE

1 Ahmed Kathrada was later charged in the Rivonia Trial and served life imprisonment with Nelson Mandela on Robben Island.
2 Secretary of the NIC and a treason trialist.
3 A passionate Unity Movement member.
4 Winnie Madikizela-Mandela.
5 Chief Albert Luthuli's widow.

CHAPTER SIX

1 Ismail called Fatima, his future wife, 'Behn', or sister, until they were married.
2 The founder of Pakistan. He negotiated independence for Pakistan with the British.
3 A Bengali freedom fighter.

CHAPTER EIGHT

1 The defeated Old Guard established the Natal Indian Organisation as a moderate organisation that could collaborate with the government.

CHAPTER NINE

1 Bengu was a traditional herb doctor from Ladysmith whom the authorities hoped to train into a major African leader whom they could influence, and, through him, the African people. In this way they hoped to evade any discussions with the ANC leaders of the day.
2 The Surah Al-Fateha is regarded as the summary of the entire Quran. It is also referred to as the essence of the Quran, hence its popularity among

275

Muslims, who recite it at almost every community occasion, such as weddings, funerals and engagements.
3   A soft drink, often made with milk.
4   'Fatima, the daughter of Moosa Meer, to Ismail, the son of Chota Meer.'
5   Food given to the bride to tide her on her journey to her in-laws.

CHAPTER TEN

1   The pass laws; the Separate Representation of Voters Act; the Suppression of Communism Act; the Bantu Authorities Act; the Stock Limitation Regulations; and the Group Areas Act.

CHAPTER TWELVE

1   Twentieth-century novelist, activist and social philosopher.

CHAPTER THIRTEEN

1   Dr M Motala of Pietermaritzburg, Ismail's second cousin.
2   Fathu's non-biological mother and Ismail's cousin.
3   Fathu's sister-in-law, her oldest brother Ismail's wife.
4   Dr Hilda Kuper, celebrated anthropologist and close friend.
5   Fathu's third brother, a doctor.
6   A huge boy doll in corduroy trousers that Fathu's brother Ahmed bought her.
7   A medical doctor and on the COD executive.
8   A reformist Hindu group.

CHAPTER FIFTEEN

1   A lawyer and last NIC president before its banning.
2   A philosophy lecturer at the University of Natal who was very active in the anti-apartheid struggle. He had great influence on the students and worked closely with trade unions. He was assassinated in 1977.
3   Victoria Mxenge, a civil rights activist and lawyer who was assassinated by reactionaries.
4   Aiden Walsh, a friend of Andrew Verster's.

CHAPTER SIXTEEN

1   The pilgrimage to Mecca which all Muslims are expected to make at least once.
2   Someone who is undependable.
3   A pilgrim's guide during the Haj.
4   An important event in the performance of Haj. It is obligatory for all pilgrims to reenact Hazra's agony by running between the two hills. This is referred to as 'sai'.
5   Noonday prayer.
6   Call to prayer.
7   Exorcising these Satans from within oneself and undertaking to lead pure and compassionate lives. This is another Haj ritual, the purpose of Haj being self-purification and liberating oneself from evil.
8   Prayer at sunset and last prayer of the day.

GLOSSARY

ALWIDA: farewell
ARYA SAMAJ: a reformist Hindu group
AZAAN: call to prayer
BAAS: boss
BAI: elder sister
BAJEE: father
BEHN: sister
BHABIE: sister-in-law
BHAI: brother
BHAIYA: brother
BHAJ POD: food given to the bride to tide her over on her journey to her in-laws
BRAAI: barbecue
CALIPHATE: see Khilafat
EDIE: money
ESHA NAMAAZ: last prayer of the day
FARISHTAS: angels
FARIYA: neighbourhood
FATEHA: Islamic prayer suitable for all occasions
FIJR NAMAAZ: the first of the five Islamic prayers, performed at dawn
GADEE: car
GOJIE KUTHRIE: dirty bitch
GORA LOG: white people
HAJ: pilgrimage
HARAAM: forbidden
HARTAL: day of prayer
HERRENVOLK: master race
HOU LINKS: keep left
INYANGA: traditional herbal doctor
JALSA: reception/celebration
JAMAT KHANA: prayer space
KHILAFAT: the struggle to maintain the autonomy of Muslims under the jurisdiction of the Caliph in the face of British domination
KURTAS: long shirts
KUTUM: clan
LADOOS AND BURFEE: sweetmeats

MADRESSA: school
MAGRIB NAMAAZ: prayer at sunset
MANZILS: destinations
MITHAI: sweetmeats
MOLVI: teacher at a madressa
MOULANA: Islamic scholar and teacher
MUALLIM: a pilgrim's guide during Haj
MURABBA: the Gujarati version of jam
MUSAFFAR KHANAS: travellers' lodges
MUSALLAH: prayer mat
MUSHAIRA: a gathering of Urdu poets
NAMAAZ: prayer
NAMAAZ AWDNIES: head scarves
NAWAB: nobleman
NAZAR: evil eye
NIKAH CEREMONY: marriage ceremony
PADMA SHREE: highest award given by the Indian government in recognition of exceptional talent or contribution to society
PATHILAAS: pots
PURI PATHA: an Indian savoury
PURNA SWARAJ: complete independence
QAWALI: traditional music recital
SAI: a ritual commemorating the agony of Hazra, who was left in the desert by Ebrahim with her infant son, Ishmael
SARANGEE: violin
SARVODAYA: Gandhi's hut in Phoenix, Durban
SATYAGRAHA: non-violent form of resistance
SETH: trader
SHERBET: a soft drink, often made with milk
SIJDA: prostration
SIRDAR: overseer of the workforce
SOLO: a sweet rice dish
TABLA: drum
TAMASHA: spectacle
TAWAAF: ambulations
TOPI: fez
UMFUNDISI: Zulu word for teacher
UMKHONGI: marriage co-ordinator
UNANI MEDICINES: alternative Islamic medical practice
URUMBU: a lizard-like reptile
USTAAD: teacher
VOHRA: Gujarati-speaking Muslims from Surat, India, and its environs
VOLK: nation
WEESEE: food contract with the cooks on a ship
ZOHAR NAMAAZ: noonday prayer

INDEX

Abantu Batho 153
Abdurahman, Dr 15, 16, 18, 38, 39, 40, 120
Abrahams, Peter 37, 147
Adam, Farid 184, 185, 194
Adam's Mission 102, 129
Advance 170
African Chronicle 30
African National Congress (ANC) viii, x, 38, 57, 58, 67, 75, 79, 80, 84, 89, 90, 116–23 *passim*, 141, 143, 144, 148, 149, 151, 167, 171, 175, 215, 241
African People's Organisation (APO) x, 38, 67, 75, 79, 90, 122, 124, 167
Afriki, Moulana 4, 5, 6
Agong, King Yangdi-Pertuan 255
Ahimsa viii, 81
Ahmed, Hawa H 37
AI Kajee (Pty) Ltd 8
Aiyar, PS 30, 32
Alberts, Vera 44
Alexandra bus boycott 93
Aligirh College 105
All Africa Convention (AAC) 151
Amin family 2, 3
Amra family 18
Amra, Cassim 36, 37, 38, 41, 60, 70, 71, 140, 189, 243
ANC *see* African National Congress
Andrews, Reverend CF 19, 26
Andrews, WH 38
Angalia, Cassim 26, 47

Angalia, Mohamed 14, 25, 26, 34
Anglo-Boer War 3
Anti-Asiatic Land Act 48, 51
Anti-Pass Campaign 93, 215–16
Anti-Segregation Council 51, 87, 150
Anti-War Campaign 58–60
apartheid 109–12
APO *see* African People's Organisation
Arabic Study Circle 213
Arenstein, Roly 43, 130, 131, 139, 177, 217, 220, 221
Arya Samaj 214
Asher, B 27
Asian Relations Conference 106
Asiatic Land and Trading Bill 46, 49
Asiatic Land Tenure Act 49, 92, 103
Asiatic Land Tenure and Indian Representation Bill 92
Asmal, Mohamed 185
Asvat, EA 48
Asvat, Zainab viii, 81, 95, 98, 99, 100, 101, 113, 182, 241
Ataturk, Kemal 74
Atlantic Charter 50
Attlinger, Advocate 110
Avalon Cinema 56, 64, 101, 134
Azad, Moulana Abul Kalam 28, 253

Bákie 153
Ballinger, William 16
Baloyi, BG 38
Bantu Education Act 148
Bantu National Congress 118
Bantu Social Centre 144
Bashir, Molvi 132
Bassa, Cassim 214
Bawa, Ahmed 229
Benson, Mary 212
Bernhardt, Ian 214
Bernstein, Lionel 113, 194
Berrange, Vernon 110, 181, 183, 197, 198, 211
Beyleveld, P 173
Bhabha, Essop 96
Bhabha, Jamila 96, 100, 113
Bhagwan family 139
Bhagwan, Denis 169
Bhagwan, Devi 169
Bhamjee, Yusuf 263
Bhayat, Ahmed 8
Bhayat, Chotie Bai 73, 95, 113
Bhayat, Zohra 95, 96
Bhoola, Ahmed 69, 71, 80, 81, 82
Bhugwan family 204
Biko, Steve 227
Black Consciousness 225, 226, 227, 230
Black Power 225
Black Women's Federation 214, 227
Blitz of Bombay 29
Bloom, Harry 40, 60
Bodasingh family 224
Bombay Chronicle 27
Bopape, David 93, 121, 197

279

Bopape, JW 147
Bose, Subhash Chandra viii, 105, 253
Botha, PW 260
Boyd, Leo 116
Bramdaw, Dhanee 29
Brandt, Willy 252
Brookes, Dr Edgar 118
Brown, Peter 169
Brown, Val 226
Brutus, Dennis 214
Budhoo family 9
Buirski, Comrade 4
Bundhoo, Mrs D 212
Bunting, Brian 241, 242
Bunting, Sonia 241
Burne, Swart, Hudson and Rindle 189
Buthelezi, Mangosuthu 58, 117, 120, 129, 132, 169, 264
Buzme Adab 102

Cachalia, AM 28
Cachalia, Amina Bai 243
Cachalia, Maryam 113
Cachalia, Molvi IA vii, 28, 72, 73, 74, 75, 84, 91, 93, 95, 104, 113, 117–18, 143, 153, 243
Cachalia, Yusuf vii, 73, 77, 84, 91, 113, 143, 144, 167, 171, 229
Cafe de Move On 37
Calata, Reverend JA 181
Caliphate *see* Khilafat
Call, The 36
Cape British Indian Council 15
Cape Standard 30, 91
Cape Town Agreement 32, 34
Carlisle Street Government School 22, 58
Carrim, Yunus 261
Castle, Barbara 207
Cato Manor 83, 116, 117, 216, 221
Cele, Wilson 36
Central Housing Board 70
Chacha, Adam 7, 8, 9

Chacha, Desai 3, 4, 12, 13
Chacha, Karodia 11, 23
Chacha, Mullah 26
Chacha, Sardiwala 4
Champion, AWG 13, 15, 16, 17, 24, 38, 40, 58, 80, 116, 120, 128
Chari, RT 117, 143
Chetty, AS 170
Chetty, BT 87
Chetty, Dr 186–87
Chetty, Dr Thegie 88
Chiba, Laloo 253
Cho Cho, Lotchi 161–62
Chou En-lai 171
Choudree, Ashwin 113, 114, 115, 187
Christopher, Albert 31, 34, 35, 40, 42, 47
Christopher, Gadija 139
Christopher, Mrs 218
Christopher, Zulie 94
Class Areas Bill 33–34
Clayton, Dr Geoffrey 212
Coaker, John 181
CODESA 260–61
Cohen, Mr 160–61
Collins, Canon 212
Colonial Born and Settler Indian Association (CBSIA) 32, 34, 35, 46
Colonisation Commission 32, 34
Coloured People's Organisation 175
Coloured People's Congress (CPC) 224
Combined Ratepayers Association 147
Commissioner for Asiatic Affairs 109, 110
Communist Party of South Africa (CPSA) viii, x, 16, 36, 38, 42, 44, 45, 56, 66, 67, 70, 72, 75, 78, 79, 82, 90, 92, 93, 122, 123, 124, 147, 149, 155, 167, 169
concession stores 2
Conco, Dr Wilson 191

Conco, Shiemie 191
Congress Alliance 120
Congress Education Committee 115
Congress High School 115
Congress Movement 167, 223
Congress of Democrats (COD) 67, 167, 171, 175, 205
Congress of the People (COP) 154, 167, 168, 169, 170, 171–75, 184, 211
Coopan, Dr 71
Coopasamy 7
Cooper, Saths 231
Council for Human Rights 100
CPC *see* Coloured People's Congress (CPC)
CPSA *see* Communist Party of South Africa
Cry, the Beloved Country 159
Cultural boycott 214
Curries Fountain 87, 102

Dadoo, Dr Yusuf vii, 22, 38, 39, 47–49, 50, 58, 59, 62, 64, 66, 67, 72–73, 74, 75, 81, 87, 88, 89–93, 99, 100, 101, 106, 110, 111, 113, 147, 151, 151, 171, 209, 241, 242
Dadoo–Xuma–Naicker Pact 90, 118, 120
Daily News 39, 66
Dartnell Crescent school 225
Darul Uloom 4
Davidson, Dr 137, 187
Day of Volunteers 141, 143
Dayal, Swami Bhawani 32, 33
De Jaager, Lotjie 3, 15, 19
De Klerk, FW 192, 252, 260
De Villiers, Leslie 36, 45
Defence and Aid Fund 152, 180, 189, 198, 205, 212
Defend Free Speech Convention x
Defiance of Unjust Laws Campaign 74, 120, 141–55, 152, 169, 196 213

INDEX

Democratic Education Advancement League (DEAL) 262
Department of Asiatic Affairs 109
Desai, Sulieman 48
Deshmukh, High Commissioner 92
Detainees Care Group 218
Devodutt, Harry 55
Dhlomo, HIE 121, 122
Didcott, John 189, 237
District Six 83
Dlamini, Steven 191, 217
Docrat, AKM 36, 45, 62, 70, 87, 145
Doctors' Pact *see* Dadoo–Xuma–Naicker Pact
Dome magazine 54
Drill Hall 180, 181, 182, 193, 198, 205, 207, 212
Drum 147, 192
Dundee 1, 2, 5, 57, 150, 151
Dundee and District Courier 14
Dundee Theatre Supper Club 57
Dunlop Strike 40, 70–71
Durban 21–30, 144, 145
Durban and District Women's League 139, 154
Durban Central Prison 67, 104, 146, 217
Durban City Council 70, 125
Durban Indian Child Welfare Society 129, 226
Durban Indian Girls' High School 226
Durban International Club 119
Dutt, Palme 56

Fakroodeen family 245, 247
Falkirk Iron and Steel Workers' Union 40, 47
Falkirk Strike 40, 70–71
Federation of Progressive Students (FOPS) 78, 79
First, Ruth 75, 78, 181
Fischer, Bram 56, 75, 82, 110, 113, 121

Fordsburg 72, 111
Fort Hare University 105, 149
Forum 121, 168
Free Speech Rally 122
Freedom Charter 154, 167–75, 184, 197
Freedom Day Rally 122
Freedom Day strike x, 122, 123, 124
Funde, Eddie 254

Ganas, Mr 88
Gandhi, Feroze 61
Gandhi, Indira 37, 60–67 *passim*, 82, 83, 84, 253
Gandhi, Manilal 28, 61, 62, 64, 67, 74, 111, 171, 174
Gandhi, Mohandas viii, ix, 2, 8, 10, 25, 26, 31, 33, 39, 42, 48, 61, 64, 66, 69, 79, 81, 85, 88, 97, 99, 100, 105, 106, 107, 110, 112, 145, 153, 223, 253
Gandhi, Priyanka 84
Gandhi, Rajiv 82, 83, 84, 253
Gandhi, Rajmohan 253
Gandhi, Sonia 66, 82, 84
Gandhi, Sushila Behn 28, 62, 220
Gangat, Ismail 218
Gardee 153
Gawe, Reverend WS 181
Gcabashe, Thulani 165
Ghalib 1, 35
Ghetto Act 89, 95, 103
Giyana, Reverend 160
Godfrey, Irene 41, 94
Godfrey, JW 31, 40, 46
Goga, Ebrahim 131
Gokhale, Professor Gopal Krishna 10, 12
Goldie, Andrew 42
Goldie, Fay King 36, 42
Gollancz Left Book Club 42
Gool, Cissy 38, 39, 101
Gool, Dr AH 33, 38
Gool, Dr Goolam 38, 150

Gool, Halima 150
Goonam, Dr K 27, 41, 44, 47–49, 70, 95, 99, 100, 101, 111, 131, 132, 134, 135, 235
Gordhan, Pravin 241
Govender, Lutchmee 96, 99
Govindjee, Dayabhai 49
Graphic 196, 207
Great March of 1913 10
Great Salt March 11
Green, Mr 88, 98, 111
Group Areas Act 33, 125, 130, 138, 168, 262
Group Areas Board 181
Guardian 30, 58, 123, 128, 153, 170
Gumede family 139
Gumede, Archie 191
Gumede, Dr MV 164, 165
Gupta, Chandra 62, 65

Habibullah Commission 10
Haffejee family 39
Harmels family 113, 189
Harry, PM 22, 36, 47, 62, 70
Harrypersadh, Bobby 192
Hartal 141
Hashim, Enver 218
Hawthorne, Margaret 205
Hawthorne, Michael 205
Hellman, Dr Ellen 209
Hertzog, JBM 17, 19
Hindu 27
Hindu Youth Movement 47
Hlapane, B 194
Hofmeyer, JH 39
Hooper, Marie Louise 191–92
Horwich, Ike 212
Horwood, Owen 239
Howard College 54
Howick Falls 63
Human Sciences Research Council 71
Hurbans, Gopalal 138, 151, 167, 178, 190, 191, 198
Hurley, Archbishop 169

ICU *see* Industrial and Commercial Workers Union
Immigrants Regulation Act 109, 110
Immorality Act 157, 194
India Independence Day 56–58
India League 61, 67
Indian Child Welfare Society 139
Indian Congress *see* Natal Indian Congress, South African Indian Congress, Transvaal Indian Congress
Indian National Congress 10, 33, 37, 39, 98, 253
Indian Opinion 16, 26, 27, 28, 33, 61, 64, 153, 172, 174, 207
Indian Views 8, 16, 19, 22, 23, 25–28, 33, 37, 38, 47, 53, 57, 58, 70, 150, 153, 207
Indira Gandhi Memorial Conference 82
Industrial and Commercial Workers Union (ICU) 13, 16, 58
Inkatha Freedom Party (IFP) 230, 233, 234
Institute for Black Research 214, 228
International Club 69, 102
Irving & Johnson 42
Islamic Propagation Centre 160
Ismail, MH 8, 9

Jabavu, Professor DDT 16, 119
Jada, I 153, 171
Jalianwala Bagh 15, 103
Jawoodeen 4
Jeewa brothers 14, 26
Jinnah, Mohamed Ali 105
Johannesburg 69–85, 144
Johnson, Hewett 37
Jongwe, Dr 141
Joseph, Helen 181, 194
Joseph, Paul 181, 185, 194
Joshi, J 101

Juma Masjid 10
Junod, Violaine 78, 127–28, 136, 171, 177, 191, 192, 201, 205

Kadalie, Clement 13, 16, 80
Kajee, AI 27, 31, 32, 33, 34, 35, 39, 40, 42, 46, 47, 61, 64, 95
Kallenbach, Herman 10, 62, 79
Kalloo 5
Kally, Ranjith 189
Karis, Tom 256
Kark, Dr Sydney 139
Kathrada, Ahmed (Kathy) vii, 75, 76, 77, 78, 113, 118, 122, 123, 171, 185, 261, 264
Kathrada, Essop Ba 247
Kazi's Agencies 8
Kesari 27
Khama, Tshekedi 77
Khan, Omar 26, 28, 105, 132
Khan, Sir Mahomed Zafrullah 125
Khan, Toti 88
Kharwa, Sulieman Ismail 14
Khilafat movement 10, 13, 14
Kholvad House vii, 50, 75, 83, 128
Khuzwayo, Clement 15
King Alfred School 226
Koestler, Arthur 168
Kotane, Moses 38, 113, 119, 121, 147
Kumaramanglam, Parvathi 62–63
Kuper, Hilda 137, 139, 140, 154, 169, 177, 191, 192, 204, 205
Kuper, Leo 137, 139, 169, 177, 191, 192, 196, 205
Kutako, Hosea 77
KwaZulu-Natal Legislative Assembly 261

Laher, Ebrahim 153
Lakhani Chambers 57, 88
Lawrence Committee 51

Lawrence, Harry 55
Lawrence, VL 145
Lax, Jacqueline 36
Lazarus, Gertrude 41
Leader xii, 29, 106, 153, 262
Left Book Club 38, 42, 67, 69
Lembede, Anton 84, 113, 251
Letele, Dr and Mrs 197
Liberal Party 168, 169, 171, 205
Liberal Study Group 36, 41, 44, 62, 66, 67, 68, 69, 71, 88, 92, 120, 121, 147
Liberation History Foundation 262
Limbada, Dr AI 149, 150, 151, 152
Lipman, Alan 204
Lloyd George, D 34
Loskop Killer 14, 15
Lowen, Dr 78, 117, 118
Luthuli, Albertina 183, 191
Luthuli, Chief Albert John 22, 56–58, 112, 117, 120, 128, 143, 144, 145, 151, 164, 165, 167, 169, 171, 178, 183, 191, 198, 208, 216, 217, 218, 221, 223, 224
Luthuli, Nokukhanya 84, 191

Mabizela, Stanley 253
Mac the Master 208
Madikizela-Mandela, Winnie xi, 83, 84, 183, 191, 227, 229, 261
Magazine Barracks 44, 63
Magid, Brenda 221
Mahabane, Reverend Z 16
Mahabeer family 161–62
Mahabeer, R 110
Maharaj, Kundanlal 19
Maharaj, Mac 241
Maharaj, Puran 189
Maharaj, Shewlal (Frank) 19
Maharaj, TS 264
Maistry, Mr and Mrs 230
Makiwane, TX 194
Malan, DF 112, 121, 125, 143, 192, 197

INDEX

Malinga's school 7
Mall, Hoosen 6
Mall, Judge Hassan 105, 189, 197, 214, 230
Mall, Salehba 4
Mandela, Eveline 183
Mandela, Nelson vii–xii, 76, 80–84, 113, 119, 120, 121, 122, 123, 124, 142, 143, 144, 148, 171, 178, 180, 181, 183, 202, 208, 216, 224, 250–53, 260
Mandela, Winnie *see* Madikizela-Mandela, Winnie
Marie, Bobby 228, 235, 237, 263
Marie, Maia 264, 267
Marie, Zen 263, 267
Marks, JB 93, 119, 120, 121, 123, 147, 207
Marxism viii, 81
Masabalala, Samuel 13
Masekela, Barbara 253
Mashoba, Reverend George 3, 13, 15, 16, 19
Master, Ismail 4, 18
Matthews, Joe 179, 181
Matthews, Professor ZK 167, 181, 198
May Day Unity Committee 67
Mayat, Dr Mohamed 134, 135, 230
Mayat, Julu (née Bismillah) 134, 230
Mayat, Khatija 101
Mbeki, Thabo 256–57
Mbeki, Zanele 257
McCords Hospital 164, 165, 187
McDonald, Mrs 54
Mda, AP 121, 148, 251
Medh, SB 28
Meer, AC 9, 15, 17, 18, 19, 21, 23, 31, 32, 53, 54, 71, 102, 105, 105, 107, 145, 228, 245, 246, 247, 249, 262
Meer, Afoo 11
Meer, Ahmed [forefather] 1, 21, 243

Meer, Ahmed (Hajee Bhai) 106
Meer, Ahmed [MI's son] 138, 219
Meer, AI (Ahmed) 3, 4, 14, 18, 21, 23–24, 25, 29, 31, 35, 53, 54, 87, 89, 94, 102, 104, 105, 107, 113, 116, 128, 130, 139, 155, 201, 214
Meer, Alif 21, 27, 29
Meer, AM [MM's son] 9, 35, 102, 105
Meer, Amina (Gorie Bai) 9, 21, 27, 29, 106–7, 228, 262
Meer, Äpa 3, 14, 23, 25, 107, 113, 127, 130, 137
Meer, Ayesha 6, 21, 23, 45, 105, 107, 127, 246
Meer, Baby 132, 228, 262
Meer, Bhabi 135, 136
Meer, Bhaboo 94, 95, 96, 101–2, 137, 217
Meer, Bhai 240, 242, 257
Meer, Bubbles 105
Meer, Budie 95, 96, 101, 184, 262
Meer, Cassim 1, 11, 71, 107
Meer, Chota (CA) 1, 2, 3, 4, 12, 13, 14, 15, 17, 19, 21, 22, 23, 262
Meer, Chotie Mamie 246
Meer, EM 9, 21, 29, 35, 102, 105
Meer, Farouk 228, 229, 262
Meer, Fatima [sister] 21, 107
Meer, Fatima (Fathu) x, xi, 66, 104, 105, 106, 125, 127–40, 163, 165, 177, 178, 182, 185–89, 201, 202, 205, 206, 213, 214, 217, 219, 220, 221, 222, 225, 226, 232, 233, 234, 262, 263, 267
banning orders 153–55, 171, 227, 234–37
Defence and Aid Fund 212
detention 228, 229, 232
Haj 245–49

Mandela's biographer 82, 251, 260
Non-European Unity Movement 149, 150, 151
resistance campaign 94, 95
Riots, 1949 117
social issues 214, 227, 230, 233, 234
sociology 196
travel abroad 239–40, 256, 257
Meer, GH 71, 72
Meer, Haroon 9, 21
Meer, Haroun 139
Meer, HC (Hussain) 15, 17, 21, 23, 105, 107
Meer, Iqbal 146, 242
Meer, Ismail [MI's son] 104
Meer, Ismail [nephew] 138
Meer, Ismail [uncle] 1, 4
Meer, Ismail Chota (IC)
arrest for treason 157
articles 109, 113
banning 147, 153, 213, 214
CPSA membership 16, 42
Defiance Campaign 141–55
detention 216–22
early education 4–7, 17, 22
engagement and marriage 130, 131–32
first arrest 65–66
Freedom Charter keynote address 209, 210
Haj 245–49
high school 22, 24, 53
imprisonment 146–47, 178–80
journalism 24, 25–28, 29, 30, 91
legal practice 157–65, 168
'listing' 167, 170, 213, 214
passive resistance 87–107
political activism 31–52
trade unions 40–43
travel abroad 240–57
Treason Trial 177–214
university 53–55, 69–70, 78–79
Meer, MC 23

283

Meer, MI (Moosa) 4, 10, 14–35 *passim*, 43, 48, 53, 54, 55, 58, 71, 73, 91, 94, 96, 101, 102, 104, 105, 106, 132, 133, 136, 138, 139, 177, 195, 201, 218
Meer, Mohamed Ahmed 1–2, 10, 21, 101, 106, 131, 243–44, 262
Meer, Moosa Mohamed 105
Meer, Munir 138
Meer, Nash 246
Meer, Rashid 106, 137, 177, 185–87, 188, 189, 198, 215, 221, 226, 227, 228, 229, 236, 240, 257, 260, 262–63
Meer, Salim 146, 263
Meer, Sarah 1
Meer, Shafique 146
Meer, Shamim 134–35, 139, 167, 178, 189, 192, 198, 219, 221, 225, 226, 262, 263, 264, 267
Meer, Shehnaz 137, 154, 177, 189, 192, 198, 217, 221, 222, 226, 241, 262, 263, 264, 267
Meer, Siddiek 240, 257
Meer, Sulaiman 1
Meer, Unus 104, 138
Meer, YC (Yusuf) 53, 73, 75, 107
Meer, Zainab 262
Meer, Zohra 21, 23, 45, 101, 246
Meer, Zubie 240, 241, 257
Mehta, NV 37
Mehtar, Farooqi 19, 27, 34, 60
Mhlongo, Aron 194
Mia, Molvi 71
Mia, Moulana Abed 4, 5
Milne, John 170
Mineworkers' strike, 1946 93
Minty, AI 109
Mji, Diliza 124
Mji, Dr 197
MK Gandhi Library 56, 64, 67
Mkhize, Bertha 139, 217

ML Sultan Technical College 115
Mofokeng, Theresa 145
Mohamed, Amod 105
Mohamed, Dr Mahathir 254, 255
Mohamed, EV 171
Mohamed, Ismail 235, 236, 237, 238, 265
Mohamed, OH 180
Moodley, NG 41, 69
Moodley, Strini 231
Moola, AM 152
Moorges, Freddy 178, 179
Moosa family 265
Moosa, Ismail 9–10
Morar, Nathoo V 57
Moroka, Dr 90, 122, 142
Mota, Amjaloo 4
Motala, AM 55–56
Motala, Chota 23, 130, 178, 180, 181, 185, 190, 195, 198, 212, 230
Motala, Dr MM 170, 207
Motala, Mrs Choti 212
Motala, SM 21
Mphele, Nphutu 253
Msimang, Selby 13
Mungal family 131, 133, 139, 193
Mungal, SB 170
Munsamy, Kay 217
Murray, Dr Andrew 209, 210, 211
Muslim Gujarat 14
Muslim Institute 39
Muslim League 98
Mxenge, Victoria 233

Nabie, Mr 131
Naby, Shahadat 189
Nagdee, Essop 77
Naicker, Dr GM 170, 171, 197
Naicker, Dr Monty 9, 22, 47–49, 51, 70, 75, 87, 88, 89, 90, 92, 95, 96, 97, 99, 100, 106, 107, 111, 118, 120, 143, 145, 146, 150, 151, 152, 155, 167, 179, 180, 189, 190, 191, 198, 207–9, 212, 217, 220
Naicker, Marie 190, 191, 212
Naicker, MC 218
Naicker, NT 171, 190, 191, 218
Naidoo, Bobby 96
Naidoo, Dr MB 115
Naidoo, HA 22, 36, 38–45 *passim*, 47, 62, 64, 70, 71, 91, 101, 131
Naidoo, HK 69
Naidoo, Mannie 145, 171
Naidoo, MD 87, 89, 96, 97, 99, 100, 111
Naidoo, Mrs PK 96, 113
Naidoo, Mrs SRR 212
Naidoo, Narainsamy 153
Naidoo, RD 40
Naidoo, Sarojini 11, 12, 33, 34, 85, 96, 106, 107
Naidoo, Sirkari 32
Naidoo, VG 150, 151
Nair, Billy 145, 217, 218
Nakasa, Chamberlain 27
Nakasa, Nat 27
Nana, SM 48, 49, 89
Naraidu, Aubrey 138, 139, 189
Natal Advertiser 29
Natal Indian Association (NIA) 25, 46, 47, 49, 59
Natal Indian Congress (NIC) viii, x, 10, 15, 17, 25, 27, 32–35 *passim*, 40, 42, 46, 57, 87–124 *passim*, 129, 138, 141, 144, 148, 150–55 *passim*, 170, 171, 184, 211, 213
Natal Indian Organisation (NIO) 118, 152
Natal Law Society 69, 70, 109
Natal Teachers Association 41, 53, 70
Natal Witness 17, 30
Natal Working Committee 205
Nathie, Solly 93, 153, 202
National Bloc 46, 49, 51
National Day of Protest x, 141, 144

INDEX

National Joint Consultative
    Committee 175
National Party 121
National Union of South
    African Students
    (NUSAS) 54, 92
Nationalist Bloc 67
Native Representative Council
    (NRC) 149, 151
Ndlovu, Jim 5
Ndungane, Bishop 142
Nehru, Indira *see* Gandhi,
    Indira
Nehru, Jawaharlal viii, 27, 37,
    58, 60, 61, 64, 65, 81,
    84–85, 90, 91, 105,
    106, 107
Nel, Oom 3
NEUF *see* Non-European
    United Front
NEUM *see* Non-European
    Unity Movement
New Age 123, 153, 184, 207
New Outlook 27–28
Ngubase, Solomon 196, 197
Ngwevela, SM 147
Nhlapo, Amos 196
NIC *see* Natal Indian Congress
NIC Youth Congress 214
Nkobi, Thomas 253
Nkomo, William 251
Noel-Barham, Peter 237
Non-European Conference 38
Non-European United Front
    (NEUF) 38, 39, 46, 47,
    48, 49, 51, 59, 61, 64, 65,
    66, 67, 70, 72, 75, 93, 120
Non-European Unity
    Movement (NEUM)
    xi, 148–51
Nowbath, Ranji S 29
NUSAS *see* National Union of
    South African Students

Ohlange High School 237
Omar, Abu Hassan bin Haji
    254
Omar, Essop 9
Orient Club 35, 55

Osman, Moulana Ahmad
    Mia 4
Osrin's cinema 48

PAC *see* Pan African Congress
Padayachee, Roy 241
Paddison Commission 10
Pahad, Amina vii, 72, 73, 81,
    84, 95, 99, 113, 180, 182,
    208–9
Pahad, Aziz 95, 180, 241
Pahad, Essop 95, 180
Pahad, Goolam vii, 72, 73, 81,
    84, 113, 121, 180, 182, 243
Pahad, Ismail 95, 180
Pahad, Nasim 95, 180
Pahad, Zunaid 95
Palmer, Dr Mabel 37, 54, 69, 70
Pan African Congress (PAC)
    148, 215, 223
Pandit, Vijayalakshmi 125
Pappet, Seymour 149
Parents' Committee, UDW
    230, 231
Parents' Committee, Soweto 227
Parker, Aida 39, 66
Parsee Rustomjee Hall 64
Paruk, EM 24, 39
Paruk–Lockhat wedding 50
passive resistance campaign 30,
    48, 81, 87–106, 109–12,
    119, 141, 149, 152
Passive Resistance Council
    (PRC) 76, 91, 92, 93, 94,
    95, 99, 101, 111
Passive Resister 30, 75, 91
Patel, Abdul Haq viii, 81
Patel, Dr Vallabhbhai 79, 89
Patel, EI 48
Patel, Manilal Galal 153
Patel, Mrs Bhailal 9
Patel, Suryakala 103, 113
Patel, Zubeida 96
Pather, Mrs Veeramah 96, 99
Pather, PR 31, 34, 40
Paton, Alan 159, 168, 169,
    192, 212, 235
Paton, Dorrie 169, 191, 192
Peer, Amina 21, 127

Peer, GH 21
Pegging Act 46, 49, 51, 92
Perumal, Mr 206
Peter's Lounge 37
Peters, Billy 89
Peterson, Hector 228
Petterson, Senator 118
Phoenix Settlement 28, 62,
    227, 238
Phoenix Settlement Working
    Committee 169
Pillay, Kanabaran 196
Pillay, Krishensamy 100
Pillay, Nad 186
Pillay, Nessa 69
Pillay, RA 100, 110
Pillay, Thumba 241
Pinetown 104, 125, 131
Pinetown Relief Committee 117
Pirow, Oswald 207
Pistorious, Professor 198
Plowright, Mr 164
Pochee, Mahomed 101
Pochees Cycle Works 101
Podbrey, Pauline 36, 40, 41, 44
Pollak, Dr Hansie 209
Ponnen, George 22, 36, 40, 41,
    42, 44–45, 62, 70
Ponnen, Indira 45
Ponnen, Marsha 45
Ponnen, Vera 205
Poovalingam, Pat 169, 189
Poovalingam, Sakunthalay 169
Pope John Paul II 252
Port Elizabeth 141, 143, 144
PRC *see* Passive Resistance
    Council
Pretoria Agreement 51

Rafesath, Mr 170
Raidoo, Abba 79
Rajab, Habib 230
Ramawthar, Minnie 41
Ramohanoe, CS x, 90
Rampura Regiment 55
Ramsevak, Sirdar 12, 13
Ramsunder 40
Randeree 39
Rao, Rama 125

Rao, Sir Benegal Narsing 125
Rasool, Wahajar 193
Ratepayers Association 155, 213
Rawat Bio Hall 47
Red Square vii, 22, 95, 97, 101, 103, 106, 112, 144, 145
Reddy, Sir Kurma 9
Reddy, SV 41, 111
Reddy, Venget 190
Reddy, Zainab 191, 196
Reeves, Bishop Ambrose 212
Resha, Robert 171
Residents Association, Umlazi 233
Riotous Assemblies Act 172
Riots, 1949 116, 141
Robeson, Paul 171
Rooknoodeen, Hajee 8
Roosevelt, Eleanor 212
Rosenburg, Mr 181
Round Table Conferences 15, 18, 32–34
Royal Picture Palace 47
Rubin, Harry 43
Rubin, Sarah 38
Rumpff, Judge 184
Russell, Martin 192
Russell, Mr 146
Rustomjee, Sorabjee 31, 33, 34, 40, 47, 49–51, 59, 61, 90, 91, 101

Saab, Hafez 246
SACTU *see* South African Congress of Trade Unions
Sader, Dr AH 101, 151, 167
Saheb, Amod 3, 4
SAIC *see* South African Indian Congress
Saleh, Salim 113
Saloojee, Molvi 153
Sampson, Anthony 198
Sapru, Sir Tej Bahadur 33
SASO *see* South African Students Organisation
Sastri College 23, 24–25, 29, 53, 69, 94, 115, 128, 129, 226
Sastri College Alumni Association 261

Sastri, VS Srinivasa 15, 24
Satchel, Reverend WH 56
Scott, Rev Michael (Bajee) 75, 76, 77, 78, 100, 101, 113, 241
Seedat, Dawood 36, 37, 38, 41, 58, 59, 60, 61, 62, 64, 66, 67, 68, 217, 218, 222
Seedat, Dr Cassim 17
Seedat, Fatima 60, 61, 145
Sema, Moulana Cassim 4, 6
Seme, Dr 84
Seth, Mahomed 11
Sewpersadh, George 228, 229, 235
Shanley, Dorothy
Shanley, Errol 181
Sharpeville massacre 216
Shaw, George Bernard 54, 56
Shearer, Advocate 221
Shearer, Judge 237
Shifa Hospital 230
Sibiya, Reverend JM 118, 145
Siddiqi, Moulana Bashir 4
Sigamoney, BLE 42
Sigamoney, Reverend BTE 141, 142
Simelane, Stalwart 145, 146, 191, 218
Singh, Baijnath 3
Singh, Debi 36, 41, 70, 76, 88, 89, 96, 98, 100, 112, 113, 114, 116, 125, 143, 151, 167, 178, 190, 197, 198, 232
Singh, George 51, 118, 214
Singh, Jay 145
Singh, JN vii, viii, x, 56, 69, 70, 71, 75, 76, 78, 80, 81, 87, 89, 91, 93, 95, 96, 97, 98, 99, 104, 110, 112, 115, 119, 131, 132, 169, 191, 217, 224, 261
Singh, Radhi 41, 131, 169, 191, 262
Singh, Ramsevak 3, 4, 15, 16, 19
Singh, Ranjith 3, 19

Singh, Sir Kunwar Maharaj 26, 31
Sischy, Benny 100
Sisulu, Walter x, 113, 119, 120, 121, 123, 143, 144, 148, 197, 251
Sita, Nana 84, 144, 153, 167
Slovo, Joe 56, 75, 78, 113, 121, 181, 241
Smuts, JC 33, 49, 51, 60, 90, 91, 92, 97, 112, 121
Sneddon, Professor Elizabeth 54
Sontonga, Enoch 16
South African Congress of Trade Unions (SACTU) 167, 224
South African Federation of Non-European Trade Unions 42
South African Indian Congress (SAIC) viii, x, 15, 18, 33, 38, 40, 67, 89, 90, 106, 119, 123, 124, 143, 155, 167, 175, 241
see also Natal Indian Congress, Transvaal Indian Congress
South African Indian Review 30
South African Institute of Race Relations 118
South African Indian Council 230
South African Students' Organisation (SASO) 227, 230, 231
Soweto 83
Soweto Revolt, 1976 227–28
sports boycott 214
Srinivassan, Professor 239
St Aidan's Hospital 134
St Alban's Mission 76
St Anthony's school 225
St Joseph's Home 76
state of emergency 215–24
Statesman 27
Steenkamp, Colonel 228
Stimpson, Robert 142, 143

INDEX

Strydom, Mr JG 173
Sugar Workers Union 45, 131
Sultan, ML 114–15
Suppression of Communism Act 123, 147, 154, 172, 223
Surat 2, 9, 11, 21, 243
Surat Hindu Association Hall 62
Sussex University 227, 230
Sutcliffe, Dr Mike 264
Swanepoel, Captain 218
Swart, CR 155
Sykes, Paul 56

Tabata, IA 150
Tabete, Detective Sergeant 185
Tambo, Oliver x, 119, 120, 142, 171, 208, 251, 230
Tayob, Dr 262
Ten Point Programme 149, 150
Thatcher, Margaret 241
Third Non-European Conference 15
Thomas, Ephraim 17, 22
Thomas, Glynn 78
Thompson, Reverend DC 181
Thorpe, Joe 169
TIC *see* Transvaal Indian Congress
Timol, Beaver 36, 62
Tin Town Relief Committee 227
Tolstoy Farm 79, 96
Too Late the Phalarope 159
Trade Union Action Committee 171
Trade unions 40–43

Transvaal Indian British Association 15
Transvaal Indian Congress (TIC) x, 28, 48, 49, 56, 72, 74, 75, 76, 79, 87, 89, 90, 91, 92, 93, 95, 97, 106, 121, 123, 124, 185, 212
Transvaal Indian Youth Congress 185
Transvaal Law Society 109
Treason Cage, The 198
Treason Trial 152, 177–214, 222, 223
Tsantsi, Reverend 144
Turner, Rick 233

UDF *see* United Democratic Front
Umkhonto we Sizwe 224
UNISA *see* University of South Africa
United Democratic Front 230, 233
United Party 121
University of Cape Town 227
University of Durban-Westville 226, 230
University of Natal 42, 53, 69, 128, 150
University of South Africa 226
University of the Witwatersrand 71, 78, 127, 128
University Students Bursary Committee 79
Upliftment Clause 32

Vadival, A 145
Vahed law company 189

Valod, EM 89
Van den Heever Commission 118
Van den Heever, Justice 117
Van Niekerk, Mr 211
Van Papendorf, G 209
Van Riebeeck, Jan 141
Vania, Ahmed Mohamed 243
Verster, Andrew 226, 229, 235
Verwoerd, HF 112, 173
Victoria Picture Palace 40
Victoria Street Market 29
Vilakazi, BW 58
Vorster, John 67

Warriner, CR 25
Warwick University 226
Waschbank 1–20 *passim*, 21, 35, 267
Waterford School 226
Waterval Islamic Institute 71
Webb, Beatrice and Sydney 37
Webb, Maurice 118
Weinberg, Nana 229
West, Albert 26
Williams, Cecil 214
Wilson, Boris 148
Wolpe, Harold 78, 149
Wolpe, Howard 256
Women's Action Group 98
Women's Liberal Study Group 41
World War II 55, 66

Xuma, Dr AB 90, 91, 101, 106, 112, 118, 119

Yengwa, Bonnie 191
Yengwa, MB 132, 143, 191, 218, 241